CW01111851

THE ANALYSIS OF CREDIT
Foundations and development of corporate credit assessment

THE ANALYSIS OF CREDIT
Foundations and development of corporate credit assessment

Alexander Bathory

McGRAW-HILL Book Company (UK) Limited

London · New York · St Louis · San Francisco · Auckland · Bogotá
Guatemala · Hamburg · Lisbon · Madrid · Mexico · Montreal
New Delhi · Panama · Paris · San Juan · São Paulo · Singapore · Sydney
Tokyo · Toronto

Published by
McGRAW-HILL Book Company (UK) Limited
MAIDENHEAD · BERKSHIRE · ENGLAND

British Library Cataloguing in Publication Data
Bathory, Alexander
 The analysis of credit: foundations and
 development of corporate credit assessment.
 1. Credit—Management
 I. Title
 658.8′8   HG3751
 ISBN 0-07-084938-2

Library of Congress Cataloging-in-Publication Data
Bathory, Alexander
 The analysis of credit.
 Bibliography: p.
 Includes index.
 1. Credit—Management.   I. Title.   II. Title:
Corporate credit assessment.
HG3751.B385   1987   658.8′8   87-2060
ISBN 0-07-084938-2

Copyright © 1987 McGraw-Hill Book Company (UK) Limited. All rights reserved. No part of this publication may be reproduced, stored in a retrieval system, or transmitted, in any form or by any means, electronic, mechanical, photocopying, recording, or otherwise, without the prior permission of McGraw-Hill Book Company (UK) Limited, or of the original copyright holder.

12345 AP 8987

Typeset by Latimer Trend & Company Ltd, Plymouth
Printed and bound in Great Britain at the Alden Press, Oxford

CONTENTS

Foreword	vii
Preface	ix
Acknowledgements	xiii

Part One   Broad views and developments in credit analysis — **1**
1. Definition and purpose of credit analysis — 3
2. Examination of traditional ratios — 26
3. Standard and hybrid ratios in basic analysis — 55
4. The development of ratio-based models in credit analysis — 75

Part Two   Problems in the computation and interpretation of data — **103**
5. Development of a ratio-based, multiple sector insolvency forecasting model — 105
6. The calculation of short-term surplus funding — 138
7. The significance and treatment of deferred taxation — 171
8. The radical treatment of off-balance-sheet exposures — 183

Part Three   The correlation and treatment of company data — **199**
9. Data sources — 201
10. Varied corporate credit assessments — 260
11. Data collection and assessment in a large corporate — 282

Part Four   Towards the perfect credit analysis — **291**
12. Credit analysis in lending operations — 293
13. Bank analytical and forecasting routines for medium to large corporate credit applications — 319
14. The perfect credit analysis — 344

Bibliography	357
Appendix I. Table of computations and formulas	359
Appendix II. Glossary of reporting, analytical and accounting terms and references	366
Index	379

FOREWORD

by
Sir Kenneth Cork, GBE, DLitt, FCA, FICM
President
Institute of Credit Management

Credit management, as the Institute of Credit Management has taught, and is continuing to teach, is a sophisticated and complicated profession in its own right.

The skill required is the marrying of an assessment of risk, so as not to deny credit being given, with the need to see that the risk is proper in relation to the reward to be obtained by supplying a particular organization.

This book, *The Analysis of Credit*, is not for amateurs. It is for the dedicated professionals. It is an extremely comprehensive and well thought-out work which few could contemplate writing unless they were possessed of an analytical mind and extreme financial skills.

The book itself is worthy of a long period of study. Large organizations and their financial policies are analysed so as to enable the reader to assess not only the financial standing of a business, but its entire future profitability.

I have said in the past, in a jocular way, that when a company is in difficulty, if you read the chairman's report and turn that report into a cashflow, if the company were able to carry out what the chairman said it would carry out, then with its balance sheet and likely facilities, it would have ended up in insolvency.

This book gives you the art of analysis. In fact, it turns you into a detective working mainly from published criteria. It is even more appropriate to the investment manager of a fund. I would like to think that investment managers put the same study into their investments as the credit manager would do, once he has mastered this volume.

The difficulty is going to be that both the fund manager and the credit manager are very busy people with large numbers of cases coming to them upon which to make decisions. They would, therefore, be unable to put the time into full analysis of each customer on each occasion. However, where there is a major customer and a large sum of money involved, they should do so.

Here you have the opportunity to have case studies from international conglomerates, small companies, banks, assorted financial institutions logically worked out, with various solutions given in each case and the ultimate solution highlighted.

Most credit managers have to operate on flair; but flair, I think, comes from a detailed knowledge of the basic facts and principles of credit management, or any other science. You cannot paint an impressionist or unorthodox picture, so I believe, unless you have learnt the basic artistic skills at a normal college of art.

A quick decision, therefore, only comes from experience, knowledge, and training. Those who master this book will have those skills. For credit managers, I think the value lies in the fact that the book can be dipped into until there is time to master the whole procedure. To dip into a book, there must be a very quick reference to what you are looking for, and this has been provided.

For instance, if you want to know the difference between 'net worth' and 'net assets', or need to have a list of the documents required for borrowing, this is the book for you. Similarly, if you want to understand the 'acid-test ratio' and its value, again, this is your book.

I have no hesitation in recommending credit managers or anyone concerned with the management of a business to study this book; and in certain cases, I think companies might well give their credit managers a sabbatical in order to master it!

Kenneth Cork

PREFACE

As a coherent discipline, credit analysis is still in its infancy. With this in mind, *The Analysis of Credit* was written to examine corporate analytical methods critically and to develop certain new assessment techniques.

Accordingly, the book discusses in detail a range of accepted financial assessment methods. From these, optimal techniques are correlated in a way intended to be both logical and practical. Credit analysis should, we argue, be regarded as the central commercial consideration. Effective credit management, after all, underpins profitability. Credit analysis, however, is a working tool. It must, therefore, be theoretical, technical, practical, and instinctual if it is to reflect commercial realities. In this writing, we try to consider analysis from each of these standpoints before making recommendations as to how prudent commercial practice can best be served by examinations of creditworthiness.

The foundation of credit analysis is the interpretation of accounting statements. Thus, a working knowledge of accounting principles is essential. While this is not an accountancy textbook, key accounting principles effectively shape the book. Some of the more abstract of these concepts are treated at length, notably, deferred tax, capitalization of leases, and provisions for contingent liabilities and off-balance-sheet exposures.

Analysis does not, however, stop with the reading of accounts. We, therefore, pay considerable attention to sources of data and information-gathering techniques. From these, analysts can sharpen their understanding of the ways in which companies operate.

Throughout the book we stress the importance of synthesis. Credit analysis frequently calls for the collection of large amounts of data. Sense must be made of it. We suggest that data should be best examined in a variety of ways, and at different levels—a concept we call 'dimensionality'. Eventually, these dimensional views must be brought together in a comprehensible synthesis. We argue that this kind of summing-up is best accomplished by financial models. We then show how such models can be constructed. In the course of the text, we build, develop, and test new models concerned with risk description, solvency, and debt-cover.

The literature on credit analysis is sparse. This book will help to supplement the writings on a subject that has now become a main concern of banking and commerce. As noted before, *The Analysis of Credit* is not designed as an accounting text. It is not a course in financial model-building; nor is it an introduction to statistics. The book, however, draws on all three areas and shows how they structure modern credit analysis. The source materials used are given in detail at the end of each chapter and in the Bibliography. A study of these sources will assist in amplifying the scanty critical work on the subject.

Analytical problems need easy-to-understand illustrations and solutions. It is a waste of time and intensely aggravating to be unable to follow a text without cudgelling one's brains. We have, accordingly, provided formulas, justifications, definitions, and many examples of all discussion points. A Glossary of Analytical Terms as well as a Table of Computations and Formulas have been supplied for reference. Also, the detailed Index will enable readers to locate items of interest quickly.

This book is not concerned with consumer credit. It examines the foundations and general development of corporate credit assessment. In particular, we discuss credit analysis as carried out by theorists, companies, banks, reporting agencies, factors, and credit-insurance underwriters. This is not intended to be an exhaustive list. In view of our interest in short to medium-term credit applications, secured and unsecured, this list will serve as indicative only.

Our writing argues that credit is vital to today's economy. Effective credit assessment forms the heart of credit-granting. In this book, credit analysis is treated at its most basic economic level—one company granting credit to another, and with what effects. We feel that this narrow view best answers the needs of working credit managers and loan officers.

In many cases, we have been outspoken concerning 'received ideas' and 'traditional' analytical procedures. Some, in our view, are ill-conceived. Others are merely stupid. Where we have criticized, we have attempted to suggest better alternatives. These alternatives are not, however, intended to be taken as gospel. If this book stimulates other practitioners in further development of key analytical procedures, a useful function will be fulfilled.

Until very recently, credit analysis in its fullest form has been carried out almost solely in banks. The general commercial public has either known nothing about the subject or has tended to confuse analysis with sales-ledger management and accounts collection. Additionally, few distinguish between a company status report and a credit analysis. This work aims to explain the analysis of credit and bring the benefits of analysis to the commerical public. If credit analysis is all that we claim it to be, it is, in fact, the alpha and omega of credit management. Credit management is, of course, integral to all the other main business functions such as product development, sales and marketing, cash management, and accounting. Many of the examples in this writing illustrate the informational links credit analysis can provide between these business functions.

Important as it is, the structure of credit has become fragile and precarious. Over the last few years, we have seen unprecedented levels of company failures, bank collapses, and sovereign defaults. Economic recovery is still awaited. The credit expansion, nevertheless, continues unabated. The nature of credit binds the fortunes of economies on all levels more closely than ever before. This interdependence only increases the fragility of credit. For its strengthening and continuation, it is essential that accurate assessment of credit risk be developed beyond its current capacities. This book indicates problem areas requiring radical and quick solutions—e.g. the management of off-balance-sheet exposures. This and other development areas will be greatly benefitted by computerized analytical functions. Others will not. The point cannot be made too strongly that the computer is a tool of the human mind, not a substitute for it. By the same token, a mystical reliance on 'gut feeling' or predigested ideas that are merely 'received' must be anathema to real analysis.

Credit analysis is no respecter of persons. Bankers, for obvious reasons, have come to regard their analytical skills highly. In many cases, these opinions are warranted. In many other instances, bank analysis is antediluvian. A good many poor credit decisions have been hidden by reschedulings, moratoria, and a range of other devices to delay the impact of loan losses on balance sheets. This legerdemain is not so readily available to companies. It is interesting to note that since Myers and Forgy's bank evaluation scoring model research in the 1960's, the most important analytical developments have come from the universities and the corporate sector.

Since Altman's work in 1968 on corporate-insolvency forecasting, new liquidity concepts, performance measurements, statistical routines, and financial models have proliferated, changing the focus of credit analysis from a static to a dynamic discipline.

Important developments in accepted accounting practice in the UK and US have contributed materially to the making of more accurate and indicative credit assessments. We examine some of these developments along with the differences between UK and US accounting standards.

Government interference has tended to harm economies. In the UK, government interference has likewise harmed credit analysis. Mythical distinctions are made between 'large' and 'small' companies. So-called small firms are allowed reporting exemptions. These result in the production of modified accounts. For analysts, these modifications greatly dimish the value of accounting statements—the formation of a true and fair view of financial condition. With the possibility of further modifications to company accounts, a continuing concern of credit analysis must be the overcoming of information gaps. As part of the new ground broken in this book, we suggest certain estimating procedures and financial models that help in bridging these gaps.

In summary, *The Analysis of Credit* attempts to give an overview of corporate credit appraisal techniques. With hope, the book will serve as an aid to practitioners as well as a stimulus to further research in the discipline.

Alexander Bathory, MA, MICM
Trade and Commercial Credit Corporation Limited
London

ACKNOWLEDGEMENTS

In preparing this book, valuable and appreciated assistance was received from the following:

A. W. Brooks, FCIS, FICM—Credit Manager, Phillips Petroleum Company Europe-Africa

J. A. Cooper, AIB, MICM—Manager, Cash Management, Gulf Oil (Great Britain) Limited

Sir Kenneth Cork, GBE, D Litt, FCA, FICM—President, Institute of Credit Management

J. Dawson, FICM—Former Director of Public Affairs, Dun & Bradstreet Limited

N. W. F.-R. Dungan—Executive Director, Merrill Lynch Europe Limited

T. A. Godfrey, MICM—Credit Manager, Arbuthnot Factors Limited

A. Hammond, AIB, MBIM—Assistant Head of Banking Training, Barclays Bank PLC

The Rt Hon The Earl Howe, MA, AIB—Manager, Barclays Bank PLC

D. L. Howson, FCIS, FICM—General Manager and Underwriter, Trade Indemnity PLC

I. A. Marshall, CA, MICM—Chairman, Trade and Commerical Credit Corporation Limited

C. A. McCartan, MC, MICM—Marketing Manager, Trade Indemnity PLC

Ms I. Sarandacos, MA—Former Economist, Trade Indemnity PLC

D. W. Plevin, BSc, MBA, MICM—Director, QUI Credit Assessment Limited

I. Ross—Head of Library Department, Trade Indemnity PLC

A. G. Trypanis, BA—Head of Credit, Banque Indosuez

M. N. Wright, AIB—Director, Arbuthnot Factors Limited

Views advanced in this book are not necessarily representative of those persons who have provided assistance or of their organizations unless explicitly stated.

Part One

BROAD VIEWS AND DEVELOPMENTS IN CREDIT ANALYSIS

1

DEFINITION AND PURPOSE OF CREDIT ANALYSIS

Credit analysis is the assessment of ability and willingness to meet deferred payment obligations. Applications for deferred payment take many forms, among them:

1. Trade credit
2. Bank loans
3. Issuance of debt securities
4. Cash acceleration finance, e.g. factoring
5. Mortgages
6. Credit insurance to cover buyer insolvency and delayed settlements

Analytical assessment is largely, but not wholly, numerically based. The numerical data on which analysis operates is taken from a range of sources. The chief sources are:

(a) accounting statements
(b) data lodged for public inspection, e.g. registered indebtedness
(c) representations from directors or managers seeking the credit
(d) financial and other types of private investigations
(e) rating agencies, e.g. Standard & Poor's Corporation
(f) credit and financial reporting companies, e.g. Extel Statistical Services Ltd
(g) credit analysis companies, e.g. Trade and Commercial Credit Corporation Ltd
(h) economic and market reports, e.g. periodic reports issued by Trade Indemnity PLC or Midland Bank PLC
(i) financial and general press information
(j) unaudited financial statements, e.g. Interim accounting extracts produced by public companies
(k) special financial statements produced in support of particular credit applications, e.g. cashflow projections and sales forecasts in support of a bank accommodation
(l) description of internal credit management and general management procedures and aims, e.g. descriptions produced for factoring or for credit insurance 'audits'
(m) intercompany or industry-sector intelligence, e.g. Trade Protection Association exchanges of information between members
(n) interbank intelligence
(o) trade references
(p) bankers' opinions and references

In analysis, the data gained from these sources can be subjected to computational routines.

The programme of computational routines is continually expanding in order to provide more indicative and accurate findings. Thus, effective credit analysis is not merely a matter of learning a list of calculations or procedures.

Traditional and newly-developed computational routines are used in analysis to furnish performance indicators of all kinds as well as forecasts. Examples of performance indicators could be:

1. Assessments of measurements of profitability
2. Liquidity judged against specific credit exposures
3. Credit periods allowed customers

Forecasting can be used to provide such information as:

1. Future sales
2. Future cash inflows
3. The probability of failure due to insolvency

The purpose of credit analysis—or the carrying out of selected and systematic routines—is to determine as dispassionately as possible whether or not an applicant is willing and financially able to accept credit in specific amounts according to specific terms and conditions. In other words, is it likely that the amount and the terms of the credit will be honoured?

In this writing, we are concerned only with corporate applications for credit. These are requests for credit from companies made to other companies (suppliers) or to providers of finance. In examining corporate credit analysis, we shall consider a range of existing procedures and develop new procedures concerned with specific problems.

The point should be made that credit analysis has no hard and fast routines. It varies with the type of credit and the kind of institution providing the credit. Analysis of credit is not, therefore, like algebra, in which there is a menu of agreed assumptions and methods of calculation. The basic assumptions and computational routines of credit analysis vary in the way suggested earlier, and also grow in response to the development of new financing instruments.

Analytical assumptions

Effective credit analysis must mirror the real world as we know it. If analytical findings fail to do this, the findings will violate common sense. All assessment processes in credit analysis call for some measure of human judgement. Whilst many computations and forecasts can, and should, be performed by computers, human judgement must select the computer inputs. Of course, seasoned judgement of one kind or another should also inform the programs on which the computers operate. Seasoned judgement presupposes a backlog of practical experience. This backlog of experience is thorough familiarity with the real world in respect of a certain problem or set of problems.

No human judgement process can be totally dispassionate. Having said that, the most experienced and prudent judgements should, in credit analysis, seek to minimize emotional responses and rely, wherever possible, on fact and extrapolations from fact.

From the earlier list of analytical sources, it is clear that the collection of facts is a prime duty of good analysis. Facts vary in recency, depth, proveability, and relevance. The judgement or treatment of them is thus the second duty of analysis.

Credit analysts are not normally ultimate decision-makers. Analysts' chief functions tend to be:

(a) to supply information to decision-makers
(b) to keep watching briefs on existing credits' performance
(c) in banks, to assist marketing and new business development officers in the design of credit instruments

In essence, the credit analyst's work is technical. It therefore has its own jargon drawn from an amalgam of banking, accountancy, and statistical terminologies. Over the last decade, borrowings from the computer world have contributed to this 'credit-speak'.

Because the real world does not stand still, decision-makers must make decisions quickly. In many cases they will not be financial specialists. Accordingly, it is important that good credit analysis be both concise and fully comprehensible. It must speak to decision-makers in their own languages. It must summarize what are often complex problems and clarify what was previously obscure. It must seek always to highlight key information from an indiscriminate mass of data. Above all, good analysis must make both intelligent and practical recommendations to decision-makers. Thus, the guiding spirit of effective credit analysis is deliberate simplification. Likewise, the ultimate criterion of good credit analysis must be common sense.

Let us look at some simple solutions to analytical problems stemming from our previous assumptions.

Credit analysis should mirror the real world

If we were asked to prepare a sales forecast for a financially sound and well-managed company selling attractively-priced and popular products in a buoyant market, our forecast would not mirror the real world if we predicted a sharp downturn in sales in the short term. Such a prediction would run counter to the facts we were given. This is not to say, however, that the company's market, as well as sales impact, may not have peaked. If so, we might be correct in predicting a drop in sales provided that we can justify our assumptions about the company's market, as well as its sales and marketing impact. Accordingly, whenever divergences between a body of facts and a forecast of facts arise, analysts should attempt to justify their opinions.

Violation of common sense

If we are asked to provide the 'nicest' (in the sense of most indicative) measurement of a company's liquid funds for use in its day-to-day operations, we would violate both general and accounting common sense if our measurement of liquid resources was a larger quantity than the company's net current assets as posted in its balance sheet. Net current assets, or working capital, is a 'generous' measurement of liquid funds for day-to-day use. We are being asked to provide a nicer measurement. It must, therefore, be less than working capital. This means that some quantities or proportions of quantities must be deducted from current assets *before* deduction of current liabilities.

In speaking of accounting common sense, we are bound to assume as a matter of course that audited accounting statements, being independently validated, are in default of any proof to the contrary, 'true and fair'. Audited accounting quantities or 'facts' must then be regarded as reflections of the real world in which a particular company operates. Audited figures are thus the analyst's numerical touchstone. To dispute audited fact requires considerable justification. The availability of further facts on which to base such justification is normally not practicable for analysts, working as they are, at some remove from the companies they examine.

Seasoned judgement in analytical selection

If we are asked to build a financial model to predict the possibility of corporate collapse due to insolvency, we must begin with a selection of the model's component parts. To do this, we would have to ask what main financial movements most contributed to solvency or insolvency. The seasoned judgement in such a case would not only rely on personal opinions, but would take prior research into account. Both prior findings and personal contributions to the problem would require testing. The purpose of this testing would be to see whether or not actual events show beyond a reasonable doubt that the final list of model components do, in fact, make up the main financial flows that most contribute to solvency or insolvency. The building of a list and its testing calls for inductive and deductive reasoning. Apart from selecting the most reasoned and empirically sound list of quantities, the 'seasoning' of our judgement in making our selection presupposes a thorough knowledge of the framework in which companies' financial conditions are encapsulated. This framework is, of course, accountancy—and, in particular, the interpretation of accounting flows.

Dispassionate judgements

In most instances, credit analysts should seek to make non-emotional judgements. If we are asked to consider the capital adequacy of a company, our first consideration will be to ask the question, 'Adequate for what purposes?'. Our next consideration will be to try and assess the company's current capital position. For instance, do we see a net deficiency of assets in the balance sheet? Does the company's current and long-term financing look adequate as at accounting date? What about the future? Is the cost of capital being met at present by the company? What is the interest cover? The answers to such questions will be largely factual and established from the company's accounts. Leaving aside, for the present, any discussion of accounting frailties, the most direct answers to our questions will be given by making certain computations. None of these entails any appreciable emotional response; merely experienced-based judgement to select the most indicative quantities on which to build the most indicative ratios.

An emotional response to a question about the adequacy of capital in a particular company could be something along the following lines:

The sectoral averages for capital adequacy in companies of this type show higher rates of return on capital employed and less gearing than our subject company. From this we can deduce that our company's capital adequacy is not particularly good.

Such a finding is fraught with problems—some of which are caused by lack of dispassionate judgement. Firstly, it is no more than a received idea and in no manner an empirical fact that industry averages say anything significant about the performances of individual companies operating in those industries or sectors. To base a judgement on a received idea implies that one emotionally espouses that idea when supporting facts have not been adduced.

Secondly, return on capital employed is only one measurement ratio which can be used as an indicator of profitability as well as capital adequacy. If a company is new (and does not have sizeable reserves made up of called-up capital, reserves, and latest profits), yet the company has earned high net profits in its latest period, the return on capital employed (ROCE) will be necessarily very high in percentage terms. But will this high percentage tell us very much about capital adequacy? Will it not tell us more about trading conditions and good luck?

Even given the latest profits and existing reserves plus share capital, what does this tell us about the company's future foreseeable capital needs? And what do these future needs have to do with other companies' capital needs even if they are operating in the same industry sector?

Thirdly, gearing, like other corporate data is largely idiosyncratic. Companies operating in the same sector may differ greatly in gearing—and for perfectly justifiable reasons. High gearing, accordingly, does not tell one much in itself concerning capital adequacy. A company's capital resources may be extremely adequate because of the proportionally high mix of borrowed capital to equity capital. Again, behind the basic assumption that high gearing in some way signifies inadequate capital resources, we see a received idea which may not be borne out by facts in individual cases such as this example.

Fourthly, analysts should be wary of using emotive attributes such as 'good'. Whole philosophies have been written around the meaning of good. 'Good', as credit analysts should use the word, should imply pragmatic benefits. In this way, if companies exist primarily to make profits, then whatever contributes positively to profitability will be held 'good', as profitability fulfils a company's prime function. In certain instances, it would be perfectly possible to argue that a small capital base including a high level of gearing will contribute to certain companies' profitability in the best way. That is to say, a small and highly-geared capital base will be the most adequate for some companies. If an analyst uses an attribute like 'good' which normally has a high emotive overtone, he must be careful to justify the 'goodness' in so far as possible. These justifications, like all others in credit analysis, should be based on fact drawn from accounting statements of a reliable kind, and forecasts based on the most common sense and reasonable probabilities drawn from the real world external to accounting statements. Above all, justifications, wherever feasible, should be based on particular instances at hand and not on industry, sectoral, or other such generalities.

Deliberate simplification

To maximize the speed and accuracy of decision-making, good credit analysis will deliberately summarize and simplify data. If a proposition cannot be cast in simple terms it is not a proposition worth considering. Simplicity need entail neither loss of accuracy nor nuance. An analytical report can enter into great technical detail, but quick and accurate

8 BROAD VIEWS AND DEVELOPMENTS IN CREDIT ANALYSIS

decision-making will be best served by analysts presenting their summaries and recommendations before detailed treatment of the subject. In conventional mathematics, computational routines are abbreviated by universally accepted symbols; in credit analysis, there will be few such universally accepted notations. Analysts must, accordingly, show or describe their assumptions, divergences from fact, forecast outcomes, and the like, at some stage of a report. Notwithstanding, the most important part of an analysis is its findings and not its workings.

To illustrate the point, consider the two opinions as to a company's solvency that follow. Which would be most appreciated and most useful to a commercial credit manager?

OPINION 1

In brief, our financial model showed that debt-service ability was non-existent; profitability had declined over the period in question and was very low for the last year; capital resources in the latest year were slim and that without strong profits in the next year, the company's capital could well be insufficient for even its existing turnover; and that liquidity had worsened and was presently inadequate to meet day-to-day requirements once stocks had been deducted from working capital. The model scores for both years indicated a company well within the risk area of an insolvent crisis.

OPINION 2

In brief, our financial model $Y = k \left(\sum_{x_{1-5}} \right)$ showed X_1 at 0.4; X_2 at 1.3; X_3 at 2.7; X_4 at 0.1; X_5 at 0.8. After weightings, we obtained scores of -15 and -34, both falling into 'at risk area'. In the fifth component, we normalized net current assets before inputting.

Net current assets before inputting

Opinion 1 discusses the workings of the financial model in respect of the company's main financial flows contributing to solvency/insolvency. Whilst none of these flows was quantified, as the weighted end ratios would mean nothing in isolation to the credit manager, the significance of each ratio was noted briefly. This opinion also gave the credit manager an idea of trend. Quantities were noted to be declining and key flows had deteriorated. In operating the model, the analyst attempted to compute a rigorous measurement of liquidity by normalizing stock from current assets. Nevertheless, he avoided use of the technical term 'normalizing' and spoke of deducting stock from working capital. The credit manager to whom he is speaking will certainly know about stock and about working capital. He may have been puzzled by normalizing, nettings-out, and net current assets. The individual ratio movements together with the model's total scores for the company were so poor that the analyst stated that the firm was greatly at risk of an impending insolvent crisis—not merely that the firm was, or that it was about to be, technically insolvent.

Opinion 2 was far briefer and gave the model's formula as well as listing what the credit manager could only suppose to be the subject company's latest year's ratios on these financial flows. The ratios in isolation show no trend. Nor do they in, and of themselves, tell the credit manager anything—unless he is perfectly and immediately familiar with the composition of the individual ratios. Can one assume that this sort of technical information will be instantly recalled from memory or even that the credit manager should be expected to unravel the analyst's shorthand by consulting a key?

It was noted that model scores were −15 and −34. Do these apply to the later and prior year respectively? We cannot be sure. Thus, what might have been a useful index of trend turns out to be a puzzle that the credit manager must take time to work out.

Finally, the analyst mentions that in 'the fifth component, we normalized net current assets before inputting'. Firstly, the language is technical. Secondly, it wilfully obscures a simple procedure. Thirdly, it provides no justification for the normalization. Fourthly, it does not state what was deducted from what in the normalizing. And fifthly, the sentence construction makes the meaning of the sentence very unclear.

Presumably, the analyst meant that before inputting data (a dreadful neologism in itself), he deducted whatever he deducted from current assets before deducting current liabilities in order to arrive at a nicer measurement of working capital.

Whilst Opinion 1 is by no means perfect, Opinion 2 is extremely flawed. Opinion 1 does make clear to the credit manager that the company is about to undergo an insolvent crisis with all the attendant implications. Opinion 2 may have reached the same conclusions mathematically, but does not say so. The numbers, in other words, have not been interpreted. Opinion 2 is not only a skeleton, but a rachitic one. By contrast, Opinion 1 must be a figure by Rubens.

Intelligent and practical recommendations

Commercial credit managers, and others having to make decisions on a high number of applications, require intelligent and practical guidance from analysts. A recommendation will be intelligent if it satisfies the following criteria:

(a) it is an accurate interpretation of the most accurate and most recent data
(b) it is constructive in so far as possible
(c) it is expressed succinctly and significantly
(d) it is informed by knowledge of the subject and its pertinent ramifications

A recommendation will be practical if the advice it contains can be carried out in the real world, and notably, the world of business.

Two analytical recommendations follow. Let us consider their intelligence and practicality.

RECOMMENDATION A

Its 1983 accounts show the company to be illiquid and dependent on overdraft borrowings as well as trade creditor financing. We recommend, accordingly, a reduction in monthly exposure to £20,000 with this amount covered by a bank guarantee until further review.

RECOMMENDATION B

Its 1985 accounts show the company to be illiquid mainly due to the service of high levels of bank borrowings. This is coupled with apparent over-reliance on trade creditor financing.

Indications are that a down-turn in the company's market is imminent. If this happens, illiquidity will almost certainly reach dangerous levels. We therefore advise you to reduce the company's monthly credit from £150,000 to £20,000 on strict 30 day terms. If any arrears develop over the next six months, we recommend dealing with this firm on a cash with order basis to replace the £20,000 p.c.m. credit.

Recommendation A appears to be based on accounts that are three years old. No forecasts have been made to attempt to update the 1983 figures. No mention is made of liquidity trend. The analyst recommends a reduction in credit exposure but does not state what the previous exposure was. This would have been helpful to the credit manager who looks at hundreds of accounts and cannot carry all customers' credit limits in his head. Next, this recommendation does not suggest particular terms relevant to a reduction in exposure. Presumably, if he is concerned enough to reduce exposure, the payment terms may also have to be altered with the alteration in credit limit. Finally, the analyst advises that the new and reduced exposure be secured by a bank guarantee.

We were told, however, that the company is highly dependent upon bank overdraft. Is it practical to suggest that the company's bankers will be happy to subordinate any prior claims or charges they hold in favour of a trade creditor? If the company is as illiquid as the analyst indicates, the bank is probably allowing it borrowings on a secured overdraft. This facility will most likely be secured by means of a fixed and floating charge over the business or by directors' personal guarantees. The suggestion, therefore, of looking to the subject's bankers for a guarantee is both naïve and impractical.

Recommendation B, on the other hand, is based on up-to-date figures (1985 accounts). It specifies the causes of illiquidity and analyses them, e.g. over-reliance on trade creditor financing. That in itself implies lax payment performance and poor cash inflows. Also, bank indebtedness is noted. It is plain that the analyst has calculated the cost of this borrowing. He has arrived at his opinion concerning bank debt servicing presumably by computing gross cash inflow against bank debt or by means of another indicative flow.

Also, Recommendation B speaks of short-term market developments relevant to the company. The analyst forecasts an even severer cash famine if the market falls. Such an assumption in no way violates common sense. It is almost truistic. It does, however, help put the subject company's perilous liquid condition into perspective.

A sharp drop in credit exposure is recommended and 30 days terms are specified. Because the analyst is so clearly expecting the worst, he stipulates a total cancellation of the credit facility and replacement of it with cash terms should any arrears develop over the next six months—the six months apparently reflecting short-term developments both in the company and in its market.

Spreadsheets and the treatment of data

The orderly and informative arrangement of data is of great importance to analysts attempting to arrive at overall views of companies' financial conditions. The point should be made at once that there is no generally recommendable spreadsheet for all credit applications. One credit analysis may also require more than one spreadsheet.

The purpose of a spreadsheet is to rearrange, and in some cases, to restate, quantities normally found in accounting statements. Spreadsheets, or spreads, rearrange and restate for the following reasons;

(a) to point out main financial flows not already apparent from accounting statements, e.g. gross cash flow
(b) to make clearer key financial movements, e.g. debt-service ability
(c) to provide both particular views and overviews of companies' financial conditions, e.g. liquidity as a function of total assets, or synoptic model scores in insolvency prediction

Effective spreadsheets should be drafted for specific purposes. Analysts will gain quicker and clearer views if spreads relating to particular purposes are kept separate and not amalgamated into one document. The spreadsheet should follow one of the main tenets of credit analysis—to simplify deliberately—and not to obscure. Thus, if an analyst requires holistic model scores, key performance indicators, e.g. financial and operating ratios, and main financial flows, e.g. net cash flow or working capital, it would be sensible to produce three separate spreadsheets. Results and interpretations of these spreads can then be brought together in a particular section of the credit analysis, and salient items can be mentioned again in the summary or opinion.

Limitations of space normally mean that analysts will not be able to note many important computations on the spreadsheets themselves. For this reason, it is good practice to keep working papers and attach them to the relevant spreads. For example, if asked to calculate hybrid quantities such as current debt (where current debt signifies bank and other financial creditors plus any government departmental creditors, e.g. Inland Revenue or VAT), the analyst will be well-advised to keep notes as to the items under current liabilities he chose to represent current debt in order easily to justify his computation. For instance:

Creditors: Amounts falling due in one year   100,688

The notes to the accounts will itemize these current liabilities:

Overdraft:	40,275
Trade creditors:	35,241
Social security:	25,172
	100,688

Given our definition of current debt, the analyst would sum:

Overdraft:	40,275
Social security:	25,172
	65,447 = current debt

Working calculations of this type should be kept to hand in the event further explanations are needed. This can be particularly important when quantities other than accounting numbers are fed into computers.

Detailed spreads providing key financial flow information should take a form along the following lines:

	+/−%	£'000s 1985	1984
Gross cashflow			
Profit after taxation			
+			
Depreciation			
+			
Increase in deferred taxation			
+			
TOTAL GROSS CASHFLOW			
Tangible net worth			
Total assets			
−			
Intangible assets			
−			
Total liabilities			
TANGIBLE NET WORTH			

Spreads providing financial model information vary widely. For ratio-based models which are a common type of formula, data should take a form similar to the following:

Model: $\mu = k(a+b+c)$
Where μ = debt capacity, k = ratio weights (constant), and
a = Net cashflow/current debt
b = Funds generated from operations/current liabilities
c = Normalized working capital/total assets

	+/−%	£'000s 1985	1984
a: *Net cashflow*			
Profit after taxation			
Depreciation			
Increase in deferred taxation			
Less dividends			

	+/−%	£'000s 1985	1984
TOTAL NET CASHFLOW			
a: *Current debt*			
Overdraft			
Taxation			
Other			
Other			
TOTAL CURRENT DEBT			
NET CASHFLOW/CURRENT DEBT:			

We mentioned earlier that different credit and other types of financial applications should be spread in varying ways. For instance, it is hard to read the data spread for a company producing only modified accounts when this data is arranged sparsely over the spreadsheet one would use for a company producing full audited statements. A completed spreadsheet should avoid looking sparse or 'bitty'. One quantum of information should flow logically, if possible, from another. Figure 1.1 shows a computerized spreadsheet used for all credit accounts in the sales ledger of a major company.

Our immediate feeling must be that this spreadsheet is, in fact, harder to read than any set of accounting statements. The information it tries to convey is spread indiscriminately. There is an attempt apparent here to try and convey every piece of information that can be extracted from accounts. In a sense, this is commendable; but in a more important sense, it is a waste of time and effort. Not all information is needed for what is, after all, a short-term, practical application—the granting of monthly trade credit in varying amounts.

What, for example, is the sense of computing three gearing ratios in such applications? What is achieved by carrying out decimals to six places in ratio measurements? Is an acid-test of 0.862565 truly more informative than 0.863 or 0.9? The six decimal places show misapplied sophistication. Neither current nor acid-test (liquid) ratios are anything other than a rough guide to solvency and liquidity. Solvency is more accurately and represent-atively measured, in any event, by certain holistic models, e.g. Altman's, Taffler's, or Bathory's. These models rely not solely upon balance-sheet data but flow information more indicative of companies' dynamic natures. This kind of dynamism is not wholly reflected in balance sheets. Also, nicer computations of liquidity are available to analysts than the liquid or acid-test ratio. A simple example is:

Normalized working capital
Current assets—an agreed portion of stock
Current liabilities

The agreed portions of stock deducted will vary according to the type of company under consideration. Varying portions of stock truly contributing to liquidity by quick turnover can be made along the following lines:

Manufacturing companies
Assumption: 75% of stock normally represented by raw materials and work-in-progress (WIP) and thus not readily saleable.
Therefore
Accept only 25% of stock in current assets.

Retailing companies
Assumption: 25% of stock is normally represented by slow-moving and/or obsolete items not readily saleable.
Therefore
Accept only 75% of stock in current assets.

Non-specific or combined operations
Assumption: For prudence, take the mean of 75% and 25% for the above classes of company—i.e. 50% of stock normally representing readily saleable items.
Therefore
Accept 50% of stock in current assets.

If Figure 1.1 is intended to be a spreadsheet to be read in order to illuminate accounting statements, it must fail. For trade credit management purposes, what can the sense be of

BALANCE SHEET ANALYSIS

DATA £'000s	Year 1	Year 2	Year 3	Year 4	Year 5
Financial year	280284	280285			
Sales	7283	9161			
Pre-tax profit (loss)	87	42			
Fixed assets	136	143			
Current assets	782	1046			
Current liabilities	764	1037			
Trade debtors	651	884			
Stock	123	129			
Trade creditors	718	620			
Overdraft	46	413			
Ext. loans (not inter-co) in C.L.	0	0			
Inter-co loans in C.L.	0	0			
Directors' loans in C.L.	0	0			
H.P. & leases in C.L.	4	0			
Ext. loans (not inter-co) long term	0	0			
Inter-co loans long term	0	0			
Directors' loans long term	0	0			
H.P. & leases long term	0	13			
Deferred taxation (on B/S)	39	27			
Depreciation	28	40			
Post-tax profit	56	28			
Cost of sales	6693	8530			
Capital commitments	0	0			
Continent liabs and cont. def. tax		14			
Intangibles	11	41			
Increased in deferred taxation	20	12			

RATIOS

Capital employed	154	152	0	0
Nett worth	115	112	0	0
Tangible nett worth	104	57	0	0
Current ratio	1.023560	1.008678	ERR	ERR
Acid test	0.862565	0.884281	ERR	ERR
Profit margin	1.194562	0.458465	ERR	ERR
Prime ratio	56.49350	27.63157	ERR	ERR
Total borrowing as % of total assets	5.446623	35.82842	ERR	ERR
External borrowing as % of total assets	5.446623	35.82842	ERR	ERR
Stock turn	6.164355	5.139722	ERR	ERR
Debtor turn	32.62597	35.22104	ERR	ERR
Creditor turn (by cost of sales)	39.15583	26.52989	ERR	ERR
Creditor turn (by sales)	35.98379	24.70254	ERR	ERR
Bankers' ratio	74.67532	73.68421	ERR	ERR
Gross cashflow	104	80	0	0
Current debt	50	413	0	0
Current debt serviceability	208	19.37046	ERR	ERR
Gearing I	15.05235	10.80038	ERR	ERR
Gearing II	12.77641	5.035335	ERR	ERR
Gearing III	1.960784	0.756938	ERR	ERR
Model score	58.85661	12.71893	ERR	ERR

Figure 1.1 Specimen company credit analysis spreadsheet

having random profit and loss items in balance-sheet data? What will a lone depreciation figure tell analysts or credit managers? Figures to be truly informative should be compared with other figures or summed or deducted to give flow rather than static quantities. For a credit manager or analyst, the depreciation item noted in Figure 1.1 does not 'speak'. But it can be made quite eloquent in the following examples:

A.

Gross cashflow
Profit after taxation: 5,000
+
Depreciation: 16,000
+
Increase in deferred taxation: 20,000
TOTAL GROSS CASHFLOW   41,000

Depreciation contributed 39% to GCF and suggests that the company may have a comparatively high investment in fixed assets.

B.

In modified accounts where no depreciation figure is given we can calculate backwards for depreciation. Once calculated, depreciation will enable us to determine gross cashflow.

Fixed assets: 25,678.00

The accounting number above gives no differentiation of classes of fixed assets, e.g. freeholds, leaseholds, land, equipment.

Assumption:
Freeholds/leaseholds/land: Depreciated @ 2%, reducing balance basis over 50 years
&
Equipment: Depreciated @ 20%, reducing balance over useful life
Therefore
For fixed assets showing no differentiation, take the mean of 2% and 20%, i.e. 11% and depreciate @ 11% on a reducing balance basis.

Computation: $\dfrac{\text{Fixed assets} \times 11}{89} = $ depreciation in latest period

The fixed assets noted above are posted net after estimated depreciation of 3,174 for the latest period has contributed to gross cashflow.

The computational procedures for arriving at depreciation need not be noted in the spreadsheet. But depreciation, either known or arrived at, should be displayed for some greater purpose than it has in Fig. 1.1. This spreadsheet shows another questionable item: cost of sales. Full accounting statements will show what we must, in the absence of any notes to the contrary, accept as the direct costs of sales. Indirect costs and establishment costs are noted subsequently in the profit and loss account after gross profit has been arrived at:

Turnover:	190,000,000
Cost of sales:	150,456,000
Gross profit:	39,544,000
Establishment costs:	28,478,234
Profit on ordinary activities:	11,065,766

The distinction between direct and indirect costs of sales is clear in the above illustration. Modified accounting statements, however, will not give a profit and loss account, and full accounts will often fail to provide sufficiently detailed breakdowns on the profit and loss account to enable analysts to distinguish accurately between direct and indirect costs. Consider the following profit and loss account of Monsanto PLC:

	1983 £'000s
Turnover:	371,227
Cost of sales:	296,845
Gross profit:	74,382
Selling and distribution costs:	10,964
Administration expenses:	9,183
Other operating income:	(5,783)
Other operating expenses:	4,023
Share of profit of associated company:	(544)
	17,843
Profit on ordinary activities before interest:	56,539

No notes clarify whether or not the selling costs posted together with distribution expenses are represented by sales commissions paid in the period or any other items which could arguably be treated as direct sales costs. Nor do we know the breakdown between these selling and distribution costs. Furthermore, what part of administration expenses is represented by salaries and wages and directors' remuneration? Some of these items could possibly be direct sales costs. Have proportions of such items already been taken into cost of sales noted under turnover?

The simple option, of course, is to treat this profit and loss account exactly as it has been set out, accepting cost of sales as total direct costs and taking all expense items after gross profit as indirect costs of sales. In practice, this easy option is often the most sensible once analysts have reassured themselves of the quality both of the subject company and of the auditors.

The *direct* cost of sales is extremely important not only in computing and assessing gross profit, but also in assessing a company's payment performance, albeit roughly. A very approximate computation of payment to trade creditors can be made by:

$$\frac{\text{Trade creditors}}{\text{Direct costs of sales}} \times 365 \text{ days}$$

Monsanto's 'trade creditors' turnover' would thus be:

$$\frac{£'000s}{} $$
$$\frac{13,857}{296,845} \times 365 = 17 \text{ days}$$

providing that the figure noted as cost of sales in the profit and loss account represents total direct costs of sales. If there were any additional direct costs, e.g. any direct labour and sales commissions, the trade creditor turnover figure would be shortened.

Figure 1.1 includes the cost of sales item apparently on the understanding that direct costs only are represented as we see later computations of 'creditor turn'. Are these creditors trade creditors only or are they trade and sundry creditors? The main points here are that particularly in abridged or modified accounts, the accurate computation of direct sales costs will prove extremely difficult in most cases, if not impossible. Also, these abridged and all too common accounting statements will often fail to note a breakdown of current liabilities. Thus, accuracy in determining trade creditors as well as direct costs of sales will not be practicable. For these reasons, we argue that as these items appear in Figure 1.1, they are overly ambitious—particularly in a company supplying credit to a high percentage of small firms producing only modified statements.

Next, we see provision for 'model score'. If the model used by this company is a multiple-ratio formula, it would be more informative to give the separate ratios first, and then the holistic scores. Such an arrangement would serve both to tie together the fragmented information in the data and ratios sections as well as showing clearly the contributions to model scores made by the component ratios.

Finally, ratios are defined as comparisons of one quantity with another:

$$5 \text{ peaches}/10 \text{ pears} = 0.5$$
$$\text{or}$$
$$50\%$$

Why, then, has capital employed been included as a ratio? Or the two net worth measurements? Possibly, they are added for the computer's convenience. Nevertheless, they should be elsewhere on the spreadsheet.

In summary, spreadsheets are credit analysts' most important tool. Whether manually operated or computerized, they should make the interpretation of accounting statements quicker and easier. Trend in one form or another should be noted. Numbers should be rounded-up in most cases. £7·6 m is easier to digest than £7,568,431.12. Decimal places should not be carried out to absurd degrees in what are only very approximate measures, e.g. current ratio or acid-test. Data should be grouped cohesively and logically to give an idea of flows and their interaction. Financial models using spreadsheet data should be set out in full where model components will provide further flow information. Spreadsheet information should be restrained. No spread can convey total information; it should illuminate. An endless and indiscriminate mass of data only obscures. The essential questions a spreadsheet should ask are:

1. What are the main flows not already apparent from the accounting statements?
2. What are the assumptions on which any re-statements or reconstructions of numbers or flows will be made?

3. What kind of comparisons of numbers or flows will be most useful to the type of credit application in question?
4. What kind of synopsis or 'total view' will the spreadsheet afford?

At the heart of a spreadsheet lies synthesis and antithesis. This is easily illustrated. Certain key financial indicators are not at once apparent in accounting statements. Gross cashflow, for one, is a composite quantity represented by the sum of profit after taxation, depreciation, and the increase in deferred taxation. The summing of these quantities gives a synthesis: gross cashflow. But gross cashflow is most informative as a quantity if compared with, say, current liabilities, another composite. The comparison will indicate whether or not a company's current obligations due for payment at accounting date could have been serviced solely from cash coming into the company. The comparison process is an antithesis, i.e. two quantities have been placed in opposition for measurement purposes. Ratios in this way are antithetical. The enlightening process of synthesis and antithesis should inform the entire spreadsheet.

MODEL: $Y = 0.20(X_1 + X_2 + X_3 + X_4 + X_5)$
Company name:
Year ending:

	%	19--	19--

Gross cashflow
   Profit after taxation
   Depreciation
   Increase in deferred taxation
TOTAL GROSS CASHFLOW

Current debt
   Overdraft
   Current portions of loans
   Taxation
   Government agency creditors
   Others
TOTAL CURRENT DEBT
PROFIT BEFORE TAXATION
CAPITAL EMPLOYED

Equity:
   Called-up capital
   Profit and loss account
   Reserves
   Others
TOTAL EQUITY
CURRENT LIABILITIES

Total assets
   Fixed assets
   Intangible assets
   Current assets

TOTAL ASSETS
Total liabilities
  Current liabilities
  Long-term liabilities
  Capital contracts entered into
  Contingent liabilities/portion thereof
  Other
TOTAL LIABILITIES
Tangible net worth
  Total assets
  Less
  Intangible assets
  Less
  Total liabilities
TOTAL TANGIBLE NET WORTH
WORKING CAPITAL

MODEL KEY: X_1 = gross cashflow/current debt
               X_2 = profit before taxation/capital employed
               X_3 = equity/current liabilities
               X_4 = tangible net worth/total liabilities
               X_5 = working capital/total assets $0.20 = k$(multiplier)

Figure 1.2 A purpose-built spreadsheet for operation of an insolvency-prediction model

Ratio	19--/computations		19--/computations	
X_1	_____	= _____	_____	= _____
+				
X_2	_____	= _____	_____	= _____
+				
X_3	_____	= _____	_____	= _____
+				
X_4	_____	= _____	_____	= _____
+				
X_5	_____	= _____	_____	= _____
TOTALS:	_____ X0.20 =	_____	_____ X0.20 =	_____

Basis points change over the period:

Figure 1.3 Separate or appended spreadsheet for model workings

Figures 1.2 and 1.3 illustrate a logically cohesive spreading of data needed to operate a simple financial model. The data is arranged so that either on computer, or manually, the analyst can form something of an overview of the subject's financial condition following the company's main flows. The workings of the model are made visible in Figure 1.3 so that the analyst can assess each ratio component and its variance over the period. Both spreads are based firmly on the principle of synthesis and antithesis discussed earlier. In this way, composite quantities are calculated and the resulting numbers are given real dimension by spreading them against relevant quantities. Trend is provided throughout the spreads both by juxtaposing two years' worth of figures and by computing percentage increases or decreases. The synoptic model scores which are the *raison d'être* of the spreadsheets will be noted as whole numbers and their trend highlighted by the change in basis points over the two years.

Credit analysis: Summary of assumptions

We have discussed the basic assumptions on which the analysis of credit is based. To summarize, they are as follows:

1. Findings must mirror the real world.
2. Common sense should never be violated.
3. Collection of good-quality, recent data is important, but selection of relevant data is more important.
4. Effective analysis should be comprehensible to final users (decision-makers), and concise to facilitate making decisions.
5. Effective analysis depends largely upon numerical criteria. However, not all analytical criteria are quantifiable with good effect, e.g. management capability. Experience and seasoned judgement can bridge the gap.
6. Credit analysis as a discipline depends upon a thorough familiarity with accepted accounting practices.
7. Judgements, numerical-based and others, should be linked with fact wherever possible; and judgements should be kept as dispassionate as analysts are able to make them.
8. Practical analysis should seek deliberately to simplify.
9. Intelligence and practicality should be the hallmarks of analytical opinions and recommendations.
10. If statements of account are the credit analyst's prime source of reliable data, the spreadsheet is his most useful tool in correlating and interpreting the data.
11. Spreadsheets should be purpose-built and easy to read. Data selection for spreading should be highly discriminating. Every item should serve a purpose. That purpose ought to be plain from the spreadsheet. Spreads should provide what accounting statements have not. The principle of synthesis and antithesis should inform the whole of a spreadsheet. Ultimately, effective spreads afford accurate synopses.

To summarize further, credit analysis is all about asking particularized questions and making informed extrapolations and forecasts from the answers. Very few 'received ideas' cannot be seriously questioned. Our previous remarks on corporate idiosyncracy is a case in point. In that instance, it is arguable that the questioning can be as valuable as the answering. Formulation of any opinions in credit analysis should be based on justification. Justification, wherever possible, must be tied firmly to fact and not to hypothesis.

Credit comes in many forms. We can summarize them by distinguishing the following main types:

(a) trade credit
(b) loans (including mortgage advances)
(c) funding devices, e.g. issuance of debt securities
(d) purchase of debt for cash acceleration purposes, e.g. factoring
(e) buyer settlement delay and insolvency insurances, e.g. credit insurance

Varying kinds of credit analysis will be performed by principals involved in granting these credits. In the course of this writing, we shall look at some of these applications in detail.

Ultimately, all credit analysis seeks to answer the following questions:

1. Has the subject enough liquid resources to honour the credit obligation in full and according to terms?
2. What quantifiable margin of safety will there be if the credit is granted?
3. Do the subject's current and forecast prospects look adequate for future service of the credit?
4. Given that the subject is financially able to support the credit, is he also willing to honour the obligation?

Credit paradox

Perfect liquidity in an ideal world would rule out the need for credit. Companies seeking credit are companies that need cash. The need for cash does not always reflect illiquidity or an insufficiency of cash with which to discharge obligations. Many companies with adequate cash purposefully defer payments to all but the most pressing creditors in order to maximize interest income. Others will postpone settlements to creditors in order to use cash for acquisitions of all kinds. Yet other companies suffer from periodic or chronic cash famines. Some are either on the brink of insolvency or are outright insolvents. All companies have come to expect credit. All credit rests on a paradox. Simply, companies that most need credit are the poorest credit risks. Accordingly, companies who least require credit are the best (least risky) credit propositions.

Risk, therefore, cannot be eliminated from credit decisions. Risk, in financial terms, must vary. No business is static. Commercial dynamics cause companies to make profits, break even, and sustain losses. Risk is not only inherent in any historic accounting, but also, in any post-balance-sheet activity.

Risk, in analytical terms, centres around:

1. Delayed payments
2. Buyer insolvency
3. Disruptions in normal commercial routines, e.g. divestiture
4. Unacceptable commercial practices, e.g. over-reliance on trade creditor financing
5. Political or extraordinary events, e.g. revolutions, wars, fires or floods
6. Currency movements and foreign exchange
7. Failure of guarantee mechanisms, e.g. collapse of bank providing documentary credits, or avoidance of guarantee, e.g. documentary terms not complied with
8. Adverse economic and market conditions

Items 1 and 2 constitute ultimate risks while items 3 to 8 contribute to delayed payments or to outright insolvency and collapse, and must be regarded as proximate risks.

In sum, however, the overriding credit risk is simply not getting paid at the proper time. An ultimate concern with risk must underlie analytical opinions and recommendations. Throughout the remainder of this book, we shall be examining different types of risk and attempting to take them into account in forming analytical judgements.

Distinctions between trade and financial institutions' credit

Credit applications differ primarily in use, scale, and term. These differences notwithstanding, important distinctions can be drawn between intercompany credit (trade credit) and the wide range of credit facilities provided to companies by banks and other financial institutions. The use to which 'financial credits' are put, the scale or monetary size of the facilities, and the term or periods over which the credits are extended, all differ significantly. Let us consider a few examples:

1. *Sample bank credit facilities*

Credit	Scale	Use	Term
Documentary credit	Invoice value	Payment guarantee	30–180 days
Term loan	say, £50 k–£1 m	Property purchase	10–20 yrs
Syndicated loan	say, £1 m–£200 m	Oil development	5–15 yrs
Note issuance facility	£100 m–£1 bn	Refinancing programme	say, 5–10 yrs
Multiple facility:	say, £100 m–£1½ bn	Refinancing/cash/ standby credit	
Euronote issuance			say, 1–2 yrs
short-term advances			say, up to 1 yr
standby credit facility			say, up to 5 yrs

2. *Sample financial institution credit facilities*

Credit	Scale	Use	Term
Forfaitage	Invoice/contract value	Payment guarantee/cash acceleration	6 months–6 yrs
Invoice-discounting	Portion of sales ledger	Cash acceleration	monthly
Confirming house credits	Invoice value	Shipment and cash acceleration	up to 180 days
Leasing	Cost of equipment	Capital purchasing/ maximization of cashflow	useful life of asset

3. *Sample commercial or trade credit facilities*

Credit	Scale	Use	Term
Buyer credit facilities	say, £500+	Maximization of buyer purchasing power and cashflow	30 days+
Credit limit	Variable	As above	variable

Apart from the variance in facilities, use, size, and term of commercial and financial institutional credit, another difference obtains. Both banks and other financial institutions tend to be in a privileged position as regards credit applicants. Borrowers do not normally regard borrowing as a right. The more experienced borrowers such as large corporates and sovereign states appreciate that their creditworthiness will always be a prime factor determining the amount, term, and cost of credit. Experienced and large-scale borrowers are thus at pains to improve or maintain their credit ratings and general financial status.

Financially aware companies of all kinds and sizes know that, despite the general aggressiveness of banks and other providers of capital, credit applications must be supported by reasonable, up to the minute, and comprehensive financial data, including audited accounts and management information. Some may regard theirs as more attractive borrowing propositions than others, but all but the very stupid know that lenders are bound to demand proper documentation including forecasts or projections before advancing the credit.

Banks and other providers of capital, therefore, have easier access to full information for analysis than providers of trade credit. Though deplored by supplier companies and by professional bodies such as the Institute of Credit Management, trade credit is now seen as a right and not as a privilege.

This has been caused by internationally troubled economies giving rise to intense and often imprudent market competition. Government intervention, both in businesses and in national economies, together with the world-wide erosion in corporate and bank liquidity, must be regarded as main contributing factors in our currently unprecedented expansion of credit.

In such a climate, companies not only expect credit, but they often must have it in order to survive illiquidity, inadequate capitalization, and near or outright insolvency. It is now accepted commercial common sense for companies to buy from whatever supplier can offer them the lowest prices and the longest credit.

Accordingly, applicants for trade credit facilities rarely come prepared to convince suppliers that the credit is anything but an arrangement for buyers' convenience. They know better than to suggest that the credit is needed to substitute for working capital. They certainly know better than to suggest that their companies intend at the outset of trading to delay settlements to trade creditors as long as possible in any event. Nor are many of those companies most in need of trade credit those most able to prepare viable documentation for such a financial proposition.

Thus, supplier companies are, in practice, very restricted in the quality and quantity of information they can expect to receive from credit applicants. Additionally, most companies are, to a degree, locked into their banking relationships. Even few major suppliers could claim the same with respect to their buyers. Applicants for bank credit are, for this reason, somewhat obliged to wait at the banks' convenience for decisions. No banker worth his salt will allow himself to be pressured into over-hasty decisions. If the information backing up a credit proposition is insufficient, the banker will ask for more information. If this is not forthcoming, the credit will be turned down. To borrowers, this is common knowledge, and even commoner experience.

On the other hand, providers of trade credit must content themselves, in the main, with a quality and quantity of back-up information that no responsible banker would countenance. On the basis of such information, by whatever experience he has of the market, and by any first-hand knowledge he may have of the customer, the credit manager must make extremely rapid decisions. If the decisions are not made quickly, existing and potential customers will go elsewhere. It is worth noting also that many individual credit decisions taken by supplier companies are substantially greater than the total discretionary powers of some branch bank managers.

Very possibly, banks have lost considerably higher volumes of money through poor lending decisions than supplier companies making 'wrong' credit decisions. Furthermore, despite the highly unsatisfactory informational climate behind the granting of trade credit, the analytical function in the general commercial sector has developed quickly over the last decade by way of compensating. Interestingly, there is a greater cross-flow of analytical research and information in the general commercial sector than in the banking and financial institutions who tend to regard analytical assessment routines as strictly confidential. It is hoped that the remainder of this book will make analytical developments in both sectors clearer.

Sources

Bathory, A., *Predicting Corporate Collapse*, Financial Times Business Information, 1984, p. 3.
Edwards, H., *Export Credit*, Shaws Linton, Wantage, 1980, p. 299.
Euromoney October, 1985, pp. 404, 410.
Finanz AG 'Forfaiting', Credit Suisse Special Publications, Vol. 47, II, February, 1982, passim.
Robinson, R. I., *The Management of Bank Funds*, McGraw-Hill, New York, 2nd edn, 1962, Chapters 12, 14.
Swiss Bank Corporation *Foreign Exchange and Money Market Operations*, Zurich, 1980, passim.

2

EXAMINATION OF TRADITIONAL RATIOS

The collective wisdom of the ages is rarely totally mistaken. Traditional credit analysis has, since the early nineteenth century, been based on the interpretation of financial and operational ratios. In short, traditional analysis has depended upon synthesis and antithesis. The distinction should, however, be made at once, between traditional credit analysis and the simple, and often simple-minded, interpretation of accounts. Traditional credit analysis has not had a long tradition. The systematic examination of accounting, and other financial statements, and the recasting of quantities in ratio form has been practised more frequently by stockbrokerage firms than by commercial banks and supplier companies. The analytical emphases used by stockbrokers focus on yield, return on investment, gearing, market capitalization, price earnings per share (PER), dividend yield, cover, net asset value (NAV), and payout, i.e. gross dividends distributed as a percentage of profit after taxation.

As discussed earlier, the emphases of bank, financial institution, and supplier companies' credit analysis lie in different directions. These are:

1. Solvency
2. Liquidity
3. Cashflow
4. Profitability as a main determinant of retentions and cash inflow
5. The amount and priority of debt obligations
6. Various measures of 'free' or working capital
7. Effect of external conditions on the subject company
8. Purpose of the credit
9. Term of the credit
10. Structure of the credit
11. Security for the credit

Of these, the first six are especially well-expressed by ratio measurements. Whereas, stockbrokerages are concerned primarily with investment ratios, bank and trade credit grantors are concerned mainly with a reading of operational and financial ratios.

Operating ratios show how companies are trading. They are not concerned with companies' financial structures. Financial ratios, on the other hand, measure the internal and external financing elements of companies and compare these with trading. Traditional analysis uses a well-established list of operational and financial ratios. It observes and comments on the trend between two or more accounting periods.

Operating ratios

The chief operational ratios are concerned with profitability, return on capital, amount of trading done in respect of a given capital base, credit periods allowed customers, approximate payment periods to creditors, stock turnover, proportion of stock financed by supplier companies, amount of credit allowed the subject by its suppliers, trading balance, the amount of capital required to finance the business in addition to funds tied up in fixed assets, and various measurements of overtrading.

Profitabilty

The main financial flows of any company to some degree overlap. Ratios will, to the same degree, show an overlap both in respect of the quantities used to build the ratios and in the supposed end-products of the measurements. For example, the two main profitability indicators (ratios) are:

$$\frac{\text{Profit before interest and taxation}}{\text{Turnover}}$$

This is the computation for profit margin where the margin is expressed as a percentage. Also:

$$\frac{\text{Profit before interest and taxation}}{\text{Capital employed}}$$

being the 'prime ratio' indicating not only profit before interest charges and taxation as a function of permanent capital used to run the business, that is, profitability, but also, as ROCE, or return on capital employed, that is, a measurement of return on investment.

In this way, ratio measurements can often be used interchangeably. Strictly speaking, profit margin is computed by trading profit/sales, where:

Trading profit = Profit before taxation and interest charges, the company's share of the profits of any associated companies, and income from investments.

And

Sales = Turnover excluding VAT and any other sales-based taxation, e.g. excise duty, and excluding any intergroup sales, i.e. sales to group or associated companies.

Superficially, high profit margins will always be the desired goal. High margins can, however, entail a low market share. For this reason, in large, capital-intensive retail operations in particular, managements will sometimes settle for low margins in return for higher market penetration or share. Low margins can also be caused by closure, expansion, or divestiture costs. These points having been made, low margins normally tend to indicate weak performance.

Holmes and Sugden make the point that better than average margins are generally seen as signs of good management, but unusually high margins may mean that the company is 'making a packet'. This type of performance will tend to attract more competition unless significant barriers to entry obtain. Since the 1970s, the increasing competition in housebuilding, banking, and business information, to name a few examples, have sharply eroded margins.

Profit margins are also used as important assessment tools by corporate predators in making acquisitions and in effecting takeovers. Forecasts of future profitability on estimated sales are multiplied by would-be acquirers to arrive at offer prices.

Accounting measures profits in terms of sales made and costs incurred. This, however, says nothing of cash generated nor consumed. Accounting turnover is based on the value of goods or services rendered to customers in a given period irrespective of whether or not settlement has been received in that period. Likewise, costs or expenditures incurred in a period are calculated on the cost of materials, services or labour consumed in that period irrespective of whether or not settlement for these costs has been made. Accounting statements are thus made up on an accruals basis and not on a cash basis.

Accordingly, it is not uncommon for companies to show attractive profitability yet fail due to shortages of cash. Measuring profitability in various ways along with other connected flows is thus an important business of credit analysis. Supposed profitability should, therefore, be considered together with cashflows. These cashflows can be computed in different ways which will be outlined subsequently. In the case of a company showing strong levels of profitability yet in danger of collapse due to cash famine, investigation of the funds flow (statement of source and application of funds) statement can warn analysts of this possibility. The funds flow analyses the movements of cash into:

Total cash generated from operations
Cash movements in working capital
Cash used in capital expenditures
Cash required by external financings

For the calculation of totals generated from operations, depreciation is added back to the profit figure in the profit and loss account. The accountant in doing this spreads the cost of an asset over its expected useful life. This device ensures that the impact of the depreciation charge is not taken by profits earned in only one period. The impact on profits is thus reduced.

In cash terms, the capital expenditure occurred at the time that the asset was acquired. Having taken the outflow into account at the time of the expenditure, it will be necessary to add back depreciation to profit if outflow is not to be overstated.

Some analysts measure profit margin using trading profit before deduction of depreciation. Also, as Holmes and Sugden point out, this computation normalizes any distortions caused by depreciation in making intercompany comparisons. When such an approach is favoured, trading profit should also be taken before deduction of hire charges in order to bring a company that leases rather than owns plant and machinery on to a comparable basis. Holmes and Sugden favour treating depreciation as a cost and deducting it from any calculation of profit. Accordingly, they will make *ad hoc* adjustments in cases of unduly high or low depreciation charges in lieu of adding back every company's depreciation charge.

Profit margins represent the relationship between a business's sales and its costs. To give dimension to margins, they should be considered together with cashflows. For example:

	Company A		Company B
ROCE:	14%	ROCE:	14%
Profit margin:	30%	Profit margin:	30%
Gross cashflow:	£2 m	Gross cashflow:	£10 m

The £8 m difference in gross cashflow between Company A and Company B will lead analysts to look closely at the difference in investments in fixed assets, taxation effects, and capital bases. At first sight, the £10 m GCF must be more attractive for credit propositions than the £2 m inflow.

Return on capital employed

The computation is: $\dfrac{\text{Profit before taxation and interest charges}}{\text{Capital employed}}$

This ratio is often called the prime ratio as it is the prime indicator of profitability. It shows whether or not the company is generating a level of profits commensurate with the amount of capital resources invested. It is a function both of profit to sales and of the rate of capital circulation in number of times per accounting period. Capital employed is not always the same quantity as net assets. In Figure 2.1, we see that net assets stand at £178,151 in the company's 1985 balance sheet.

	Notes	1985	1984
Fixed assets			
Tangible assets		141,321	139,526
Research and development expenditure		15,773	26,164
		157,094	165,690
Current assets			
Stocks	1	32,966	36,056
Debtors	2	60,244	55,613
Money market deposits		7,424	2,705
Cash at bank and in hand		7,506	1,345
		108,140	95,719
Current liabilities			
Trade creditors		43,313	37,571
Sundry creditors		6,192	6,445
Taxation and social security		9,883	1,418
		59,388	45,434
Net current assets		48,752	50,285
Total assets *less* current liabilities		205,846	215,975
Creditors: Amounts falling due after more than one year (including loans)	3	23,110	74,007
Provisions for liabilities and charges	4	4,585	11,868
Net assets		£178,151	£130,100

Represented by:
Capital and reserves

Called-up share capital	2,504	2,504
Share premium account	22,514	22,514
Other reserves	89,309	89,309
Profit and loss account	63,824	15,773
	£178,151	£130,100

Figure 2.1 Balance sheet as at 31 December 1985.

Net assets are represented by capital and reserves of £178,151 for this period. Yet capital employed being the permanent or long-term capital used to finance the business, must take into account not only called-up share capital and reserves, but also any taxation and long-term loan capital used to finance operations for more than the current accounting period (in this case, one year). To compute this ratio, since interest charges are being excluded from the calculation of profit before taxation and interest charges, the capital sum of such items as bank overdrafts which are deemed for this exercise to be long-term, hard-core borrowings, i.e. long-term capital, these charges should, therefore, be included in capital employed. Accordingly, the capital employed computation is:

Creditors: Amounts falling due after more than one year (including loans):	23,110
+	
Provisions for liabilities and charges:	4,585
Long-term finance:	27,695

and adding this sum to shareholders' funds, i.e. capital and reserves:

Capital and reserves:	178,695
+	
Long-term finance:	27,695
Capital employed:	205,846

where restating the capital employed in this example lowers ROCE. The next example shows a modified balance sheet where the above computational routine is not required:

Balance sheet

Fixed assets	1,188
Current assets	
Debtors:	7,272
Cash at bank and in hand:	16,897
	24,169
Current liabilities: Creditors: Amounts falling due within one year	14,770
Net current assets	9,399
Net assets	10,587

Capital and reserves
　Called-up share capital:　　　　　　　　　　　　　　　　10,000
　Profit and loss account:　　　　　　　　　　　　　　　　　 587
　　　　　　　　　　　　　　　　　　　　　　　　　　　　10,587

In this example, the company has no long-term creditors being used to contribute financing to the operation. Total assets and liabilities are represented by shareholders' funds, or capital and reserves of 10,587. In this balance sheet, the proprietorship ratio (shareholders' funds/capital employed) = 100 per cent, whereas in the previous example (Figure 2.1), the proprietorship ratio = 86.5 per cent:

$$\frac{\text{Shareholders' funds (net assets)}}{\text{Restated capital employed}} \text{ or } \frac{178,151}{205,846} = 86.5\%$$

Without restatement, the proprietorship ratio would have been 100 per cent and this figure would have taken no account of long-term taxation and finance liabilities.

For trading purposes as measured by operating ratios, capital employed can thus be taken to include long-term financings, as these items will provide a proportion of a company's total capital resources on which the trading is based. Accordingly, in Figure 2.1, capital employed is not identical to net assets.

For these reasons, in calculating capital employed for trading purposes, analysts take the following items into account:

　　　　　　　Called-up share capital
　　　　　　　+
　　　　　　　Profit and loss account
　　　　　　　+
　　　　　　　Reserve accounts
　　　　　　　+
　　　　　　　Creditors: Amounts falling due after one year
　　　　　　　+
　　　　　　　Taxation and other deferred liabilities

Nicer calculations of capital employed can be made, and Holmes and Sugden suggest:

　　　　　　　Share capital
　　　　　　　+
　　　　　　　Reserves
　　　　　　　−
　　　　　　　Intangibles
　　　　　　　+
　　　　　　　All borrowings including bank overdraft
　　　　　　　+
　　　　　　　Minority interests
　　　　　　　+
　　　　　　　Deferred liabilities (excluding government grants)
　　　　　　　−
　　　　　　　Associates and investments

If, however, capital employed is taken to signify long-term or 'permanent' capital used to finance the business, Holmes and Sugden's treatment of overdraft borrowings and other borrowings falling due currently (i.e. within the accounting period in question) must be open to question. Whilst their calculations will yield a total financing computation, we do not view it as strictly long-term or permanent as shown by the more traditional computation for capital employed given previously.

Trading profit, when compared with capital employed, none the less indicates profitability according to the numbers used, either on a trading or on a group or overall basis. Strong profitability coupled with maximum cash inflows constitute any company's most effective preventatives to insolvency. Additionally, the return on capital employed (ROCE) indicates:

1. A guide for investments or business start-ups where rates of return on long-term capital can be assessed. Very simply, if an investor can obtain a high ROCE or a low ROCE on two investments, he will normally choose the investment offering the high return, other considerations being equal, e.g. risk. Often, higher ROCE will be found in less capital-intensive businesses. Thus, ROCE may be higher in a consultancy operation with not much money tied up in fixed assets than in a bank where high levels of investment in technology are required.
2. Levels of performance. Chronically low ROCE may indicate poor performance. In groups of companies, an overall low ROCE can suggest possible disposal of poorly performing subsidiaries when those companies do not form integral parts of the group.
3. Levels of attractiveness in acquisitions. Acquisitions can be attractive if ROCE is high, and in some instances, when ROCE is low. In the latter cases, potential buyers may estimate that acquisition costs will be cheap and that new management will be able to effect better margins and higher rates of return on the investment without undue trouble.
4. Safety margins in respect of the costs of finance. When ROCE is less than the cost of borrowing, additional borrowings will reduce earnings per share (EPS) unless the extra money can be employed in areas where ROCE is higher than the group average.
5. Vulnerability of margins to market developments. If ROCE is low, even short-term market downturns can obliterate positive return on capital.
6. Pricing levels. Changes in ROCE can indicate something of a company's pricing of goods or services. Persistently fine ROCE can suggest competitive undercutting of prices in order to capture greater market share. Similar sized companies' ROCE can be examined to assess the differentials in rates of return on capital, levels of turnover, and profit margins to bear out suspicions of overly competitive pricing.

Another operating ratio used to measure profitability is asset turnover. It is computed as follows:

$$\frac{\text{Sales}}{\text{Capital employed}}$$

Asset turnover shows how often and fully a business is using its capital. Normally, the more fully or intensively the capital is being used, the better. By this token, higher or rising ratios tend to indicate better performances. In other words, a company is doing greater volumes of business in respect of its capital resources. Again, this ratio, as in the case of others, should not be considered in isolation. A company could, for instance, show improving asset turnover ratios merely by not investing in certain fixed assets needed to keep its operations up to date. In this case, Holmes and Sugden point out that depreciation will steadily erode the company's capital base, improving the asset turnover ratio without any improvement in sales. Another common example of a misleading improvement in asset turnover would be where a bank compels a company to reduce its borrowings on overdraft. Asset turnover will show improvement due to a reduction in capital employed. The company in question, however, may suffer a loss in market share forced by the reduction in external financing. Trade creditor financing may be increased to compensate for the reduction in bank facilities. Depending upon how analysts interpret capital employed, asset turnover may show a higher multiple when, in fact, the business is more straitened.

Following from this, large increases in asset turnover can often signify overtrading. In attempting to do more business than its capital base can finance, the overtrading company will suffer shortages of cash. For this reason, it is well to look at the asset turnover alongside various liquidity indicators as:

Working capital
Gross cashflow/current liabilities
Fixed assets/capital employed
Acid-test ratio, i.e. current assets—Stock/current liabilities
Normalized or non-normalized working capital/total assets

If reductions in capital employed allow, in some instances, for fallacious or misleading asset turnover ratios, it will be wise to consider the ways in which permanent capital can be reduced. There is nothing inherently wrong or financially unhealthy with any of them. That having been said, it is important for analysts to try and determine why capital reduction devices were used, whether or not the devices were effective in respect to overall financial soundness of the company, and to what extent such reductions should be added back in some cases or restated in others for analytical purposes. Basically, there are four capital reduction devices:

1. Leasing of assets
2. Factoring operations including invoice-discounting
3. Forfaiting of capital equipment/goods
4. Stand-by financings

Of these, items 2 and 3 constitute forms of debtor financing for cash acceleration. Leasing likewise maximizes cashflow by keeping capital free that might otherwise have been tied up in the purchase of fixed assets. Stand-by credits provide term financing at cheaper costs than normal bank loans, and provide greater flexibility in terms of hedging and drawn-down options, without having to take an entire amount of loan capital into the balance sheet when not all that amount is required in a given period. All these devices are intended to maximize liquidity.

Leases should be considered both in respect of current portions due for payment in a given period and total long-term liabilities under the leases. Some audited accounting statements will give both exposures. All should give current portions of leases and other types of hire finance, e.g. hire purchase, under current liabilities in the balance sheet. The notes to the accounts will, in many cases, e.g. large private companies and public limited companies, give total leasing liabilities. Exposure Draft 29 called for financial leases to be capitalized and included in balance sheets. When this becomes a requirement, leasing will cease to be an important off-balance-sheet financing device, though the beneficial effects on cashflow will remain.

For credit managers particularly, the computation of a company's credit periods allowed customers (or, more accurately in many cases, taken by its customers) is of great importance in determining the cost of credit as well as averaged periodic income from receivables. Debtors' turnover or 'debt-turn' is calculated as follows:

$$\frac{\text{Debtors}}{\text{Sales}}$$

and to express debt-turn in days (collection periods):

$$\frac{\text{Debtors}}{\text{Sales}} \times 365 \text{ days in the year}$$

For trade credit purposes, a nicer computation can be made, given sufficient information in the accounts by:

$$\frac{\text{Trade debtors}}{\text{Sales}} \times 365 \text{ days}$$

Accordingly, in a company whose latest turnover was 4,000,000 and whose trade debtors totalled 480,000, debt-turn would be:

$$\frac{480,000}{4,000,000} \times 365 = 44 \text{ days}$$

Using the debtors/sales ratio given above, we can see that trade debtors represented 12 per cent of turnover. Holmes and Sugden suggest that in practice, a figure of 20–25 per cent is normal where payment terms are set at end of the month following delivery. From the present example, we can thus see that the 44 days collection period is comparatively quick and that with trade debtors representing only 12 per cent of sales, the company will probably show reasonable liquidity.

Collection periods as indicated by debt-turn must be related to particular industry sectors to make them significant. Thus, without using cash acceleration financing such as factoring or forfaiting, a shipyard would show long collection periods due to long manufacturing and delivery times, as well as high value orders. On the other hand, a retail grocery business, where most purchases are made for cash, will show a quick debt-turn. To make sense of debt-turns, they should be compared with the debt-turns of similar companies operating in the same sector.

Thus Company 1 (a retail grocery chain) shows a debt-turn of 0.874 or less than one day, but until we compare this turnover with similar multiple grocery businesses, say Companies 2 and 3 which show debt-turns of $1\frac{1}{2}$ days and 0.9 days respectively, we cannot make any truly informative value judgement on Company 1's performance in this respect. Of course, in this example, Company 1's debt-turn is the quickest. We can, therefore, assume a slightly higher relative level of liquidity in Company 1 and a higher level of cash sales. But these assumptions are superficial. Higher levels of cash sales may or may not indicate higher levels of profitability. Also, not all companies operating in the same industry sector require the same levels of liquidity due to differences in capitalization, scale of operations, product ranges, and market location. Accordingly, to make any but superficial assumptions about debt-turn in such an example would be unwise.

More informative is the comparison of a company's debt-turn over several accounting periods. Consider the following example:

	Company A		
	1985	*1984*	*1983*
Debt-turn:	54 days	58 days	65 days
	Company B		
Debt-turn:	54 days	60 days	75 days

What assumptions can be made? Firstly, we see that debt-turn in both companies has been reduced over a three year period. Superficially, we may assume that higher liquidity has been achieved by both companies due to the quicker collection of accounts receivable. This, in itself, serves as an indication of tighter credit control. We can see also that Company A has reduced its debt-turn by 7 days from 1983 to 1984 and by a further 4 days from 1984 to 1985, an aggregate 11 days for the three year period. Company B has reduced its debt-turn by a sharp aggregate 21 days for the same period, with 15 days being saved from 1983 to 1984 and 6 days further for 1984 to 1985. Company B has thus made higher reductions from year to year and a higher aggregate reduction in debt-turn for the three year period.

Without further information from accounting statements for the two companies, we cannot make many significant judgements. We can, however, suggest that on the face of it, Company B appears to have more effective credit control over its receivables than Company A. This credit control may be the result of conscious policy or of necessity. Company B may be starved of cash and illiquid to the point of being unable to meet its obligations as they fall due. Were that the case, the favourable trend in its debt-turn only partially masks extremely serious problems. Company A, on the other hand, shows a systematic though less total reduction in debt-turn. In this instance, the lesser reduction might be the 'healthier' one.

In prior studies on characteristics of corporate insolvency by the present writer and by others, it has become apparent that in their final stages, insolvent companies often show tighter credit control because of their need for cash. In the penultimate stages of insolvency before collapse, debt-turns are accordingly reduced sharply. Also, total amounts of trade debtors can decrease sharply as less sales are made in the closing stages of a company's life.

The following example makes this clear:

	X Ltd				
	In liquidation—1982				
	1981	*1980*	*1979*	*1978*	*1977*
Turnover:	1.1 m	1.4 m	2.0 m	2.6 m	3.2 m
Debt-turn:	57 days	68 days	84 days	86 days	83 days

In this example, tighter credit control has been achieved systematically or accidentally over a falling turnover as the company becomes increasingly straitened for cash prior to collapse in January, 1982.

Despite the apparently tighter credit control, overall levels of liquidity decreased:

	1981	1980	1979	1978	1977
Current ratio:	0.4	0.5	0.7	0.8	0.9
Acid-test ratio:	0.2	0.3	0.4	0.5	0.7

Accordingly, reductions in debt-turn are in general terms beneficial. However, they can indicate cash famine due to various causes. They can also indicate an illiquid company's reliance on unhealthy levels of discounts for cash as well as self-defeatingly tight credit policies shown to customers. When credit terms are not attractive, customers will take their business elsewhere. Overly tight credit thus suggests possible drops in turnover as shown in the last example. In brief, to make intelligent judgements about debt-turn, analysts should look at debt-turn alongside:

(a) sales over x periods
(b) liquidity indicators over x periods
(c) solvency indicators over x periods
(d) debt-turns of other companies operating in the same sector over x periods

If we are able to calculate the frequency with which a company settles with its trade creditors, we could appreciate the differences between 'debt-turn' and 'creditor-turn' in terms of cashflow. This difference in cash would be either positive, that is adding to the liquidity of the company, or negative, in which case the company would be paying out more to its trade creditors in a given period than it was receiving in settlements from its trade debtors. This, of course, would lower overall liquidity. Finally, a balance might be achieved showing a stasis. Because of the continual and variable nature of trading in its widest sense, such a stasis would be unnatural and betoken a company functioning at less than par rather than on a true equilibrium.

The ratio creditors/sales furnishes our starting point. This can be refined to:

$$\frac{\text{Trade creditors}}{\text{Sales}}$$

and would furnish an approximation of the time creditors allowed the company to settle its accounts. This assumes, as Holmes and Sugden point out, that stock levels and profit margins are fairly steady, and that the character of the business is not highly seasonal.

Further refinements are possible provided that a company's accounts disclose cost of sales figures. To be truly informative, these costs of sales should take into account not only direct costs but relevant indirect costs such as sales commissions, portions of staff remuneration, and so forth. Unfortunately, few accounting statements, save those for public companies, provide such detailed profit and loss information.

Analysts must then make reasonable assumptions. Firstly, that the auditors, when posting costs of sales under turnover, have taken into account both direct and relevant indirect costs. Secondly, when no costs of sales are posted in the profit and loss account, that reconstructive data may be found in the notes to the accounts to enable a rough estimate to be made as to total costs. In theory, such a reconstruction might be done from notes on staff and directors' remuneration, sales commissions, profit margins, and gross profit. In any event, the final estimate would be only the roughest of approximations. Note that the profit and loss account is constructed in the following manner:

Sample profit and loss account
TURNOVER
Direct cost of sales
GROSS PROFIT
Direct expenses
DIRECT PROFIT
Establishment and general overheads
Dividends received
TRADING PROFIT
Interest charges
PROFIT BEFORE TAXATION
Taxation
PROFIT AFTER TAXATION
Dividends paid
RETAINED PROFIT/(LOSS)

The key question is how much of the direct expenses are to be added to the direct costs of sales? Arriving at such an estimate is impossible when working with modified accounting statements. With the full accounts of a public company, better estimates can be obtained. Take for example, Monsanto PLC's 1983 profit and loss account shown in Figure 2.2.

Abbreviated profit and loss account/Monsanto PLC

	1983/£'000s
Turnover	371,227
Cost of sales	296,845
Gross profit	74,382
Selling and distribution costs	10,964
Administration expenses	9,183
Other operating income	(5,783)
Other operating expenses	4,023
Share of profit of associated co:	(544)
	17,843
Profit on ordinary activities before interest	56,539

Figure 2.2 Abbreviated profit and loss account

In this example, the analyst wishing to determine total costs of sales, i.e. direct costs plus relevant indirect sales costs, might add the cost of sales posted under turnover to selling and distribution costs. This still leaves a doubt as to how to treat remuneration expenses involved in making the sales. A note in the accounts discloses total remuneration costs of £25,707,000. A portion of turnover may be represented by work-in-progress, in which event direct and relevant indirect costs will have been taken into account. Possibly, the most accurate course of action will be the easiest and most straightforward and we assume that total sales costs in this case are:

Direct cost of sales:	296,845
+	
Selling and distribution costs	10,964
TOTAL SALES COSTS	307,809

We discover from another note to the accounts that trade creditors total £13,857,000. We can therefore construct the following ratio to give a rough idea of settlement time to the company's trade creditors:

$$\frac{\text{Trade creditors}}{\text{Total sales costs}} \times 300 \text{ days}$$

The values, accordingly, would be:

$$\frac{13,857}{307,809} \times 300 = 13\tfrac{1}{2} \text{ days}$$

The same company's debt-turn is:

$$\frac{31,056}{371,227} \times 300 = 25 \text{ days}$$

Comparing the creditor-turn with debt-turn, we see an $11\tfrac{1}{2}$ days' differential in favour from a cashflow point of view to Monsanto's trade creditors. The analyst should now consider this differential against liquidity indicators to check for any serious impairment.

Liquidity indicators

Working capital:	£49 m	down 3% on prior yr
Current ratio:	1.8	down 0.31 points on prior yr
Acid-test ratio:	1.2	down 0.1 points on prior yr
Gross cashflow:	£74 m	up 325% on prior yr
CGF/current liabilities:	1.2	up 0.82 points on prior yr

Whilst gross cash inflow was increased sharply in the latest year, we can see from the above figures that the company's overall liquidity on these indicators fell.

Comparing debt and creditor-turns over the two years, we see further corroboration of the interpretation of the above data.

	1983	1982
Trade creditors-turn:	$13\tfrac{1}{2}$ days	12 days
Trade debtors-turn:	25 days	32 days

We note that debt-turn has been reduced over the two years. This reduction will have contributed to the company's sharply increased cashflow as seen above. It will also have compensated in a degree for the slight downturns in current and liquid ratios. Note, too, that the differential in debt and creditors'-turns in 1982 was 20 days. The company has thus narrowed the drift between payments to trade creditors and receipt of settlements from trade debtors by some $8\frac{1}{2}$ days. Considering these figures on an overall basis, better balance has been achieved though there is still scope for reductions in debt-turn. Nor are there any serious impairments to overall liquidity, despite the 3 per cent drop in working capital. Both current and acid-test ratios indicate adequate balance between current assets and current liabilities. At this point, it should be noted that 'adequacy' of balance between current assets and current liabilities, as is the case with other measures of adequacy, should be viewed relatively. Thus, in respect to itself in a 'closed system', Monsanto's balance and liquidity appears adequate. In examining these figures in respect of an 'open system', the same figures may not be adequate. For instance, would the working capital figure of £49 m be adequate to support a credit exposure of £$7\frac{1}{2}$ m on 60 days terms? Could gross cashflow contain such an exposure given the company's various classes of current liabilities?

Making operational indicators more informative

From the above observations, it will be clear that credit analysis must proceed from a consideration of a company's figures first in relation solely to its prior figures; and secondly, analysis will then attempt to build in the exposure under question to see to what degree, if at all, it can be serviced.

Although we disagree radically, many analysts would argue for a three-fold procedure. In this, a company's figures would be considered in respect of prior years' results, the credit exposure under question, and results for other companies of similar size operating in the same industry sector.

We disagree on two grounds:

1. Corporate idiosyncracy: Both logically and in actuality, no two companies are alike in any truly significant senses.
2. Credit propositions are particular: Applications for credit are from individual companies addressed to particular suppliers/lenders. Whether another company's figures will support a particular credit other than the applicant's figures to hand must be totally irrelevant to the sanction of the present application.

If a subject's general financial condition is the first consideration of analysis, looking at an applicant's figures in relation to a credit exposure is, in our opinion, the second and most salient step in credit analysis. Thus, in the earlier calculations of Monsanto's debt and creditor-turnovers, whilst informative in themselves, the figures and the end-products of our calculations only 'speak' significantly for credit purposes when we consider them against a particular exposure. Secondly, the figures speak when considered against the credit grantor's own cashflows, notably, working capital, debt and creditor-turns.

In considering both the grantor's cash requirements and the applicant's, thought should be given to the utilisation of working capital—that is, the surplus or deficiency of current assets over current liabilities. Every type of business will have its own optimum level of working capital to sales. The relationship of working capital to sales can indicate the frequency with which working capital is being used to underpin sales. When the ratio increases, greater utilization is normally indicated. Too high a rate of working capital turnover, however, suggests that too much business is being done on too slim a working capital base. The ratio is expressed as a multiple:

$$\frac{\text{Sales}}{\text{Working capital}}$$

A nicer measurement of how much free capital is needed to underpin sales in addition to the capital tied up in fixed assets is:

$$\frac{\text{Working capital}}{\text{Sales}}$$

where the ratio is expressed in percentage terms. Holmes and Sugden take working capital to include:

> Stock
> +
> Trade debtors
> −
> Trade creditors

This, however, may be an unduly limiting notion of surplus or 'free' capital. For instance, it takes no account of cash/bank balances or near-cash items such as marketable investments, or even sundry debtors. If a strictly 'trading' balance is sought, Holmes and Sugden's computation is more easily justifiable.

For credit purposes, however, it is more important to try and obtain a broad and truly representative view than a narrow and precise view in most instances. The inclusion of 100 per cent of stocks in working capital is, in our opinion, to err in the opposite direction. Stock in most companies will be composed of goods for sale or resale, work-in-progress, raw materials, and goods that are, in fact, obsolete and unsaleable or saleable only at discounted prices. By and large, then, a more indicative computation for the working capital/sales ratio would be:

> x% of stock representing goods for sale or resale
> +
> Trade debtors
> +
> Cash/bank balances
> +
> Marketable investments
> +
> Sundry debtors
> −
> Current liabilities

In this computation, we are concerned neither where the working capital comes from (that is, whether it originates from trading or from other activities), nor whether the current liabilities are trading or other types of obligations. We are concerned only with the most representative indication of free capital available, with which sales can be financed. Accordingly, our ratio could be expressed:

$$\frac{\text{Normalized current assets} - \text{current liabilities}}{\text{Sales}}$$

where the percentage answer will necessarily be less than the non-normalized ratio working capital/sales first mentioned.

Again, analysts working with modified accounting statements will generally not have sufficient information to allow a normalization of stock in the way suggested above.

Treatment of stock in normalized ratios and other quantities

Practically speaking, 100 per cent of stock is rarely quickly realizable for cash. Thus, taking 100 per cent of stock into working capital or other computations designed to give truly indicative measures of liquid funds will be distortive.

Where detailed information of stock is not available, the treatment of stock in analysis must depend upon certain assumptions. Provided that the assumptions are experience-based and make sense, more indicative measurements should result.

We could, for instance, reasonably assume that companies can be classed as:

Manufacturing companies
Retailing companies
Non-specific or combined operations
Service companies

Of these, service companies are taken to mean operations in which stock, as such, plays no significant part in the sum of current assets, e.g. an invoice-discount company or theatrical agency. Of the remaining three types, experience very broadly suggests:

MANUFACTURING COMPANIES

Seventy-five per cent of stock is normally represented by raw materials and WIP and is, therefore, not quickly realizable for cash. Accordingly, take 25 per cent of stock at posted value plus balance of current assets. Normalized working capital will be the resulting difference between the restated total of current assets and current liabilities.

In this assumption, and in the following examples, analysts should always utilize any particular knowledge they may have in favour of generalities.

RETAILING COMPANIES

Twenty-five per cent of stock is generally represented by slow-moving and/or obsolete items which are not readily realizable for cash. Therefore, take 75 per cent of stock at posted valuation, plus balance of current assets. Normalized working capital will be the resulting difference between the restated total of current assets and current liabilities.

NON-SPECIFIC OR COMBINED OPERATIONS

Take the mean between 75 per cent (retailing companies) and 25 per cent (manufacturing companies), i.e. 50 per cent to account for stock quickly realizable for cash. Accordingly, take 50 per cent of stock at posted valuation, plus the balance of current assets. Normalized working capital will be the difference between restated total current assets and current liabilities.

As suggested earlier, these recommendations will not apply where exact itemizations of stock are given in the accounts. In these cases, analysts should use the precise figures given.

FINANCIAL RATIOS

Operational ratios were concerned with measuring how companies traded. Financial ratios measure companies' financial structure and indicate how these structures relate to trading. Holmes and Sugden and others divide financial ratios into two broad groups:

1. Gearing ratios
2. Liquidity ratios

As mentioned earlier, gearing is the relationship of loan capital to capital employed. Loan capital refers to external financial commitments such as bank loans, and does not include provisions such as a deferred taxation account. The proprietorship ratio noted earlier measures the relationship between shareholders' funds and capital employed, showing the owners' equity in the operation. It is thus a gearing ratio. Apart from the proprietorship ratio, sometimes called the banker's ratio, gearing can be measured in the following ways:

DEBT RATIO

The debt ratio measures loan capital to capital employed. It is illustrated by the example in Figure 2.3.

		1986
FIXED ASSETS		527,614
CURRENT ASSETS		
Stock and WIP:	374,580	
Debtors:	347,424	
Taxation recoverable:	11,759	
Cash:	1,093	
	734,856	
CURRENT LIABILITIES		
Creditors:	353,197	
Taxation:	—	
Bank overdrafts	184,273	
	537,470	
NET CURRENT ASSETS		197,386
		725,000
DEFERRED TAXATION		(21,504)
NET ASSETS		703,496

Represented by:	
Share capital:	100,000
Reserves:	250,000
Profit and loss account:	90,884
Debenture stock:	20,000
Loans:	242,612
CAPITAL EMPLOYED	703,496

Figure 2.3 Balance sheet as at 31 January 1986

Of these balance-sheet items, the following would be taken into debt:

Bank overdrafts:	184,273
Debenture stock:	20,000
Loans:	242,612
TOTAL DEBT	446,885

For this illustration, we will take capital employed to be the net assets total of 703,496. Deferred taxation represents funds available to the company. Accordingly, it is included in the computation.

The debt ratio would thus be:

$$\frac{446,885}{703,496} = 0.635 \text{ or } 64\%$$

By most canons, the company would be said to be highly-geared as debt represents over 50 per cent of capital employed.

Capital employed is constituted by debt and equity capital itself. Accordingly, a nicer operational gearing measurement would be debt to equity. Holmes and Sugden point out that this ratio gives a better indication of the effect of gearing on equity income, known in North America as the 'leverage effect'. The ratio, they continue, can be distorted by the varying treatments of deferred taxation. Using the example in Figure 6, the debt/equity ratio would be:

Debt:		446,885
Equity:		
Share capital:		100,000
Reserves:		250,000
Profit and loss account:		90,884
		460,884

Debt/equity ratio: $\quad \frac{446,885}{460,884} = 0.969 \text{ or } 97\%$

This shows clearly that the balance between debt and equity is very fine and confirms the indications of the debt/capital employed ratio, that the borrowing powers of the company appear to be almost fully reached given the shareholders' own investment in the business.

The level of gearing apart, what will constitute 'healthy' gearing must vary from company to company and from industry to industry. It is plain that certain types of business require high levels of gearing, not only to begin operations but to continue trading. A bank is a good example. A producer of heavy equipment is another; and a petroleum exploration company is possibly the best example. In all these types of business, profit margins tend to be fine as profits are closely related to sales and the cost of money. Large injections of capital are required at irregular intervals to finance research and development, or as in the case of banks, to maintain or restore liquidity. In the case of publically-owned entities, cash calls can be made, share issues floated, placements can be made, debt securities can be sold, and funds can be borrowed in an ever-increasing assortment of forms. For private companies, some of these options are not permitted. They cannot, for instance, offer their shares to the public. Most private companies will not be credit-rated highly enough to issue commercial paper or sell debt securities in the capital markets. For private companies, placements and loans are the most usual methods of providing capital injections. Given that such injections dilute equity, it is still a totally different question as to whether the dilution of equity is prudent, cost-efficient, and necessary.

It is axiomatic that the greater the gearing the less the owners' control in the business. In some businesses, this control is more important than in others. The question of control should, in our view, focus on management control rather than financial control. Two different types of control are exerted by both. A large public company's management control lies not in the owners (the shareholders), but in the management of the company—its managers and directors. To another extent, financial control is also exercised by management. To still another extent, external financial control is exercised on the company by its institutional providers of capital, notably banks. For these reasons, it is not very informative to speak without particularizing about the importance of equity when the effective control exerted by equity-holders in the company is spread widely over the general public. The company's management may or may not hold shares in the enterprise. Notwithstanding, the management runs the company, and unhappily for credit analysts, the quality of management is not easily quantifiable. Its cost-efficiency in choosing the optimal type of gearing or means of financing activities is more readily measured.

The interest cover ratio shows the extent to which profits can decline before a company will fail to meet current interest charges from its current profits. The ratio is calculated as follows:

$$\frac{\text{Profit before interest and taxation}}{\text{Interest}}$$

From the following example, we can see that Amos Hinton & Sons PLC's interest cover according to its 1984 profit and loss account was:

(abbreviated) £'000s	*1984*
Turnover	125,656
Costs of sales excl depreciation and other income	(121,814)
Operating profit	3,842
Depreciation of tangible fixed assets	(1,701)
Net interest payable	(231)
Profit on ordinary activities before taxation	1,910

The computation being:

Profit before interest and taxation = Op profit:	3,842
Less	
Depreciation	(1,701)
	2,141
Interest payable (net of interest receivable)	231

Ratio: $\dfrac{2,141}{231} = 9.3$

The ratio shows that the company's 1984 net interest payable was almost ten times covered by profits even after deduction of depreciation. In an extremely volatile market (multiple off-licences and supermarkets with own brands) the company's financing charges are easily contained by profits alone. If we examine the firm's balance sheet, we find that capital employed stands at £13,395,000 and equity totals £13,090,000. This gives a proprietorship ratio of 98 per cent. Debt for this company totalled £3,454,000 in 1984. The debt/equity ratio thus works out at 26.4 per cent which must be regarded as low gearing in general and particularly low gearing for the subject's industry sector.

As approximate guides for assessing solvency and liquidity, analysts have, since the early nineteenth century, relied on a calculation of the current and acid-test ratios. The computation for the current ratio is:

$$\frac{\text{Current assets}}{\text{Current liabilities}}$$

with the result expressed as a multiple. Thus, using the accounts in Figure 6, for example, the company's proportion of current assets to current liabilities would be:

$$\frac{734,856}{537,470} = 1.367 \text{ or } 1.4$$

'Acceptable' cover for current liabilities has necessarily altered over the last twenty years, in particular as borrowing in all forms has become both more customary and more necessary. Traditionally, providers of capital and credit managers looked for cover of 2.1 in subjects' current ratios. A ratio of 1.1 is currently regarded as 'classical'; and in many sectors, especially in those industries based on cash sales, e.g. food retailing operations, current ratios of about 0.9 down to 0.5 can be regarded with some justification as adequate. The current ratio measures the most dynamic or 'living' section of a balance sheet in the sense that both current assets and current liabilities 'mature' in one accounting period (normally a year) or under. The accurate reflection of these items' currency, however, is difficult for such a ratio to give. As some current assets mature, i.e. are paid, as in the case of trade debtors, new current assets arise; in this example, more trade debtors. Similarly, as some current liabilities are extinguished, such as trade creditors, new trade creditors replace them. A constant equilibrium would thus be relatively impossible to maintain. Particularly in seasonal businesses, the balance between current assets and current liabilities necessarily varies with trading volumes, stockpiling, and any additional establishment overheads, i.e. extra staff. The current ratio provides only a snapshot of a balance as at a certain accounting date. It does not indicatively reflect the dynamic process inherent in all functioning companies.

In general, then, the current ratio is subject to some serious frailties. These are:

1. The dynamics of trading are not reflected indicatively.
2. As a measurement of solvency, the ratio measures only short-term (12 months and under) items, leaving out of account long-term considerations such as paybacks from extended projects and financial commitments. Also, as a measure of solvency the current ratio includes stock indiscriminantly.
3. Even as a rough measurement of solvency or liquidity, the ratio gives only an historical indication. This may be extremely out of date if the accounting statements are old.
4. As a measure of trading balance and liquidity, the ratio is again indiscriminant, adding sundry current asset items to trade debtors and adding other sundry current liability items to trade creditors, thus covering the more useful ratio:

$$\frac{\text{Trade debtors}}{\text{Trade creditors}}$$

5. Finally, as an index of solvency, even technical solvency or insolvency, a single ratio measurement cannot seriously be taken as an accurate or even particularly indicative measurement. Multiple financial flows taken singly, severally, and, above all, simultaneously make up the most accurate 'holistic' or 'synoptic' determination of solvency/insolvency.

An area in which the current ratio may be judged more useful might be in assessing the efficient use of capital. For instance, too high a current ratio, say 5.1, might suggest in some cases that stock and/or debtors are too high. Depending upon the real liquid nature of these items, high proportions of capital tied up in stocks or debtors may suggest that if, for example, the company is suffering from a cash rather than a working capital shortage, stocks could or should be run down and tighter credit control should be exerted over the debtors to restore liquidity in cash terms to easier levels.

If, on the other hand, the current ratio is treated as Holmes and Sugden suggest, as 'a broad indicator of a company's short-term financial position', in lieu of a measurement of solvency, a better case can be made for use of the ratio. We are still left, as with all ratio measurements, with the question of how to interpret the quantities. Interpretation of the current ratio must be related to the following considerations:

THE COMPOSITION OF THE CURRENT ASSETS

Of central interest to the analysis of a company's short-term financial position will be the liquidity of that position. Accordingly, the mix of current assets between liquid and less liquid items is important. In general, current assets will include:

Trade debtors
Sundry debtors
Quoted investments
Cash at bank and other balances, e.g. deposit accounts
Cash in hand
Stocks and work in progress
Directors' current accounts
Amounts due from group companies

The liquidity in these classes of current asset items varies widely. For instance, trade debtors, usually reckoned to be companies' most singly valuable current asset may mask many difficulties. Queried or disputed invoices, for example, could not be readily expected to be realized for cash. As credit terms and the quality of credit management varies from company to company, trade debtors as a whole will be more liquid in some companies than in others. Allowance should be made for the fact that even the tightest credit control cannot always result in prompt observance of payment terms. Thus, if in general a company's terms are net 30 days, settlement dates for its trade debtors account will still stretch beyond 30 days on an averaged reckoning because of the replacement of debtors or the augmenting of debtors with new debtors. Also, and more interestingly, buyer companies will normally attempt to take as much credit as they can. On an aggregate reckoning, the extra days taken here and there by a whole sales ledger mount up and add days if not weeks on to debt-turn. On the other hand, if the level of trade debtors is low in comparison with other balances than cash or investments, analysts can see a warning of illiquidity. If trade debtors are low and cash and investments are high, credit control may simply have been effective and settlements were received quickly. One must suppose, however, that the cash resulting from prompt settlements is at least in large part being used to finance new sales. These new sales will result in additional trade debtors. Accordingly, a persistent low trade debtors/current assets ratio, or a declining one, suggest that even if sales are being made, work is not being finished and invoiced. This could indicate production, management, distribution, or financial problems. Finally, trade debtors may include what are, to all intents and purposes, bad debts. Where bad debt provisions have not been made in the profit and loss account and balance sheet, analysts should attempt, whenever possible, to net out any doubtful debtors in assessing the quality of current assets. As often as not, this information will not be available. An aged debtor analysis can be of help in determining how out of line from the norm certain debtor accounts have become. It is not possible to construct such an analysis from published accounts. However, when a list of aged debtors is available, any accounts greatly exceeding the agreed credit terms should be examined carefully. The payment delays may be caused by a variety of factors:

(a) Queries or disputes
(b) Buyers' illiquidity
(c) Exporting difficulties, e.g. improper compliance with documentary credits' forms, currency controls
(d) Accidental or 'natural' causes interrupting normal settlement procedures
(e) Buyers' insolvency
(f) Changes in buyers' corporate structures, e.g. a management buyout or takeover interrupting normal procedures
(g) Buyers' receivership or liquidation
(h) Banking delays not caused by non-compliance with advised procedures.

Internal credit managers and sales ledger staff should, of course, be well-aware should any of these factors obtain. External analysts may have no inkling unless an aged debtor analysis provides evidence of extraordinary settlement delays. Both for internal and external credit staff, it is important that financial assessments be carried out on companies that delay settlement beyond acceptable limits and without acceptable reasons. Even in cases of liquidation, analysis of the company's latest figures should give analysts an idea of priority creditors, charges over assets, and any amounts available for unsecured creditors. This last, of course, will be made available later in the liquidator's statement of affairs.

THE COMPOSITION OF CURRENT LIABILITIES

Normally, current liabilities include items of the following kind:

> Trade creditors
> Sundry creditors
> Bank overdrafts
> Portions of long-term loans repayable in the period
> Other loans currently repayable
> Taxation:
>   PAYE and Social Security
>   Corporation tax
>   Advance corporation tax
> Proposed final dividend
> Bills of exchange payable
> Amounts owed to group companies

Of these, the key issue must be the creditors' rankings on the time-scale of payment. Some current liabilities will crystallize more quickly than others. Some will be more easily postponable than others. Still others will be preferred creditors or priority creditors and, accordingly, must be paid in order of priority of preference. To a degree, it is fair to argue that the total volume of any creditor's account may make that class of creditor more important from the liquidity standpoint notwithstanding that class's priority. The analyst would, therefore, lay greater emphasis on trade creditors than on taxation in the following account:

Current liabilities	
Trade creditors	500,000
Sundry creditors	2,000
Overdrafts	10,000
VAT creditor	7,500
PAYE and Social Security	8,900
	528,400

In the above example, taxation represents 16,400. Tax creditors enjoy preferred status. These items comprise only 3.1 per cent of total current liabilities. Ninety-five per cent of total current liabilities are represented by trade debtors. We would hope that, in the same company's current assets, we would, see a proportionally high level of trade debtors resulting in a favourable trading balance. In the above example, the analyst might be less concerned with the relatively low level of preferred tax creditors than might ordinarily be the case, and be more interested in the extremely high level of trade creditors if a higher level of trade debtors does not create a favourable trading balance.

Looking more closely, the analyst might then try and construct a table of priority for these current liabilities. At the outset, however, he knows that 95 per cent of total current liabilities are unsecured trade creditors. Unless details can be had on the sundry creditors, we must assume that they will rank behind either preferred and priority creditors or possibly, behind trade creditors. A preliminary ranking, assuming the company is not in liquidation or receivership, would be:

Debt priority schedule

Preferred—Inland revenue (PAYE/Social Security):	8,900
Preferred—HM Customs and Excise (VAT):	7,500
Priority—Bank (overdraft if secured):	10,000
Priority—Sundry creditors if secured:	2,000
Trade creditors if unsecured:	500,000
	528,400

Holmes and Sugden suggest that the key factor in analysing the 'imminence of current liabilities' is the determination of whether or not the company has capacity for further borrowings. Given a proportionally greater and healthy mix of current assets, the company in the example above might be well below its borrowing capacity. In assessing this capacity, account should also be taken of any existing long-term debt as well as off-balance-sheet financing items, e.g. leasing commitments. Overdraft and/or other borrowing limits, however, are rarely disclosed in accounting statements.

KNOWLEDGE OF A COMPANY'S TRADING PATTERNS

Before particularly telling observations can be made concerning the relationship of current assets to current liabilities, some care must be taken to ascertain as much as possible about a company's trading patterns and the main trading characteristics of its particular business. For instance, a toy manufacturer might offer a set of accounts as at 31 December from which a current ratio of 2.1 could be calculated. If one examines the composition of current assets which so generously cover current liabilities and sees that a high proportion of current assets is represented by stock, the analyst might not feel that anything was amiss—if he did not have some prior knowledge about the seasonal character of the toy manufacturing industry. With hope, one would expect to see stocks at a very low level after the Christmas period, or 31 December. With some feel for the seasonality of the toy industry, the analyst could then question why more stock has not been sold. If high volumes of sales have not been achieved over the Christmas season by the toy manufacturer, when are they more likely to be achieved? In brief, it would appear that the manufacturer is going to be in some difficulty despite his strong year-end current ratio.

But again, before conclusions are hurriedly reached, it is wise for the analyst to check the trend shown over several years by the current ratio, other ratios, and the company's main financial movements. Is the high level of stocks a usual feature? In other words, what is the composition of current assets at year-end in prior periods? If stocks are deducted from working capital, does the company appear illiquid? If so, to what degree? What is the composition of the stocks themselves? Are most of the stocks represented by work-in-progress and raw materials? How much stock is made up of finished goods for sale? Most of these questions can be answered either by a closer inspection of the accounts or by the subject company supplying further information. How trustworthy this latter class of information is must be another consideration. But most importantly for the present discussion, what about the type of toys the company manufactures and sells? Are they the sort of products that one might reasonably expect to sell large quantities of over the winter months and particularly over Christmas? Possibly the company manufactures children's surf-boards. If so, it might make financial sense to buy in raw materials in the winter months to allow both for manufacturing time and accumulation of sufficient stocks for spring and summer sales campaigns. Such questions can only be answered by a working knowledge of industries.

Without relating subject companies to particular industry characteristics, intelligent credit analysis is impossible. This is not to say that sectoral or industry comparisons with a subject company of dissimilar product-ranges, capital structure, asset-size, and turnover will make ratio-based analysis any the more informed. Both causes and effects, even if they lead to similar financial conditions cannot say anything greater than showing in ratio or quantity form that a company is above, below, or on par with the rest of its sector. Any such outturn leaves corporate idiosyncracy out of account. The following figures are outturns:

	'000s		
	Company 1	Company 2	Company 3
Net profit:	60	60	60
Current ratio:	2.1	2.1	2.1
Net assets:	150	150	150

These outturns are identical. If each of the three companies operated in the same industry sector, what would the identities tell us? If we subsequently learn that the sectoral averages are:

Net profit: 65
Current ratio: 1.1
Net assets: 500

what are we to deduce? (a) our subjects fall below the industry average in net profits, broad solvency and liquidity measurement, and total net assets. And (b) that because our subjects fall below the average, they must be regarded as poor performers or 'weak' in respect of these three measurements.

As logically inescapable as these conclusions may be, they cannot be held to be very significant for they take no account of differences in the three companies' sales volumes, gearing, composition of current assets and current liabilities, normalized working capital, off-balance-sheet commitments, industry characteristics with respect to stock, seasonality, or multiple product lines. They take no account of margins, hard measures of liquidity, tangible net worth, R&D, and future sales and profits forecasts.

Also, though our subjects fall below the 'average', how many companies and what kind of companies contributed to the average? If our subjects fall below the average, is this average truly indicative? Furthermore, though the average has not been reached, are the three companies achieving their end results from widely divergent beginnings? What were the increases or decreases in reserves? What differences in equity obtained between the three?

Credit analysis is not normally geared around such three-fold comparisons. An analysis is performed on a particular company applying for new credit or more credit. Idiosyncracy is thus the hallmark of intelligent analysis. In short, it makes very little difference what the financial outturns of an industry sector may be. It makes all the difference in the world what the financial outturns of a subject company are. These outturns and the trends giving dimension to them will suggest whether or not the company will be able to support the credit.

ACID-TEST RATIO

The acid-test or quick or liquid ratio is traditionally supposed to indicate a harder measurement of liquidity than the current ratio. The acid-test is calculated by:

$$\frac{\text{Current assets} - \text{stock}}{\text{Current liabilities}}$$

The rationale is simply that stock may or may not be quickly realizable for cash. It is accordingly deducted from current assets to provide an indication of current asset items readily convertible to cash should all current liabilities crystallize at the same time.

The rationale is faulty on three counts:

1. It is open to question whether x per cent of stock may not be very quickly converted to cash, e.g. raw materials and goods for sale or resale as opposed to WIP.
2. The acid-test assumes unjustifiably that all other current assets will be quickly convertible to cash.
3. The assumption is made that all current liabilities will crystallize at the same time. This runs counter to common sense and accounting sense. As some liabilities crystallize and are discharged, other will arise to take their place in varying degrees—provided that the company is trading. The same type of movement is apparent in current assets as noted earlier.

Let us consider the sample abbreviated balance sheet below:

CURRENT ASSETS	Notes	'000s
Stock	1	300,000
Trade debtors		250,000
Sundry debtors	2	13,400
Cash at bank		6,700
Directors' current accounts		67,100
Amounts due from assoc co		100,000
		737,200
CURRENT LIABILITIES		
Trade creditors		320,000
Sundry creditors	3	15,600
Amounts owed to group cos		250,100
Taxation		133,456
Proposed dividend		10,000
		729,156

Notes:
1. Stock
Raw materials	50,000
Work-in-progress:	200,000
Finished goods:	50,000
	300,000

2. Sundry debtors
Rental arrears:	10,000
Hire of equipment:	3,400
	13,400

3. Sundry creditors
Leases and HP	15,600
	15,600

This company's acid-test ratio will be:

$$\frac{737,200 - 300,000}{729,156} = 0.5$$

The ratio itself assumes that any multiple less than 1 indicates a company that could not meet all its outstanding current obligations simultaneously. The company shown above would thus be in dire straits. We have already questioned the common sense in assuming all current obligations would crystallize for payment at the same time. A more sensible and indicative liquidity measurement might be:

Normalized liquidity ratio

$$\frac{x\% \text{ or classes of stock} + y\% \text{ of remaining current assets (or selected classes of quickly realizable current assets)}}{p\% \text{ of classes of trade creditors} + q\% \text{ or selected preferred and priority creditors}}$$

Using values from the earlier example, the same company's normalized liquid ratio might be:

A

Stock

Accept raw materials:	50,000
finished goods:	50,000
	100,000

Selected current assets

Accept trade debtors:	250,000
cash at bank:	6,700
sundry debtors:	3,400
dir current A/cs:	67,100
	327,200

Total accepted current assets: 427,200 (numerator)

B

Trade creditors
Accept say 80% of trade creditors as prior measurement of creditors' turnover is very short, therefore,
Trade creditors: 256,000
256,000

Selected preferred and priority creditors
Accept sundry creditors: 15,600
taxation: 133,456
149,056

Total accepted current liabilities: 405,056 (denominator)

The normalized liquidity ratio would thus be:

$$\frac{427,200}{405,056} = 1.055$$

The quantity and quality of information provided in this last example is about average for all but modified accounts. The difference in results obtained between the standard acid-test and the normalized liquidity ratio is manifest. We contend that the acid-test measurement is non-informative because it is based on erroneous assumptions. The acid-test showed a considerably illiquid company, whereas the normalized ratio, based on more realistic assumptions, showed a reasonably liquid company.

In computing the normalized ratio, we have simply omitted irrelevant quantities. For instance, would it be sensible to assume that were large groups of a company's current liabilities to crystallize simultaneously, the management would dare settle outstanding intercompany accounts before preferred or priority creditors? By the same token, would it be sensible to assume that were the company called upon suddenly to settle large portions of its current obligations, that various current assets such as directors' current accounts would not be fully or partially paid in cash? We have treated these items accordingly in the computations.

Such computations and suggestions for normalizing are merely rough guides. The exact percentages or classes of items for inclusion in normalized ratios should depend upon analysts' first-hand experience of the subject and its business. In the above example, readers will note that the normalized liquidity ratio gives a higher measurement than the ordinary current ratio of 1.011. This is due to the omission of intercompany accounts. Adding net intercompany outstandings to current liabilities would drive the normalized ratio to 0.77.

$$\frac{427,200}{405,056 + 150,000} = 0.7696$$

To include intercompany balances in this way, violates common sense in that it does not reflect the way in which most companies would act if faced with large proportions of creditors demanding settlement.

There is, accordingly, an argument for omitting intercompany accounts from a computation of current ratios.

Sources

Bathory, A., *Predicting Corporate Collapse*, Financial Times Business Information, 1984, Chapter 5 passim.
Bathory, A., *Departure from Fact: The Restatement of Accounting Numbers in Standard Credit Analysis, Credit Management*, Institute of Credit Management, mid-October, 1984, p. 24 sqq.
Fadel, H., and Parkinson, J. M., 'Liquidity Evaluation by Means of Ratio Analysis', *Accounting and Business Research*, Vol. 8, No. 30, Spring, 1978.
Holmes, G., and Sugden, A., *Interpreting Company Reports and Accounts*, Woodhead-Faulkner, Cambridge, 1983, Chapter 23, pp. 163–173.
Horrigan, J. O., '*A Short History of Financial Ratio Analysis*', *Accounting Review*, 1968, passim.
ICC Business Ratios, *Industrial Performance Analysis*, 8th edn, ICC Information Group, 1983, passim.

3

STANDARD AND HYBRID RATIOS IN BASIC ANALYSIS

As ratios fulfil certain key analytical criteria, they are accepted generally as prime constituents of credit analysis. The key analytical criteria are:

1. Ratios are syntheses made up of antitheses. Synthesis and antithesis, as discussed earlier, both display and suggest quantifiable data in the most informative manner. The ratio format itself is thus a miniature of the whole analytical process.
2. Ratios are common-size reductive devices. For comparison, and contrasting a range of different quantities, ratios automatically reduce both extremely small and large numbers to lowest numbers or multiples. Thus a comparison of 345,678 to 567,902 would be expressed by the ratio 0.6 which is more easily assimilable.
3. Ratios express findings in significant ways, notably, as percentages or as multiples. In so doing, they highlight whilst summarizing.
4. If one ratio measurement contributes significant information, it follows that more than one ratio will contribute additionally significant information. This is demonstrable when one ratio is compared with another—possibly causing the analyst to temper an original opinion or interpretation. Accordingly, financial models composed of several interrelated ratios stand to contribute particularly high levels of significant information.
5. If ratios are combinative with significant results—as they indeed have proven to be over a wide range of applications—those ratios having predictive power inherently or because of their combination with other ratios in a certain way, provide forecasts which are highly accurate within acceptable degrees of variance. Altman's *Z*-Score model is a good example.
6. In their forecasting role, ratios can effectively do away with some detailed and time-consuming analytical routines, e.g. cashflow projections or transaction analyses. Obviating such routines can be beneficial when the full accounting information needed to complete the routines is neither complete nor recent. Also, ratio forecasting can be beneficial to grantors of trade credit where subject companies do not always know that their financial condition is being examined. In these cases, requests for further data would not, practically speaking, always be either well-received or received at all. Bank analysts may have the time and the data necessary to perform certain long-winded analytical routines; commercial analysts have neither.

It stands to reason that some ratios either taken singly or severally will satisfy these key criteria of analysis better than others. Trainee analysts sometimes imagine that the more exhaustive the list of ratios they compute, the better their analysis. This is certainly not the case. Ratios should always be selected for their relevance and significance. In considering whether a company's working capital (taken in the widest sense as opposed only to net current assets) will support an exposure, is it at all relevant to compute tangible net worth to total liabilities? Indeed, in such a case, the intelligent analyst might question the relevance of calculating net current assets as a key indicator.

There is no definitive master-list of accepted ratios. Ratios can be invented or built for any purpose. Thus, some will be of wider importance than others. Yet other inventions will be foolish in the sense of being trivial or misconceived for their original purposes. There are, however, various operating and financial ratios in common use. Many of these widely-accepted ratios have already been discussed in this writing. For the sake of convenience, these can be called 'standard ratios'. Briefly, key standard ratios are:

Operating ratios
Trading profit/turnover
Trading profit/capital employed
Turnover/capital employed
Stocks/turnover
Debtors/creditors
Trade debtors/trade creditors
Trade debtors/turnover × 365
Trade creditors/costs of purchases
Trade creditors/turnover
Working capital/turnover

Financial ratios
Debt/equity
Equity/capital employed
Profit before taxation and interest/capital employed
Current ratio (current assets/current liabilities)
Acid-test ratio (current assets—Stock/current liabilities)
Loan capital/capital employed
Profit before interest and taxation/interest
Turnover/net fixed assets

This list does not pretend to be exhaustive. Different industries will have other key standard measuring devices especially suited to particular businesses. The important point is that various ratios are accepted as standard measuring tools in all sectors. As financial analysis becomes more sophisticated, new ratios are bound to be developed to fulfil particular requirements. Together with the standard ratios, hybrid ratio measurements have thus come into use. The development of hybrid forms follows logically from the shift away from accrual-based analyses to cashflow analysis.

Hybrid ratios

As indicated, hybrid ratios have tended to be cashflow oriented rather than accrual-based. An analyst is typically less interested in measuring the relationship of current assets to current liabilities than in trying to determine to an acceptable degree of probability that a subject company's cash inflow will be able to support not only its existing debt-burden, but a future debt-burden including a specific credit exposure. This is a cashflow consideration which can be looked at in varying ways. The construction of a hybrid ratio is a good initial way of starting.

In this case, the analyst is not particularly interested in cash resulting from extraordinary items such as an asset sale or a taxation credit. He is, on the other hand, vitally interested in the company's normal trading activities and their resulting cashflow. Ideally, the analyst will have not only historical accounting information but also management data on which to build his computations. Both types of data can, of course, be used in the ratio. For the moment, let us suppose that only historical accounting data is available.

Accordingly, he might build a ratio along the following lines:

Numerator

Profit on ordinary activities after taxation but before extraordinary items
+
Depreciation
+
Increase in deferred taxation

This would give a measurement of gross cashflow before any gains/losses on items not forming part of the company's ordinary trading activities. Let us, therefore, call the numerator normalized gross cashflow (NGCF).

Denominator

In forming the denominator of the ratio, the analyst has some latitude. For instance, is he trying to measure preferred debt obligations? Or preferred and priority-status creditors? Or trade creditors? Or possibly, total current liabilities? Remembering also that the numerator as suggested above was composed purely of historical quantities, does the analyst want to introduce a new or non-historical quantity into the denominator? That non-historical quantum would, of course, be the credit exposure under consideration. For the sake of simplicity, let us assume that at this stage the ratio is to be kept purely historical. Accordingly, the ratio denominator might be composed on the following lines:

Preferred + priority creditors + x% of trade creditors

The denominator is, therefore, composed by normalized current debt (NCD) and the hybrid ratio would be:

$$\frac{NGCF}{NCD}$$

To provide for a projection beyond the purely historical measurement given by this ratio, the analyst might add a quantified assumption of future cashflow from ordinary activities to the numerator and add the credit exposure in question to the denominator. The resulting ratio would indicate the extent to which normalized current debt including the exposure could be 'serviced' from projected gross cashflow from ordinary activities. The accuracy of the finished ratio will be directly proportional with the accuracy of the forecasting assumptions added to numerator and denominator. The new ratio would thus be:

$$\frac{\text{NGCR} +/- p}{\text{NCD} +/- q}$$

Other examples of hybrid ratios in common use are:

Ratio	Measuring
$\dfrac{\text{Tangible net worth}}{\text{Total liabilities}}$	Cumulative profitability
$\dfrac{\text{Equity}}{\text{Current liabilities}}$	Capital adequacy
$\dfrac{\text{Pre-tax profit}}{\text{Capital employed}}$	Annual profitability
$\dfrac{\text{Totals generated from operations}}{\text{Current debt} + \text{exposure}}$	Priority debt-service ability and comfort margin
$\dfrac{\text{Normalized working capital}}{\text{Total assets}}$	Liquidity

Of these, the fourth hybrid is defective in that the comfort margin for a given credit exposure is pitted against not only historical current debt items (when the exposure in question may or may not enjoy preferred or priority status), but also, no adjustment for future earnings from operations has been made to the numerator which is purely historical. The information this ratio provides is thus very limited and very approximate. The same criticism will, of course, be levelled at any ratio or other indicator itself based on assumptions such as sales forecasts or the cashflows resulting from future sales. By contra, we firmly believe that it is better to make forecasting assumptions provided they are based on as much fact as possible and provided that these assumptions have been clearly noted in the analyses. Other analysts or decision-makers can then agree or disagree with the initial findings.

Earlier, we spoke of the combinative property of ratios. Simply, ratios can be placed together in various groupings. These groups can be weighted or unweighted and summed. The sum can be made to provide synoptic views, such as:

Overall liquidity
Solvency
Averaged free capital
Risk description

Composite ratios

Standard and hybrid ratios can be arranged in groups to produce formulas or financial models. Such models can have varying specific purposes and applications. In general, however, ratio-based models are used to obtain:

Synoptic views—That is, views whose constituent parts are considered singly, severally, and simultaneously, e.g. an insolvency forecasting model

Averaged views—That is, views whose constituent parts are summed and divided by the number of parts to obtain an average or indicative picture of the whole of those constituent parts, e.g. a 'free-capital' model

'What if?' type models can be ratio-based or otherwise. The 'answers' to 'what if' propositions can be single, several, synoptic, or averaged. By and large, the most useful 'what if' applications will be synoptic. For instance, the question, 'What if sales fell by 3.5 per cent over the next 12 months and direct costs of sales rose by 1.2 per cent? What would the expected margin be and what effect would this have on the company's balance sheet, in particular, its capital and reserves? This is a complex question calling for a plugging-in of new values and restatement of the company's interaction of main financial flows. The need to follow the effects throughout the whole financial system of a drop in sales and a rise in costs of sales is apparent. While certain 'answers' to the questions will be seen looking at resulting individual flows, others of a more far-reaching nature will not be so apparent until the entire restatement has been completed when the full ramifications of the model's assumptions can be appreciated. Remembering that one of the main purposes of modelling or, indeed, of credit analysis, is to furnish concise, overall views as well as particularized views, the person operating the 'what if' model, in this case, will want an overall view or synopsis of the company's financial condition resulting from the two assumptions fed into the model. The 'what if' type model outlined here is not, however, designed to be synoptic in the same degree as, say, an insolvency forecasting model making no future assumptions but merely summing main financial flows, weighted or unweighted, on the premise that corporate insolvency is a complex outcome made up of several flows and their interaction. This premise additionally entails the assumption that corporate insolvency cannot be accurately determined using unsummed or individual measurements alone. This is the premise and entailment on which such varying holistic models as Altman's *Z-Score* and Bathory's Model are based.

In examining the uses and workings of composite ratios, let us first consider the simplest purpose to which a group of ratios can be put. This is to obtain an average and, with hope, indicative view of a company's particular class of flow. By particular class of flow, we understand such movements as:

Debt-service ability
Capital adequacy
Free capital for day-to-day use
Cash inflow/outflow

None of these is measurable in a definitively final form by consideration of one quantity or one ratio alone. Each class of flow can and should be looked at from as many relevant viewpoints as possible. The averaging process resulting from the ratio or quantity groupings provides the means for so doing.

Furthermore, each class of flow contributing, say, to capital adequacy, must be related to some antithetical number. This relation will highlight the degree of adequacy. For instance, we could see that by placing tangible net worth over total liabilities, a cover or adequacy indicator of 2.1 might obtain. That would be one ultimate or long-term view of a company's capital adequacy. We might, however, like also to consider the company's adequacy of capital in the current or short term. This could be done by placing equity over current liabilities. Obviously, we are constructing ratios to highlight measures of capital adequacy. We could then try and group the ratios in the following way:

$$\frac{\text{Tangible net worth}}{\text{Total liabilities}} + \frac{\text{Equity}}{\text{Current liabilities}}$$

Assuming that the sum of the two ratios equals 100 per cent, we might decide that for our purposes, the company's short-term position was more crucial. In weighting the two ratios, the relative importance of short-term adequacy could be assured by weighting ratio two higher than ratio one, say, as follows:

$$\frac{(\text{TNW/TL}) \times 0.20 + (\text{E/CL}) \times 0.80}{0.100} \quad \text{or } 100\%$$

The use of such arbitrary weighting distorts at the same time as contributing 'power' to the model. Provided that the analyst or model-builder fully appreciates that the weightings calculated by whatever means deform results in order to highlight them, model results can be used indicatively and divorced from what has become to some users a species of magic midway between statistics and witchcraft. Weightings, then, should be used as pointers or schematic indicators to highlight important areas of analysis. There are no 'correct' ratio or constituent weightings, statistical-based or other. The selection or computation of weights is arbitrary. The indicative usefulness of weights must accordingly be assessed against common sense—in these cases, what we know about the real functioning of the subject company both internally and with respect to its market. Weighted ratios in models should, therefore, give synopses or scores that do not clearly violate common sense. In this way, any group of weighted ratios that gave a higher averaged free capital to a company greater than the company's net current assets as seen in its balance sheet, would have to be considered suspect. In model-building, analysts will often have to work backward from such points of reference as, say, net current assets, to test the common sense of their findings. In this case, the model-builder would see that adjustments were made to his ratio weights to bring down the synoptic measure of free capital to no greater amount than formal working capital in the accounts, and probably, far less.

The criticism of arbitrary weightings is thus quite plain. Arbitrary weighting of ratios or other quantities is wholly artificial and distortive to a greater degree than simple averaging. In our opinion, this criticism has not yet been satisfactorily answered. If variable weights are used merely as highlighting devices and noted as such, the problem appears less troublesome. When weighting, statistical-based or other, is used for predictive purposes, e.g. insolvency forecasting, the problem grows more acute and open to a good many questions.

In these areas of credit analysis, practitioners should remember that the central concerns are less with numerical accuracy than with indicativeness based on historical performance in the widest sense. This indicativeness will be sharpened in direct proportion to:

(a) the accuracy of computation of the ratio constituents
(b) the realism of the assumptions behind the weightings

Firstly, if we are concerned to measure, say, debt-service ability, it is plain that our computations of the financial flow or flows that are to service the company's debt must be calculated accurately. So, indeed, must be the debt. Care must be taken even at this computational stage not to measure long-term debt against short-term cashflow. The mismatch would make results uninformative. The possible exception to this might be some break-up type measurement such as tangible net assets over total liabilities. But such a wide measure providing what is, in essence, a worst possible outcome, should most indicatively be used together with other ratios where the individual measurements could be summed.

Secondly, the realism of the assumptions behind ratio weightings refers to the non-distorting quality of the weights. It is self-evident that the weightings in Example 2 below are more distortive than those in Example 1, assuming equal importance of the three flows in each example.

Example 1
$$\frac{(a+b+c)}{x}.50 + \frac{(t+u+v)}{y}.50$$

Example 2
$$\frac{(a+b+c)}{x}.99 + \frac{(t+u+v)}{y}.01$$

By this token, it is clear that the equal weightings in Example 1 serve only as an averaging mechanism—Example 1 being restatable as:

$$\frac{\frac{(a+b+c)}{x} + \frac{(t+u+v)}{y}}{2}$$

The distortive quality of arbitrary weights, however, should not necessarily rule out their careful use. Such weights can be used with good illustrative effect in focusing on particularly important flows, such as short-term cash inflow for the servicing of short-term priority debt obligations.

Let us now look at an example of a simple ratio-based model to indicate averaged capital cover for a credit exposure. The basic assumption informing this model is simply that analysts look at a credit exposure against a subject company's latest historical main financial flows to judge to what degrees, if any, the exposure would have been contained. This assumption, of course, is imperfect in that the credit exposure should be looked at not against historical data but current information. Current data is not always possible or practical to obtain—especially for non-bank analysts. The secondary assumption, then, is that the company's latest historical data is a more accurate foundation in analysis than a totally new and unvalidated set of forecast data. If this assumption appears supine, it is still infinitely more prudent and, in our view, more indicative, than basing credit opinions upon forecasts amounting to total restatements of companies' accounts. The imperfection of these two assumptions and the degrees of non-indicativeness to which they subsequently give rise rest squarely on the age of the historical data used. The older the data, the more error-prone the credit opinion.

Those caveats having been made, let us, for the sake of argument, go on and build a model to measure averaged capital cover. The purpose of the model will be to measure the amount average spare capital can decline before the company cannot meet its obligations including a credit exposure under consideration.

For simplicity, let us choose four main measures of spare or free capital; say,

Net cash flow
Net current assets
Normalized working capital
Net totals generated from operations

Note that each of these flows is the product of the deduction of one quantity from another. This could be expressed in the finished model either as $x-y$ or x/y. It is perhaps easier for our purposes to express the model components as completed nettings-out, i.e. $x, y, z,$ and so forth, bearing in mind that their sum will be the numerator against the credit exposure as a denominator. This serves to express the finished model as one ratio instead of five ratios. The model formula can then be expressed in a straightforward way:

$$AVC = \frac{(a+b+c+d)/4}{x}$$

Where AVC = Averaged capital cover
and
a = Net cash flow
b = Net current assets
c = Normalized working capital
d = Net totals generated from operations
and
x = credit exposure
and
4 = divisor for averaging

The formula could be expressed even more simply by:

$$AVC = \frac{0.25 \left(\sum_{x_{1-4}} \right)}{y}$$

Where AVC = Averaged capital cover
and

x_1 to x_4 = the variable net flows
0.25 = the averaging constant multiplier
y = credit exposure
$\sum$ = the sum of x_1 to x_4

Examining the finished formula, we can see that equal weighting has been given to each of the four flows. This can be justified on the following grounds:

(a) Each flow is a current or short-term flow indicating cash coming in against cash going

out of the company. The resulting net amounts are all valid measurements of free capital.
(b) Because we do not know which, if any, of these measures may be the most important in servicing the credit exposure along with existing obligations, we propose averaging as a reasonably indicative way of taking all the main flows into account.
(c) We do not know following on from (b) what rankings in degrees of importance or 'power' to ascribe to secondary flows.
(d) Averaging is less distortive and more indicative than unequal weighting.

At this point, mention should be made of prior research in the question of ratio weighting by Myers and Forgy. Their studies of bank analytical models showed that equal weightings used in forecasting routines provided superior discriminating powers to statistically calculated weights assigned to individual ratios. In our opinion, Myers and Forgy's findings have not been overturned by the subsequent use by Altman and Taffler of multiple discriminant weights for predictive purposes. Whilst Altman and Taffler obtain high degrees of predictive accuracy with multiple discriminant-based models, equally high degrees of predictive and indicative power have been obtained in far less time and cost by equally-weighted models, predictive and classificatory. The use of statistical-based weights calls for well-defined industry sector samples of similar asset size. The calculation of these weights requires specialist statistical routines. These are best carried out and tested on computer. Thus, these types of weightings call for specialist skills, equipment, and testing time. Furthermore, their scope of operation is considerably limited. For these reasons, and when looked at against the ordinary demands both in time and money of commercial credit departments we opt for equal weighting or no weighting for basic applications to be carried out manually by analysts in the ordinary course of their work.

Finally, we feel it is important that analysts understand fully each assumption they make. No one but the statistician calculating special weights will understand either the assumptions or the entailments of the assumptions made in such exercises. The analyst using what is no more than a software package often has no idea of the ratio components, much less their weightings. He cannot, therefore, understand what he is calculating, how he is making the calculations, or what the final scores mean or entail—apart from repeating parrot-fashion received ideas from the software package's manufacturers. In some cases of this kind, credit decisions may be made on accurate and indicative criteria, but the analyst or user of the package does not know this. He is working blind. In other cases, the model assumptions and weightings may be faulty. The resulting credit decisions taken on the model's findings will, therefore, stand a good chance of being faulty. The buying-in of a software analytical package can, in these ways, hoodwink analysts into laying aside their brains when they are not thoroughly familiar with and agree to the workings and underlying assumptions of the computer models.

So far, we have not bothered to define precisely the computations we wish made in the terms:

Net cash flow
Net current assets
Normalized working capital
Net totals generated from operations

Let us now propose working definitions where the definitions will yield net measures of free capital. Accordingly:

Let net cash flow represent:
>Profit after taxation
>\+
>Depreciation
>\+
>increase in deferred taxation
>−
>Dividends
>−
>Current liabilities (ex proposed dividend)

Let net current assets represent:
>Current assets
>−
>Current liabilities

Let normalized working capital represent:
>Ex stocks:
>Raw materials and consumables
>\+
>Finished goods and goods for resale
>\+
>Balance of current assets
>−
>Current liabilities

Let net totals generated from operations represent:
>Totals generated from operations
>−
>Current liabilities

Using information taken from Monsanto PLC's 1983 consolidated figures (Figure 3.1), we can assign values to the model's components and arrive at an averaged measure of free capital against which an exposure can be placed.

Let the proposed credit exposure be £5 m at any one time.
The computational routines are thus:

($y = £5$ m)

Ratio	Description	Computations	£'000s
X_1	NCF − CL	Profit after taxation:	55,247
		Depreciation:	18,663
		Increase in def taxation:	—
		Gross cashflow:	73,910
		Dividends	—
		NET CASHFLOW:	73,910
		CURRENT LIABILITIES:	59,388
			14,522

X_2	CA − CL	Current assets:	108,140
		−	
		Current liabilities:	59,388
		NET CURRENT ASSETS:	48,752
X_3	NWC	Stock:	
		Raw materials and consumables:	11,376
		Finished goods and goods for resales:	17,649
			29,025
		+	
		Balance of current assets:	75,174
			104,199
		−	
		Current liabilities:	59,388
		NORMALIZED WORKING CAPITAL:	44,811
X_4	NTG − CL	Totals generated from operations:	76,473
		−	
		Current liabilities:	59,388
		NET TOTALS GENERATED:	17,085
Sum total X_1 to $X_4 =$		125,170 × 0.25 = AVC	14,522
			48,752
			44,811
			17,085
			125,170

$$AVC = \frac{£31,293}{5,000} = 6.26 \text{ or expressed as a \%}$$

the £5 m exposure represents 16% of averaged free capital cover

This simple model and others designed along similar lines have the virtue of synopsis as they look at several main flows singly, severally, and simultaneously. The final results thus give a particularly fair view considering the problem is examined from every relevant known angle. Ideally, models should be used jointly with standard analysis as a convenient way of bringing together differing but related strands of information.

The alternative to a model such as the one just described, would be for the analyst to calculate all the main financial flows not immediately apparent from the subject's accounts and to pit the credit exposure against all of them and note the results. He is still left to interpret these results—not only individually but in some manner of summary form. This procedure is not only extremely time-consuming both in respect of computations and individual interpretations of them, but also, a long-winded approach lays itself open to inconsistencies in final interpretations and summary. This is true not so much from the standpoint of computational error, but from the human mind's difficulty in setting up multiple logical problems and deducing logically consistent answers to each of the problems acceptably and simultaneously. Allowing for error in basic assumptions, the formulaic or

MONSANTO p.l.c. AND SUBSIDIARIES

Consolidated profit and loss account for the year ended 31st December 1984

	Note	1984 £000	1983 £000
Turnover	1	398,906	371,227
Cost of sales		295,249	296,845
Gross Profit		103,657	74,382
Selling and distribution costs		11,410	10,964
Administration expenses		10,559	9,183
Other operating income		(11,933)	(5,783)
Other operating expenses		2,647	4,023
Share of profit of associated company		-	(544)
		12,683	17,843
Profit on ordinary activities before interest		90,974	56,539
Interest receivable	4	(4,872)	(3,427)
Interest payable	5	1,742	4,841
		(3,130)	1,414
Profit on ordinary activities before taxation	2	94,104	55,125
Taxation charge (credit)	6	24,608	(122)
Profit on ordinary activities after taxation		69,496	55,247
Extraordinary charges	7	1,870	7,196
Retained profit for the year	18	67,626	48,051
Retained by:			
Company		65,909	47,546
Subsidiaries		1,717	505
		67,626	48,051

A separate profit and loss account for the holding company has not been presented as provided by Section 149(5) of the Companies Act 1948.

6

Figure 3.1 Part of Monsanto PLC Annual Report 1984[17]

MONSANTO p.l.c. AND SUBSIDIARIES

Consolidated balance sheet at 31st December 1984

	Note	1984 £000	1983 £000
Fixed assets:			
Tangible assets	8	135,051	141,321
Investments	9	73,779	15,773
		208,830	157,094
Current assets:			
Stocks	10	42,373	32,966
Debtors	11	85,133	60,244
Investments — short term bank deposits		7,712	7,424
Cash at bank and in hand	12	8,453	7,506
		143,671	108,140
Current liabilities —			
Creditors: amounts falling due within one year	13	56,294	59,388
Net current assets		87,377	48,752
Total assets less current liabilities		296,207	205,846
Creditors: amounts falling due after more than one year (including loans)	14	22,666	23,110
Provisions for liabilities and charges	15	27,764	4,585
Net assets		245,777	178,151
Capital and reserves:			
Called up share capital	17	2,504	2,504
Share premium account		22,514	22,514
Other reserves		89,309	89,309
Profit and loss account	18	131,450	63,824
		245,777	178,151

Figure 3.1 (*continued*)

MONSANTO p.l.c. AND SUBSIDIARIES

Statement of source and application of funds for the year ended 31st December 1984

	1984 £000	1983 £000
Source of funds		
Profit on ordinary activities before taxation	94,104	55,125
Depreciation and obsolescence	19,832	18,663
Loss on disposal of tangible fixed assets	254	2,685
Total generated from operations	114,190	76,473
Adjustment re conversion of associated company to subsidiary	-	20,619
Proceeds from sale of tangible fixed assets	610	14,729
	114,800	111,821
Application of funds		
Increase (decrease) in stocks	9,407	(3,090)
Increase in debtors	24,889	4,631
Decrease (increase) in creditors falling due within one year	4,582	(14,504)
Total increase (decrease) in working capital	38,878	(12,963)
Net expenditure on tangible fixed assets	14,426	6,408
Increase in tangible fixed assets on acquisition of subsidiary	-	31,464
Increase in fixed asset investments	58,006	10,228
Taxation paid	10	62
Decrease in creditors falling due after more than one year	444	50,897
Expenditure charged against provisions for liabilities and charges	3,107	14,479
	114,871	100,575
Net (application) source	(71)	11,246
Movement in net liquid funds		
Increase in current investments	288	4,719
Increase in cash at bank and in hand	947	6,161
(Increase) decrease in bank overdrafts	(1,306)	366
	(71)	11,246

Figure 3.1 (*continued*)

MONSANTO p.l.c. AND SUBSIDIARIES

Notes on the financial statements continued

		1984 £000	1983 £000
Note 10	**STOCKS**		
	Consolidated:		
	Raw materials and consumables	11,476	11,376
	Work in progress	4,940	3,941
	Finished goods and goods for resale	25,957	17,649
		42,373	32,966
	Company:		
	Raw materials and consumables	11,476	11,007
	Work in progress	3,302	2,835
	Finished goods and goods for resale	19,062	13,148
		33,840	26,990

		1984 £000	1983 £000
Note 11	**DEBTORS**		
	Consolidated:		
	Trade debtors	35,775	31,056
	Amounts owed by group companies:		
	Holding company and fellow subsidiaries	34,906	22,282
	Other debtors	8,153	4,188
	Prepayments	6,299	2,718
		85,133	60,244
	Company:		
	Trade debtors	16,952	12,266
	Amounts owed by group companies:		
	Fellow subsidiaries	1,349	397
	Subsidiary companies	70,114	79,449
	Other debtors	8,011	3,979
	Prepayments	6,209	2,467
		102,635	98,558

Figure 3.1 (*continued*)

MONSANTO p.l.c. AND SUBSIDIARIES

Notes on the financial statements continued

Note 12   CASH AT BANK AND IN HAND

The balances include interest bearing current accounts on which market rates are paid.

		1984 £000	1983 £000
Note 13	CREDITORS: AMOUNTS FALLING DUE WITHIN ONE YEAR		
	Consolidated:		
	Bank overdrafts	1,376	70
	Trade creditors	14,099	13,857
	Amounts owed to group companies:		
	Fellow subsidiaries	25,234	29,386
	Corporation tax	190	8
	Other taxation and social security	10,997	9,875
	Other creditor	-	67
	Accruals and deferred income	4,398	6,125
		56,294	59,388
	Company:		
	Bank overdrafts	1,376	49
	Trade creditors	12,507	13,634
	Amounts owed to group companies:		
	Holding company and fellow subsidiaries	36,010	58,993
	Subsidiary companies	3,145	313
	Taxation and social security	14,889	13,506
	Accruals	4,841	5,965
		72,768	92,460

16

Figure 3.1 (*continued*)

MONSANTO p.l.c. AND SUBSIDIARIES

Notes on the financial statements continued

		1984 £000	1983 £000
Note 14	CREDITORS: AMOUNTS FALLING DUE AFTER MORE THAN ONE YEAR		
	Loan stocks:		
	5% Guaranteed loan stock 1992/97	1,500	1,500
	6¼% Guaranteed loan stock 1992/97	1,500	1,500
	5% Sterling/Dollar convertible guaranteed loan stock 1982/86	10,800	10,800
	Less: Stock cancelled on conversion	10,510	8,677
		290	2,123
	Other loan at interest rate of 5% repayable in 1986	12,093	10,704
	Amounts owed to holding company:		
	Wholly repayable between 1 and 2 years	7,283	7,283
	Consolidated and company	22,666	23,110
	Loans are repayable as follows:		
	Between 1 and 2 years	19,666	-
	Between 2 and 5 years	-	20,110
	Over 5 years	3,000	3,000
		22,666	23,110

5% and 6¼% Guaranteed loan stocks 1992/97.

These stock are unconditionally guaranteed by Monsanto Company in sterling as to principal, premium (if any) and interest and rank *pari passu* with each other and with 5% Sterling/Dollar convertible guaranteed loan stock 1982/86.

The company may at any time purchase all or any part of the 5% or 6¼% stock in the market or by tender available to all stockholders of the relevant class or classes alike at any price. The company may at any time after 31st May 1992 redeem the whole or any part of the 5% stock at £105 per cent. or the 6¼% stock at par. The company is obliged on 31st May 1997 to redeem any 5% stock outstanding at £105 per cent. and any 6¼% stock outstanding at par.

5% Sterling/Dollar convertible guaranteed loan stock 1982/86.

This stock is unconditionally guaranteed by Monsanto Company in sterling as to both principal and interest. The last day for conversion was the 31st May 1984.

The company may at any time purchase convertible stock in the market or by tender available to all stockholders alike at any price.

The company may redeem at any time the whole or any part of such stock at par and is obliged to repay any convertible stock outstanding on 31st May 1986 at par plus accrued interest.

Figure 3.1 (*concluded*)

model format provides the most effective tool in this species of problem solving. Naturally, the efficacy of the model depends upon the rightness of the assumptions on which the model is composed.

To make these statements clear, let us consider the credit exposure of £5 m at any one time against Monsanto's main flows. From the results, let us see what difficulties may arise merely in trying to assess the degree to which the exposure is contained, in this case, by Monsanto, where all the flows noted are inter-related as they are in any company.

We can begin by noting the company's main flows as well as more static quantities normally used by analysts in assessing optimal exposure. As with the averaged capital cover model, we use the company's 1983 consolidated figures given earlier in Figure 3.1.

SPREADSHEET
Credit exposure: £5 m at any one time

Accounting number/or Financial flow	Value (£'000s)	Others	Cover for exposure (as a multiple)
Turnover	371,227		74.2
Profit on ordinary activities before taxation	55,125		11.0
Retained profit for the year	48,051		9.6
Capital and reserves	178,151		35.6
Equity	178,151		35.6
Capital employed	205,846		41.2
Working capital	48,752		9.8
Gross cashflow	73,910		14.8
Net cashflow	73,910		14.8
Liquid current assets	75,174		15.0
Current ratio		1.8	
Acid-test ratio		1.3	
Return on capital employed		27.5%	
Retentions	153,133		30.6
Net assets	178,151		35.6
Debt-turn		31 days	
Trade creditors' turnover		17 days	
Stock turnover		32 days	
Cash and near-cash items	14,930		3.0
Totals generated from operations	76,473		15.3
Total source of funds	111,821		22.4
Net source of funds (after application)	11,246		2.2
Movement in net liquid funds	11,246	+905%	2.2

Figure 3.2 Standard computational analysis

This spreadsheet is by no means exhaustive. It virtually ignores trend as would be shown by comparison of two or more years' figures. What information is given relates chiefly to asset cover and liquidity using quantities already discussed in this writing. From this tabulation, as small as it is, what cover for the £5 m exposure should be selected? Is the proposed exposure safe? If so, to what degree?

Even from the above data such questions are not impossible to answer, though the answers do not come readily. The average cover expressed as a multiple would be 21.9 (372.9/17). But into this average we have taken various items indiscriminately. The criticism that can be made at this point is that the greater amount of 'discrimination' used, the greater the possibility of error. To our minds, this type of criticism minimizes the true sense of discrimination—that is, a selection process based on knowledge rather than opinion and common sense, namely, a thorough familiarity in this case with the way in which main financial flows interrelate in making up a company's overall financial condition as at accounting date. This sort of discrimination, of course, implies a prior knowledge of accounting practice.

Naturally, some species of discrimination will be more effective than others. With these qualifications, the argument for quantity rather than quality when applied to interpretation of batches of data, in our view, has nothing whatever to recommend it for all the reasons discussed earlier.

Trend in respect of ratios and other indicators

In credit analysis, a ratio or any other performance indicator is of limited value without a notion of trend. Whilst in the final analysis, sensible credit decisions are geared mainly around a company's latest audited results and any reasonable but prudent forecast results, it is dangerous to attempt forecasting without knowledge of past results and the basic direction these past results have taken the company. Also, no one would prefer to advance credit to a declining company rather than to a strengthening company. As we operate in a highly imperfect world, credit must very often be given to ailing companies because of the very nature of credit examined before. Nevertheless, an appreciation of trend—or the direction in which a company is going—helps to focus our minds on risk rather than 'containment' of the credit alone.

This is illustrated very simply. Working off 1985 audited figures, an analyst is asked to assess working capital cover for a £1 m at any one time exposure. The subject company is a computer manufacturer. The 1985 accounts show a working capital of £6,459,000, giving a cover of 6.4 where the credit ranks as $15\frac{1}{2}$ per cent of net current assets. The exposure is thus contained by surplus capital on this measure. Whether or not the cover is optimal must be another question. Working with only these figures, the proposition may not look out of court. Consider, however, Figure 3.3 in which five years' net current assets have been noted along with percentage increases/decreases and working capital/exposure ratios.

The prior years' figures along with the trend, illustrated here in a variety of ways, gives dimension. This dimension (or depth to the 1985 figure noted earlier) shows clearly the adverse effects of overtrading or not enough profitable trading on the company's liquidity over a five year period. Analysts familiar with the computer industry will be able to read further into these trends. Why, for instance, when this market has been extremely buoyant until very lately, has the company's liquidity on this measure dropped so sharply each year?

	(£'000s)				
	1985	1984	1983	1982	1981
Working capital	6,459	7,342	10,741	20,500	36,740
Exposure cover (as multiple)	6.4	7.3	10.7	20.5	36.7
Trend (% +/−)	−12	−32	−46	−44	
Trend (base index 100)	17.6	19.9	29.2	55.8	100.0
Trend (graphic)	—	—	—	—	—
Trend (graphic)	<	<	<	<	
Trend (averaged)	−33.5%				

Figure 3.3 Trend of ratios and other indicators

Is the possible overtrading here due to an ineffectual attempt on the part of the company to capture greater market share? Is the deepening erosion of working capital due to poor credit management? Poor stock control and turnover? Or is the basic trend really one of a dying company—i.e. a firm selling less and less and selling on increasingly poor margins?

The computations or illustrations of trend are very simple and only one method need be noted. This is calculating trend from a base index (in the above example, 100). The computation is:

Divide each year's figure by that of the first year and multiply the result by 100.

This method can be of greatest use when dealing with very large figures in that the resulting trend will reduce and make these figures less cumbersome visually.

Sources

Bathory, A., *Predicting Corporate Collapse*, Financial Times Business Information, 1984, Chapter 7, pp. 100–101.
Cohen, K. J., and Hammer, F. S., *Analytical Methods in Banking*, Richard D. Irwin, Homewood, Illinois, 1966, Chapter 6, pp. 124–127.
Holmes, G., and Sugden, A., *Interpreting Company Reports and Accounts*, Woodhead-Faulkner, Cambridge, 1983, Chapter 23, pp. 157–161 (trends).
Myers, H., and Forgy, E. W., 'Development of Numerical Credit Evaluation Systems', *Journal of American Statistical Association*, Vol. 50, September, 1963, pp. 797–806.

4

THE DEVELOPMENT OF RATIO-BASED MODELS IN CREDIT ANALYSIS

Credit analysis and current informational climate

The point has been made earlier that effective and accurate credit analysis must be based on a fairly wide range of pertinent and up-to-date information. In later chapters, we shall examine many of the ancillary, though important, kinds of data. At present, however, we want to consider audited accounting data only. This, as has been made clear, provides the most important type of information in a discipline that is chiefly numerical.

Analysts will either work off 'standard' spreadsheets in use by their firms or will often be required to develop their own spreads. The development of spreadsheets is no more than the search for:

(a) greater speed in analysis
(b) greater relevance in analysis
(c) greater accuracy in analysis
(d) new foundations for newly-developed analytical methods

We have discussed items (a) to (c). Item (d) forms the prime focus for this Chapter. New spreads for new methods are something of a chicken-and-egg business. Which comes first? The analyst casting around for new spreading techniques will sometimes group items in such a way that will suggest further correlation of facts into financial models. At other times, the search for particular solutions to general problems, such as the determination or prediction of insolvency, or the quantification of truly indicative measures of working capital, will suggest what information must be spread and in what form.

In a significant sense, the greater the quality and quantity of data at the analyst's disposal, the better the credit opinion. Following on from this, the analysis of public companies and other large corporations, e.g. nationalized industries, does not present analysts with the same types of problems as the assessment of small firms and private companies.

The quality and quantity of information available (immediately and free of charge) on public companies is considerable. Basically, the sources are:

1. Annual reports and accounts
2. Interim reports and accounts
3. National and trade presses

4. Market intelligence
5. Stockmarket reports
6. Credit ratings, e.g. Extel, Standard and Poor's, Moody's
7. Information/Public Relations Departments of the companies themselves
8. Share prices
9. Agency reports, e.g. Dun & Bradstreet

These, along with trade and bank references, furnish providers of credit with good quality data on which to base computations and make decisions.

In the case of small firms and private companies operating in the United Kingdom and in North America, for example, the compilation of good quality data is extremely difficult and, in some cases, costly, for all but banks who can demand whatever financial and management information they need before considering loans. In the United Kingdom (Northern Ireland excepted), all companies are obliged to lodge their audited accounts annually at registries in London, Edinburgh, or Cardiff. In North America, only public corporations are obliged to file accounts for general inspection.

The reporting requirements for private companies in England lead the world. But this does not say very much. Accounts tend to be made up as late as possible, with the standards varying very widely from company to company. Schedule 8 of the Companies Act, 1985, grants certain reporting exemptions to small companies. These small companies produce 'modified' accounts for lodgement at the Registries, even though full accounting statements have been produced from which the modified versions derived. The full accounting statements normally remain with the shareholders and directors of the firms.

Credit managers and analysts generally agree that both the age and the depth of modified accounts sharply diminish their potential value as assessment tools. The main difficulties encountered in modified statements are the omission of key accounting numbers, e.g. turnover, and itemizations or schedules, e.g. current liabilities listed by class.

The Department of Trade and Industry is currently proposing to reduce further the reporting requirements which small companies are obliged to lodge for public inspection. Briefly, the reasons are:

1. Audits impose undue costs on small businesses. The level of cost is said to be a matter of concern to many companies.
2. Audited accounts are not held to be essential in protecting the interests of shareholders in owner-managed firms. The DTI states that shareholders should normally be able to form a view of their companies' affairs without being required to commission an independent audit.
3. Audited accounts are held by the DTI to be of insufficient importance to creditors to justify their cost of preparation for small firms. The information such audits provide is historical and, therefore, out of date. The DTI goes on to state that the audited accounting statements of small companies are of limited practical use in assessing creditworthiness.
4. Audited information is held to be of questionable value as in the case of small firms, the auditors have had to accept much information supplied by the directors or managers 'on trust'.
5. Apart from the real cost burden imposed on small companies, the 'cost of the audit is disproportionate to the benefits it provides'.

The idiocy of these assertions is breathtaking. Firstly, it is both common knowledge and borne out by empirical studies that corporate balance sheets have come to show great and ever-increasing reliance upon trade creditor financing. This development goes partly in hand with the global expansion of credit, and partly as a result of banks' reluctance to take the risks of providing long-term capital to businesses. Whether rightly or wrongly, bank financing, especially in the small business sector, has become secondary in a great many cases to the credit terms the businesses can arrange with suppliers. It is the supplier credit which thus often determines whether or not the firm will stay in business. The importance of trade creditor finance both to large and small firms is self-evident. A recent example is Sinclair Research, rescued by its trade creditors and not by its bankers. It follows, then, that whatever is done to harm the whole credit apparatus, will serve to restrict the volume of credit. The DTI proposals offer several options in eliminating the statutory audit for small companies. If accounts are to be scrapped or further modified, the information available to potential credit grantors will be unworkably poor. Both the quality and the quantity of credit will be quickly reduced as a result. The options proposed by the DTI are:

(a) Abolish the audit requirement for small companies all of whose members are directors.
(b) Abolish the requirement for all small companies below a certain size, though not for all small companies as presently defined.
(c) Abolish the requirement for all small companies and leave it to members to decide the company's policy on audits in light of its particular circumstances.

Apart from the enforced or permitted minimizing of information vital to the analysis and granting of credit, these options are demonstrably silly. The first option is based on the wrong assumption that company directors of small enterprises can accurately appreciate the total financial condition of their companies at any one time. Do directors carry around in their heads such items as direct and indirect sales costs' totals, accruals and prepayments? It is often such items that cause managing directors the greatest surprise in their own audited accounts. Even financial directors of consummate skill would need formal accounting statements, audited or unaudited, as points of repair and reference. No director alive can form accurate holistic assessments of his company in any but the most general terms. Given the exigencies of today's business world, fuzzy pictures are not good enough.

The second option is a can of worms. Attempts at 'defining' a small firm must be purely arbitrary. The government's present criteria for smallness are trivial and meaningless and will remain so. Moreover, and more interestingly, this 'sop' to small business could backfire in that company expansion and firms seeking public status or quotations could be discouraged from these courses by what appear superficially to be easy options.

The third option is largely reiterative. It is also simple-minded as it shows that the DTI is flatly ignorant of how credit assessment is carried out. It is naïve to assume that small firms will commission a special audit at the request of suppliers. The best that suppliers could hope for would be species of management data (in this case, unaudited accounting statements extracts). When confronted with such information, credit grantors will necessarily apply considerable scepticism. This wariness will result in less credit being sanctioned. In these circumstances, less credit does not mean safer credit. The credit and the risk attaching to it will, on the contrary, be inversely proportional.

Summing up, were the scrapping proposals to be made law, the granting of trade credit to all but large corporations and public companies would be made well-nigh impossible. Impossible from the informational point of view and from the costs involved in obtaining necessary supplementary information. Unaudited data and/or further modified information supplied by companies themselves would necessarily be of questionable value. Trade credit, which is axial to the continued development of capitalism, would be made dearer, scarcer, and riskier. Given the current state of our economy, the end result would be unprecedented levels of company failures.

Accounting requirements for small companies are currently too lax for informed credit assessment purposes. Further relaxations could encourage more window-dressing and outright falsification by the unscrupulous.

The Inland Revenue, HM Customs and Excise, banks and credit insurers will always require independently validated accounts from large and from small firms. Proper internal records and accounts must, therefore, be done by firms regardless of any DTI rulings on the matter.

The DTI's proposals are unresearched, unquantified, and unsubstantiated. For instance, audit costs vary widely. Companies are free to find the service at the cost most suited to themselves. It is untrue and misleading to hold that historical accounts are uninformative. The whole of credit analysis shows that historical data can be made to yield higher quality information for better credit judgements than any other body of numerical or non-numerical data.

Against this background of modified statements and possible scrapping of accounting information, credit analysts, particularly those in commerce, as opposed to banking, need to develop new assessment techniques to draw more information from less data. Given this scenario, it is counter-productive to think in terms of 120 page spreadsheets and elaborate financial models. Concision, relevance, and ease of operation must be the by-words of corporate credit analysis. Also, the costs of analysis must be justified against the amounts of credit. Specialist procedures and new technologies may be easily cost-justified against certain large bank advances. The same is rarely true in trade credit applications. The most valuable tool in this area has always been the human brain. The new assessment methods developed by the human brain should be capable of being implemented with a pencil and a piece of paper—not a mainframe. The time and cost-justifications for software assessment applications depend largely upon volume of inputs and volumes of accounts for analysis. Accordingly, computerizing assessment routines and financial models can be justified in terms of cost and time-saving when either large volumes of credit applications occur, or when assessment routines as bought-in by way of back-up for existing procedures. Provided that analysts understand the ready-made packages, computer back-up to human assessment can prove of considerable value. More mystique attaches to computers than to any other tool. A computer is merely a large and powerful calculating machine. It is not capable of the fine adjustments that the human mind can make on an *ad hoc* basis. The ability to make *ad hoc* adjustments and interpretations from highly variable data is the key to effective credit analysis. If, then, computers can provide answers to the rules, credit analysts should be able to provide answers to the exceptions.

Ratio-based models as a means of augmenting scanty information

Illuminating spreadsheets, deeply informative status reports, and key accounts data will not, in most situations, be available to credit analysts—especially those working in the commercial sector. High proportions of any sales ledger are represented by companies producing poor quality or modified accounts for inspection. In theory, credit departments can request supplementary details. In practice few do, and fewer get them. There is thus a need for credit analysts to develop new and better assessment procedures for the vetting of existing accounts and the analysis of potential accounts.

Standard and hybrid ratio-based models are an effective means of augmenting modified and other poor quality data. As with all other financial models, they should be used in conjunction with and not instead of formal assessment procedures coupled with first-hand experience of the applicant whenever possible.

Ratio-based models are not intended to be substitutes for spreadsheets. Spreadsheets can be used to drive models as we have shown earlier. Bearing this in mind, let us attempt to construct a model to be used after the completing of a spreadsheet for the interpretation of a company producing modified accounts. The spreadsheet will show the component parts of the company's main financial flows. The model will then try to treat the spreadsheet data in such a way as to give form to the prime question of credit analysis—what is the risk involved in providing credit to this company?

Risk can be quantified in a range of ways. Briefly:

(a) loss of the total amount of the exposure at any one time
(b) loss of the principal and interest
(c) loss of interest only
(d) possibility of arrears increasing permitted exposure
(e) internal effect of any of the previous items on the credit grantor's financial condition calculated in terms of loss of earnings, bad debt provisions, reduction in liquidity, increased administration costs, overall reduction in profit margins
(f) where exposure is insured, possibility of higher premia for subsequent insurance
(g) external additional costs, e.g. collection fees and legal fees
(h) loss of both earnings and inventory
(i) loss of market share
(j) in cases of buyer insolvency, possible domino effect

Of these, the prime consideration of risk must be loss of the total exposure at any one time. This would include arrears of varying kinds and would also (apart from items f, g, and j) give the basis for any financial provisions necessary.

Firstly, is the risk in financial terms acceptably absorbable by the credit grantor? Secondly, if one is, for instance, willing to grant £5 m credit at any one time to one customer, how does this £5 m stack up against the customer's latest audited results? No one in his right mind would advance credit of such proportions to a company producing only modified accounts. Accordingly, the credit limits or exposures assessed for modified accounts companies are more modest. The risk assessment principle, however, is the same. How does the credit exposure stack up against the customer's latest audited results?

This risk question itself is a ratio in form. A ratio-based risk description model would, accordingly, seem to be the most immediately helpful tool for analysing the spread data of companies producing modified accounts or less than full accounting statements. Use of such a model after completion of the spreadsheet would assist in reducing the amount of time spent in the analysis of disproportionally small credits. If the model shows that the proposed exposure is overly risky, the credit application can be either turned down or reconsidered further to the supply of additional information.

Underlying assumptions of the risk description model

Before determining what data is to be spread, it is necessary to make certain assumptions about companies producing modified accounts or less than full accounting statements. First, and most importantly:

1. Large credit exposures should not be sanctioned without the benefit of full financial information implied by full audited accounting statements. What companies consider to be large will necessarily vary. For the sake of argument, £5,000 per calendar month might generally serve as an upper limit for our present purposes.

    It then follows that the developed model will be a risk classification tool especially suitable for grouping modified and less than full accounting information companies into classes of risk.

2. It is neither possible nor practical for analysts to attempt sales and other types of forecasting to amplify historical data in such cases. Accordingly, the completed model will operate over historical data.

3. To particularize risk (one's own credit exposure along with existing obligations against available assets rather than a summary of assets and liabilities as at last accounting date as in the case of some types of insolvency prediction), credit exposure should be incorporated in the model's workings—i.e. added to the subject's existing obligations.

4. The type of risk examined by this model will be the subject's degree of ability or inability as at its latest accounting date to meet its existing obligations plus the proposed credit exposure. The model is thus non-predictive; simply diagnostic using an obviously artificial base assumption:

    (a) That the subject company's classificatory liquidity at its latest accounting date depended not only upon its existing commitments but also, the proposed credit exposure when judged against its available assets.

    (b) The justification for making this artificial assumption the basis of operation is that it is the same assumption that analysts tacitly make in carrying out credit assessment where particular exposures are in question. That is, the exposures are pitted against the subjects' latest historical data. While the assumption is not perfect (the perfect assumption would, of course, be to pit the exposure against the subject's immediate financial data, including existing obligations), we have nothing better in the practical sense. Nor is it at all likely that anything better will become available in the assessment of small exposure, poor quality, high-volume trade credit applications of the sort under discussion.

5. In general, companies producing modified and less than full statements could be said to show some, if not all, of the following characteristics:

    (a) They are shareholder-owned and managed.
    (b) They tend to be young companies—i.e. under 10 yrs old.
    (c) Capital employed tends to be less than £1 m.
    (d) Staffing levels are low—i.e. they tend to have less than 200 persons.
    (e) Because of their age and capital resources, among other reasons, they tend to rely more heavily on trade creditor financing than on formal external financing.

(f) Because modified accounts tend to conceal more than they reveal, many analytical routines and standard performance indicators, e.g. debt-turn, cannot be used in any risk description model.
6. The generally agreed key criteria to any company's progress are:

> profitability
> capital adequacy
> liquidity

7. Spreadsheet data for the risk description model should thus be based upon profitability, capital adequacy and liquidity as bases of reference.
8. Because we are here trying to describe a lot from a little, it will be reasonable to examine subjects' profitability, capital adequacy and liquidity together with credit exposure from several standpoints in the model by way of amplifying information for the sake of fairness of view.

By a closer consideration of profitability, capital adequacy and liquidity, we shall be better able to determine the format of the model spreadsheet.

Profitability

Companies owe their continued existence in the medium to long-term to their ability to generate adequate levels of profits. The contribution of the profit and loss account to reserves as well as to liquidity is the vital consideration. For small and/or new firms, profitability is crucial for the following additional reasons:

1. Reserves have not had much time in which to accumulate.
2. Without adequate reserves, the continued existence of the firm is overly dependent on monthly or short-term trading cycles. This can be further aggravated by the lack of external funding and by the seasonal character of many businesses.
3. Without a proven track record, and also, frequently without much equity, permanent capital or other types of external finance are normally not available to the firm.

For these reasons, our model might look at a subject's profitability in the following respects:

(a) Profitability as return on capital employed
(b) Profitability as a constituent of liquidity
(c) Profitability as a constituent of debt-service ability

Capital adequacy

To supplement the frequently low level of retentions in these firms, analysts will look to see realistic amounts of called-up share capital. These represent in quantifiable terms, the shareholders' involvement in the business. The general tendency has been to pay up the barest minimum of share capital and to rely on trade creditor finance, and often, on bank overdraft, to keep buoyant. The model should take some account of called-up capital. This can be done by noting shareholders' funds which include called-up capital, reserves, and the latest year's profit and loss account. The consideration of permanent capital is only one measure of capital adequacy. As suggested above, profitability as a constituent of liquidity and, in particular, debt-service ability, must also be viewed as measures of capital adequacy over the short- to medium-terms.

Liquidity

Many companies producing modified accounts will not have an 'established' turnover. They are busy trying to create one. In so doing, they will run the risk of trying to do more business than they can realistically finance. They will, accordingly, overtrade. This overtrading has the effect of reducing liquidity. As suggested before, liquidity is a function of capital adequacy and, at source, of profitability.

Turnover will not normally be posted in modified statements. The model, therefore, has to try and assess liquidity partly on the effect of sales and the costs of those sales on overall results—i.e. the net profit/loss carried forward to the balance sheet. Another measurement of liquidity could be a normalized or non-normalized computation of net current assets. As current liabilities, in particular, are not usually itemized in modified accounts, accurate normalizing is difficult. It would then appear that at least one measure of liquidity will have to be working capital or net current assets.

Modified statements will, however, normally show current assets itemized. Where stock is carried, some or all of it can be deducted from current assets before deduction of current liabilities. Thus, a partial normalization is possible as a further measurement of liquidity—for our purposes more satisfactory than the 'soft' measurement of working capital.

The three criteria as seen from other standpoints

Although the spreadsheet information in these cases is bound to be comparatively limited, the mix of debt obligations as well as notional net worth of the firm should all liabilities crystallize are other standpoints from which profitability, capital adequacy, and liquidity can be assessed.

Debt mix

Modified accounts rarely give breakdowns of types of current or other liabilities. Current liabilities may be posted as that without any notes or schedules. Off-balance-sheet obligations may not be noted. Long-term debt, if any, may not be specified in respect of repayment schedule or interest rates applicable. Nor would we expect to see any terms for directors' current accounts noted. The quality of debt information in these statements is, therefore, extremely poor.

Earlier, we spoke of current debt. This is not the same set of obligations as total current liabilities, but a selection from current liabilities of debts for priority settlement. In this definition, priority carries no legal meaning as such. Current debt items, however, include obligations to preferred and priority creditors, and are represented by such debts as a company would normally take steps to settle before making payments to trade creditors. These would be:

1. Inland Revenue
2. HM Customs and Excise

3. Bank loans (current portions repayable)
4. Borrowings on overdraft (were reductions called for)
5. Hire purchase obligations (current portions payable)
6. Leasing commitments (current portions payable)
7. Debenture or loan stock interest currently payable
8. Bills of exchange currently payable and other documentary credits
9. Other contractual financial commitments currently payable, e.g. credit insurance or other insurance premia.

Because schedules of such liability items will not normally be given in modified or less than full accounting statements, this type of priority debt cannot be accurately calculated. It is none the less extremely important for suppliers of trade credit to estimate where they stand in the settlement queue. For these reasons, the model should attempt to estimate the level of 'current debt' as defined above to ostensible liquidity, if not in ratio form, then indirectly.

On the premise that something is better than nothing, we can agree to base the estimate of current debt on prior experience of balance sheets. As credit analysts, Trade and Commercial Credit Corporation has, for instance, found that from 15 to 25 per cent of current liabilities rank as current debt items on the above parameters. As we are not concerned here with legal status of the obligations but with an estimate of amounts of money to be paid out (and thus affecting liquidity) on a priority basis (i.e. if the firm expects to remain in business and not be compulsorily wound up), let us assume that 20 per cent of total current liabilities will represent such priority obligations for the purposes of our model.

Net worth

Net assets is not necessarily the same quantity as net worth. If a firm has off-balance-sheet commitments, should some or all of them crystallize at break-up date, the resulting net worth of the company would necessarily be less than the net assets total posted in its latest balance sheet were break-up date the same as accounting date or very shortly thereafter. Were break-up some time after accounting date, the firm's assets and liabilities would have changed to reflect the normal course of trading. For this reason, the difference between net assets and net worth would be even greater.

Net worth is not the same as tangible net worth (TNW). TNW nets out intangible assets such as goodwill, technical know-how and, in some instances, capitalized research and development costs. TNW provides a harder measure of the break-up value of a company than net assets, though TNW computations in credit analysis accept valuations of assets given in accounting statements. In cases of break-up, the liquidator or receiver could find that some assets were grossly over or undervalued. If so, the company's TNW would be significantly altered as would the prices the liquidator could get for various tangible assets.

Because of these uncertainties in the computation of tangible net worth which are magnified by the lack of specific information in modified accounts, we would obtain something of a mid-way view of a firm's net worth by a straight deduction of intangible or fictitious assets from total assets before deducting total liabilities. Thus, the model's net worth figure may be less than the company's net assets figure.

This measurement of TNW, though imperfect as no account has been taken of off-balance-sheet commitments, can be used in various ratio formats to give indications of resources, profitability as a function of total liabilities, and a very wide indication of cover for all balance-sheet obligations.

Purpose and use of the model

To recapitulate, we are trying to examine singly, severally, and simultaneously the less than full or modified accounting statements of companies. We expect that these modifications will be severe. As comparatively little information will be given, the model will have to examine what information there is in several ways with respect to profitability, capital adequacy, and liquidity. In some measures, it will have to take account of debt mix and net worth in making its assessments, as these two items are important factors of the three previous key criteria of a functioning company.

The model will have to take account of a proposed credit exposure in addition to the subject's obligations as at its accounting date. Though it was acknowledged to be an imperfect assumption, it was accepted as the normal working assumption of all credit analysts in assessing a potential exposure against a set of historical data. The accuracy and relevance of the model's findings are thus directly proportional to the age and quality of the historical data.

The developed model should assess synoptically. It should be used after spreading data for a quick classification of subject companies into risk description groupings. For simplicity, let these be:

Low risk
Medium risk
High risk
No credit without further information/guarantees/other security

As these requirements entail the inclusion of several ratios in the model, the quickness and simplicity of operation depends upon few difficult calculations being called for after initial spreading of the data. We saw that a 20 per cent estimated level of current debt would be required if debt mix and its ramifications were to be considered.

As the developed model is intended to be used over many, small exposure credit accounts normally representing high proportions of sales ledgers, the model workings must be easily carried out manually or on computer.

As the model is also intended as a general diagnostic tool, it is important that it be operable over any commercial or industrial sector with the exception of banks, insurance companies, or finance houses.

Model form

Our previous considerations suggest that the model should be expressed in linear form made up of hybrid ratios summed to a total and multiplied by a constant to equalize the constituent powers of the ratios. This format is easy to operate manually and is quickly programmable for use on microcomputers.

Building the spreadsheet

By way of prudence, let us assume that the modified accounts lodged at the Registry of

Companies for public inspection consist of balance sheet only. No notes to the accounts nor profit and loss account will be available. The information gleanable from the modified balance sheet will be, accordingly, minimal. It is, therefore, a waste of time to design a detailed spreadsheet. Figure 4.1 below gives a specimen of the type of balance sheet most likely to be encountered:

BROWN AND SMITH LTD
Modified balance sheet
as at 31 December 1985

	1985		1984	
	£	£	£	£
FIXED ASSETS				
Tangible assets		118,135		109,866
CURRENT ASSETS				
Stock	1,341,553		1,303,510	
Debtors	383,445		364,757	
Cash in hand and at bank	28,586		1	
	1,753,584		1,668,268	
CREDITORS: Due within one year	1,268,180		1,244,497	
NET CURRENT ASSETS		485,404		423,771
TOTAL ASSETS LESS CURRENT LIABILITIES		603,539		533,637
CREDITORS: Due after more than one year		(12,764)		(1,296)
		590,775		532,341
CAPITAL AND RESERVES				
Called-up share capital		1,000		1,000
Retained profits		589,775		531,341
		590,775		532,341

We have relied upon the exemptions for companies' accounts available under Schedule 8 of the Companies Act 1985 and have done so on the basis that the company is entitled to the benefit of those exemptions as a small company.

_____ A. Brown
                       Directors
_____ B. Smith

Figure 4.1 Brown and Smith Ltd: Modified balance sheet

Our first problem is that no depreciation has been shown. The depreciation indicates the use the company has had from the net fixed assets posted in the balance sheet. Depreciation is also used for the computation for gross and net cashflows. What, in other words, did depreciation contribute to this company's liquidity? If depreciation is an important constituent of liquidity, how can we work backwards, as it were, and reasonably estimate depreciation from net tangible assets?

The following routines are suggested:

Freeholds/leaseholds/land
Assume depreciation @ 2% reducing balance basis over 50 yrs
The computation would then be:

$$\frac{\text{Net fixed assets}}{49}$$

Where the denominator represents 2/98ths or 1/49th.

Equipment/cars/machinery and tools
Assume depreciation @ 20% reducing balance basis over 5 yrs
The computation would then be:

$$\frac{\text{Net fixed assets}}{4}$$

Where the denominator represents 20/80ths or 1/4th.

Tangible net fixed assets (showing no differentiation)
Assume depreciation to be the mean between 2% and 20%, or 11% on a reducing balance basis
The computation would then be:

$$\frac{\text{Net fixed assets} \times 11}{89}$$

In Figure 4.1 the fixed assets show no differentiation. Accordingly, the spreadsheet should use the final computation for depreciation and the depreciation estimates for liquidity assessment by the model would be:

$$\begin{array}{cc} 1985 & 1984 \\ \frac{118{,}135 \times 11}{89} = £14{,}601 & \frac{109{,}866 \times 11}{89} = £13{,}579 \end{array}$$

These computations for approximate depreciation charges are, as stated earlier, suggested when detailed information is not provided in the accounts. Concerning the basis of the suggested depreciation charge, we have opted for a reducing balance method, rather than a straight-line method. This is done because details of fixed assets and bases of depreciation have not been supplied in the accounts, and also because it is prudent to do so. The reducing balance method will add less back to gross cashflow than might be the case with straight-line depreciation. The following figures will make this clear.

Straight-line depreciation
(on an assumed 20% per annum basis over 3 yrs)

	£'000s Annual depc'n charge	£'000s Net asset
Cost of fixed asset: £100,000		
Yr 1	20	80
Yr 2	20	60
Yr 3	20	40

Total depreciation: £60,000

Reducing balance depreciation
(on an assumed 20% per annum basis over 3 yrs)

	£'000s Annual depc'n charge	£'000s Total depc'n	£'000s Net asset
Cost of fixed asset: £100,000			
Yr 1	20	20	80
Yr 2 @ 20% × 80	16	36	64
Yr 3 @ 20% × 64	12.8	48.8	51.2

Total depreciation: £48,800

From these figures, we can see that the reducing balance method will give £11,200 less in aggregate depreciation to add back into cashflow than the straight-line computation.

The caveat should be made concerning the making of depreciation and other estimates in analysis that common sense must be the analyst's guide. It would be absurd, for instance, to depreciate a freehold building at 20 per cent on either method. The approximations suggested above should thus be used only when information concerning the mix of fixed assets has not been provided.

The accounts in Figure 4.1 give us the company's working capital (net current assets). Working capital should provide one measure of liquidity. Should the model require others, which we have suggested may be the case, let us attempt to obtain a harder measure of working capital by netting-out stock. We can do the netting-out either on a 100 per cent basis or by deducting portions of less liquid stock, e.g. raw materials and WIP. Most modified statements, however, will give no stock information of this kind. Our spreadsheet might usefully contain both. Earlier, we discussed the treatment of stock when no differentiation was provided. Briefly:

Manufacturing companies
Net-out 75% of stock

Retailing companies
Net-out 25% of stock

Non-specific or combined operations
Net-out 50% of stock

These computations will serve to give rough approximations of liquid stocks when

	£		
		Date:	
Company name:			
Accounting date:			
Credit exposure:	% +/−	19--	19--
Tangible net assets:	___	___	___
Depreciation:	___	___	___
Current assets:	___	___	___
Current liabilities:	___	___	___
Net current assets/liabilities:	___	___	___
Stock:	___	___	___
Current assets − stock:	___	___	___
Current assets − stock − current liabilities:	___	___	___
Normalized stock used in above computations:	___	___	___
Current liabilities + credit exposure:	___	___	___
Total assets:	___	___	___
Total liabilities:	___	___	___
Total assets − intangible assets:	___	___	___
Total assets − intangibles − total liabilities:	___	___	___
Net assets:	___	___	___
Tangible net assets:	___	___	___
Capital employed:	___	___	___
Equity:	___	___	___
Net profit/loss:	___	___	___
Reserves:	___	___	___
Total debt:	___	___	___
Current debt:	___	___	___

Assumptions:
Depreciation: _____
Stock: _____
Other: _____

Figure 4.2 Risk description model: Specimen spreadsheet

itemizations have not been supplied in the accounts. Where itemized stock is noted, use these figures.

Capital employed, or the total capital used to run the business on a permanent basis, should be calculated for the spreadsheet. In the course of calculating capital employed, the equity (shareholders' funds) will be noted.

Current assets and current liabilities will be noted in the balance sheet. Earlier, we spoke of adding the proposed credit exposure to current liabilities in various ratio formats. This can be carried out on the spread under the notation of current liabilities as they stood at accounting date.

From the balance sheet, we must obtain the latest year's net profit figure. This is done by deducting the prior year's profit and loss account from that of the latest year. To obtain the 1984 profit/loss figure, we need the 1983 profit and loss account which can be seen from earlier microfilm records.

The spread should note net assets. This is total assets less total liabilities as noted on the balance sheet. Accordingly, as suggested earlier, net assets may or may not be the same quantity as tangible net worth. Clearly, it would not be were intangible assets included in total assets, and off-balance-sheet liabilities not included in total liabilities.

Finally, current liabilities should be examined. If no schedule has been given, as in the example in Figure 4.1, compute current debt by taking 20 per cent of Creditors: Amounts falling due within one year.

As this spreadsheet is being designed chiefly to drive the risk description model, we propose omitting the various performance indicators, e.g. ROCE, working capital/total assets, that would otherwise be informative. Note, however, that modified accounts make the computation of many key performance indicators impossible. This, doubtless, is seen as one of the 'benefits' in producing abbreviated statements.

Our spreadsheet's format would then be along the following lines of the example in Figure 4.2.

Selection of model ratios

The form the spreadsheet has taken will assist in selecting model ratios. Also, the key criteria as suggested earlier will give us the purposes of the ratio measurement we choose. Those criteria were:

Liquidity
Profitability
Capital adequacy

Let us consider profitability first. The only profit figures we have are for net profit carried forward to the balance sheet. By placing net profit over capital employed, we have a measurement of profitability in the latest year. If we want added dimension, that is, a measurement of cumulative profitability, we could place net assets over total liabilities. This would give us an indication as at accounting date of the company's net assets in relation to its total obligations. But a harder measurement of cumulative profitability would obviously be net tangible assets over total liabilities. We thus have two profitability measures:

$$\frac{\text{Net profit}}{\text{Capital employed}}$$

and

$$\frac{\text{Net tangible assets}}{\text{Total liabilities}}$$

As we want to look at profitability from the latest, as well as from accumulated periods, let us keep both measures for the model.

For the treatment of liquidity, consider that the net profit for the latest year gave, or underpinned, the latest year's current assets. That is, trade debtors were largely a result of the latest year's sales, though not all of them would necessarily be because of settlement delays. Also, net profit might contain net interest income which if uninvested at accounting date would be represented by cash or balance at bank. To measure liquidity in the latest year, we could place current assets over current liabilities (current ratio), but this would represent a less indicative measurement in our view than net profit over current liabilities as net profit will include some items additional to current assets, e.g. surplus after accounting for depreciation and extraordinary items.

Earlier, we spoke of normalizing net current assets by deduction of stock. The resulting normalized working capital could be placed over current liabilities plus credit exposure. But this would give a wrong picture. Current liabilities have already been deducted from normalized stock plus the balance of current assets. Accordingly, we should place normalized working capital over credit exposure. This would show how much cover a hard measure of latest liquidity would afford. We, therefore, have the two following ratios to measure liquidity:

$$\frac{\text{Net profit}}{\text{Current liabilities}}$$

and

$$\frac{\text{Normalized working capital}}{\text{Credit exposure}}$$

Capital adequacy could most rigorously be measured in the short term (currently) by contrasting shareholders' funds (equity), which is made up of the shareholders' stake in the company net of long-term financings, with current liabilities—again, obligations to be met in the short term. Capital adequacy implies long-term or permanent capital. In this sense, a company's permanent capital would not be used in normal circumstances to meet short-term obligations. The acid-test ratio would, for normal trading circumstances, be a more indicative measure of capital resources. Here, however, we are concerned to look at the company's inalienable capital as adequate cover for all current obligations. The equity stake can, in many situations, provide firms with further borrowing powers, should the trading balance between current assets and current liabilities develop adversely. Very roughly speaking, if equity is greater than 50 per cent of capital employed, further borrowing might reasonably be represented by the difference between the actual level of equity to capital employed and 50 per cent.

As most modified accounts will not give off-balance-sheet liabilities, let us provide the most severe total of a firm's obligations by adding credit exposure to current liabilities. We thus have the ratio:

$$\frac{\text{Equity}}{\text{Current liabilities} + \text{credit exposure}}$$

At this early stage, it can be anticipated that the liquidity ratio normalized working capital/

credit exposure will probably produce comparatively high numbers (probably negative) to the other ratios developed. We, however, regard the ratio as important enough to accept in the model. Accordingly, so that the high negative figures thrown by this ratio do not distort the cumulative scores yielded by the other ratio components, a compensatory ratio should now be added to the model.

The credit exposures for these companies was earlier agreed to be comparatively low, from say, £1,000 to £5,000 at any one time or per calendar month. This should suggest two courses of action. First, that we let the credit exposures apply for any one time as the accounting figures themselves applied as at accounting date only. Secondly, that we judge the credit exposure against a netted-out total to assess the amount of cover. We have already used the hard measure of net worth (tangible net assets) in the ratio measuring cumulative profitability. Against our credit exposure, let us look at net worth cover from another standpoint and use net assets (total assets less total liabilities). It is hoped that net assets will provide a significantly large amount of cover for the small credit exposures we have discussed. The resulting ratio should thus throw high positive numbers and its effect on the model should accordingly compensate for the high negative numbers thrown by normalized working capital/credit exposure. The compensatory ratio providing a measurement of 'comfort margin' for the credit is:

$$\frac{\text{Net assets}}{\text{Credit exposure}}$$

In considering the parameters for our spreadsheet, we spoke of debt-service ability in general, and of current debt in particular. To a degree, debt-service ability is already implied by the ratios:

> Net profit/current liabilities
> Normalized working capital/credit exposure
> Equity/current liabilities + credit exposure
> Net assets/credit exposure

and to a lesser degree by:

> Net profit/capital employed
> Net tangible assets/total liabilities

Debt mix can be considered in sum or in part. In sum, we could determine the total of all known obligations (current and long-term liabilities). In part, we have already discussed the importance of priority treatment obligations (current debt). To assess debt capacity, we could add total debt obligations to the proposed credit exposure and place this total against total assets. This would indicate safety margin given all known obligations including our credit, should the credit not be honoured according to terms. Such a measurement would give a rough idea of break-up value of the company, were all obligations, including our original exposure to crystallize simultaneously. The ratio then gives an indication of safety margin and debt capacity both of which are functions of liquidity, capital adequacy, and profitability. The ratio is, therefore,

$$\frac{\text{Total assets}}{\text{Total liabilities} + \text{credit exposure}}$$

Finally, the treatment of priority debt items could be measured by contrasting current debt with the financial flow that will be servicing it. Computing gross cashflow from modified accounting information will be difficult without a detailed profit and loss account showing depreciation. We can, however, arrive at a good approximation of GCF by calculating depreciation in the ways noted earlier and adding depreciation to net profit. If we note any increase in deferred taxation accounts on the balance sheet, these can be added back to net profit and depreciation. Accordingly, our priority debt-service ability measurement will be:

$$\frac{\text{Net profit} + \text{depreciation} + \text{any increase/decrease in deferred taxation}}{\text{Current debt (or 20\% of current liabilities)}}$$

We now have eight ratios ostensibly covering all main areas of concern in classifying risk with respect to modified accounts companies.

Figure 4.3 lists the ratios and summarizes what they are measuring:

Ratios	Descriptions	Measuring
X_1	Net profit/capital employed	Profitability (annual)
X_2	Net tangible assets/total liabilities	Profitability (cumulative)
X_3	Net profit/current liabilities	Liquidity
X_4	Normalized working capital/credit exposure	Liquidity
X_5	Equity/current liabilities + credit exposure	Capital adequacy
X_6	Net assets/credit exposure	Comfort margin
X_7	Total assets/total liabilities + credit exposure	Debt capacity
X_8	Net profit + depreciation/current debt	Priority debt-service ability

Figure 4.3 Risk description model: Ratios and measurements

If the model is to be a sum of these ratios multiplied by a constant to equalize the ratios' contributing powers, the resulting formula would be quickly expressed as:

$$RD = k \left(\sum_{X_1-X_8} \right)$$

Where RD = Risk description grouping
  k = the constant multiplier: 100% = 12.5 or 0.125 to sum to unity
  X_1 to X_8 = the ratio variables

The developed model is thus:

$$RD = 0.125 \left(\sum_{X_1-X_8} \right)$$

Using the accounting data from Figure 4.3, let us assign values to the model:

Ratio	Descriptions	Computation (1985)	Single scores
X_1	NP/CE	58,434/603,539	= 9.6
X_2	NTA/TL	590,775/1,280,944	= 46.1

X_3	NP/CL	58,434/1,268,180	=	4.6
X_4	NWC/C Exp	(185,373)/5,000	=	(3,707.4)
X_5	E/CL+C Exp	590,775/1,273,180	=	46.4
X_6	NA/C Exp	590,775/5,000	=	11,815.5
X_7	TA/TL+C Exp	1,871,719/1,285,944	=	145.5
X_8	NP+D/CD	73,035/253,636	=	28.7
Total:				8,389 $\times 0.125 = 1,048$

In these figures, the credit exposure has been taken at £5,000 at any one time. Ratios have not been rounded up to the nearest decimal place. Stock was accepted at 50 per cent as we were not told what type of company Brown and Smith Ltd is. From the company's balance sheet, we can see that stock represents some 77 per cent of current assets. If stock were to be wholly deducted from current assets, the effect on liquidity would, accordingly, be catastrophic. Considered singly, the NWC/C Exp ratio where stock has been 50 per cent accepted reads adversely. Note also the compensating mechanism of ratios X_4 and X_6 as discussed earlier.

We see that on the basis of these calculations the company has been assigned a score of +1,048. Until we have tested the model on a number of modified accounts companies, we cannot assess the significance of this score. The significance will become clear once the model is tested over the following types of samples:

Good risk companies: Currently trading
No auditors' qualifications
Known to pay to terms
Bad risk companies: Qualified accounts
Known for gross arrears/defaults
In receivership/liquidation

The good risk companies should be divided into an initial and a holdout sample. The bad risk companies should be divided likewise. Both good and bad risk companies should be drawn from a wide range of industry sectors and these sectors known, so that normalizing can be done as accurately as possible. Initial and holdout samples should cover the same financial years. Companies need not be of similar asset size. It is more instructive for the total sample universe to cover financial years well past, say, 1982 and 1983 so that the model's scores can be judged against subsequent events such as arrears on various accounts, receiverships, liquidations, or improvements in trading and liquidity. Samples should be in even numbers for ease in tabulating results. Scores from both samples should be arrayed on a scale of values. If the samples have been indicative, numerical bunching should be observed on the scale. These bunchings will indicate the various risk groupings:

Low risk
Medium risk
High risk
No credit without further information/guarantees and no credit

The scale or statistical array can be drawn as follows:

```
                            Negative scores  │  Positive scores
                                             │   +2,000 ⎫
                                             │   +1,500 ⎬ Low risk
                                             ├──────────
                                             │   +150 ⎫
                                             │    +99 ⎬ Medium risk
                                             ├──────────
                                             │    +30 ⎫
                                             │    +25 ⎬ High risk
                                             ├──────────
No credit without further      ⎧ −30         │
   information/guarantees      ⎩ −36         │
                                             │
                               ⎧ −190        │
              No credit        ⎩ −200        │
                                             │
```

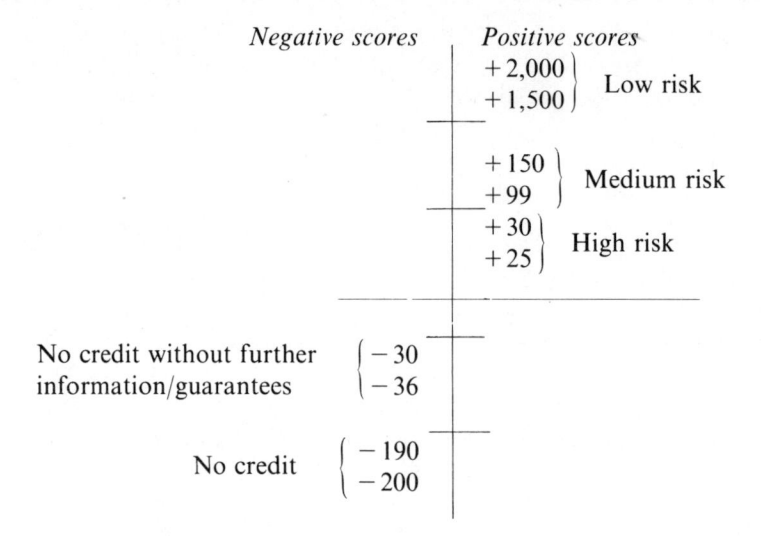

The results of a recent testing programme for this model by Trade and Commercial Credit Corporation are shown in Figures 4.4 to 4.8 that follow. For speed of data retrieval and for the sake of corroborative payment performance evidence, we used the accounts of no company in liquidation/receivership. All companies were notified to us by customers of Trade and Commercial Credit Corporation who spoke for the conduct of the various accounts. This data was kept separate from the analysis of the modified accounts for spreadsheet and model purposes. In this way, possible subjective responses to numerical data could be obviated. To minimize bias, we used no accounting data notified to us where the notifying company represented a major supplier. Payment performance was thus unlikely to be 'good', despite poor financial condition.

RISK DESCRIPTION MODEL: TESTING PROGRAMME

(All companies currently trading)

Test sample: 40 companies' modified accounts
divided into:

20 — Initial sample   20 — Holdout sample

Commercial/industrial sectors of sample companies

Food/drink/catering
Shipping
Chemicals
Farm and veterinary supplies
Printing
Paper
Exporting and general merchanting
Fertilisers and animal by-products
Company information
Footwear
Industrial wax
Adhesives
Electrical contractors

Auditors' qualifications/insolvency indicators

Of the 40 accounts examined, from the initial sample, number 17 received a 'going concern' qualification. From the holdout sample, number 14A received a material uncertainty qualification in respect of an uncrystallised contingent liability; and 18A received a 'going concern' qualification.

All three companies were classified as follows:

number 17: no credit
number 14A: high risk
number 18A: high risk

Figure 4.4 Risk description model: Testing programme

RISK DESCRIPTION MODEL: STATISTICAL ARRAY

Negative scores
(left-hand reading)

Positive scores
(right-hand reading)

```
                              2,349
                              1,191
                              1,035
                                880
                                831
                                796
                                568
                                463
                                418
                                351
                                288
                                273
                                251
                                222
                                217
                                216
                                194
                                177
                                153
                                152
                                 88
                                 68
                                 64
                                 52
                                 31
                                 26
0 ─────────────────┼───────── 0
                                 12
                                 35
                                 40
                                 56
                                 88
                                 97
                                103
                                133
                                376
                                504
                                622
                                633
                              1,022
                              1,559
```

Risk groupings according to statistical bunching		*Percentage of total sample (40)*
Low risk:	+700 upward	15%
Medium risk:	+100 to +688	35%
High risk:	+1 to +99	15%
No credit without further information/guarantees:	−numbers	35%
		100%

Figure 4.5 Risk description model: Statistical array

ANALYSIS OF INITIAL SAMPLE: TWENTY COMPANIES
Numbers: 1–20

1. Low risk: 20%
   Medium risk: 30%
   High risk: 10%

   No credit without added information and/or
   guarantees/other security: 40%
                                                                100%

2. *Profiles*

Debt capacity:	Number of total	% of sample
Excellent:	3	15
Good:	4	20
Fair:	6	30
Poor:	1	5
Very poor:	1	5
Nil:	5	25
	20	100%

Profitability:		
Excellent:	3	15
Good:	6	30
Fair:	3	15
Poor:	2	10
Very poor:	2	10
Nil:	4	20
	20	100%

Liquidity:		
Excellent:	4	20
Good:	4	20
Fair:	3	15
Poor:	2	10
Very poor:	3	15
Nil:	4	20
	20	100%

3. Average positive scores: +468
4. Average negative scores: −448
5. Assumption 1—From the sample (initial) 20 companies, 60% constituted 'acceptable' credit risks (low to high risk profiles).
   Assumption 2—From the sample (initial) 20 companies, 40% constituted 'not immediately acceptable' credit risks.

Figure 4.6 Analysis of initial sample: Twenty companies (1–20)

ANALYSIS OF HOLDOUT SAMPLE: TWENTY COMPANIES
Numbers: 1A–20A

1. Low risk: 15%
    Medium risk: 30%
    High risk: 25%

    No credit without added information and/or guarantees/other security: 30%
    ___
    100%

2. *Profiles*

Debt capacity:	Number of total	% of sample
Excellent:	2	10
Good:	3	15
Fair:	5	25
Poor:	2	10
Very poor:	6	30
Nil:	2	10
	20	100%

Profitability:		
Excellent:	3	15
Good:	4	20
Fair:	5	25
Poor	0	/
Very poor:	1	5
Nil:	7	35
	20	100%

Liquidity:		
Excellent:	0	/
Good:	3	15
Fair:	6	30
Poor:	5	25
Very poor:	2	10
Nil:	4	20
	20	100%

3. Average positive scores: +409
4. Average negative scores: −282
5. Assumption 1A—From the sample (holdout) 20 companies, 70% constituted 'acceptable' credit risks (low to high risk profiles).
   Assumption 2A—From the sample (holdout) 20 companies, 30% constituted 'not immediately acceptable' credit risks.

Figure 4.7 Analysis of holdout sample: Twenty companies (1A−20A)

AVERAGES OF INITIAL AND HOLDOUT SAMPLES: FORTY COMPANIES
Numbers: 1–20 and 1A–20A

Note: The arithmetic process of averaging is statistically distortive. This distortion is increased when averages are being calculated from averages. The numerical data that follow should be interpreted as a rough guide only for general interest.

1. *Analysis of total 40 companies:*

Risk grouping	% of total 40 companies
Low risk:	17.5
Medium risk:	30.0
High risk:	17.5
No credit without further information and/or guarantees/other security:	35.0
	100%

   (A) Of the above sample 40 companies, 65% constituted acceptable credit risks (low to high risk groupings); while 35% represented not immediately acceptable credit risks. Of this latter group, approximately 71.4% constituted credit risks that in our opinion could not be lowered adequately to become acceptable.

   (B) In making the last assumption, we regard the statistical bunching of negative scores from -1 to -60 as possibly rectifiable given further information/guarantees/other security; and scores from -70 below as being not worth your while pursuing on a time-cost basis.

2. *Analysis of total 40 profiles:*

   Debt capacity:

	% of total samples
Excellent:	12.5
Good:	17.5
Fair:	27.5
Poor:	7.5
Very poor:	17.5
Nil:	17.5
	100%

   Profitability:

Excellent:	15.0
Good:	25.0
Fair:	20.0
Poor:	5.0
Very poor:	7.5
Nil:	27.5
	100%

Figure 4.8 Average of initial and holdout samples: Forty companies (1–20, 1A–20A)

Liquidity:

Excellent:	10.0
Good:	17.5
Fair:	22.5
Poor:	17.5
Very poor:	12.5
Nil:	20.0
	100%

3. Averaged positive score: +438
4. Averaged negative score: −365

5. The difference between the analysis of the single profile results and scores and the model results and scores represents the difference between a standard credit analytical examination and a synoptic interpretation. The synoptic interpretation of the model examines singly, severally, and simultaneously. The equalised weightings used further ensure this process.

   (A) Considering the individual profiles (including debt capacity, profitability and liquidity—which measures we consider to be most salient in credit assessments of this type based on limited information of indifferent quality), we see the following indicators:

Debt capacity
65% of the total samples constituted acceptable credit risks (low to high risks). 35% of the total samples constituted not immediately acceptable credit risks (very poor to nil debt capacity).

Profitability
65% of the total samples constituted acceptable credit risks (low to high risks). 35% of the total samples constituted not immediately acceptable credit risks (very poor to nil profitability).

Liquidity
67.5% of the total samples constituted acceptable credit risks (low to high risks).
32.5% of the total samples constituted not immediately acceptable credit risks (very poor to nil liquidity).

       Scale: Excellent/good/fair/poor = acceptable risks (low to high)
            Very poor/nil = not immediately acceptable risks without further information/guarantees/other security.

   (B) Comparing the profiles analysis above with the model analyses, we see that a favourable degree of parallelism has been achieved. Model findings showed that approximately 65% of total samples ranked as acceptable risks, whilst 35% were not immediately acceptable risks. The parallelism indicates that the model is operating satisfactorily without in any way violating common sense.

Figure 4.8 (*Concluded*)

The statistical array of test scores indicates the following risk groupings for the model:

> Low risk: +700 and upwards
> Medium risk: +100 to +699
> High risk: +1 to +99
> No credit/etc.: −Numbers

Our sample company, Brown and Smith Ltd, received a score of +1,048, and thus is indicated as a low risk credit proposition—with the reservations about stock deductions as discussed before.

If Brown and Smith's balance sheet is examined, we can see the following indicators:

	% +/−	1985	1984
Working capital:	+14.4	485,404	423,771
Equity:	+11.0	590,775	532,341
Debtors and cash:	+13.0	412,031	364,758
Stock:	+3.0	1.34 m	1.3 m
Stock as % of total assets:	−1.3 pts	72%	73.3%
Working capital cover for exposure:	+12.3 pts	97.1	84.8
Net assets cover for exposure:	+11.7 pts	118.2	106.5
Current ratio:	+0.042 pts	1.383	1.341
Acid-test ratio:	+0.032 pts	0.325	0.293
Liquid assets as % of total assets: (Assuming 50% of stock included)	+0.8 pts	58%	57.2%
Liquid assets as % of total assets: (omitting 100% of stock)	+1.0 pt	22%	21%

From these figures, we can see clearly that stock is the crucial item in this firm's liquidity. High levels of liquidity here will presuppose quick stock-turn. Given a rapid turnover of stocks, the company looks a good credit risk for the small exposure of £5,000 at any one time. The above figures do not contradict in any way the model's findings. Both on 'standard' analysis as above and according to the model, the importance of stock is made clear. In all main flows, the company looks to be strengthening performance whilst at the same time providing adequate cover for the credit in question.

Sources

Argenti, J., *Corporate Collapse—The Causes and Symptoms*, McGraw-Hill, New York, 1976, passim.
Bathory, A., 'Idiocy in High Places—The Department of Trade and Industry's Proposals for the Abolition or Further Modification of Accounting and Audit Requirements for Small Firms—A Consultative Document', *Credit Management*, August, 1985, pp. 26–31.
Bierman, H. J., 'Measuring Financial Liquidity', *Accounting Review*, October 1960.
Fadel, H., and Parkinson, J. M., 'Liquidity Evaluation by Means of Ratio Analysis', *Accounting and Business Research*, Vol. 8, No. 30, Spring, 1978.
Taffler, R. J., 'The Empirical Models for the Monitoring of UK Corporations: The State of the Art', *Working Paper Series*, The City University Business School, London, No. 51, 1983.
Trade and Commercial Credit Corporation Ltd, 'Model Testing Programme—Risk Description Ratio-Based, Linear Model', Archives, January 1986.

Part Two
PROBLEMS IN THE COMPUTATION AND INTERPRETATION OF DATA

5

DEVELOPMENT OF A RATIO-BASED, MULTIPLE SECTOR INSOLVENCY FORECASTING MODEL

The work in the field of corporate insolvency prediction using multiple discriminant analysis is now well-known. This research was begun in 1968 by Edward Altman. Altman based his work on groups of appropriate financial ratios extracted from company accounting statements. His resulting Z-Score represented a holistic sum derived from the various ratios. These ratios were weighted with variable discriminant coefficients computed by an MDA programme and tested for bias and corrected using accepted statistical procedures. MDA was selected as the best means, in Altman's view, of discriminating between the characteristics of solvent and insolvent companies. The ratio weights, or discriminant coefficients, pull these allegedly distinguishing characteristics as far apart as possible on a solvency scale. Altman's first published model, designed to operate over US manufacturing concerns (quoted) of similar asset size, was expressed as follows:

$$Z = 0.012X_1 + 0.014X_2 + 0.003X_3 + 0.006X_4 + 0.999X_5$$

In which Z = the overall solvency index
and
X_1 to X_5 = the independent variables:

X_1 = Working capital total assets
X_2 = Retained earnings/total assets
X_3 = Earnings before interest and tax total assets
X_4 = Market value equity/book value of total debt
X_5 = Sales/total assets

The Z-Score model funtioned with a high degree of accuracy over the original industry sector with which it was designed to operate.

It was soon noted, however, that the differences between market capitalization of US corporations and UK counterparts varied sufficiently to make Altman's original model predictively inaccurate when applied to UK companies in the same sector. In 1972, Lis, using a sample of quoted manufacturing, construction, and retailing companies matched by industry, financial year, and asset size, established the operational use of Zeta Analysis in the UK. Lis's linear model with MDA-determined ratio coefficients was:

$$Z = 0.063X_1 + 0.092X_2 + 0.057X_3 + 0.0014X_4$$

Where X_1 = Working capital/total assets
X_2 = Earnings before interest and tax-total assets
X_3 = Retained earnings (adjusted for scrip issues)/total assets
X_4 = Net worth/total debt

This model accurately predicted at 81.7 per cent and 76.7 per cent for the two financial years with the lower percentage obtaining for the earlier period as will be subsequently seen to be a hallmark of most forecasting models. Lis's model demonstrated the superior predictive performance of multivariate models over univariate ratios. Taffler remarks that the importance of Lis's work consists in its demonstration for the first time that the Z-Score approach (using multivariate ratio groups in lieu of univariate ratios) was applicable outside the US.

In 1974, Richard Taffler's research on the *ex ante** predictive ability of the MDA-based approach developed a five-ratio model of the following description:

$$Z = c_0 + c_1 X_1 + c_2 X_2 + c_3 X_3 + c_4 X_4 + c_5 X_5$$

Where X_1 = Earnings before interest and tax/opening total assets
X_2 = Total liabilities/net capital employed
X_3 = Quick assets†/total assets
X_4 = Working capital/net worth
X_5 = Stock-turn

With c_0 to c_5 as the weights (coefficients)

Taffler's model was tested over thirty-three manufacturing companies identified as going insolvent between 1974 and 1976, from which sample 12.1 per cent or 4 were misclassified. The 87.9 per cent predictive accuracy rate was comparable with Altman's 1968 Z-Score model.

Howard Tisshaw in 1976 developed a five-ratio MDA model using the following ratios:

Earnings before interest and tax/average total liabilities
Profit before tax/sales
Net capital employed/total liabilities excluding deferred taxation
Quick assets/net capital employed
Acid-test

Whilst Tisshaw was not able to subject this model to the conventional validation tests, the study did demonstrate that it was possible to analyse the accounting statements of unquoted companies in the UK using the Zeta Analysis approach. Tisshaw's test sample consisted of privately-owned manufacturing firms.

In 1977, Taffler published studies using a linear discriminant model tested against 46 quoted manufacturing companies failing in the eight year period to the end of 1976. These companies met various criteria to ensure evenness and reliability of data. This sample was matched on a 1:1 basis by a solvent set of companies chosen according to similar size and industry. Based upon a study of prior literature and previous experience, a menu of 80 financial ratios was constructed. These were subjected to logarithmic or reciprocal transformation as appropriate. Importantly, principal component analyses were carried

---

*Ex ante: see Glossary of Terms
†Quick assets: Current assets quickly realizable for cash

out to assist format design and interpretation of the resulting model. The model, again, was driven by MDA ratio coefficients. The final ratios selected were:

Profit before tax/average current liabilities
Current assets/total liabilities
Current liabilities/total assets
No-credit interval (the measure in days the firm can continue to trade if it can no longer generate revenues)

Through the principal component analyses, these ratios were interpreted as measuring respectively:

Profitability
Working capital position
Financial risk
Liquidity

Taffler's model appears to have forecast failures with some 97.6 per cent accuracy over the sample tested (41 of the 42 finally accepted test companies) with an averaged lead-time of $3\frac{1}{4}$ years provided by the Z-Score after first going negative to the appointment of a receiver or liquidator.

Taffler, in writing on empirical models for the monitoring of UK companies (1983), makes the important point that 'such an analysis does not constitute a test of the predictive ability of the model as is conveniently rather loosely argued but of its classificatory ability'. He goes on to say that, 'An at risk Z-Score is not a prediction *per se* of failure within a specified time frame but a description of a company as having a financial profile more similar to a group of previous failures, which is a necessary but not sufficient condition for financial distress, than to a group of sound firms.' Taffler adds that in evaluating the operational utility of Z-Scoring, the percentage of firms classed as 'failing' is equally important as *ex ante* tests of the model's misclassification probabilities. The true *ex ante* predictive ability arises when the events forecast are the financial distress or improvement of a firm within the next year. (Taffler, R. J., *Empirical Models for the Monitoring of UK Corporations: The State of the Art*, 1983, pp. 15–16.)

Five further statistical-based models using an assortment of ratios have been well documented since 1977. All these models, forecasting with varying degrees of accuracy, have been designed to operate over defined industry sectors. If it is to be considered seriously that such models have a high degree of operational utility, the following criticisms must be effectively answered:

1. Highly-specialist statistical skills are required to weight and test the models. These programmes are, for practical reasons, viable on computers only. Additional staff is thus required.
2. The MDA and regression analysis models mentioned have been designed to operate only over certain industry sectors. Their practical use to all but theoreticians is, therefore, strictly limited.
3. The basic assumption of MDA that insolvent firms exhibit distinguishing financial characteristics from solvent companies, is trivial. If the assumption is correct, as far as it goes, the justification for complicated statistical 'prediction' routines over extremely limited test samples is unclear.

4. If the above criticism is valid, then accurate classification of the more or less self-evident characteristics in a synoptic form is more to be desired than true *ex ante* predictive power.

The whole discriminating function of MDA can be countered by an empirically straightforward computation of companies' main financial flows. For instance, in examining 40 UK firms of which 20 were insolvent (in liquidation, receivership, going concern qualifications, or trading with the continued support of qualification) and 20 were solvent (still trading and with no auditors' qualifications), for the financial years 1981 to 1984, the following distinguishing characteristics were found to apply to the insolvent set:

1. Developing inability to service current debt from operating income
2. Current profitability extremely low or non-existent
3. Losses tend to increase
4. Reserves show gross depletions and are inadequate, when present, to discharge current obligations in the event of a break-up
5. Marked deterioration in tangible net worth, if any
6. The company is illiquid for the discharge of current obligations

Restated simply, these characteristics are merely:

1. Inability to service debt
2. Inability to make significant profits
3. Likelihood of increasing losses
4. General illiquidity
5. Reduction in net worth

These can hardly be news. They all, either singly or severally, hark back to the chief determinants of a company's existence:

Profitability
Capital adequacy
Liquidity

Accordingly, a synoptic classificatory model composed of selected ratios should, if based on these three main conditions, as well as related conditions such as debt-service ability, accurately 'predict' insolvency from full or modified accounting data. Furthermore, for such a model to have real operational utility, it would have to be usable over multiple industry sector companies. It would also need to avoid specialist statistical-based weighting and testing routines. It would have to be operable manually as well as easily programmable for microcomputers.

Using these guidelines, we published in 1984 a study developing a corporate insolvency forecasting model based on five ratios summed and multiplied by a constant. (*Predicting Corporate Collapse: Credit Analysis in the Determination and Forecasting of Insolvent Companies*, Financial Times Business Information, 1984.) In tests after completion of the model and subsequently in daily use at Trade and Commercial Credit Corporation, the model has classified with around 97.5 per cent accuracy.

The model is operable over all industrial sector companies save banks, financial institutions, and insurance companies. It takes no account of asset size due to the common-reductive power of the ratio format. The model's workings are non-proprietary and have, accordingly, been programmed successfully for a number of banks and credit-granting companies.

From a short-list of 24 standard and hybrid ratios, drawn up as the best performers in previous studies of our own and of others, we tested in various combinations and eventually selected six ratios. We then made a total of 40 test runs with a five ratio model when it was found that the two liquidity ratios in the six ratio model were merely reduplicative. Prior studies by Altman, Myers and Forgy, Cohen and Gilmore indicated that total predictive power is as effective using fewer rather than many variables. We then carried out 10 further runs using only five ratio models measuring profitability (annual and cumulative, capital adequacy, debt-service ability, and liquidity. Of these, the following ratios were chosen as being the most easily accessible from published accounting data and as providing apparently the highest predictive or classificatory power. The financial years over which testing ran were 1980 to 1981. The final ratios were:

X_1 = Gross cashflow/current debt
X_2 = Pre-tax profit/capital employed
X_3 = Equity/current liabilities
X_4 = Tangible net worth/total liabilities
X_5 = Working capital/total assets

And the model formula was:
$$Y = 0.20 \left(\sum_{x_{1-5}} \right)$$

The model's workings, taken either individually or synoptically, do not present information contrary to that offered by companies' accounting statements. Being essentially classificatory, it rearranges main flows and compares them schematically in a manner wholly complementary with audited data. The purpose of this rearrangement is to give added dimension and significance to the accounting statements. In other words, the whole of a subject's dynamic processes are viewed simultaneously.

Bathory's Model is a multi-purpose analytical tool. It was designed to be used over all industry sectors save banks, insurance, and finance houses. The model is used with best effect in conjunction with companies' standard credit analytical routines as a simple way of bringing them together interpretively for further consideration. The model was tested initially over a small sample of 40 companies. 'Predictive', in the sense of classificatory correctness, was measured at 95 per cent. These results were encouraging. There is no reason why such levels of accuracy should not be maintained, though the verification is difficult out of a non-academic or controlled testing programme. This is so, largely because in the case of companies receiving poor or negative model scores, many events may supervene, either rescuing the companies from insolvent crisis and collapse, or precipitating their failure. Acute insolvency does not automatically entail collapse. Companies can prolong their existence by many stratagems, consciously or not. However, in the cases of chronically ailing companies, the model scores will accurately reflect from year to year the extent and the nature of their financial difficulties, giving credit-grantors clear warning of likely outcomes.

For our present purposes, perhaps the most interesting aspect of this model and others is the process of selecting constituent ratios or other indicators. The selection process should be rational and, thus, non-mysterious. Until a more effective method is found, model-builders have relied upon the results of prior studies in components' efficacy and on the testing in groups or multiples of their own hybrids. Both best performers from previous research and the new constituents are tested alone and together in varying groups over controlled samples. From these runs or tests, a short-list of best performers arranged in the most effectively performing groups are chosen. Adjustments to any of the constituents can be made at any time throughout the process, but this entails extensive retesting of the adjusted individual constituents singly and severally over the same controlled samples. An example of such an adjustment might be varying ways in which cashflow was computed. Another frequent difficulty for model-builders is the computation of working capital. In the case of Bathory's Model, however, prior studies by Fadel and Parkinson showed that for the model's ultimate purposes, working capital/total assets gave the best predictive results in the measurement of liquidity. These findings, together with the necessity of keeping computational routines as straightforward and quick as possible, suggested use of working capital in its traditional form (current assets—current liabilities) as a numerator. In this case, Fadel and Parkinson's capital employed (as the denominator) was changed in favour of total assets, where it was reasoned that liquidity as a proportion of a company's total assets would give a nicer indication of liquidity than a comparison of the proportion of liquidity (working capital) with total resources (capital employed which includes long-term external financings).

Wherever possible, ratio constituents should indicate related concepts. For instance, in choosing a ratio to measure capital adequacy, the ratio finally accepted will also indicate to a degree cumulative profitability—that is, the balance made up of past profit and loss accounts as this quantity (retentions) is the point of reference for determining whether or not such items as called-up capital are adequate for the company given its present size, commitments, and levels of trading.

Using Bathory's Model, let us examine how the final ratio constituents were selected and what flows they are each measuring.

$$X_1 = \frac{\text{Gross cashflow}}{\text{Current debt}}$$

This ratio is a hybrid and was chosen as the best measurement in the grouping with which to indicate the company's ability to service short-term, important debt obligations. These obligations were termed 'current debt' and form part of any company's total of current liabilities. We defined current debt earlier and gave examples. Briefly, this class of debt included priority and preferred creditors such as bank debt (including overdraft, secured or unsecured), taxation (including value added tax), and leasing or hire purchase repayments due within the agreed accounting period. This class of debt was argued to be important, as such items would tend to receive priority treatment (i.e. settlement) in the event of concerted demands made on a company by its creditors. Very simply, current debt would be the obligations a company would reasonably wish to meet before settling other debts. The thinking behind this is that banks, governmental bodies, and finance companies are conventionally supposed to be more readily willing and able to wind-up debtor companies than trade creditors. Although this supposition is, by no means, always the case, experience shows that as a working hypothesis, it is significant.

To service current debt, gross cashflow was selected on the grounds that a dynamic rather than a static measurement was desired. Dynamic measurements more accurately reflected the way in which companies actually functioned than static measurements. For this reason, a cashflow measure was seen as more indicative as a debt-servicing quantum than a number such as working capital which, although simultaneous (in the sense of presenting a snapshot of surplus funds at one time) gives no indication of flow, and the sources of that flow, apart from a whole class of current assets and current liabilities. Different computations of gross cashflow were considered, including use only of net profit carried forward to balance sheet. This last was considered to be flawed in that dividends and other distributions may already have been deducted and also, that depreciation and the deferred taxation account, if any, had not been added back as sources of cash. Accordingly, we computed the most representative measure of gross cashflow as the sum of profit after taxation, depreciation, and the increase in the company's deferred taxation account over the period.

The resulting ratio was an adaptation of Fadel and Parkinson's cashflow/interest charges and cashflow/total debt. Gross cashflow/current debt seemed, in our opinion, to provide nicer indications in that debt-service was particularized as was the flow ostensibly servicing it. Furthermore, the new ratio was clearly a measurement of an important area of solvency in that it showed the scope or margin left for further borrowings against normal trading receipts. X_1 thus served a dual purpose, indicating both priority debt-service ability as well as latitude for increased priority obligations. Both of which appeared to us as crucial in any consideration of overall solvency.

$$X_2 = \frac{\text{Pre-tax profit}}{\text{Capital employed}}$$

In any consideration of solvency, the final holistic score assigned by a model is given more meaning by comparing it with the score assigned for the previous period. In this way, the trend is shown. Analysts would naturally be more concerned in cases where the trend was adverse than where the trend showed improvement or strengthening. This type of trend is particularly telling in a company's net profit or loss for the year; these results being the product of the firm's trading and other activities as well as the net effects of its management. Profit before taxation, in our view, gave a fairer approximation of these results than profit after taxation, as the level of taxation was, to a large degree, directly proportional to the earnings ability of a firm. This can be qualified, of course, by taking account of the purchase of capital assets leading to exceptional first year tax allowances, the effect of tax losses forward, or by various tax minimization measures such as bonus payments to directors or payments into a pension fund before year-end. These, however, all impose analytical difficulties where full information is not to hand. Nor, in our view, is the effort productive of more truly indicative net results. We, accordingly, chose profit before taxation as the number including trading and extraordinary items plus any net interest earnings as the fairest measure of a company's annual earnings ability. To highlight annual profitability, we placed pre-tax profit against the total funds required to generate that profit: capital employed. Capital employed represented both equity and loan capital. Previous research showed that this ratio performed well for Altman, Fadel, Parkinson, and Whittington as a predictor in various groupings.

$$X_3 = \frac{\text{Equity}}{\text{Current liabilites}}$$

For X_3 we adapted the conventional gearing ratio loan capital/equity, feeling that in its new form, the ratio gave a nearer indication of a firm's capital resources in the face of its total current (short-term) obligations. Equity, for this reason, was selected rather than capital employed. X_3 was also a variant on Fadel and Parkinson's gearing ratio substitutes: long-term debt/total equity (shareholders' funds) and total debt/total equity.

Our equity measure represented the sum of called-up share capital and reserves (distributable and non-distributable) and this ratio was seen to perform well. Interestingly, certain fixed assets revaluations which would be noted as non-distributable reserves, could be expected to provide for a higher measure of capital adequacy were there a run on the company by its creditors or in the event of a winding-up. This type of measurement of capital adequacy is schematic. A company under pressure to meet all or most of its current obligations would, of course, look to make settlements or compositions with creditors from current assets first before granting charges over fixed assets or giving floating charges over the undertaking.

Realizable balances would be held as current assets, e.g. cash, stocks, deposits, debtors, or as fixed assets, such as buildings or land. Equity, as such, being a means of financing these assets is merely a schematic summary of the dispositions of assets and liabilities set out elsewhere in the statement of account. For these reasons, the measure of capital adequacy selected represented a summary more than a servicing indicator.

Current liabilities included all obligations due within one accounting period, including trade creditors, overdrafts, taxation, and unpaid dividends.

$$X_4 = \frac{\text{Tangible net worth}}{\text{Total liabilities}}$$

This ratio was selected as a measurement both of capital adequacy and of cumulative profitability. It is an adaptation of Cohen and Gilmore's ratio, retentions/total liabilities. The model previously looked only at annual or latest year's profitability. This needed the extra dimension of past profits/losses to judge the total effect of the company's workings. Thus, a measurement of cumulative profitability was needed. Past profits would contribute to equity. In this sense, the ratio measuring cumulative profitability would also give an indication of capital adequacy by contrasting total historical earnings and called-up capital with some measure of liabilities. Concerning this last, if we were to use a cumulative measurement of earnings and capital—i.e. worth—we would be obliged to compare this with a cumulative measurement of liabilities.

In prior studies, Altman measured cumulative profitability with retained earnings/total assets. He argued rightly that this measurement takes into account the age of a firm. The younger a company, the less time it has had in which to amass cumulative earnings. It will accordingly be at greater risk of insolvency resulting from trading downturns or other adverse developments than older firms, which have had more time in which to amass earnings. Altman's reasoning has been borne out in every succeeding study of corporate failure incidence where the highest levels of collapse are always among young companies.

Bearing this in mind, we wanted a harder measurement of cumulative profitability than retained earnings alone. We wanted the harder measurement both for the sake of a rough indication of break-up value in the event of a run on the company by its creditors, and also an indication of added value contributed by revaluations. For these reasons, we wanted a worth measurement rather than a total earnings measure. Of the various common worth measurements, net asset value, capital employed, multiples of equity, and tangible net worth, we chose tangible net worth as being the hardest as well as the most truly indicative of a firm's approximate break-up value. TNW would, of course, be based on retained earnings as well as any revaluations. The selection of TNW presented some analytical problems. TNW is calculated in varying ways. Accordingly, we stipulated the hardest, most schematic computation, reckoning that this would give the most accurate (pessimistic) figure for a company in distress. The computation was:

Total assets
Less
Intangible assets
Less
Total liabilities including all long-term debt, capital commitments contracted and/or entered into, and all contingent liabilities

$$X_5 = \frac{\text{Working capital}}{\text{Total assets}}$$

We now had ratio measurements for current debt-service ability, annual profitability, capital adequacy, cumulative profitability, and needed only an indicator of liquidity to complete the model.

Liquidity, as such, was indicated in various measures by the measurement of debt-service ability and margin. That measurement, however, gave a very specific indication. We now required a broader measurement, possibly, a more truly indicative one, to consider liquidity as a function of the whole company, that is, the net effect of its surplus day-to-day funds as a function of its various assets.

To keep computational routines as simple as possible, any liquidity (surplus) funds measurement should avoid normalization provided that the measurement performed predictively well in a group of ratios. Working capital was seen as having performed with higher predictive accuracy when used as a numerator or ratio constituent than a wholesale current ratio or acid-test both by Altman and Merwin. Fadel and Parkinson, accordingly, compared working capital with capital employed to show a company's liquid position as a percentage of its investment in fixed or investment assets. In our opinion, a broader view would be achieved by placing working capital against a company's total assets which would show the percentage surplus day-to-day funds occupied in a firm's total assets available. We, therefore, accepted the traditional computation of working capital for X_5's numerator and called for total assets as the denominator.

Because of the number of external and internal developments that can supervene, vitiating true *ex ante* predictive ability of any financial model concerned with solvency scoring and forecasting, we have been concerned to sharpen Bathory's Model as a classificatory device for risk description of companies producing full accounting statements. This refocussing does away with much of the tedious and time-consuming test programmes necessary for predictive models. By concentrating on risk classification based solely on historical results, subsequent model tests are easier to run from the standpoint of data collection. Effectively, similar financial years, asset size, industry sectors, and selection of ratios as best performers in varying groups can be subordinated to the development of harder measuring devices. The hardness of these measuring devices (both the ratios used and their constituent parts) refers to the obtaining of the most netted-out positions possible as well as to the degree of computation involved in achieving these positions. The composition of a risk description model, as seen earlier in this writing, however, still depends in our view, on a synoptic treatment of those main financial flows concerned with a company's solvency. Accordingly, Bathory's Model which is based on profitability, capital adequacy, and liquidity as the prime contributors to solvency can be maintained as a core from which to develop other risk classification models.

Akin, in some respects, to the alchemist's dream of finding a formula to transmute base metals into gold, credit analysts tacitly look for a financial model to do all their computational spreading and give a wise answer that cannot be gainsaid, though all researchers and theoreticians in this field have been at pains to stress that whatever model is used or developed, sole reliance should not be placed upon model findings. These findings are best used along with the results of ordinary analysis. This ordinary analysis, however, is the result of spreading data in various formats and of restatement of accounting numbers. Thus, in lieu of saving time, model-builders have tended to add to analytical time.

Secondly, financial models can be built to provide answers to many questions simultaneously. For instance, Bathory's Model was constructed to answer the question: What is the quantifiable degree of risk that a company will fail due to insolvency within an accounting range of two years? Such an application can be extended to ask: What is the company's quantifiable degree of risk of failure within two accounting years when my credit is added to its other obligations?

Thirdly, given the right spreadsheet format/s, will not such an extended model effectively take the place of any other analytical routines such as the computation of main operational and financial ratios and the calculation of trends? Were this so, no spreading of data need be done apart from that needed to operate the model.

Finally, for trade credit applications in particular, no practitioner would seriously urge disregarding such supplementary data as trade references, bank references and opinions, management information, personal interviews; and where analysis was done on an existing account, a review of payment performance and general conduct of the account to date. Such supplementary data is argued to bridge the gap between often out of date or non-current accounting information and time of analysis. In practice, supplementary data does bridge the gap in a manner of speaking. It does not, however, accomplish this either very accurately (in the quantifiable sense where accounting data has been independently validated by auditors) or in the sense of fullness of data. Trade references, for example, are extremely particular in that they speak only of the conduct of a specific account and of a specific credit limit allowed that account. The source and the amount of the trade reference necessarily contribute elements of bias. It is truistic to argue that most companies would not give as trade referees other firms that they felt would speak badly of them. Moreover, if the trade reference does not speak of very similar or identical figures (credit limits/exposures) to one's own, its significance is questionable. Other frailties in supplementary information obtain, and it is well to mention them.

Where the applicant for credit is an existing customer whose latest accounts are not sufficiently recent, how informative of the applicant's true and current financial position is an examination of his payment performance with one's company? It may be extremely indicative. But on the other hand, if one's own credit control is lax, the applicant's payment performance is bound to show arrears and slow payments. It is beyond the realms of common sense to believe that without proper credit control, firms will automatically observe trade credit terms to the letter. In other words, the poor payment performance may say nothing beyond an indictment of one's own poor control and collection procedures, and say nothing whatsoever about the applicant's financial ability to contract further obligations.

Bankers' references and opinions, despite the central and privileged position of banks in companies' financial affairs, speak normally only of the conduct of companies' accounts with the bank in question. These references cannot judge a company's outstanding commitments which the bank has no way of knowing. Even if the bank holds the subject's latest accounts, the banker will still not be aware of the company's immediate position *vis-à-vis* current assets and current liabilities. The banker may know that such and such a liability was discharged by the company, but he still does not necessarily know that a new liability has been taken on as part of the normal course of trading. Likewise, companies may spread their cash, deposits, and marketable securities around a range of banks. Thus, the risk is run that a bank reference will speak only for balances held at that bank and consequently fail to present a full picture of the subject's resources. Finally, while bankers' opinions and references can be of great value—especially when assessing foreign trade transactions and credits, the provision of bank references is an entirely non-profitable, ancillary service that banks are expected to give. They do not, in the main, tend to give this service with any degree of speed, willingness, thought, or from the vantage point of kaleidoscopic knowledge. The clearing banks' record in these respects is outstandingly poor, begrudging, slow, and simple-minded. Paradoxically, largely because of their computerization, these banks have little first-hand 'feel' or knowledge of their customers. As their record of lending to businesses is poor enough to have given birth to a large variety of venture capital and other quasi-loan institutions, the references they are able to give will tend to be a mere parroting of formulas, e.g. a respectably constituted company, or a glance at the latest statement to see whether overdraft limit has been exceeded. If so, the subject's assets will be noted to be 'fully employed'. The opacity and unfairness of such references can make them of minimal use to analysts. In mitigation, banks tend to answer the questions put them. An opaque bank reference will be the usual result of a flat request for a reference on Jones Limited. If, however, the credit manager or analyst asks for answers to specific questions, such as Jones's liquidity, his capacity for x or y amount of unsecured credit, some indication of his total capital resources, and conduct of his bank account/s over x years, a detailed and useful bank reference can sometimes be expected. The point here is the detailed and useful bank reference will still be extremely limited in value from the trading position of Jones, his treatment of trade creditors, his probity, and so forth. The bank's privileged position as the chief repository of Jones's financial outcomes does not enable it to speak as an oracle. It can normally speak only for the conduct of Jones's bank account and/or loan account.

Management information in the form of unaudited figures necessarily varies widely in respect of quality and quantity. For public companies, the production of unaudited interim figures can be of considerable help to analysts in bridging the gap between latest audited accounts and the present. For private companies, the production of unaudited figures at varying intervals must be viewed with caution. For example, how frequently have such management figures been generated? Are they produced simply for the sake of convincing one to sanction such and such a credit? Or are they produced at regular intervals for the internal consumption of management? Obviously, management accounts and other information will be truer and fairer in most instances if the latter condition obtains. Next, is the management information manually or computer-generated? If manually produced, the opportunities for bias, error, fraud, or special pleading are easier. If computer-generated, the information given by the computer will most likely be drawn from a range of separate books of entry and other sources such as sales ledger, purchase ledger, nominal ledger, assets register, cash book, and so on. The opportunities for error or fraud are less.

The degree to which management information truly bridges the gap between latest audited accounts and the present also depends upon the degree to which management figures approximate full accounting statements. Full accounts carry their own synoptic view of a company's varied financial flows. Models help to restate and interpret this in-built synopsis. When managment accounts' formats approximate or are identical to the company's audited accounting statements, and when the management data is felt to be reliable, the gap is bridged most effectively.

Perhaps, the most vexed area of supplementary information is personal experience of the applicant. This personal experience can take the form of visits, interviews, telephone or telex conversations, market or trade association intelligence, and the appraisal of the conduct of an account if the applicant already trades with one's company. All these are fraught with opportunities for bias, error, and want of experience. More than the other types of supplementary data, personal experience is difficult or impossible to quantify significantly.

Traditionally, it is an area of information most relied on by analysts working in commercial environments, liquidators, receivers, and management consultants. Allegedly significant financial and trading conclusions are drawn from the shabbiness of waiting rooms, the managing director's Rolls-Royce, the beautiful display of marble and potted palms, the courtesy of staff, the clutter or lack of it on executives' desks, even the flying of a Queen's Award to Industry flag. The point here is that each of these so-called significant items can be used in logical argument to demonstrate what one wishes to demonstrate. Each is thus totally open to bias.

Accordingly, the arguments' conclusions will be informed only by bias expressed as supposition. These suppositions will not be corroborated by fact until audited accounting results are available covering the period in which the personal assessment was made. For example, a company may have small, bare, and generally shabby premises, harried staff with cluttered desks, and no receptionist to welcome you. A common view of such an enterprise might be that it is on its financial knees. When one subsequently sees the managing director arrive in his Rolls-Royce for the meeting with you, the first impression can be extended. Not only is the company in apparent financial need, but its managing director is milking it of much-needed funds to equip himself with a luxury car. Such personal impressions (or collection of them) may adversely influence a potential credit sanction. This would be bad and unfair mistake if it were later seen that the company maintained a conscious policy of trimming all overheads that were not strictly necessary to the conduct of its business. This might account for the shabby premises. The same company might also have been something of a market maker or innovator, in which case, it stands to reason that its staff was extremely busy. The absence of a receptionist could have been due to the fact that visitors to the company were generally not expected nor encouraged. Were this so, the managing director's Rolls-Royce might well have been a justifiable expenditure in providing the company's chief executive with a comfortable, reliable, and impressive means of calling on suppliers and customers. Above all, every one of these impressions might easily be justified and explained in financial terms by the company's next set of audited figures. If one felt sorry for the harried staff having to work in ugly surrounding, the same staff may have been compensated by large salaries and bonuses or commissions. The company may have generated proportionally high profits *and* remained extremely sound financially. In other words, the total effect of everything one considered to be 'anti' might well, in the final reckoning, be seen to be 'pro'.

For these reasons, personal experience must be treated with great care. Whenever possible, such experience should be related to independently verified results to see how the two stack up. If they appear significantly at odds, possibly, important changes are taking place at the company. But these changes should ideally be interpreted by direct questions and some type of proof in quantifiable form rather than by divine inspiration.

Taken as a whole, all the traditional supplementary data considered so far must be seen as a mixed bag by analysts. Nor is it a very reliable or easily interpretable body of information. The amassing of such data is extremely time-consuming. While data collection of all types is an important and central skill for credit analysts, it is, after a certain stage of development, akin to a pianist's ability to read music. Certainly, he must learn to read notes correctly, but the point at issue is how well he plays the piano, and perhaps, the ultimate consideration is how well he interprets the notes he plays. The same is true for analysts. Thus, after trainee analysts learn how to collect data, supplementary or otherwise, their worth as analysts must be determined by their ability to read and interpret this information. Whereas musicians will always need to read notes in order to learn the pieces they play, credit analysts have at their disposal various means of delegating data collection, particularly of the supplementary kind, to external agencies. In many respects, the commission of data collection to third-party agencies cuts down on the possibility of bias, error, incompleteness, and triviality. These agencies are status, credit, and financial reporting companies, investigators, collectors, and independent companies of credit analysts. Costs in employing such firms is more readily and easily justifiable than a total reliance on in-house facilities. In addition, these companies can claim professional expertise and experience along with the impartiality of third-parties to the credit applications in question. In a later chapter, we shall examine some of these facilities and how they can be effectively combined with internal analytical operations.

Assuming for the moment that supplementary bridging data will be collected and interpreted intelligently, we are still left with the problem of expanding a financial model that will assess risk accurately, that will include a potential or existing credit exposure, that will possibly make some forecasting assumptions as part of the analysis of the exposure, and that will significantly reduce the indiscriminate spreading of historical data.

Earlier, we argued that a consideration of solvency was axial to this type of examination. In the remaining parts of this chapter, we will go on to develop a format for the type of model suggested in the previous paragraph.

Computation for debt-cover: An expansion of Bathory's Model

For credit assessment purposes, the chief value of a financial model is its ability to measure debt-service ability. Insolvency represents a class of outcomes when a company cannot meet its obligations as those obligations fall due. For effective credit assessment, the central problem would thus appear to be the quantification of debt-service ability, or debt cover, both according to latest historical data and also, on forecast data.

Bathory's Model is concerned with the classification of insolvency. It groups companies according to holistic scores on array of solvent and insolvent scores (solvency scale). The component ratios in the model are, accordingly, classificatory, based as they are, on purely historical accounting data. Given the supervention of no extraordinary events such as a total recovery in profitability due to wholesale reorganization/divestiture, or an unlooked-for market downturn, to name two, the model indicates both the latest year's synoptic solvency and prior year's synopses, thus presenting a picture of trend. Given no extraordinary phenomena, the latest results plus the trend in scores provides a good classificatory forecast of solvency or insolvency. We argued before that corporate solvency is in itself the sum total of companies' main financial flows. Solvency is thus the ultimate consideration when examining companies.

That having been said, credit intervals (used here in the sense of the terms over which credits extend) are, particularly in the case of trade credit facilities, far shorter than the periods in which it is customary to assess solvency. Bathory's Model, for instance, considers solvency at yearly intervals. Trade credit intervals, however, are normally monthly or quarterly. Some, of course, are denominated 'at any one time'. These last are especially comparable with year-end results (or with any other periodic results) which are snapshots taken at one time only, i.e. accounting date.

Because of the central importance of the consideration of solvency to credit assessment, but also because of the most immediate problem of debt-service ability, we can use a solvency classification model and enlarge upon it in ways calculated to highlight or stress debt-service ability.

To begin with, it is perhaps, as stated earlier, overly crude to place various historic flows over a putative credit exposure to measure cover. The historic flows are past whereas the credit exposure is either currently existing or potential. Thus, like is not being compared with like. An adjustment needs to be made; and this would be:

$$\frac{\text{Forecast flow}}{\text{Exposure}}$$

In theory, this is simpler than in practice. There can be no agreement on the most accurate methods of forecasting. But in general terms, two points concerning forecasts should be made at this stage:

1. Forecasting should follow the double-entry system on which modern accountancy is based. That is, for every debit, there should be a corresponding credit. The size of these correspondences is the key difficulty. Merely because we forecast a 10 per cent increase in sales, need we also forecast a 10 per cent increase in costs of sales? Clearly, the answer is no, and our ultimate profit figures will reflect whether the correspondences were treated as *pari passu*, directly or indirectly or inversely proportional.

    By forecasting following double-entry principles, we understand that provision must accordingly be made for 'the ripple effect' in the treatment of main financial flows. Any deviation therefrom should be justified and noted.
2. The most reasonable forecasts are those that assume the supervention of no extraordi-

nary events. By their nature, we cannot reasonably predict a catastrophe or an extraordinary piece of good fortune. Accordingly, reasonable forecasts should attempt to extend what we already know from observation of results, possibly normalized, over the longest intervals or periods available. In this way, a forecast based on five years' results is likely to be more indicative, all things being equal, than one based on two years.

From these two points, there follow several important considerations. Firstly, ripple-effect forecasting can be carried out more quickly and easily on ratio quantities than by calculating something akin to an audit trail through quantities of accounting numbers. Secondly, trend or normalized trend of one kind or another can be very quickly and easily done by adjustments to the ratios' numerators and denominators. A final point should be made. We believe it is more useful and more immediately significant for analysts to gain a feeling for the comfort margin or amount of cover for their exposures than to classify the historic or forecast results of companies even when these forecasts include their credit exposures as part of total liabilities. In other words, analysts want to know, first and foremost, the amount of times free capital can decline before a company will fail to meet its forecast obligations including the putative credit exposure. From the credit-grantor's point of view, classification or prediction of insolvency must be of less moment. Briefly, this is because insolvency comes in many shapes and forms. Many insolvent companies continue to trade. Insolvency has been described as 'technical', 'acute', 'chronic', and 'terminal'. For model-testing purposes, insolvent companies have been firms selected on the following bases:

In liquidation
In receivership
'Trading with the support of' qualification
'Going concern' qualification
'Trading with the continued support of parent company' qualification

Further to the Cork Report's recommendation on the establishment of an administrator for troubled companies, 'In Administration' may shortly become another insolvency criterion for testing purposes.

In the proposed expansion of Bathory's Model, we are thus trying to alter the model's purpose from the identification and classification of insolvent companies to the forecasting of debt cover where this debt cover includes an actual or potential credit exposure. We choose Bathory's Model as being structured on the basic or synoptic result of companies' main financial flows: solvency or insolvency. We choose this model also because it is ratio-based and we can more easily make adjustments to numerators and denominators than attempting to make calculations for the ripple effect through quantities of accounting numbers. An expansion of this model will necessarily call for a more particularized and detailed spreading of data. Particularly with regard to the forecasting elements in the expanded model, an intelligent reading of supplementary data should be more informative in light of the greater body of information available. Simply, purely historical data will be extended by the forecasts. The supplementary data should then help to refine or controvert those forecasts.

Debt-service ability includes assumptions about liquidity. Profitability includes assumptions about capital adequacy. Earlier, we argued that the three main financial movements in the life of any company were:

Liquidity
Profitability
Capital adequacy

By selection of certain ratios, we should be able to combine the notion of capital adequacy with liquidity and profitability, helping to minimize the number of ratios called-for by the expanded model. Liquidity indicators can also notionally include debt-service ability measurements. It is, thus, clear at the outset that the ratios for the expanded model must be hybrid. It is also clear that an expansion of the model need not necessarily therefore entail use of more ratios than the original version.

X_1 of the original model measured current debt-service ability by placing gross cashflow over current debt. This ratio also includes a notion of liquidity as well as an indication of cashflow remaining with which to service non-priority debt items.

If we deduct current debt from gross cashflow and place this quantity over credit exposure, we have a crude approximation of flow remaining for the service of exposure alone. But this ratio is flawed as the numerator is historic whilst the denominator is current or potential. This can be 'corrected' by substituting forecast gross cashflow and current debt totals for historic totals in the numerator.

We are then confronted with the problem of how to make the forecasts. As a basic premise, let us assume the supervention of no extraordinary events. Thus, we could let the forecast quantities equal the averaged trend percentage increases/decreases in those quantities as taken from historical data with the average percentage used to extrapolate the forecast quantities.

An easy alternative which will throw lower figures, and may, for that reason, appear more prudent, is to take an average of the differences between the years in question and add that average to the final year.

The two computational methods are illustrated in Figure 5.1

Averaged % trend

	1985	1984	1983	1982	1981
	£150	£100	£57	£40	£30
+/−%		50.0%	75.4%	42.5%	33.3%

Sum of %'s: $\frac{201.2}{4} = 50.3\%$

150 × 50.3% = £75.45
           +£150.00

1986 forecast: £225.45

Averaged amounts trend

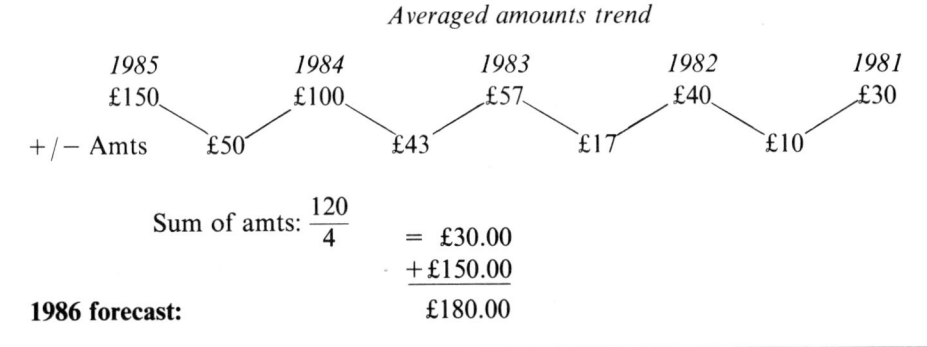

```
    1985        1984        1983        1982        1981
    £150        £100         £57         £40         £30
+/− Amts  £50         £43         £17         £10
```

Sum of amts: $\frac{120}{4}$ = £30.00
                              +£150.00
1986 forecast: £180.00

Figure 5.1 Trend computations for forcasting purposes

To smooth the divergence between these two computations, the analyst can take the average forecast figure in each case and compute the mean:

$$\begin{array}{r} 225.45 \\ +180.00 \\ \hline 405.45 \end{array}$$

$$\frac{405.45}{2} = £202.73$$

The smoothed forecast for 1986 would thus be £203, showing a 35.3 per cent upward trend on the 1985 figure of £150.

A final averaging possibility for these purposes is to compute the harmonic mean between the percentage trend and the sum of amounts trend figures. The harmonic mean will throw a lower figure than the smoothed forecast figure noted above.

Harmonic mean of a set of numbers, is the reciprocal of the arithmetic mean of their reciprocals. Accordingly, if the numbers in question are X and Y, their reciprocals are $1/X$ and $1/Y$. The arithmetic mean will be:

$$\frac{1}{2}\left(\frac{1}{X} + \frac{1}{Y}\right) = \frac{1}{2}\left(\frac{X+Y}{XY}\right) \Rightarrow \frac{X+Y}{2XY}$$

The harmonic mean of X and Y is therefore:

$$HM = \frac{2XY}{X+Y}$$

If we let $X = 225$ and $Y = 180$,

$$HM = \frac{2 \times 225 \times 180}{405} \Rightarrow \frac{81,000}{405} = £200$$

The criticism can be made that in averaging once much less two or three times, distortion will result. 'Distortion in what?' must be the answer. In computing these trends for forecasting, we have no other information save historical figures over five years, in this case.

If analysts are privy to market intelligence information, economic or management financial data, doubtless, forecasting becomes more accurate. Here, our basic assumption is accordingly that given no external or supplementary information, the common sense premise is for the analyst to use historical trend over the longest period possible to make his forecasts. In order that we err on the side of pessimism rather than optimism (which would be more dangerous in credit sanctions), we select that method of averaging the historical information that will throw the lowest figures. Accordingly, forecasts for the model in question will be made taking the harmonic mean of averaged percentage trend and averaged sum of amounts trend. In the first ratio of the expanded model, we shall, accordingly, let μ = the harmonic mean of the two trends.

We now have the first ratio component of the expanded model. Essentially, it takes the improved form of net forecast flow/credit exposure, and can be written:

$$\frac{\mu GCF - \mu CD}{e}$$

Where μ = the harmonic mean of averaged % trend and averaged sum of amounts trend
GCF = Gross cashflow
CD = Current debt
e = Credit exposure

And the ratio can be read as

$$\frac{\text{Forecast net cashflow after forecast priority current debt}}{\text{Credit exposure}}$$

The treatment of working capital is important in any consideration of liquidity. We have already seen that working capital can be interpreted in varying ways. Three discussed to date have been:

Net current assets
Normalized working capital
Averaged free capital

As net current assets will, in essence, furnish the basis or point of reference for the others, let us examine averaged free capital. Earlier, this was defined as the sum of the following quantities multiplied by the constant 0.25:

Net cashflow − current liabilities
Current assets − current liabilities
Normalized working capital
Totals generated from operations − current liabilities

The ratio averaged free capital/credit exposure will thus indicate a strict measure of net liquid funds available to service the exposure. As in the case of our first ratio, this second is flawed in that historic data are being compared with current or future data. The ratio can be adjusted by a forecasting of averaged free capital where the restated ratio would be:

$$\frac{\mu AFC}{e}$$

Normalized working capital is a less speculative measure of net liquid funds from which credit exposures can be serviced. Normalization, in this case, nets out those portions of stock agreed to move comparatively slowly. The netting-out gives a truer picture of stock quickly realizable for cash for the settlement of obligations. Accordingly, the normalized working capital figure is already a net quantity and offers a nicer approximation of this type of liquidity than straight net current assets. Note also, that in the computation for averaged free capital cover, the provision is made for net current assets in any case. To provide for the necessary adjustment to normalized working capital to bring it into the same time-scale as the credit exposure it is intended to service, the third ratio can be written:

$$\frac{\mu \text{NWC}}{e}$$

It is important to measure profitability from an annual and a cumulative viewpoint. So far, we have three ratios measuring the ultimate effects of profitability, namely, liquidity, capital adequacy, and debt-service ability historically and according to forecasts. The model workings will thus show whether profitability has been achieved at the expense of liquidity (for instance, as in cases of overtrading) or whether profitability has augmented liquidity and the service of debt.

Let us first consider cumulative profitability. Ratio X_4 in Bathory's Model measured the accumulated retentions of a company as a percentage of its total commitments including off-balance-sheet items. It also netted-out intangible assets such as capitalized research and development expenses or technical know-how. As we are concerned with flows from which a credit exposure is to be met, let us forecast tangible net worth and compare this with forecast total liabilities including the credit exposure. Our fourth ratio would, therefore, be:

$$\frac{\mu \text{TNW}}{\mu \text{TL} + e}$$

If we are to measure annual or latest profit performance, we can reasonably place profit before taxation and interest over capital employed. This is ratio X_2 of Bathory's Model. It is unnecessary to apply any forecasting to this ratio as we wish here to assess historical data only. The cumulative profitability ratio discussed before serves to give the forecast dimension to this expanded model. Accordingly, our fifth ratio would be:

$$\frac{\text{PTP}}{\text{CE}} \times 100$$

The sum of the five 'expanded' ratios multiplied by the constant 0.20 should give forecast debt cover for the exposure. This final figure should indicate the amount of times cover can fall before a company will fail to meet its total forecast obligations including the potential exposure. The expanded model can thus be written:

$$\Delta = \left\{ k \left(\sum_{X_{1-4}} \right) + k(Y) \right\}$$

where
Δ = debt cover
$k = 0.20$
$\sum$ = the sum of ratios x_1 to x_4
e = credit exposure
X_{1-4} = harmonic ratios
Y = non-harmonic ratio

and where the harmonic ratios are described as follows:

$$X_1 = \frac{\mu GCF - \mu CD}{e}$$

$$X_2 = \frac{\mu AFC}{e}$$

$$X_3 = \frac{\mu NWC}{e}$$

$$X_4 = \frac{\mu TNW}{\mu TL + e}$$

and the non-harmonic ratio is:

$$Y = \frac{PTP}{CE} \times 100$$

For the harmonic ratios, μ = the harmonic mean of averaged % trend and averaged sum of amounts trend as noted earlier.

The spreading of data for operation of this model is considerable. Two points follow. First, the comprehensive spreading ensures that the main flows and salient numbers used in standard credit analysis will be highlighted before being cast in ratio form. The ratio content will be high and mainly hybrid, providing better insight into synthetic and antithetical analysis than many conventional and static measures such as current or acid-test ratios. Secondly, because of the detailed computational work in operating the expanded model, entailing spreading four or five years' worth of results, it is unlikely to be a time-saving device as such, except in the analysis of large exposures.

As in the case of its prototype, the expanded model can be 'read' singly, severally, or simultaneously. The 'simultaneous' or holistic figure Δ will arguably be of most value to analysts in forming a credit opinion.

Possibly, the most concise formats for spreading the data required for this model will be two-fold: one spreadsheet for the computation of flows and notation of various accounting numbers; and the other for computing trends and the harmonic means deriving from them.

Figures 5.2 and 5.3 give suggested spreads:

	Item	1986	1985	1984	1983	1982	1981
1.	Profit after taxation:						
	+						
2.	Depreciation:						
	+						
3.	Increase in def. tax:						
4.	Gross cashflow:						
5.	Overdraft:						
	+						
6.	Loans:						
	+						
7.	Taxation:						
	+						

Figure 5.2 Expanded model (debt-cover) accounting data (spreadsheet 1).

	Item	1986	1985	1984	1983	1982	1981

8. HP/Leasing:
   +
9. Other priority debt:
10. Current debt:
11. Gross cashflow
    Less
12. Current debt:
13. Gross cashflow
    Less
14. Dividend
15. Net cashflow:
16. Current liabilities:
17. Net cashflow
    Less
18. Current liabilities:
19. Current assets:
    Less
20. Current liabilities
21. Working capital:
22. Total stocks:
    Less
23. Work-in-progress:
24. Net stocks:
    +
25. Current assets
    Less
26. Current liabilities
27. Normalized working capital:
28. Totals gen. from ops:
    Less
29. Current liabilities
30. Net totals gen from ops:
31. Pre-tax profit:
32. Equity:
    +
33. Long-term financings:
    +
34. Deferred taxation:
    +
35. Provisions:
36. Capital employed:
37. Fixed assets:
    +
38. Investment assets:
    +

Figure 5.2 (*continued*)

	Item	1986	1985	1984	1983	1982	1981
39.	Current assets:						
40.	Total assets:						
41.	Current liabilities:						
	+						
42.	Long-term liabilities:						
	+						
43.	Capital commitments:						
	+						
44.	Contingent liabilities:						
45.	Total liabilities:						
46.	Total assets						
	Less						
47.	Total liabilities						
48.	Tangible net worth:						
49.	Intangible assets:						
	Averaged free capital						
	17−18						
	+						
	21						
	+						
	27						
	+						
	30						
50.	____ × 0.25 =						

Figure 5.2 (*Concluded*)

A

Averaged percentage trend

	1986	1985	1984	1983	1982	1981
Accounting number/flow: %+/−		____	____	____	____	
Sum of percentages:	$\dfrac{\quad}{4} =$					

B

Averaged sum of amounts trend

	1986	1985	1984	1983	1982	1981
Accounting number/flow: Differences		____	____	____	____	
Sum of differences:	$\dfrac{\quad}{4} =$					

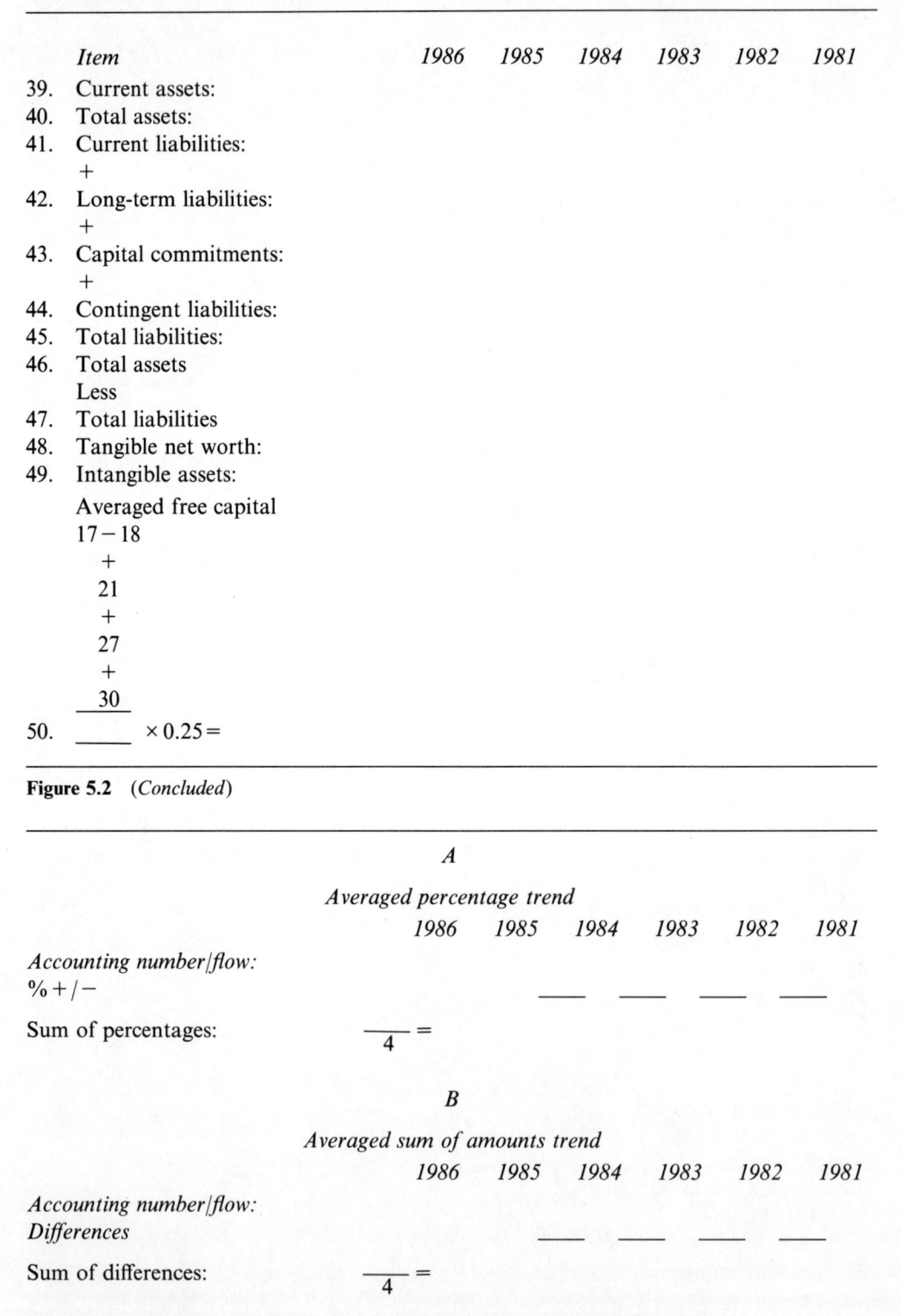

Figure 5.3 Expanded model (debt-cover) trend computations (spreadsheet 2).

C

Harmonic mean computation

	1986	1985	1984	1983	1982	1981
Formula: HM = $\frac{2AB}{B+B}$						
Harmonic mean:		___	___	___	___	

Figure 5.3 *(Concluded)*

We shall now operate the expanded model, applying a credit exposure of £5 m at any one time. We have already seen the 1984 accounting statements of Monsanto PLC and subsidiaries. Accordingly, it will be expedient to operate the new model over Monsanto's prior results for the year ending 31 December 1979 to 1983, thus giving the model five years' data from which to forecast debt cover for financial 1984/5 (i.e. the classifying or predictive range of two accounting periods assumed by Bathory's Model). Figure 5.4 sets out condensed spreadsheet data for the Group. We propose computing the expanded model score and then considering this information against a 'standard' credit analysis for the Group spanning the financial years 1983/4, and interims for 1985.

Assigning values to the model:

$$\Delta = \left\{ k \left(\sum_{X_{1-4}} \right) + k(Y) \right\}$$

we have:

£'000s

$\Delta \Rightarrow$

$$\left\{ 0.20 \left(\frac{126-17}{5} \right) + 0.20 \left(\frac{32}{5} \right) + \right.$$

$$0.20 \left(\frac{49}{5} \right) + 0.20 \left(\frac{205}{5} \right) +$$

$$\left. + 0.20 \left(\frac{55,125}{205,846} \times 100 \right) \right\}$$

and therefore $\Delta = 13.5$

where averaged forecast available capital can decline 13.5 times before the company will fail to meet its forecast obligations including the £5 m credit exposure.

In our view, the first criterion against which to judge the working of the model is the 1984 working capital figure for Monsanto: £87.4 m. Against this measurement of "free capital" the £5 m exposure would have 17.5 cover. Against Monsanto's 1983 working capital figure of £48.8 m, the exposure would have 9.8 cover. The two years' working capital figures would thus provide the £5 m exposure an averaged 13.7 cover. The harmonic mean of the two years' working capital would be 12.6. The model has thus given debt cover 0.9 points

128 PROBLEMS IN THE COMPUTATION AND INTERPRETATION OF DATA

Trend 1 = Averaged percentages
Trend 2 = Averaged sum of amounts

£'000s

	Derivatives	1983	1982	1981	1980	1979
Gross cashflow:		73,910	11,077		(12,839)	(5,535)
GCF Trend 1:	190,688	62,833	(5,947)	17,024	(7,304)	
GCF Trend 2:	93,771	+567	−35	29,863	−132	
H Mean:	125,993			+233		
Current debt:		9,953	628		8,421	8,284
CD Trend 1:	47,476	+1,485	+118.1	288	+1.7	
CD Trend 2:	10,370	9,325	340	−96.6	137	
H mean:	17,064			−8,133		
Normalized working capital:		44,811	42,762	36,879	19,543	34,578
NWC Trend 1:	52,250	+4.8	+16	+89	−43.5	
NWC Trend 2:	46,860	2,049	5,883	17,336	−15,035	
H mean:	49,453					
Averaged free capital:		17,085	(25,663)	(49,966)	(84,971)	(67,008)
AFC Trend 1:	26,994	+167	+49	+41.2	−27	
AFC Trend 2:	38,108	42,748	24,303	35,005	−17,963	
H mean:	31,569					
Total liabilities:		92,253	133,035	148,995	202,515	219,752
TL Trend 1:	78,231	−31	−11	−26.4	7.8	
TL Trend 2:	68,997	−40,782	−15,960	−53,520	+17,237	
H mean:	73,313					
μTL + e:	78,313					
Tangible net worth:		172,981	128,374	133,069	86,187	78,398
TNW Trend 1:	214,496	+35	−3.5	+54	+9.9	
TNW Trend 2:	196,627	44,607	−4,695	46,882	7,789	
H mean:	205,378					
Pre-tax profit:		55,125	41	(4,832)	(29,344)	(4,196)
Capital employed:		205,846	204,107	219,956	212,537	227,887

Fig. 5.4 Condensed spreadsheet data. Monsanto PLC and subsidiaries

above the harmonic mean, 4 points below the actual working capital figure for 1984, and 3.7 points above the 1983 working capital figure. The model score for debt-cover is thus averaging 2.9 points' divergence between the three criteria.

The salient fact emerging from this is that the model is providing a prudential forecast of debt-cover, in this instance, only 0.9 points below that indicated by the Group's 1984 working capital figure, where working capital can sensibly be assumed to be a leading indicator of potential cover for additional debt.

A secondary, but none the less interesting, point is that the model's forecasting ability takes no account of market conditions, management capability, or other supplementary credit information. This will, doubtless, be construed as a weakness by some practitioners. The model takes into account only the Group's audited results. Purposely, the interpretive element in spreading these results has been kept to the minimum. The quantification of current debt, tangible net worth, and the normalization of working capital—to mention a few areas—entail interpretive judgement. Again, this degree of interpretive judgement may be viewed as potentially dangerous by some analysts. In our opinion, these elements of interpretation have been clearly set forth and justified both in this text and elsewhere. They are thus not, in and of themselves, misleading. Their ultimate justification is that they help the accounting statements of a company 'speak' in ways that mirror the real flows inherent in any functioning company.

We will now continue by examining the individual parts of the model to check whether the components' findings in any way violate common sense—that is, what we know of ways in which the financial flows of companies move, and also, what we know from the subject's audited accounts. The model's findings can best be assessed against standard analytical procedures. Our examination will be made clearer by looking at the model's harmonic and standard ratios in order.

$$X_1 = \frac{\mu GCF - \mu CD}{e} \Rightarrow \frac{109}{5} = 21.8$$

The group's gross cashflow showed a sizeable increase (567 per cent) from 1982 to 1983. After deduction of current debt items, this measure of cashflow stood at £64 m for 1983 and £10.4 m for 1982. These figures provide cover for the £5 m exposure in the ratios of 2.1 for 1982 rising to 12.8 for 1983. Note that both amounts of cover fall below the forecast (μ) cover provided by ratio X_1 of the expanded model. This cover stood at 21.8, representing an increase of 9 points over the notional cover given by the 1983 GCF/CD ratio. The significance of this is that X_1 of the expanded model, whilst aiming at the most prudent measurement of net debt cover, still affords, in this case, an apparently wider margin from which the credit exposure is to be serviced. The latitude here is, of course, considerably influenced by any extreme values taken into the averaging computations. That is to say, in mathematical terms, the mean is highly sensitive to extreme values. By calculating sums of amounts average ($\bar{X}$), percentage increases/decreases averages (%) and taking the harmonic mean ($\mu\bar{X}$), we smooth the deviations between the three. From Monsanto's 1984 accounts, we compute GCF at £89.3 m, a 21 per cent increase on GCF in the prior period. This provides cover for the exposure in the ratio of 17.9, but is not truly indicative as priority debt has not been deducted. After netting-out current debt of £12.6 m, the 1984 GCF left to service the £5 m exposure stands at 15.3. Accordingly, X_1 of the expanded model offered cover 6.5 points above the 1984 figures; and the deviation is accounted for by μ. $\bar{X}$ for the six years' results would have produced the following figures:

    CGF: £28.8 m
    CD: £6.7 m

giving a notional 4.3 cover for priority debt. In this instance, the putative cover is demonstrably silly as Monsanto clearly has, in 1982 and 1983 alone, managed CD cover at 7.4 and 7.1 respectively.

Current Debt totals have, in fact, fluctuated widely over the six years in question. The following percentage increases/decreases make this clear:

	1984	1983	1982	1981	1980	1979
Current Debt: (% +/−)		+26	+1,485	+118	−97	+1.7

$\bar{X}$ would, therefore, equal +307 per cent. Taking this percentage of 1983 current debt and adding the same back gives the following high mean:

    Trend 1
    307% of £9,953 =   £30,556
    +1983 CD   9,953
                      £40,509

The sum of amounts (increases/decreases) over the period produces the following mean:

    Trend 2
    $\frac{4,275}{5} =$ 856
    +1983 CD   9,953
                £10,809

The harmonic mean of these two extremely divergent figures would be:

$$\text{(£'000s)}$$
$$HM = \frac{2 \times 41 \times 11}{52} \Rightarrow £17.3$$

Where the deviation from X_1 in the expanded model is some 4.5 points. To make this comparison, however, is not, strictly speaking, comparing like with like. The interesting point is that despite the non-inclusion of the credit exposure (e) in current debt in these averages, the forecast cover for CD+e given by the model exceeds μ taken over a longer averaging period (that is over five instead of four years).

X_2 of the expanded model measures e against the hybrid, averaged free capital.

$$X_2 = \frac{\mu AFC}{e} = \frac{32}{5} \Rightarrow 6.4$$

Averaged free capital is a weighted amalgam of the following:

    Net cashflow − current liabilities
    +
    Current assets − current liabilities
    +

Normalized working capital
+
Totals generated from operations − current liabilities

The sum is multiplied by 0.25 for equalized weighting, and the result (AFC) is intended to indicate surplus funds available after meeting total current obligations. Any net surplus of this kind makes sense only in respect of *additional* debt applied to it for service or of balances earning interest for the company. As a projection in itself, AFC (and working capital) is faulty in that AFC is calculated only for a company's accounting date. Future measures of AFC will necessarily vary with the totals and the composition of current assets and current liabilities. To provide for the necessary adjustment, we have used μ which casts AFC into the future mode, matching e which is potential credit exposure at any one time.

Monsanto's AFC improved over the six year period as follows:

(£'000s)	1984	1983	1982	1981	1980	1979
Averaged free capital:	57,896	17,085	(25,663)	(49,966)	(84,971)	(67,008)
% +/−	+239	+167	+49	+41.2	−27	

The percentage trend masks the AFC deficiencies from 1979 to 1982, though it is plain that these deficiencies are being 'repaired' in a systematic way by the Group. By contrast, Monsanto's working capital balances, being a far less rigorous measurement of surplus funds, show:

(£'000s)	1984	1983	1982	1981	1980	1979
Working capital:	87,377	48,752	50,285	44,622	27,072	42,778
% +/−	+79.2	−3	+13	+65	−37	

Roughly speaking, these figures would parallel the AFC figures were a linear graph to be drawn. The AFC balances, however, are negative balances until 1983. The 1984 balance does not, of course, feature in the original spreadsheet computations. The essential trend in surplus capital on these two measures is thus preserved.

As working capital is itself a net quantity, let us see the cover it would have provided the £5 m exposure—bearing in mind that the ratios obtained are faulty as working capital has no notion of futurity. The 'cover' on these balances would have been:

(£'000s)	1984	1983	1982	1981	1980	1979
Working capital cover:	17.5	9.8	10.1	8.9	5.4	8.6

Such figures are reassuring, if absurd. They are reassuring in that apparently reasonable cover is afforded for the potential credit exposure. This, however, ignores the fact that other exposures (future obligations) will combine to reduce the apparent (historic) cover sharply as part and parcel of the company's normal trading. The working capital cover figures are absurd because they present an utterly false picture, the lineaments of which are flawed at the outset. The key point here is simply that without taking into account the forecasting element, interpretative and imprecise as it may be, very little significance can be attached to purely historic data.

The forecasting element, as we have seen from this as well as from prior studies, can be achieved by various ratios in special groupings. The predictive models of Altman, Lis, and Taffler serve as examples. Forecasting can also be done by reasonable assumptions based on past performance over varying periods. From the trend assumptions computed from this data, extrapolations can be made with varying degrees of prudence. External factors such as market conditions can be incorporated as can other supplementary data. An example of the former type of model relating only to numbers (accounting data) is the expanded model under discussion.

Normalized working capital, arguably, offers a nicer indication of funds available to meet credit exposure than working capital. Again, the niceness is vitiated by NWC's lack of futurity.

X_2's cover for the £5 m exposure was 6.4 which is not generous. It deviates by -2.2 points from the arithmetic mean offered by working capital cover, 8.6. In this case, μ has lowered or reduced the expected net liquid cover for the £5 m exposure. Likewise, $\bar{x}$ offered by NWC for debt cover was 7.2. This deviates by 0.8 points from μAFC. It is thus clear that the combination of the AFC computation plus μ serve to yield a more prudential measurement of net liquid available funds. At this stage, it may still appear that X_2 is faulty in that the denominator does not include forecast current liabilities as well as credit exposure. Note that current liabilities have been netted-out of all four numerator constituents and that the net balances have been projected by μ. In this way, forecast current liabilities as well as forecast current assets and their net balances have been treated in four ways as part of AFC. Also, forecast current liabilities are included in μTL + e, the denominator of ratio X_4.

Monsanto's gross and net cashflows as debt-service measures look very bleak until 1983, the final year of our computations for the expanded model. The net cashflow (NCF) figures are:

(£'000s)	1984	1983	1982	1981	1980	1979
Net cashflow:	89.3	74.0	11.1	17.0	(13)	(5.5)
Less						
Current liabilities	56.3	59.4	45.4	62.1	72.6	69.8
	33.0	14.6	(34.3)	(45.1)	(85.6)	(75.3)

Over six years, this would provide an $\bar{x}$ cover of -32.1; over five years, -45.1. These figures, of course, obscure the fact that, apart from the adverse turn in 1980, the Group has steadily improved this measure of debt cover both by increasing cash inflows and by reducing obligations. The year 1982 serves as a good example. NCF was down by 35 per cent and current liabilities were cut by 27 per cent. These two movements accounted for the 24 per cent reduction in net deficiency shown above.

As no dividend payments apply for this Group during the period in question, GCF and NCF are identical. Analysts are fond of measuring exposures against both flows without deducting current liabilities. The cover provided the £5 m exposure on this measure would be:

	1984	1983	1982	1981	1980	1979
Exposure cover:	17.9	14.8	2.2	3.4	-2.6	-1.1

The arithmetic mean of the six years is 5.8 or 0.6 points below X_2 and 16 points below the cover forecast by X_1 where current liabilities have been taken into account.

X_4 considers the five years results known and forecasts for the next year, 1984. The cover given by this ratio was the finest in the model and stood at 2.6. X_4 took μTNW and compared it with $\mu TL + e$. In essence, the ratio is reduplicative in that total liabilities have been accounted for twice: once as a reduction from total assets to give tangible net worth in the numerator; and once again as a forecast to be added to credit exposure in the denominator. This has the effect of reducing TNW cover. TNW as a debt-servicing medium or 'flow' must be regarded as more schematic than practical in all save security-taking for medium to long-term obligations. TNW is not, strictly speaking, available for the settlement of debt apart from break-up situations. Bearing in mind the slim 2.6 cover noted before, let us see the cover provided by TNW divorced from any forecasting:

(£'000s)	*1984*	*1983*	*1982*	*1981*	*1980*	*1979*
Tangible net worth:	233.6	173.0	128.4	133.1	86.2	78.4
Cover for e:	46.7	34.6	25.7	26.6	17.2	15.7

The arithmetic mean is 27.8 which shows ample cover—leaving out of account future liabilities of all classes. $\bar{X}$ is therefore 25.2 points higher than the forecast cover of 2.6 provided by X_4.

Y of the new model makes no forecasts, being concerned solely with profitability in the latest period. The ratio is PTP/CE. Because of the sharp upturn in 1983 profits, and because X_5 ignores previous performance, Y gives the highest multiple in the model, 26.8. Profitability is undoubtedly the most significant of all financial flows in that by earning the highest profits possible a company will increase reserves and liquidity. X_4 examined TNW which, of course, is in itself a measure of cumulative profitability. Because Monsanto's past profitability, as distinct from its other flows examined so far, was largely non-existent prior to 1983 (1982 showed a profit of £41 k only), and X_4 returned a predictably low measurement (2.6). Y, on the other hand, compensates in two ways. Firstly, by virtue of its measurement of per cent rather than times cover (multiple), Y provides a relatively high number, which despite the equalized weightings makes latest (annual) profitability a key determinant of model scores—almost 40 per cent of the total model power in Monsanto's case. Secondly, Y views profitability in an actual rather than a forecast measure. This, of course, gives dimension to the findings of X_4 at the same time as tempering the forecasting element (μ) of X_4 with actual earnings ability given prominence. Taken in sum, the compensatory mechanism at work between X_{1-4} and Y ensures that model findings will be synoptically indicative. This is especially important in credit applications where debt-service ability must be the prime consideration. Profitability, as such, does not provide adequate information about comfort margins left for the servicing of debt. Neither does a profitability measure, in and of itself, say anything of liquidity—or the illiquidity brought about by overtrading. Finally, profitability makes only a veiled reference to the capital adequacy of a firm. High profitability can, in other words, be due to good luck, brilliant management, and splendid products priced well, with the whole operation financed adequately, or the high margins can be due to disproportionate earnings off an inadequate capital base. Overtrading, in such a case, would be a symptom of the undercapitalization. A firm may not necessarily overtrade, but still may have insufficient capital for expansion. Capitalization, accordingly, can be considered both from current and long-term standpoints.

The most important indicator of the expanded model's performance must be a comparison of its individual and holistic findings with Monsanto's 1984 results. These, after all, were the results being forecast. Figure 5.5 gives a tabulation.

Ratio	Description	1984 values (non-µ)	(£'000s) Scores	Model findings (µ)	Deviation (points)
X_1	GCF−CD/e	$\frac{89{,}328 - 12{,}563}{5{,}000}$ = 15.4		21.8	+6.4
+					
X_2	AFC/e	$\frac{260{,}744 \times 0.25}{5{,}000}$ = 13.0		6.4	−6.6
+					
X_3	NWC/e	$\frac{82{,}437}{5{,}000}$ = 16.5		9.8	−6.7
+					
X_4	TNW/TL+e	$\frac{232{,}563}{124{,}930}$ = 1.9		2.6	+0.7
+					
Y	PTP/CE	$\frac{94{,}101}{296{,}207} \times 100$ = 31.8		26.8	−5.0
Synoptic score: (unweighted)			78.6	67.4	−11.2
Synoptic score: (×0.20)			15.7	13.5	−2.2

Figure 5.5 Tabulation of expanded model's performance. Monsanto PLC and subsidiaries

Summary

Figure 5.5 shows that the expanded model forecast Monsanto's 1984 figures holistically within a deviation of −2.2 points. As we are considering only extrapolations made from historical data, we cannot account for whatever internal or external factors enabled the group to turn in holistically stronger results than those forecast. The model's accuracy, however, is significantly high. The model gave a forecast debt cover of 13.5 whilst the company's actual results suggested a cover of 15.7. Most interestingly, the two profitability measurements X_4 and Y provided the most accurate forecasts with respective deviations of +0.7 and −5.0. X_3 measuring normalized working capital over exposure showed the highest deviation: −6.7 points, followed by X_2 indicating averaged free capital over exposure. As both measures are highly speculative in terms of what or what not to include in the computations, the relatively high degree of deviation is not overly surprising. X_1 measuring net liquid funds servicing ability for the particular exposure showed a deviation of +6.4. The deviation is possibly accounted for by the speculative element in determining current debt which is deducted from gross cashflow. Apart from deviation due to speculative elements already mentioned, forecasting (µ) predicated not only on speculative computations but also, on historic trends, accounts for the variances. In sum, the final −2.2 points deviation from the group's 1984 figures is, in our opinion, numerically tolerable—deviating as it does on the side of prudence—as well as highly satisfactory from the forecasting standpoint.

Debt-cover, as understood by the model, is synoptic, applying to all the measurement components of the model. These components aimed at summing the most salient financial flows of the company. These flows were taken to be profitability, liquidity, capital adequacy, and debt-service ability. Both forecasting devices and potential credit exposure were added in all but one profitability measure (Y). The synoptic score indicated that Monsanto's forecast cover for debt including a £5 m exposure could fall in the ratio of 13.5 before obligations could not be met. Prudential measures taken by the model included compensatory ratios (X_1 and Y), the reductive element of equalized weighting, use of the harmonic mean in the treatment of trend, and adjustments to all ratios save Y to 'match time', i.e. to bring past, present, and future time into alignment. Thus, purely historic data was not contrasted with present or future data.

The model score indicates that ample cover for the £5 m exposure should exist over the subsequent two accounting periods. Monsanto's 1984 audited results indicate that such cover existed. When the Group's 1985 results are published, it is likely that available cover will continue to exist, if not increase, given the Group's increasingly strong position in the market.

Most importantly, the model findings in no way violate common sense according to the Group's past performance and forecast performance. Possibly, the forecasts provided by the model err on the side of pessimism rather than optimism. Generally speaking, in credit analysis, this is to be desired.

The operation of the model, despite the detailed spreading of data and computations required, give the analyst a synopsis of the varied important financial flows and performance indicators contributing to the results of a large company and its subsidiaries. Piecemeal examination of individual flows, accounting numbers, and performance indicators, on the other hand, cannot afford the same degree of analytic cohesion provided by a holistic model. Ideally, this model should be used together with supplementary data and individual examination of historic information. Practically speaking, such intensive analysis is not always possible. In that event, use of a wide-ranging and forecasting measurement model minimizes the risk of overlooking important facts. The spreadsheets leading to model inputs, as well as the individual ratio findings and the synoptic 'score', all serve to highlight companies' financial condition from a variety of levels. The consideration of concepts, such as profitability, from different angles can only result in a more truly indicative treatment of those concepts. Treatments that are more indicative necessarily result in more effective credit opinions.

Sources

Bathory, A., *Predicting Corporate Collapse*, Financial Times Business Information, Chapter 8, pp. 115–148.
de Mesquita, A. G., *Questions and Answers: Business Mathematics and Statistics*, Longman, London, 1978, p. 131.
Monsanto PLC, *Annual Report and Accounts*, 1979–1984.
Shock, J. *Capital Allowances*, Oyez, London, 1984, pp. 37–96.
Townsley, J., and Jones, R., *Numeracy and Accounting*, Polytech Publishers, Stockport, 1979, Chapter 30, pp. 303–322.

Date	Purpose	Builder	Formula	Weighting
1968	Forecasting insolvency/collapse quoted mfr cos. US	Altman	$Z = 0.012X_1 + 0.014X_2 + 0.003X_3 + 0.006X_4 + 0.999X_5$ $X1$:WC/TA $X2$:Ret Earnings/TA $X3$:EBIT/TA $X4$:Mkt value equity/Bk val of TD $X5$:Sales/TA	MDA
1972	Forecasting insolvency/collapse unquoted and quoted concerns UK	Lis	$Z = 0.063A + 0.092B + 0.57C + 0.001D$ A:WC/TA B:EBIT/TA C:Tot re earnings/TA D:Tot net worth/TD	MDA
1974	Forecasting insolvency/collapse quoted mftg concerns UK	Taffler	$Z = c_0 + c_1X_1 + c_2X_2 + c_3X_3 + c_4X_4 + c_5X_5$ $X1$:EBIT/opening TA $X2$:TL net cap emp $X3$:Quick assets/TA $X4$:WC/net worth $X5$:Stock-turn	MDA
1977	Forecasting insolvency/collapse listed industrial concerns UK	Taffler	$Z = c_0 + c_1X_1 + c_2X_2 + c_3X_3 + c_4X_4$ $X1$:PTP/Average CL $X2$:CL/TL $X3$:CL/TA $X4$:No credit interval	MDA
1984	Forecasting insolvency/collapse multiple-sector concerns/quoted and non-quoted US/UK	Bathory	$Y = 0.20 \left(\sum x_{1-5} \right)$ $X1$:GCF/CD $X2$:PTP/CE $X3$:Equity/CL $X4$:TNW/TL $X5$:WC/TA	Equalized

Figure 5.6 Resumé of main financial models discussed

Date	Purpose	Builder	Formula	Weighting
1985	Risk classification/mod accts cos/multiple sectors US/UK	Bathory	$RD = 0.125\left(\sum x_{1-8}\right)$ $X1$:NP/CL $X2$:WC-stock/exp $X3$:Equity/CL+exp $X4$:NP/cap emp $X5$:Net tang assets/TL $X6$:NA/exp $X7$:TA/TD+exp $X8$:NP+depcn/CD	Equalized
1985	Solvency classification/mod accts cos/multiple-sectors US/UK	Bathory	$YP = 0.20\left(\sum x_{1-5}\right)$ $X1$:NP+estd depcn/CD $X2$:NP−extraord items/cap emp $X3$:Equity/CL $X4$:NTA/TL $X5$:Normalized WC/TA	Equalized
1986	Averaged free capital–cover multiple sectors UK/US	Bathory	$AFC = 0.25\left(\sum x_{1-4}\right)/y$ $X1$:NCF−CD $X2$:WC $X3$:Normalized WC $X4$:Tots gen from ops-CL	Equalized
1986	Forecasting debt-cover/ multiple-sectors/ UK/US	Bathory	$\Delta = 0.20\left(\sum \mu x_{1-4}\right) + (Y)$ $X1$:µGCF−µCD/exp $X2$:µAFC/exp $X3$:µNorm WC/exp $X4$:µTNW/TL+exp Y :PTP/cap emp × 100 µ = harmonic mean of $\bar{x}$ and $\overline{\%}$ trends	Equalized

Figure 5.6 *(Concluded)*

6

THE CALCULATION OF SHORT-TERM SURPLUS FUNDING

Net working assets

A variety of computations exist for the measurement of net liquid surpluses. These include such quantities as:

1. Working capital
2. Gross cashflow
3. Net cashflow
4. Normalized working capital
5. Net working assets
6. Working worth
7. Averaged free capital

These measures quantify current, or short-term, cash or near-cash items to be used in financing operations. Additionally, these as well as other measures can be cast in ratio form to give proportion to the measurements. Examples of such ratios are:

Working capital/total assets
Gross cashflow/current debt
Net cashflow-current debt/trade creditors
Normalized working capital/credit exposure
Net working assets/turnover
Working worth/current liabilities
Averaged free capital/working capital

Broadly speaking, each of these measurements is concerned with liquidity. Items 1, 2, 3, 4, and 7 have been discussed earlier in this writing. Let us now consider the concept of net working assets, as set forth by the analyst R. Hale in his book, *Credit Analysis*, 1983. Hale proposes a distinction between current and less-current liabilities. For instance, dividend payment is viewed as a current liability item, but not as a 'working account'. Working accounts, according to Hale, are assets or liabilities that move with the level of turnover. These would include:

Accounts receivable
Accounts payable
Stock (including WIP)

Excluded from these accounts are cash and short-term debt. This is justified on the grounds that the computation of net working assets (NWA) is made to find cash or the want of it from purchasing, manufacturing, selling and collection of the proceeds. This, Hale calls cash from operations. NWA are calculated as shown in Figure 6.1.

Beginning balances: February 1, 19X0		ending balances: April 30, 19X0
Inventories	$960	$1,430
Work-in-progress	1,425	1,960
Accounts receivable	2,400	4,175
Accounts payable	(853)	(1,042)
Accrued expenses	(460)	(745)
Net working assets	3,472	5,778
Cash	250	350
Plant and machines	6,400	6,000
Total net assets	10,122	12,128

Three months to April 30: Sales	$4,000
Cost of goods sold	(1,500)
Depreciation	(400)
Other expenses	(94)
Profit before tax	2,006

Cash from operations, however, is not so easily found, and we must first perform a simple transaction analysis, recording the sales and expenses as follows:

	Cash	Assets Net working assets	Plant	Liabilities and owner's equity
February 1, 19X0	$250	$3,472	$6,400	$10,122
1. Sales		+4,000		+4,000
2. Cost of goods sold		(1,500)		(1,500)
3. Depreciation			(400)	(400)
4. Other expenses		(94)		(94)
5. Cash from operations	+100	(100)		
April 30, 19X0	350	5,778	6,000	12,128

Figure 6.1 Computation of net working assets. Reproduced by permission of John Wiley and Sons Inc.

As Hale observes in Figure 6.1, cash from operations cannot be easily determined without performing a transaction analysis (see Figure 6.2). Cash from operations can also be determined by adding back depreciation to net profit and deducting the change in NWA:

Net profit:	2,006
Depreciation:	400
Gross cashflow:	2,406
Less	
Change in NWA:	2,306
Cash from ops:	100

Hale points out that the notion of gross cashflow as net profit plus depreciation is valid only when there is no change from period to period in NWA. As NWA necessarily fluctuate with the normal operations of the business and inflation, the likelihood of nil change in NWA is remote.

	19X8	19X9	19X0
Cash	$9	$15	$25
Inventory	210	295	436
Accounts receivable	240	336	470
Net plant	400	525	650
	859	1,171	1,581
Accounts payable	126	177	247
Accrued expenses	100	143	201
Short-term debt	83	181	353
Owner's equity	550	670	780
	859	1,171	1,581
Sales	1,714	2.400	3,360
Cost of goods sold	1,028	1,440	2,016
Selling general and administrative expense	257	360	420
Depreciation	88	125	175
Research and development	100	136	190
Earnings before taxes	241	339	559
Taxes	(120)	(169)	(279)
Net income	121	170	280
Dividends	50	50	70
Retained earnings	70	120	110
Net working assets	224	311	458
Working capital	150	145	130
Capital expenditure	224	250	300

Figure 6.2 Transaction analysis. Reproduced by permission of John Wiley & Sons, Inc.

At the end of the proverbial day, what does NWA along with the distinction between funds from operations and cash from operations tell us in a credit analytical sense? Funds from operations are defined by Hale as sales less the costs of sales and other cash-related expenses. Cash from operations is found by deducting the change in NWA from funds from operations.

In our view, Hale's total concept is interesting but practically speaking, flawed. From the general analytical standpoint, the purpose in examining the sources of corporate funds is to measure debt-service capacity. This capacity or ability can be taken to apply to individual flows, such as gross cashflow, or from reservoirs to which flows contribute, e.g. balances at bank. The analyst with an understanding of how companies work will know that the available funds from which obligations are met are necessarily composite. A debt, in other words, can be settled in full from cash derived from a variety of sources. From the analyst's point of view, then, it is a key consideration that all or at least many of the potential/actual sources of cash either currently perform optimally or are, at the very least, forecast to perform sufficiently well to allow the company to meet its current obligations including the credit in question.

Hale distinguishes between cash and net working assets, and this distinction appears at the outset on his exposition. In practical terms, however, cash will be of far greater import to grantors of credit than the schematic balance between accounts receivable and accounts payable. As the analyst will rarely, if ever, be privy to adequate current information as to settlement times between receivables and payables, he approximates by the computation of creditor and debt-turn, as we have already seen. To make what is an artificial distinction between cash and trading balances, appears to us to say nothing significant about real net liquid funds to finance the business in the short term.

Secondly, Hale's inclusion of stock plus WIP, though justified by the concept it is trying to demonstrate, does not give analysts any the clearer picture of liquidity. If, in other words, stock is to be included in a treatment of liquid assets, surely it is incorrect to take work-in-progress into the calculation. From a menu of items making up stock, say, raw materials, consumables, WIP, goods for sale and resale, the strictest normalization would allow only raw materials and consumables as truly liquid assets in most manufacturing businesses. In other operations such as retail groceries, goods for sale would be allowed. The treatment of stock is, accordingly, varied of necessity. On the other hand, the wholesale acceptance of stock into what is intended as a liquidity-based concept (NWA/cash from operations) is, in our opinion, faulty.

Thirdly, the concept itself is abstruse. The most practicable concepts are simple. To 'operate' Hale's concept leading to a statement of cash from operations (which, strictly speaking, leaves out of account cash balances in the calculation of NWA), requires three main sets of computations: restatement of balance sheet for computing NWA; restatement of profit and loss account and possibly notes to the accounts for sales and sales-related data, e.g. depreciation; and finally, preparation of a transaction analysis. Why go to such trouble when the basic concept of NWA and cash from operations may or may not be the sole source of funds for the settlement of debts? In all probability, Hale's cash from operations will not be the only source. His concept, accordingly, runs counter to the all-inclusive notion of funding. This, as we have suggested, considers the total sources of funds, chiefest among them, profit from trading, net interest receivable, and gains from asset sales and credits from extraordinary items. Treating these all-inclusively can alter the standard notion of gross cashflow. Hale, on the other hand, is making distinctions of a very different order. In essence, he appears to be concerned with a current trading assessment. In the long-term, no one would gainsay the importance of assessing whether or not a company can fund its short as well as long-term debt solely from trading. Asset sales and tax credits cannot be expected to keep contributing to cash inflows on an annual basis. The crucial consideration, however, must lie with operational assessment as well as trading assessment. Notwithstanding the importance of a company's trading performance and the cash proceeds from it, the company's total operating performance is more important in judging whether the firm can meet current and potential obligations. In brief, Hale's concept of NWA and determination of cash from operations must be regarded as only parts of a total picture. A better (in the sense of being more representative) view of liquid funds is gained by a computation of normalized working capital from which portions of stock have been removed along with any other current assets that are questionably quickly realizable for cash. A more complete picture of earnings—which are the source of cash—can be gained by an analysis of profit and whatever items represented it. An all-inclusive view of profit would take into account extraordinary gains/losses. Debt priority schedules, if adequate information is available, and gross cashflow computations tell the analyst more about the results of total operations. Even without reference to holistic models, these standard analytical tools provide more relevant information more quickly and easily than the somewhat jejune restatement of accounts that Hale has proposed.

Hale's basic motive in proposing these restatements is, however, a perfectly sound one. He is trying to convert accrual accounting information into cashflow information. This mirrors a general and salutary trend in credit analysis as a discipline

Working worth

A more attractive and judgementally simple concept centring on the computation of short-term surplus funds for credit purposes was advanced by the analyst J. Coleshaw in 1984. This is the calculation of working worth. Working worth is compared with the results of a four-ratio formula calling for balance sheet, non-normalized data. From the ratio-based formula, Coleshaw evolved a scale of risk ratings against which percentages of working worths can be used to assign credit limits.

Coleshaw initially attempts to measure the general liquidity and the stability of a balance sheet by using the following ratio-based formula:

> Ratio 1: Current assets/current liabilities
> Ratio 2: Current assets-stock/current liabilities
> Ratio 3: Short-term debt/equity
> Ratio 4: Total debt/equity

Ratios 1 and 2 are the familiar current and acid-test ratios. Short-term debt in ratio 3 is taken to mean current liabilities, while in ratio 4, total debt is interpreted as total liabilities and equity is represented by called-up capital plus reserves. The formula thus operates:

$$(CA/CL + Quick\ Assets/CL) - (CL/E + TL/E)$$

The point is made that considered as individual ratio groupings, an inverse relationship obtains between the two groups in that ideally, the liquidity measures should be as high as possible whereas the debt/equity measures should be as low as possible. Additionally, it is argued that because this formula operates with four ratios, unrealistic emphasis cannot be placed on any one ratio measurement.

Figure 6.3 shows examples of four companies' data run through the formula. Coleshaw's interpretation of the results follows.

THE CALCULATION OF SHORT-TERM SURPLUS FUNDING 143

	Example 1	Example 2	Example 3	Example 4
Current	2 (:1)	1 (:1)	0.8 (:1)	1.5 (:1)
Quick	1 (:1)	0.5 (:1)	0.4 (:1)	1.0 (:1)
ST Debt/Equity	0.75 (:1)	1.25 (:1)	2.9 (:1)	2.5 (:1)
Total Debt/Equity	1.25 (:1)	2.00 (:1)	2.9 (:1)	3.5 (:1)
Score	−1	−1.75	−4.6	−3.5

Figure 6.3 Working worth: Analysis of data (1). Reproduced by permission of the Institute of Credit Management

Examples	1	2	3	4
working capital	300,000	800,000	(10,000)	100,000
net worth	800,000	300,000	100,000	(10,000)
working worth	550,000	550,000	55,000	55,000

Figure 6.4 Working worth: Analysis of data (2). Reproduced by permission of the Institute of Credit Management

Rating	Risk description	Level of confidence	Working worth %
−4.6 or less	High	Low	0
−3.9 to −4.59	----	----	2.5
−3.2 to −3.89	----	----	5
−2.5 to −3.19	----	----	7.5
−1.8 to −2.49	----	----	10
−1.1 to −1.79	Limited	Medium	12.5
−0.4 to −1.09	----	----	15
−0.3 to −0.39	----	----	17.5
1 to 0.29	----	----	20
1 or more	Low	High	25

Figure 6.5 Working worth: Analysis of data (3). Reproduced by permission of the Institute of Credit Management

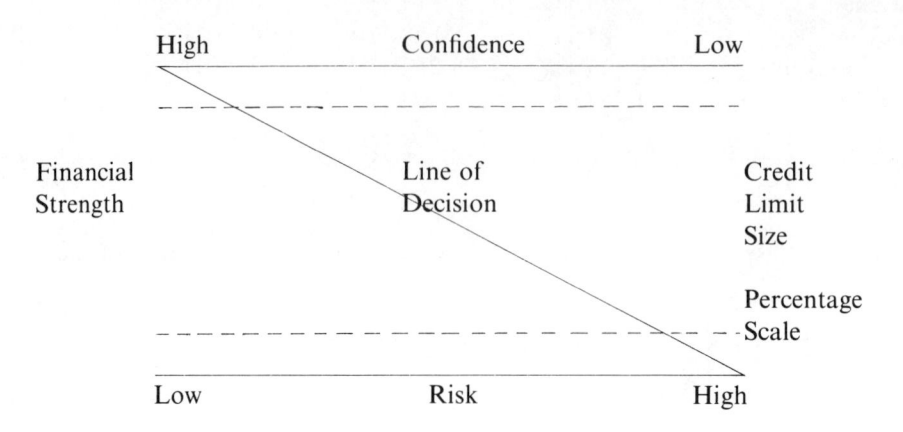

```
                High         Confidence        Low
                ─────────────────────────────────
                ─ ─ ─╲─ ─ ─ ─ ─ ─ ─ ─ ─ ─ ─ ─ ─ ─
                      ╲
      Financial        ╲   Line of           Credit
      Strength          ╲  Decision          Limit
                         ╲                   Size

                                             Percentage
                ─ ─ ─ ─ ─ ─ ─ ─ ─ ─ ─ ─ ─ ╲─ ─ ─Scale

                Low          Risk          High
```

Credit decision graph

Figure 6.6 Working worth: Analysis of data (4). Reproduced by permission of the Institute of Credit Management

Example 1 shows a 'normal' state in which current assets are adequate to discharge current liabilities according to ratio 1; and according to ratio 2, even after deduction of stock. Ratios 3 and 4 indicate that total debt on both measures only marginally exceeds net worth (Coleshaw's equity measure). Coleshaw then 'reasonably assumes' that prospects look favourable for this company. Strictly speaking, of course, no forecast element has been taken into account by the static ratios used throughout the formula. Secondly, example 1 being a snapshot or static picture of the company as at its accounting date, has not been, at this stage, brought up to date by any supplementary data. Finally, no comparisons have been given for 'scores' resulting from previous accounting years. On these grounds, we should not incline towards forecasting anything, and would restrict our own interpretation of example 1 as a static, one-time only indication of the relationship between certain assets and certain liabilities. That having been said, Coleshaw's example is quite clear in its presentation of adequate asset cover on these measures. Example 2 indicates an inadequacy of asset cover (liquidity on the one hand, and debt/equity on the other). Coleshaw suggests that this inadequacy may be caused by market over-capacity, slow stock-turn, and increased borrowings. Liquidity levels are seen to be perilously low and the lower profit level shown by smaller equity in this example contrasts unfavourably with the debt mix.

Example 3 gives a worsened picture in which short-term debt cannot be serviced by current assets and where borrowing levels are extremely high. Coleshaw suggests that if this represents a private company, it is probably trading with the continued support of its bankers. If it is a subsidiary company, careful assessment of the parent will be required. Example 4 indicates a firm with an apparently high liquidity position achieved at the expense of high gearing.

Given that the operation of this type of formula gives an indication of the financial strengths and weaknesses of a balance sheet, Coleshaw points out that the assessment and determination of credit limits depends upon the following factors:

1. The circumstances giving rise to the need for credit.
2. The apparent financial capability of the potential debtor.

Coleshaw holds that if, for any reason, the credit level required by the first factor exceeds the notional level of the second, a greater credit risk is entailed.

At this stage, Coleshaw touches on the common 'yard-stick' approach to balance sheets adopted by many analysts and credit managers. Totally arbitrary limits are imposed by these methods. For instance, a potential credit limit may not exceed 25 per cent of net worth or 15 per cent of working capital, or even worse, 100 per cent of called-up capital. Reliance upon such arbitrary measures utterly rules out a consideration of corporate idiosyncracy and has the further flaw of failing to take any account of the dynamic nature of companies. By this token, no forecasting element is included in the assessment. Interestingly, Coleshaw appears to favour a yard-stick approach though his basic concept, turning as it does, on a holistic assessment of liquidity and debt/equity, greatly improves upon the common, univariate assessment measures generally assumed by a yard-stick measurement.

Having set up a table of risks suggested by his four examples in Figure 6.3, Coleshaw then advances his own yard-stick measurement: working worth. Working worth will then be looked at against the rating and risk description scales extrapolated from his initial example (and presumably, from other work in this area). From the comparison, a percentage indicator of working worth will form the yard-stick against which credit limits can be determined.

Working worth, as proposed by Coleshaw, is:

$$\frac{\text{Net assets (equity)} + \text{working capital}}{2}$$

The formula is justified on the following grounds. Firstly, the point is made that credit limits based on a single figure can be either excessively generous or restrictive. Figure 6.4 provides illustrations; and Coleshaw's point is well-founded. Secondly, the computation is justified on the grounds that increasing companies display a low level of net current assets, coupled with a declension of net assets. Given a chronic background of economic stagnation, high interest rates, and increasing insolvencies, this point too is reasonably taken. Thirdly, the averaging mechanism of Coleshaw's working worth computation gives added dimension to the commoner univariate yard-stick measurement method. This point, in our view, is undoubted.

Figure 6.6 introduces Coleshaw's credit decision graph which illustrates the main factors contributing to a credit decision. Financial strength is called the key axis. The higher the financial strength, the greater the level of confidence reposed in the company; the greater the potential credit limit, and the lower the risk. Coleshaw's line of decision, which is fixed, can be used to plot the effect on risk, confidence and size potential of the credit limit at any point by drawing vertical and horizontal lines—the broken lines on the graph. It is added that in order to make practical use of this graph, scales are needed to measure financial strength and to determine the size of credit limits. By the formulaic rating technique described earlier, and by employing working worth as his yard-stick, Coleshaw developed a matrix scale to use in conjunction with the graph. This matrix is given in Figure 6.5.

Harkening back to example 1 in his formula, Coleshaw suggests that a score of 1 indicates a healthy liquidity and debt/equity position. Example 3, with a -4.6 score showed an unhealthy position. He accordingly chooses these scores as the upper and lower limits to his rating range, and adds that, in his experience, most companies' scores fall within this range. From the credit decision graph, the credit limit size-scale is designed to recommend a percentage of working worth—the higher the rating, the higher the percentage. His range here is 0 to 25 per cent. The tacit assumption being that it would be imprudent to assign a credit limit greater than 25 per cent of working worth to any company. Of course, as a working assumption, this must be open to many questions. According to Coleshaw, companies with a rating of -4.6 and below are in all likelihood too weak to justify advancing any credit, while the rating of 1 and above justifies a higher credit limit. He points out at this stage that both the rating scale and percentage scale can be adjusted to suit personal perferences or corporate objectives.

Coleshaw then calculates potential limits for point A and B marked on the line of decision. His example assumes a common working worth of £1 m and the rating of point A is -0.4. The potential credit limit is $17\frac{1}{2}$ per cent of working worth, or £175,000. Assuming a rating for point B of -3.2, the credit limit would be 5 per cent of working worth, or £50,000. All other points along the line of decision can thus be pin-pointed by obtaining a rating, and the credit limit can be assigned by use of the percentage scale.

In sum, Coleshaw's concept of working worth is adequately flexible and simple. Despite its ultimate reliance on the yard-stick approach, the yard-stick has been somewhat broadened by the averaging process used to obtain working worth.

The concept, however, is open to a good many questions. Provided that these questions can be satisfactorily answered, working worth as a basis for the determination of credit limits can be proved a useful tool in analysis.

Most importantly, while Coleshaw is using a holistic approach both in rating and in determining working worth, has he selected the most indicative measures as ratio components in his formula as well as the best measures for his working worth computation? The central consideration of any credit facility must always be, can the debtor service the credit? Any reference to historical accounting data will necessarily limit what analysts can say about debt-service ability. Debt, however, is not serviced from equity, net assets, or tangible net worth. It is serviced from cashflows in a dynamic representation and in a static representation, such as Coleshaw's, from net surplus short-term funds. First of all, there is no reason why analysts trying to measure debt-service ability need restrict themselves to balance sheets alone. They can refer to the profit and loss account and other statements and notes. From the profit and loss account, for instance, we can compute gross cashflow or net cashflow. From the balance sheet, we can calculate any number of debt measurements or totals. Coleshaw's use of current ratio and acid-test ratio as liquidity indicators in his formula are, in our view, blunted weapons. Firstly, they are, as argued earlier, static measures. Secondly, they are wholly artificial measurements, and therefore, distortive. They do not, in other words, indicatively reflect the normal operations of a company. A considerable range of alternate ratios could be used to give a more indicative idea of a firm's ability to service debt—in this case, additional debt. Additional debt would seem to suggest use of at least one net hybrid. For example: gross cashflow/current liabilities + requested credit. Admittedly, Coleshaw is attempting to formulate credit limits by this model where none existed. In this event, such a ratio as GCF/CL + existing credit + arrears outstanding might be used where the applicant was an existing customer. Where the applicant was not an existing customer, an indicative liquidity (debt-service) measure might be: GCF/current debt + x per cent of trade creditors. Whatever liquidity measures chosen, care should be taken to make them dynamic rather than static or purely schematic.

Next, Coleshaw does not appear to focus very pointedly on debt. Debt is taken to be current liabilities and total liabilities. The key consideration here must be the priority of debt even if surplus balances exist. In speaking of priority, we are not confining ourselves to that term's legal meaning alone. We are speaking of pecking order in settlement. Net surplus balances as shown by accounting statements or ratios derived from them can only schematize. Any notions of debt priority must be made up of especially selected items measured against certain inflows. The net balances of these give a better indication of liquidity left to discharge unsecured or other non-priority obligations. These, presumably, are what Coleshaw has in mind. Accordingly, we feel it would give more representative results to measure gross cashflow against priority debt, or current debt with or without a certain percentage of other obligations, than Coleshaw's CA/CL and quick assets/CL.

Thirdly, Coleshaw does not provide for any forecasting element in his model. Use of dynamic rather than static ratios grouped in certain ways would go a way towards updating purely historical accounting data of varying ages. It would not, however, totally eliminate the age gap. This gap means essentially that on Coleshaw's formula, we are determining a present or a future credit limit on past information alone.

Fourth, does working worth as a yard-stick violate common sense? Interestingly, working worth can exceed working capital, as in Coleshaw's examples 1 and 3. These examples are possibly his crucial ones as they are derived from a normal and an unhealthy company respectively. In example 1, the healthy firm shows a working capital of £300 k and a working worth of £550 k. In example 3, working capital is a net deficiency of £10 k, and working worth stands at £55 k. The averaging process taking account of net worth causes these working worth measures. But are they, in and of themselves, reflective of the real world of companies? Firstly, do companies 1 and 3 actually have surplus liquid working funds of £550 k and £55 k respectively? Taken purely as a snapshot, working capital is surely more indicative, as schematic as it is, than such a measure. As argued earlier, no debt will actually be serviced from net worth. The use of net worth as a 'corrective' to working capital must then be misconceived. By this argument, working capital might have been averaged with normalized working capital to obtain a working worth that better reflected surplus liquid condition. In any event, the fact that in two key examples, Coleshaw's working worth figures exceed working capital cannot truly be common sensible either from the standpoint of liquidity or from the nicer standpoint of debt-service ability.

In sum, Coleshaw's yard-stick approach is neither nicely enough chosen nor is it in our opinion, wide-ranging enough with respect to the basic model or formula. These points having been made, Coleshaw determines credit limits as percentages of working worth. This procedure ensures that if for holistic scores of 1 or above, 25 per cent of working worth will be the upper limit, the credit limit itself should fall within rather than exceeding working capital in most cases. Thus, in example 1, 25 per cent of working worth would be £137,500 which would easily be contained by the working capital figure of £300,000. Effectively, on this example, 46 per cent of working capital has been given as a credit limit. Given that all credit applications must be judged individually, and also, given that working capital is a rather poor and single yard-stick in itself, the credit limit looks very high. It may be that the compensating percentage scale is still not reducing limits within common sense liquidity levels to a sharp enough degree. This presumably will be the case when net worth figures are high in respect of net current assets.

These criticisms and questions do not, however, detract from the basically common sense and multivariate approach taken by Coleshaw. In his approach, he has considered companies holistically by using a multiple ratio formula. He has also attempted to determine credit limits based on a hybrid notion of liquidity. As a notion of real liquidity, working worth must, in our view, fail as 50 per cent of the power of this measure is based on a non-liquid quantity—net worth. If working worth, on the other hand, is intended to be a true amalgam of liquidity measurement and debt-service ability (as we believe Coleshaw intends it), the notion is conceptually more valid, though still flawed as it relies upon a static quantity, net worth, instead of a flow against which debt can be more indicatively measured.

The working worth concept does, however, suggest that with certain substitutions, a similar approach might result in even fairer credit decisions. Equalized or other weightings could be used to 'smooth' component ratios. The liquidity ratios and debt-service ratios could be chosen to yield nicer measurements. For example, working capital could be sharpened by normalization. Priority debt might be used to good effect in lieu of current liabilities. Issue could be taken with Coleshaw's use of equity which he understands as the same quantity as net assets, which, in turn, he takes as net worth. Understandings as these require expansion. As a debt-servicing medium, for instance, neither is equity a truly significant medium, nor can certain non-distributable reserves, i.e. a revaluation reserve account, even be schematized as a servicing medium.

The concept of working worth can easily be 'improved' to be made more representative. For example, use of the harmonic mean would throw a lower average than a straight division by 2. In giving a lower figure, this measure of working worth might sit more easily against both working capital and whatever was chosen to place against it. By this token, the working worth average for Coleshaw's example 1 was £550 k against a working capital of £300 k. The harmonic mean, however, would be £436,364 using the original £800 k net worth figure. Better liquidity indicators might be:

Averaged free capital
Normalized working capital
Trading balance (trade debtors − trade creditors)
Trading differential (difference between debt-turn and creditors' turnover in £)

The forecasting element lacking could be easily included by averages and the computation of harmonic means from past figures. Accordingly, a new working worth formula might be along the following lines:

$$\frac{\mu AFC + \mu \text{Trading balance} - \mu \text{Current debt} + \mu NWC}{3}$$

where μ = harmonic means of historical averages.
Another possible improvement on the working worth concept might be something of an amalgam of Coleshaw's and Hale's ideas. Hale's central thesis is that cash from operations

THE CALCULATION OF SHORT-TERM SURPLUS FUNDING

rather than funds from operations furnishes companies with the main means of discharging debt. Bankers looking at safety margins for their loans will thus focus upon cashflow projections. As stated before, Hale's concept of NWA is intended to convert accrual accounting information into cashflow data. We have mentioned what we have considered to be flaws in his method of computation. Notwithstanding, Hale's central thesis is self-evidently valid. Coleshaw's work, on the other hand, suggests that more representative ratio components and more indicative free capital measurements can be used in the computation of overall risk scores and working worth.

Initially, let us consider whether Hale's net working assets can be arrived at more simply and more significantly. More simply, by cutting down on interpretive time and effort; and more significantly, by adding back quantities we know can and will be used to discharge debt. Among the foremost of these must be cash and marketable securities. Hale allows full levels of stock in the NWA computation. This, we suggested earlier, was unrealistic as varying quantities of stock were bound to be more or less quickly realizable as cash. Accordingly, let us net out slow-moving stock and add to NWA only fast-moving inventories. The concept of NWA hinges upon items that move up or down with sales. Therefore, let us in a typical set of accounts take:

Current assets
Fast-moving stock
+
Trade debtors
+
Sundry debtors
+
Prepayments
+
Cash and marketable securities

and for current liabilities, let us accept:
Trade creditors
+
Sundry creditors
+
Taxation
+
Accruals
+
Overdraft and current portions of loans payable

The difference between these current assets and current liabilities should give us net working assets. The increase/decrease in NWA from year to year deducted from funds from operations will give us cash from operations. This last will obviously be less than funds from operations which includes various non-trading based transactions.

150 PROBLEMS IN THE COMPUTATION AND INTERPRETATION OF DATA

This can then be abbreviated as follows:

> Normalized current assets
> Less
> Normalized current liabilities
> Equals
> Normalized working assets
> or
> NCA − NCL = NWA

Using Monsanto's consolidated accounts (Figure 3.1), the following values can be given to the NWA computation:

	£'000s	
NWA	*1984*	*1983*
Stock:		
Raw materials/consumables	11,476	11,376
Finished goods/resale goods	25,957	17,649
Trade debtors	35,775	31,056
Sundry debtors	8,153	4,188
Prepayments	6,299	2,718
Cash and mktble securities		
(short-term deposits)	16,165	14,930
	103,825	81,917
Less		
Trade creditors	14,099	13,857
Sundry creditors	—	67
Taxation	11,187	9,883
Accruals	4,398	6,125
Overdrafts	1,376	70
	31,060	30,002
NET WORKING ASSETS:	£72,765	£51,915
Increase in NWA:	£20,850	
Funds from operations:	114,800	
Less		
Increase in NWA:	20,850	
CASH FROM OPERATIONS:	93,950	

Our suggested alterations to Hale's NWA's format have effectively contributed £1,070,000 to Monsanto's cash from operations. Hale's format would have given NWA for 1984 of £62,916,000 (1983: £40,996,000), with an increase of NWA of £21,920,000 to deduct from funds from operations. Thus, Hale's computation would present cash from operations as about 80 per cent of total funds, whereas ours gives a higher figure of 82 per cent.

Note that in proposing the above format, we have vitiated Hale's original notion of accounting for all items that move up and down according to sales. We have omitted work-in-progress, interGroup trading accounts, and we have added back cash at bank and cash on deposit. In proposing this format, we are clearly less concerned with presenting items that move in accordance with sales than with giving a net total of liquid assets including cash. We believe that such a format gives analysts a more practical idea of monetary reservoirs for the settlement of debt.

In the computation of working worth, Coleshaw took the mean of working capital and net worth. Earlier, we suggested that a wider interpretation might be given by substituting different quantities. In this way, we could let working worth stand for:

$$WW = \bar{\mu} \text{ averaged free capital and cash from operations}$$

The harmonic mean of AFC and cash from operations should give us a figure below working capital for the latest period. Whilst this figure would be a strong indicator of monetary reservoirs for debt settlement, it still lacks the dimension Coleshaw sought for his original concept of working worth in that no mean has been taken between free capital and some measure of net worth. We can thus elect to take Coleshaw's net assets or some other measurement of net worth and make the necessary adjustments.

Net assets tend not to be the most significant measure of net worth for two reasons. First, the total assets less current and long-term liabilities making up net assets do not always take into account off-balance-sheet financings or material contingent liabilities/capital commitments. Secondly, intangible assets may be added into the total of assets. The realization of intangible assets for book value may or may not be difficult. Accordingly, we should choose tangible net worth calculated in the following manner as the final adjustment to the working worth computation:

TNW = Tangible fixed assets
+
Current assets
Less
Total liabilities
+
Contingent liabilities
+
Off-balance-sheet finance, e.g. leases
+
Capital commitments contracted and entered into

The adjusted working worth computation could then be expressed as:

$$\frac{\mu FC + TNW}{2}$$

where μFC = the harmonic mean of averaged free capital and cash from operations
TNW = Tangible net worth

Thus, if according to Monsanto's 1984 accounts, averaged free capital is £65,186,000 and cash from operations was £93,950,000, their harmonic mean would be:

$$\mu = \frac{2 \times 65.2 \times 94}{65.2 + 94} = 76{,}995{,}000$$

If tangible net worth for the company was £232,563,000 in 1984, we have the following:

$$WW = \frac{76{,}995 + 232{,}563}{2} = £154{,}779{,}000$$

Using Coleshaw's original rating scale, Monsanto's four ratios read as follow:

Current ratio:	2.5
Liquid ratio:	1.8
CL/equity:	0.23
Total debt/equity:	0.49
	5.02

and the company would accordingly represent a low risk, high level of confidence credit proposition. On Coleshaw's scale, it could receive 25 per cent of working worth as a credit limit. Using Coleshaw's suggested working worth computation, the company could thus receive a limit of £166.6 m. Using our adjusted computation, Monsanto would receive a limit of £38.7 m. This last represents some 44 per cent of 1984 working capital. The adjusted working worth limit does not violate common sense by exceeding net current assets, taking a yard-stick approach. Coleshaw's working worth limits may exceed working capital (as they have in this instance), and thus, look and feel logically odd to credit grantors.

It would appear that the adjustments made to Coleshaw's working worth concept yield prudent results in that figures fall below working capital and the surplus short-term capital measures used in the numerator are made up of wide-ranging and indicative figures (AFC and cash from operations [CO]). Furthermore, dimensionality is preserved and sharpened by usage of TNW in lieu of net assets. We believe that these adjustments intensify yet preserve Coleshaw's important concept. The adjusted working worth computation can be expressed as:

$$AWW = \frac{\bar{\mu}(AFC + CO) + TNW}{2}$$

where
$\quad$ AWW = Adjusted working worth
$\quad\quad$ $\bar{\mu}$ = harmonic mean between AFC and CO
$\quad$ TNW = Tangible net worth
$\quad$ AFC = Averaged free capital
$\quad\quad$ CO = Cash from operations
$\quad\quad\quad$ 2 = Constant averaging divisor

Projecting cashflows

For credit analytical considerations, there are essentially two types of cashflow projections. Firstly, forecasts. Secondly, resumés. As we have already noted, forecasts are extremely open to a wide range of error resulting from lack of first-hand knowledge of the operation and its market, over-optimism or over-pessimism, the supervention of extraordinary events, crudeness in forecasting techniques, misalignments in the actual flows of income and expenditure.

THE CALCULATION OF SHORT-TERM SURPLUS FUNDING

Some of these potential sources of error can be minimized by careful research, checking and rechecking of figures, conversance with and use of accepted forecasting techniques, the noting of justifications, and the preparation of a best, middle-of-the-road, and worst set of forecasts.

Concerning resumés, unless as in the case of the extended model elaborated earlier, we are attempting to forecast from a series of past figures, the cashflow projection should reflect accurately the data given in accepted accounting statements. The purpose of such

X Ltd
Cash Forecast £'000s for the (year) ended (31 December 19–2)

	TOTAL	Jan	Feb	Nov	Dec
CASH RECEIPTS					
Sales—Cash (Sch 1)					
—Credit (Sch 4)					
VAT (net receipts)					
Other income					
Sales of assets					
Other receipts					
TOTAL					
CASH PAYMENTS					
Materials—Credit (Sch 4)					
—Cash (Sch 1)					
Labour (Sch 1)					
Overheads (Sch 4)					
Taxation (Note 3)					
VAT (net payments)					
Capital expenditure (Note 1)					
Loan repayments					
Other					
TOTAL					
NET CASH FLOW (Note 2)					
BALANCE AT START					
BALANCE AT END					

Note:
1 Capital expenditure should be forecast in detail if required (Schedule 8).
2 Total cash receipts less cash payments.
3 Corporation Tax and ACT, excluding PAYE and NHI.

Figure 6.7 ABC Ltd: Cashflow projection (year 1). Reproduced by permission of 3i (Investors in Industry)

ABC Ltd
CASHFLOW PROJECTION
YEAR 1

MONTH	1	2	3	4	5	6	7	8	9	10	11	12	Total Year 1
	£'000s	£'000s	£'000s	£'000s	£'000s	£'000s	£'000s	£'000s	£'000s	£'000s	£'000s	£'000s	£'000s
RECEIPTS													
VAT receipts from Customs and Excise	—	—	—	5	—	—	8	—	—	25	—	38	38
	—	—	—	5	—	—	8	—	—	25	—	38	38
PAYMENTS													
Accounts payable	—	11	14	14	16	16	17	21	30	33	51	53	276
VAT on expenditure	—	1	2	2	2	3	3	7	10	8	11	12	61
	—	12	16	16	18	19	20	28	40	41	62	65	337
OUTFLOW FROM TRADING	—	(12)	(16)	(11)	(18)	(19)	(12)	(28)	(40)	(16)	62	(65)	(299)
CAPITAL EXPENDITURE	—	(2)	(4)	(9)	(9)	(9)	(11)	(35)	(54)	(35)	(37)	(45)	(250)
Net interest income	—	—	2	2	2	2	2	2	1	1	1	—	15
NET CASH OUTFLOW	—	(14)	(18)	(18)	(25)	(26)	(21)	(61)	(93)	(50)	(98)	(110)	(534)
OPENING REQUIREMENT	—	—	(14)	(32)	(50)	(75)	(101)	(122)	(183)	(276)	(326)	(424)	—
CLOSING REQUIREMENT carried forward to the Statement of Anticipated Funding	—	(14)	(32)	(50)	(75)	(101)	(122)	(183)	(276)	(326)	(424)	(534)	(534)

Figure 6.8 X Ltd: Cash forecast for the year ended 31 December 19–2. By permission of Deloitte, Haskins and Sells

resumés is to highlight the flow of cash during that accounting period. The flow of cash is crucial to highlight as it provides the means of support and discharge for credit.

Accordingly, on the one hand, the cashflow forecast is generally, and should be expected to be, fallible. The resumé cashflow projection, though subject to hiatuses due to lack of precise information, on the other hand, should be fundamentally accurate. Cashflow forecasts are thus speculation, albeit, with hope, informed speculation. Cashflow resumés are post mortems.

There is a tendency in credit analysis to enter into unnecessary and essentially immaterial speculation with regard to cashflows. The detail and difficulty of a large transaction analysis sheet make this clear. We have likewise seen cashflow resumés that attempt to provide so much detail that valuable time and attention is wasted. For working analysts in the trade credit sector, something of a broad brush approach is necessary if the volume normally handled by the credit department is to be reviewed effectively. Analytical routines demanded by banks, venture capitalists, and other financial institutions tend to be more specialised. This need not always be strictly necessary.

Figure 6.7 suggests a simple and straightforward format for cashflow forecasting purposes by Deloitte Haskins & Sells for entrepreneurs seeking to raise venture capital. Figure 6.8 gives the 3i suggested format for the same purpose. The 3i version is possibly more sophisticated as it calls for breakdowns of cash and credit sales as well as cash and credit payments for materials. Also, 3i provides for taxation which will be difficult and error-prone to calculate in advance. Finally, loan repayments are included in the 3i projection. These could possibly be existing loan repayments or estimated capital repayments and interest payments provided for 3i's capital. If this last applies, 3i's own margin of safety will prove less visible than it might have been had available cashflow preceded loan repayments deductions.

The Deloitte's cashflow projection (Figure 6.7) distinguishes clearly between direct and indirect costs of sales and capital expenditures. 'Payments' are represented by:

Materials
Labour
Other production costs
Marketing
Research and development
and
General and Administrative
VAT on expenditure and payments to HM Customs and Excise (which can be different)

Deducting the above payments from sales and VAT on sales and receipts from HM Customs and Excise gives the gross inflow/outflow of funds from trading. From this, capital expenditures, e.g. the purchase of equipment, is deducted. Net interest income/expenditure is added giving an opening balance. This balance is, of course, a requirement for cash and when added to or deducted from the next period's opening balance, a closing balance or requirement is obtained. This format presupposes that funding has not yet been injected, showing as it does, the funding requirement of the company from normal operations.

Cashflow resumés of historical accounting data involve the analyst in less speculation.

The safety or comfort margin for credit (including loans) can be calculated by cash from operations less capital expenditures and any required dividends and long-term debt payments less the amount of credit exposure or loan repayments.

Hale's format for this computation is:

> Net income after taxation
> +
> Depreciation and any non-cash charges
> *Funds from operations* (sub-total):
> Less
> Increases in net working assets
> *Cash from operations* (sub-total):
> Less
> Required capital expenditures
> Less
> Required dividends (if any)
> Less
> Other long-term debt payments
> *Available cashflow* (sub-total):
> Less
> Repayments of loan
> *Margin of safety*

Effects of added value on profits and cashflows

Analysts will notice information gaps of varying degrees between sales and profit in many UK company accounting statements. The following profit and loss account gives a good example:

	£ 1986
Turnover:	23,919
Net operating expenses:	20,821
Operating profit:	3,098
Interest receivable:	567
Pre-tax profit:	3,665
Taxation:	1,539
Profit after taxation:	£2,126

In the case of modified accounts, net operating expenses will often be the subject of notes. The itemizations shown by these notes will generally not be available for public inspection at the Registries.

The 1981 Companies Act offered UK firms two essential profit and loss account layouts. The first layout breaks down operating costs into the following functions:

Costs of sales
Production costs
Wages
Manufacturing costs
Materials purchase
Depreciation

Distribution costs
Shipment/delivery of goods to outlets/customers

Administrative expenses
Directors' fees
Auditors' fees
General office expenditures

The second layout presents operating costs by their nature:

Raw materials and consumables
Staff costs
Depreciation and amortization
Other external charges
Change in stock of finished goods and WIP

    These formats, according to Holmes and Sugden, reflect the increased disclosure requirements of the EEC Fourth Directive, and, therefore, bridge the information gap mentioned before. Holmes and Sugden point out that in the past, some companies included value added statements in their accounts to bridge this gap, but these companies may well discontinue the practice in the future.

    Use by analysts of the value added concept can be helpful in forecasting and projecting profits and cashflows. The concept is a simple one. The highest level of money is attracted into a business by sales, and the lowest level of money is permitted to leave the business through cost controls, and maximum efficient employment of materials. The difference between money coming in and flowing out is the added value.

    Added value is then used to pay employees and to service capital costs of interest on borrowings and depreciation. Added value also pays for profits as a percentage of total assets employed in order that future borrowings can be controlled.

    A comparatively opaque profit and loss account can thus be restated for added value assessment in the following way:

                  Turnover:
                  Less
                  Bought-in services and materials:
                  Added value (sub-total)
                  Less
                  Staff costs:
                  Plus
                  Interest receivable:
                  Less
                  Interest payable:

> Less
> Depreciation
> Less
> *Indirect expenses (administration)*:
> Profit before taxation (sub-total):

A difficulty in preparing forecasts of profits or cashflow is providing for the ripple effect. In other words, if sales increase by 10 per cent what effect will this have on profits? To answer this question and to provide for the necessary adjustments throughout the forecast accounting documents, assumptions must be made. These assumptions should be rooted as deeply as possible in a knowledge of the type of operation in question and its markets. This kind of knowledge will help analysts to avoid overly optimistic or overly pessimistic assumptions. Knowledge of operations and their markets will help to ensure that forecasts are kept within the bounds of common sense. For instance, given a working knowledge of the toy business and its markets, an analyst would not normally, and not without adequate justification, forecast a 25 per cent increase in sales during the month of February. Peak sales will probably be expected around late November/December and possibly rising again over the summer months if the company produces toys like surfboards or beachballs.

The profit and loss account, however, is extremely sensitive to much smaller increases or decreases. Profits form the chief source of cash from operations. Cash from operations, as we noted earlier, is the main reservoir for the settlement of obligations. Accordingly, without indulging in worst possible or best possible forecasts, analysts can appreciate the sensitivity of minimal increases or decreases on profits by making 1 per cent + or − assumptions. Such assumptions when coupled with a value added restatement of the profit and loss account can be useful in credit sanction in borderline cases when neither cashflow from trading nor profits adequately support a potential exposure.

To begin with, let us restate a fairly clear and healthy profit and loss account to show added value. Let us then make +/− 1 per cent assumptions at various stages and indicate the effects in percentage terms on key numbers. For this exercise, we can use Monsanto's accounts (Figure 3.1). The value-added restatement and sensitivity analysis would look as set out in Figure 6.9.

What does the isolation of added value and cost sensitivity restatement tell us? Firstly, 36.4 per cent added value has been achieved by Monsanto at accounting date, 1984. That is added value divided by turnover. This compares interestingly with gross profit to turnover of 26 per cent. These results can be compared with those for the prior period to assess the trend in gross profitability as well as added value. The added value restatement in Figure 6.9 effectively lops off £41.6 m from costs of sales, allocating this amount elsewhere in the restated profit and loss account. This 14.1 per cent reduction in direct costs accounts for the higher level of added value achieved by the operation than gross profit. In our view, the added value figure represents a nicer approximation of the group's profitability than gross profit as a sharp distinction has been forced between specific servicing of turnover by directly related expenditures and indirect expenses as well as tributary net interest income. Depreciation of almost £20 m has been allocated to its subordinate place in the restated profit and loss to remove its direct effect on trading. The restatement for added value does not, however, distort profit on ordinary activities before taxation, which remains at £94.1 m. The added value restatement is, thus, purely schematic.

MONSANTO PLC
1984 Consolidated accounting statements
£'000s

	% +/−	1984	198– with	1% +/− assumptions
TURNOVER:		398,906	402,895	+1
Bought-in materials and services:		(253,682)	(253,682)	—
ADDED VALUE:	+2.7%	145,224	149,213	
Staff costs:		(21,735)	(21,518)	−1
Indirect expenses:		(12,683)	(12,556)	−1
Interest receivable:		4,872	4,921	+1
Interest payable:		(1,742)	(1,725)	−1
Depreciation:		(19,832)	(19,634)	−1
PROFIT BEFORE TAXATION:	+4.9%	£94,104	£98,701	
Added value:		145,224	149,213	
Employees (number of):		1,840	1,822	−1
Added value per employee:	+3.8%	£78.93	£81.90	
Increase in added value per employee:		£2.97		

Figure 6.9 Added value and cost sensitivity statements (Monsanto PLC)

If added value is used in lieu of profit on ordinary activities before taxation as a profitability indicator, naturally, the margins will, in this case, be higher: 36.4 per cent to 22.8 per cent respectively. This, however, does not take into account what can be lumped together as establishment costs—all of which are expenses required to run the business, if not to service sales directly.

Arguably, the most interesting facet of the added value restatement is the cost sensitivity analysis driven by minimal 1 per cent assumptions. The figures tell us that if turnover could be pushed up by 1 per cent only to £402.9 m and costs of bought-in materials and services could be held static, added value created by Monsanto would have been 2.7 per cent higher at £149.2 m. Schematically, this is an easy and neat assumption. In practice, of course, it would be a considerable challenge to any management to increase sales whilst holding constant the direct costs of those sales. The prime method of achieving such a widening of margins would be to increase prices. This may or may not be easy to achieve depending upon the level of the original prices and the general conditions in a given market, always taking into consideration competition.

The assumptions follow with a 1 per cent reduction in staff costs. This could be achieved in a large company by the 'natural' process of retirements and staff leaving the company with management not replacing some or all of them. The 1 per cent decrease in indirect expenses could be achieved by strict budgetary control and conscious reductions in wasteful expenditures, particularly in large companies, of purchases and supplies. The assumed higher levels of added value should then help create higher levels of liquidity. Higher liquidity can be used to reduce borrowings and so decrease interest payable. If interest on deposits can be lifted by only 1 per cent due to larger deposit balances being held rather than better bank or money market rates, and interest payable on borrowings can be reduced by 1 per cent, net interest income for Monsanto would have been lifted 2.1 per cent to £3.2 m.

The analysis assumes a 1 per cent reduction in depreciation. This could be achieved by a stricter policy of investment in fixed assets, or a reduction in fixed assets due to sales thereof or non-replacement. Were all the plus or minus 1 per cent assumptions in this case achieved, Monsanto's profit before taxation would have been increased by almost 5 per cent to £98.7 m, giving the Group a 24.5 per cent profit margin and a prime ratio of 33.3 per cent in lieu of the profit margin of 23.6 per cent and 32 per cent achieved in 1984. Note too that long-term liabilities in the balance sheet might have been reduced as part of the general lift in operating performance and decline in costs. This, of course, would have the effect of reducing capital employed. In this event, Monsanto's prime ratio would be higher than the 33.3 per cent suggested above where the historical capital employed figure of £296.2 m was used as a denominator.

The sensitivity analysis further tells us that added value per employee could be increased by £2.97 per capita by a 1 per cent reduction in workforce assumed previously in the 1 per cent reduction in staff costs.

Added value modelling and forecasting

The financial analyst G. Smith has developed added value ratio-driven models for planning and forecasting purposes. His most familiar work derives from the distinction between measuring the flow and the use of money in businesses. From money flow and money usage data, he has used the following key ratios as model bases:

Profit to assets
Sales to assets
Sales to stock
Added value to sales
Added value to pay

These ratios are held to measure the main interlocked financial productivity of a company. To these ratios, sensitivity assumptions can easily be applied by way of forecasting. Smith's ratios provide the following indicators:

Profit/assets:	The overall efficiency in the employment of money to create surplus money flow
Sales/assets:	The injection of money in the operations from sales by using all assets however funded
Sales/stock:	The efficiency of use of stock in the generation of sales income
Added value/Sales:	Money remaining in the operation for each £ of sales
Added value/Pay:	The amount of money generated for each £ of pay

THE CALCULATION OF SHORT-TERM SURPLUS FUNDING 161

Concerning the last ratio added value/pay, Smith makes the valid point that the ratio is asset-linked. The higher the level of assets per employee, the higher the ratio will need to be in order to cover depreciation, interest and profit. Added value/pay also affects cash generation in terms of depreciation and retained profit. Figure 6.10 illustrates how Smith's proprietary model operates as well as the critical nature of the final ratio added value/pay. Figure 6.11 sets out how Smith uses this system to plan for improved performance. His

Profit/assets %	15	21	21	21
equals				
Sales/assets £	2.0	2.0	2.2	2.2
×				
Added value/sales	.5	.5	.63	.55
×				
Profit/added value %	15	21	15	17
depends on				
Added value/pay £	1.4	1.5	1.4	1.44
Profit improvement of 40% is				
generated by improvement in				
Added value/pay of		7.2%		
or by Sales/assets of			10%	
Added value/sales of			26%	
or by Sales/assets				10%
Added value/sales				10%
Added value/pay				3%

Figure 6.10 Proprietary model and final ratio added value/pay. Reprinted from *Accountancy*, 1983, © G. Smith

		Decisions		
Getting money in	Volume of business %	+1	+2	+1
	Prices %	+1	+1	+5
Stop money going out	Material prices %	−1	−1	+5
	Material use %	−1	−1	−1
	Company expenses %	−1	−1	+4
Efficient use of people	Manning %	−1	−12	−18
	Pay rates %	−1	−1	+5
Efficient use of money	Debtor days	−4	−4	−4
	Creditor days	−4	−4	−4
	Stock turnover %	+10	+10	+5
	Profits up %	60	129	138
	Added value/pay £1.59	+10%	+25%	+25%
	Profit/assets 4.29% up to 7.25		10%	10%

Figure 6.11 Using the proprietary model for improved performance. Reprinted from *Accountancy*, 1983, © G. Smith

model can thus be used for reviewing decision options needed to reach higher profit/assets or profit/capital employed targets. Schematically, it is then easy to evaluate key decisions taken. Positive or negative cashflow positions are shown as part of the process. His illustration gives eleven decision options and their overall effect on financial balance. The figures are based on ICI's 1981 results.

Smith interprets the performance table (Figure 6.11) as follows:

'Every 1p improvement in added value/pay is 0.15 per cent improvement in profit/assets. This table shows in the first column the sensitivity of profits to small changes, in the second column shows the decisions required to achieve a 10 per cent profit-to-assets, and in the third column shows the decisions needed to maintain profitability while absorbing cost increases.' In 1984 at ICI, the added value/pay ratio at 1.91 was up 10 per cent and earnings per share improved by 51 per cent the 1983 level. Profit/assets at 12 per cent rose 50 per cent and net borrowings showed a reduction of 17 per cent.

Conflicting interpretations of profit

Both the work of Smith and Hale appears to be founded on the current operating performance concept of profit. Advocates of this view focus on the ordinary operating activities of a company. The extreme position entailed by such a concept is that the profit and loss account includes only normal trading activities and any extraordinary items' impact or effects stemming from accounting changes would be excluded. The strength of such a view with its ultimate entailment is seen by Holmes and Sugden as facilitating comparison of strict trading positions of companies on a year-to-year basis and also, contrasting these results with those of other companies operating in the same sectors.

In our view, however, whilst Holmes and Sugden's point is valid, over-emphasis on the current operating performance concept of profit can obscure the real cashflows available to the companies in question. Obligations, as stated earlier, will, in real life, be met from a multiplicity of cash-generating sources. While it is important to note that cash deriving from asset sales or other extraordinary items cannot be expected to be recurrent, the cash resulting from them may have an appreciable and, in some cases, long-term effect on surplus liquid funds. In that event, from the credit manager's point of view (i.e. that posited on short-term trade credit sanctions), available net liquid balances from which debts can be settled will be more important than operating profit and future operational profitability.

Hale's work is, of course, mitigated to a degree by his insistence upon transaction analyses which convert accrual accounting data into cashflow information as well as the importance he places on cash from operations. However, to a degree, this last is offset by the greater emphasis placed upon it than on funds from operations. Also as noted earlier, agreement has by no means been reached as to the significance or utility of net working assets which are arrived at only after certain key balances have been excluded.

Smith's value added-based modelling, on the other hand, while being profit rather than cash oriented, takes only the broadest view of the balance sheet (in the inclusion of 'Assets' in various ratios) and lays predominant stress on profit and loss information. In mitigation of this, his system in no way rules out the effects of extraordinary items or accounting changes. Added value focuses attention on the main decision factors in business performance—cash collection, cost controls, and efficient use of people and other assets.

The other interpretation of profit is termed by Holmes and Sugden 'all-inclusive'. Advocates of such a concept believe that the profit and loss account should include all transactions bringing about a net increase or decrease in net tangible assets during the current period. Holmes and Sugden rightly exclude from these transactions dividend distributions and issues of shares. The emphasis in an all-inclusive profit and loss account is, therefore, total historical summation of net income. The models developed by Taffler, Lis, and Bathory incline toward the all-inclusive orientation as they aim at synoptic views, an important part of which must be represented by debt in various forms.

The working worth concept developed by Coleshaw is interesting both as an intellectual corrective to Hale's net working assets and cash from operations, and as working worth, as a debt-servicing medium, derives solely from balance-sheet data.

Holmes and Sugden point out that under the current operating performance concept of profit, exclusion of extraordinary items, prior period adjustments, and accounting changes' effects can lead to their possible overlooking when operating results are reviewed over several periods.

Presenting the effects of cash injections on liquidity

The credit analyst will frequently be confronted with comparatively old historical accounting data (one to two years) and unaudited interim information and supplementary data (as defined earlier). In many of these cases, the subject company may have turned in substantial losses or shown adverse trading trends. If the entity is a public company, dividends may have been paid despite the losses, causing further strain on working capital. In some cases, the dividend payments may have been increased to bolster shareholders' confidence in the company.

The erosion in overall liquidity caused by poor trading results and dividend policy can, in these cases, call for the injection of capital by share issues, private placements, banks, or ultimate companies.

	Notes	£'000s	£'000s
Turnover	1	3,119	2,615
Cost of sales		(2,222)	(1,807)
Gross profit		897	808
Net operating expenses	2	(1,000)	(771)
Operating (loss)/profit	3	(103)	37
Interest payable and similar charges	7	(120)	(133)
Loss on ordinary activities before and after taxation		(223)	(96)
Loss per share after taxation	9	(8.75p)	(3.80p)
STATEMENT OF ACCUMULATED LOSSES			
Accumulated loss at 1 November 198–		(485)	(389)
Loss for the financial year		(223)	(96)
Accumulated loss at 31 October 198–		(708)	(485)

Figure 6.12 Profit and loss account

	Notes	£'000s	£'000s	£'000s	£'000s
FIXED ASSETS					
Intangible assets	10		12		19
Tangible assets	11		1,015		971
			1,027		990
CURRENT ASSETS					
Stocks	13	585		464	
Debtors	14	1,095		1,078	
Cash at bank and in hand		1		2	
		1,681		1,544	
CREDITORS: amounts falling due within one year	15	1,480		1,848	
NET CURRENT ASSETS/(LIABILITIES)			201		(304)
TOTAL ASSETS LESS CURRENT LIABILITIES			1,228		686
CREDITORS: amounts falling due after more than one year:					
Parent Company loan	16		1,017		252
			211		434
CAPITAL AND RESERVES					
Called-up share capital	17		255		255
Share premium account			10		10
Revaluation reserve			654		654
Profit and loss account			(708)		(485)
			211		434

Figure 6.13 Balance sheet

The analytical problems in such cases are varied. Basically, they are problems of forecasting and of historical restatement. Figures 6.12 to 6.16 give the audited results of a public limited company subsidiary of an ultimate holding company. The profit and loss account discloses two years of increasing trading losses and increasing losses per share after taxation. Since the 198– accounts, two significant pieces of information are known:

1. A loss has been sustained for the six months to 30 April 198– of £378,000. This is said to include some £95,000 of exceptional, non-recurring costs.
2. The ultimate holding company is raising £2 m in the form of a Rights Issue to:
    (a) repay the parent company loan outstanding: £1,017,000.
    (b) restore liquidity level of the subsidiary company.

THE CALCULATION OF SHORT-TERM SURPLUS FUNDING

	£'000s	£'000s	£'000s	£'000s
SOURCE OF FUNDS				
Loss before taxation		(223)		(96)
Items not involving movements of funds:				
Depreciation	65		66	
Surplus depreciation released on revaluation	—		(47)	
		65	19	
Total funds absorbed by operations		(158)		(77)
Funds from other sources:				
Sale of tangible fixed assets	30		10	
Increase in creditors falling due after more than one year	765		246	
		795		256
Total source of funds		637		179
APPLICATION OF FUNDS				
Purchase of tangible fixed assets		132		31
		505		148
INCREASE/(DECREASE) IN WORKING CAPITAL				
Increase/(decrease) in stocks	121		(244)	
Increase/(decrease) in debtors	17		(72)	
(Increase)/decrease in creditors falling due within one year excluding bank overdraft	(326)			
		(188)	454	138
Movement in net liquid funds:				
Cash at bank and in hand	(1)		—	
Decrease in bank overdraft	694		10	
		693		10
		505		148

Figure 6.14 Source and application of funds

Given that the external analyst has no detailed knowledge of how the assets and liabilities of the subsidiary may be affected by this injection of cash, how can the balance sheet be restated to show the broad effects of the cash injection? Secondly, will the proposed £2 m injection be sufficient both to restore liquidity to acceptable levels and to provide adequate free capital to allow the company to turn around its adverse trading? The analytical problems are thus reconstruction of balance sheet and guesstimation of future trading and the cash demands caused by the company's normal operations.

Interest payable	£'000s	£'000s
On bank overdrafts and other loans wholly repayable within five years but not by instalments	116	128
Other interest wholly repayable within five years by instalments	4	5
Total interest payable and similar charges	120	133

Taxation

Trading losses available against future taxation liabilities, after allowing for any deferred taxation which may arise in respect of capital allowances and other timing differences, amounted to £654,000 (198—-£235,000).

Advance corporation tax written off in prior years amounting to £37,000 has not been accounted for, as it is unlikely that it can be utilised within the foreseeable future.

Stocks	£'000s	£'000s
Raw materials and consumables	251	172
Work in progress	60	58
Finished goods and goods for resale	274	234
	585	464

There is no material difference between the replacement cost and the historical cost of stocks.

Figure 6.15 Source and application of funds

As in so many analytical problems where forecasting is involved and/or where broad information gaps occur, it is a waste of time trying to enter into great detail. In general, the greater the detail, the more prone to error the detail will be. Analytical common sense, therefore, calls for broad extrapolations based both upon historical data and the analyst's knowledge of particular markets.

From supplementary sources we learn that the subsidiary's turnover level compared with that of the corresponding period reflected the highly competitive marketplace in which the company operates. The latest profit and loss account tells us that the company's two significant problems are excessively high levels of operating expenses relative to sales. The latest interims state that some £95 k exceptional, non-recurrent costs have further aggravated these balances. The same sources also state that the company has appointed management consultants who have produced a programme of options designed to reduce operating expenses, but that the company is unlikely to derive benefit from implementing these options during the current year (for which the interims represent the first six months).

Stock market sources provide information on the proposed Rights Issue. This is said to consist of 20,391,840 ordinary 10p shares at par payable in full on acceptance, on the basis of eight new ordinary shares for each share held previously. The ultimate company has agreed to take up its entitlement to 14,784,304 shares and will underwrite the balance of the Rights Issue.

Firstly, what, broadly speaking, will be the effects of the Rights Issue? The issue's net proceeds will amount to approximately £2 m. The issue will result in conversion of the

Debtors	£'000s	£'000s
Trade debtors	1,061	1,056
Prepayments and accrued income	34	22
	1,095	1,078

All amounts are due within one year.

Creditors—amounts falling due within one year	£'000s	£'000s
Bank overdraft (see (a) below)	437	1,131
Trade creditors	849	424
Other creditors	98	122
Taxation and social security	65	35
Accruals	31	136
	1,480	1,848

(a) The bank overdraft is secured by a fixed charge over freehold land and buildings.

	£'000s	£'000s
Parent company loan	1,017	252

The parent company loan is unsecured, interest-free and is not repayable before 31 October 198–

Capital expenditure
Commitments for capital expenditure approved and contracted for amounted to £56,250 (198–£NIL).

Revenue commitments
The company is committed to make the following payments in the future under leasing agreements for which no provision has been made in the accounts:—

Year	Operating leasing agreement £'000s
198–/8–	44
198–/8–	28
198–/8–	10
198–/8–	10
198–/8–	6
198–/8– and after	22

Figure 6.16 Source and application of funds

outstanding parent company loan of £1,478,430 (at interim date) into equity *and* will provide some £520 k additional funds to the subsidiary. The issue is justified on the grounds of restoring the company's capital position, rationalization of future trading activities, and provision of finance for new product lines.

A broad interpretation of the subsidiary's accounts show two clear trends. First, in general terms, losses continued and worsened. Secondly, the balance sheet, whilst registering an improvement in most indicators, does so at the expense of increasing indebtedness to the parent company. Note the parent company loan up 304 per cent to just over £1 m.

The notes to the accounts tell us that the parent company loan is unsecured, free of interest, and not repayable until October, 198–. The date would be after the proposed Rights Issue was made.

If one treated the parent company loan as an ordinary creditor, the subsidiary company is technically insolvent. Accordingly, it is in an even worse state than its poor trading results indicate. Bathory's Model assigned the company scores showing clearly the immediate risk of collapse due to insolvency. It will be recalled that this model measures the five main financial flows:

Current debt-service ability from operational inflows
Annual profitability
Capital adequacy
Cumulative profitability
Liquidity

Taken singly, the component ratios indicated the worsening in debt capacity from operating income; a sharp fall in annual profitability; increasing inadequacy in permanent capital resources; a drop in retentions; and only a marginal increase in liquidity. The model gave an erosion of some 21 basis points for the two years in question, with the company receiving a synoptic score of -1 for 198–, and -22 for the latest period. Scores of $+20$ and below to 0 indicate companies at serious risk of insolvent collapse within two accounting years.

Regarding the company's figure for total assets used by the model, it should be noted that the total assets of £2,708,000 include fixed assets, freehold land and buildings at £844,000. Two considerations apply:

1. A revaluation in 198– increased the net value by £654,000 (credited to revaluation reserve). We do not know the quality nor validity of this revaluation.
2. Notes to the accounts inform us that in the event of a disposal of this property, some £190,000 tax would become payable.

Proceeding from this information, the balance sheet after application of the Rights Issue can be broadly extrapolated as follows.

Let us set up a four-column spreadsheet on using the company's latest audited results as a base. The second column will show the interim results; the third column, the injection of Rights Issue cash; and the fourth column, the effects of the previous columns on the company's results, or the extrapolated balance sheet.

For the extrapolated balance sheet, we can assume that as the company is in the process of attempting to reduce its capital and other commitments as part of the management consultants' proposals referred to earlier, the investment in fixed assets will, at best, be reduced either by asset sales or by lack of replacement; and at worst, by holding the balance as of the latest accounting date constant. Strictly speaking, if the latter obtains, net fixed assets will show a pro rata decrease on the latest audited figures due to depreciation. As we are concerned here with only the broadest extrapolation, the effects of depreciation can be ignored. Accordingly, we assume the worst and keep the level of fixed assets investment constant in Column 4.

	£'000s			
Columns: 1		2	3	4
Audited results		*Interim results*	*Rights issue*	*Extrapolated B/S*
30 October 198–		30 April 198–	£2 m	
Fixed assets				
Intangible:	12			
Tangible:	1,015			
	1,027			1,027
Current assets	1,681			
Current liabilities	1,480			
Net current assets:	201			806
Total assets:	1,228		605	1,833
Parent company loan:	1,017	(378)	1,395	—
NET ASSETS:	211			1,833
Represented by:				
Capital and reserves				
Called-up share capital:	265		2,000	2,265
Revaluation reserve:	654			654
Profit and loss account:	(708)	(378)		(1,086)
	211			1,833

Figure 6.17 Extrapolation of balance sheet

The first effect of the Rights Issue will, of course, be seen in higher levels of short-term liquidity. After redemption of parent company loan at interim stage (total loan indebtedness: £1,395,000) the balance of the Rights Issue proceeds will be £605,000. Again, looking broadly and having no knowledge of the movements in current assets and current liabilities, we can assume for argument's sake no significant changes as the management plans mentioned above will not yet have produced results. Adding £605,000 to net current assets will boost this measure of liquidity by some 301 per cent to £806,000. Total assets less current liabilities thus stand at £1,228,000 for the audited accounts and 49.3 per cent up at £1,833,000 for the extrapolated account.

After deduction of parent company loan in the audited accounts, net assets stand at £211,000. With Rights Issue proceeds redeeming the loan at interim stage of £1,395,000, and clearing effective long-term debt from the balance sheet, extrapolated net assets total £1,833,000.

The 'financing end' of the balance sheet registers the significant increase in called-up capital due to the application of the Rights Issue. Revaluation reserve is, of course, unaffected by this funding; and profit and loss account in the extrapolated balance sheet shows the further depletion of distributable reserves due to the heavy interim losses reported at £378,000. Accordingly, a total loss of £1,086,000 is brought forward to the extrapolated balance sheet.

At this stage, the interpretation of the extrapolated figures would be based around a specific or estimated exposure. For simplicity's sake, however, we can omit these considerations. Again, speaking only in approximate terms, what effect has the cash injection on the company's balance sheet? Whilst the effect in percentage terms is significantly high, pure percentage increases or decreases can be deceptive in that they say nothing of the company's future requirements. Also, even extremely high percentage increases may leave insufficient balances. Accordingly, in the absence of other information, we might say that in this firms's extrapolated balance sheet, working capital has been greatly increased, always bearing in mind the intellectually weak assumption of static current assets and current liabilities. We might point out with a greater degree of significance that long-term debt has been expunged from the balance sheet. Capital resources, therefore, have been increased in terms of short-term liquidity and in higher amounts of paid-up share capital. None the less, distributable reserves show increased erosion. Balances here are negative, and the deficiency has grown in the extrapolated version.

Of course, the extrapolated balance sheet does not take into account improvements resulting from more profitable trading in the second half of the year, should such performance be possible. It is unlikely, however, that given the interim losses of £378,000 and prior year's loss of £708,000, the company's second half year results will go far to wipe out the profit and loss account deficit at next year-end. This view would also seem corroborated by the supplementary data concerning effects of the recent management consultancy programme.

For credit purposes, the summary view of this company's state of affairs after application of proceeds from the Rights Issue would be that the capital injection would probably only give the firm breathing space, and that after application of cash, both its long-term prospects and current trading position would still be causes for anxiety.

Sources

Bathory, A., 'Departure from Fact: The Restatement of Accounting Numbers in Standard Credit Analysis', *Credit Management*, mid-October, 1984, passim.
Coleshaw, J., 'A Simple Approach to Balance-Sheet Rating', *Credit Management*, mid-June, 1984, pp. 21–23.
Deloitte, Haskins & Sells, '*Raising Venture Capital*', Deloitte, Haskins & Sells, UK, July 1984, Appendices C & D.
Hale, R., *Credit Analysis, A Complete Guide*, John Wiley & Sons Inc., Chichester, 1983, pp. 40–64.
Holmes, G., and Sugden, A., *Interpreting Company Reports and Accounts*, Woodhead-Faulkner, Cambridge 1983, Chapters 12, 14.
Investors in Industry PLC, 'Profit and Cash Flow Forecasting', *Management Series*, undated.
Smith, G., 'Analysing Financial Balance', Annual Lecture Series, Institute of Credit Management, *Lecture Notes*, 17 February, 1986; available from G. & B. Smith Advisors Ltd. Halford House, Copse Hill Road, Lower Slaughter, Nr. Cheltenham GL54 2HY. Tel: 0451-21135.

7

THE SIGNIFICANCE AND TREATMENT OF DEFERRED TAXATION

Underlying principle

The amounts provided for deferred tax liabilities can have far-reaching effects on the balance sheet in general, and on capital adequacy in particular. Because of the complexities both in the concept of deferred tax and the treatment of deferred liabilities in credit analysis, we want at this stage to examine deferred taxation with a view to simplification and summary treatment by analysts.

Deferred tax is the best attempt to date to account for tax on profits and surpluses which are recognized in financial statements during one period, but assessed in another. Deferred tax of this sort refers mainly to postponed corporation tax and income tax in the UK and in the Republic of Ireland and, in as much as the principles are similar, to foreign taxation on profits payable by UK and Irish companies or their subsidiaries.

A range of other taxes, including value added tax (VAT), petroleum revenue tax (PRT), and some overseas taxes, are not directly assessed on profits for an accounting period. We do not, therefore, propose considering them in this book. Statement of Standard Accounting Practice 15 (SSAP 15), Accounting for Deferred Tax (Revised May 1985), directs that to provide for such deferred liabilities as these taxes may give rise, companies should follow in general the principle that deferred tax should be provided to the extent that it is probable that a liability or asset will crystallize, but not to the extent that it is probable that a liability or asset will not crystallize. This principle underpins provision for deferred taxation in general.

Accounting background

Tax payable on profits in one particular period often bears little relationship with the amount of income and expenditure appearing for that period in financial statements. This is due to the different basis on which profits are calculated for tax computations as opposed to the basis on which profits are stated in accounts.

The different basis of computing profits for tax purposes stems from:

(a) recognition that certain kinds of income are tax-free
(b) recognition that certain types of expenditure are disallowable

Recognition of these two concepts entails recognizing 'permanent differences' between taxable and accounting profits. Permanent differences likewise arise where there are tax allowances or charges with no corresponding amount in the financial statements. Also, 'timing differences' arise when there are items included in accounts of a period different from that in which those items were dealt with for tax purposes. Accordingly, for accounting purposes, revenue, gains, expenditures and losses may be included either earlier or later than they could enter into computations of profit for taxation purposes.

As discussed earlier, extraordinary items, prior year adjustments and movements on reserves are not treated in profit and loss accounts under ordinary activities, but these items may also have an impact on companies' total tax bills.

Providing for deferred tax

Deferred tax can be computed using three bases:

Nil provision or flow through
Full provision or comprehensive allocation
Partial provision

Nil provision assumes that only the tax payable in respect of a period should be charged in that period. Accordingly, no provision for deferred tax would be made. The rationale here is that any tax liability arises on taxable profits and not on accounting profits. Accordingly, it is necessary to provide for tax only on taxable profits. Moreover, any tax liability arising on timing differences will depend upon the incidence of future taxable profits. It is highly likely that these incidences will be hard to quantify.

Full provision, on the other hand, turns on the principle that accounts for a period should recognize the tax effects, current or deferred, of all transactions applying during that period.

Partial provision requires accounting for deferred tax in respect of the net amount by which it is probable that any payment of tax will be temporarily deferred or accelerated by the operation of timing differences which will reverse in the foreseeable future without being replaced. This entails that if a company does not expect reducing the scope of its operations significantly, it will often develop a hard core of timing differences. This ensures that the payment of some tax liabilities will be permanently deferred. Partial provision will then provide for deferred tax only where it is probable that tax will become payable as a result of timing differences becoming reversed. As partial provision is grounded upon an assessment of what will actually be the company's position in any period, partial provision is preferable to the other bases mentioned earlier.

Furthermore, nil provision and full provision tend to lead to a purely arithmetical approach where certainty of calculation takes precedence over a reasoned estimation of what the tax implications of various transactions will actually be.

The effect of timing and other differences on tax charges relating to reported profits would be, in the main, insignificant, were taxation not viewed as relevant to companies' performance for stated periods, that is, were the only accepted indicator of performance results before taxation. As results after tax are also widely held to be a significant performance indicator, distortion would result by accounting for deferred tax where it is probable that a liability or asset will *not* crystallize, or by not accounting for deferred tax where it is probable that a liability or asset *will* crystallize. Distortions would also occur in the balance sheet between equity and its relationship to funds from other sources.

Computational methods

SSAP 11 sets out two allowable methods of computing deferred taxation:

DEFERRAL METHOD

Amounts are taken into the deferred taxation account at the rate of corporation tax at the time. These provisions remain unaltered despite any subsequent changes in the rate of corporation tax. Accordingly, when any reversals occur, they will be treated at original rates no longer applicable. In practice, the effects of reversals and new timing differences are sometimes accounted for as one item.

Advocates of the deferral method recognize that when tax rates change, no indication of the amount of tax payable or recoverable will be provided. Any deferred credit or charge rather than a liability or asset, will represent the deferred taxation balance. By contra, when tax rates change, no need arises to alter the amount of deferred tax already provided for. Accordingly, the tax credit or charge for the period relates only to that period. It is not distorted by any prior period adjustments.

LIABILITY METHOD

Under the liability method, deferred taxation balances are maintained at the current rate of tax. Accordingly, the balance must be adjusted whenever the rate of corporation tax is altered.

Here, deferred provisions are calculated at the rate at which it is estimated that tax will be paid or recovered when timing differences reverse. The current rate of corporation tax is thus used as the 'best estimate', unless changes in tax rates are advised in advance.

The liability method, therefore, revises provisions in order to reflect actual or anticipated tax rate changes. For this reason, the tax charge or credit for a period may include adjustments of accounting estimates pertaining to prior periods. The deferred taxation account thus represents the best estimate of the amount of tax payable or recoverable were the timing differences reversed.

SSAP 15 implies that the liability method is consistent with the objective of partial provision, namely, to provide for the amount of deferred tax that will *probably* be payable or recoverable. A majority of companies accordingly use the liability method. Adjustments to the deferred tax account under this method are to be disclosed separately, and SSAP 15 directs that any major adjustments stemming from fundamental changes in the tax system be treated as extraordinary items.

Interim summary of terms

Deferred taxation represents the tax attributable to the effect of timing differences. Timing differences are differences between profits or losses calculated for tax purposes and those between profits or losses as computed in accounting statements.

Reasons for timing differences: The divergence between tax and accounting computations for profits or losses arises from the inclusion of items of income and expenditure in tax computations different from those in which they are included, or accounted for, in financial statements.

Reversals of timing differences: Timing differences originate in one period but are capable of being reversed in one or more subsequent periods. To make this clearer, let us first consider an example of a timing difference:

> A high-technology manufacturing company shows a high level of capital expenditure on plant and equipment. To remain in business, it will have to continue if not increase its capital expenditure. Because of the system of capital allowances and first year allowances, the company will have a lower than normal tax liability for the period in which the capital expenditure is incurred. As the company's capital expenditure programme will continue unabated and will probably increase, tax liability will continue to be below normal levels. Were this not the case, and capital spending decreased, the beneficial effects of first year allowances would decrease and levels of tax payable would increase beyond the normal level.

From this example, it is clear that over a certain length of time, capital allowances defers the corporation tax liability but do not reduce the total amount paid. Also, over a certain length of time, the amount of capital allowances and depreciation will be equivalent. The net effect of the capital allowances is a timing difference.

Equivalence of capital allowances and depreciation

If a high-tech company in our example spends £½ m in year 1 on a computer and depreciates this fixed asset on a straight-line basis over five years at 20 per cent, and assuming 100 per cent capital allowance, the equivalence between the capital allowance and depreciation can be seen as follows:

Year	Capital allowance	Depreciation
1	£500,000	£100,000
2	Nil	£100,000
3	Nil	£100,000
4	Nil	£100,000
5	Nil	£100,000
	£500,000	£500,000

Amounts deducted by way of depreciation do not, however, equal amounts permitted by the Inland Revenue for usage of fixed assets. For tax purposes, depreciation is written-back to profit before taxation and capital allowances are deducted to arrive at taxable profit.

Accordingly, the salient point is not the equivalence of depreciation and capital allowances, but the net effect on profits after capital allowances. If, therefore, the high-tech company made taxable trading profits of £½ m every year and corporation tax were levied at 52 per cent, we would see the following figures:

Year	Taxable profit	Corporation tax liability
1	Nil	Nil
2	£500,000	£260,000
3	£500,000	£260,000
4	£500,000	£260,000
5	£500,000	£260,000
	£2,000,000	£1,040,000

If the capital allowances in this example were equivalent to depreciation, the following figures would result:

Year	Taxable profit	Corporation tax liability
1	£400,000	£208,000
2	£400,000	£208,000
3	£400,000	£208,000
4	£400,000	£208,000
5	£400,000	£208,000
	£2,000,000	£1,040,000

On this example, the deferred taxation account would arise in year 1 and be reflected in the company's profit and loss account as follows:

Profit and loss account

Profit before taxation:	£400,000
Taxation:	£208,000
Profit after taxation:	£192,000

And in the notes to the accounts:

Note

Corporation tax payable	Nil
Transfer to deferred taxation account:	£208,000
Total tax charge:	£208,000

Deferred tax originating in this way is accumulated and included in the balance sheet either as deferred taxation or as a provision for liabilities and charges. If the latter, deferred taxation information should be disclosed in a note.

In our example, as more tax would be payable in years 2 to 5 than the tax liability posted in the profit and loss account in each year, a transfer would be made from the deferred tax account, reducing the balance at the end of year 5 to 0. Accordingly, the note in each of the four years would state:

Corporation tax payable:	£260,000
Transfer from deferred tax account:	£52,000
Total tax charge:	£208,000

Thus in years 2 to 5, the effect of the timing difference is reversed. Losses for tax purposes are losses available to relieve profits from tax. Such losses constitute a timing difference. Revaluation of assets, including an investment in an associated or subsidiary company, will give rise to a timing difference when it is incorporated in the balance sheet, in so far as the profit or loss that would result from realizing the asset of its revalued amount is taxable, unless disposal of the revalued asset and of any subsequent assets by way of replacement would not result in a tax liability, after taking into account any expected rollover relief.

Retention of earnings overseas will create a timing difference only if there is an intention or obligation to remit the earnings, and the remittance would result in a tax liability after account had been taken of any related double tax relief.

The liability method computes deferred taxation at that rate of tax estimated to be applicable when the timing differences reverse. Under the liability method, deferred tax not provided is calculated at the expected long-term tax rate.

Summary of Standard Accounting Practice in respect of financial statements for accounting periods on or after 1 April 1985

1. Deferred tax should be calculated using the liability method.
2. Tax either deferred or accelerated by the effect of timing differences should be accounted for to the extent that it is likely that an asset or a liability will crystallize.
3. The likelihood of whether or not deferred tax liabilities will crystallize should be based on reasonable assumptions.
4. When financial projections are susceptible to a high degree of uncertainty, or are not fully developed in respect of an appropriate period, a prudent view should be taken of whether or not a tax liability will crystallize.
5. The provision for deferred tax liabilities should be reduced by any deferred tax debit balances arising from separate classes of timing differences and any advance corporation tax (ACT) which may be available to offset against those liabilities.
6. Deferred tax net debit balances should not be carried forward as assets, save to the extent that they are expected to be recoverable without replacement by equivalent debit balances.
7. Deferred tax relating to any extraordinary items should be shown separately as part of the tax on extraordinary items; that is, either on the face of the profit and loss account or in a note.
8. The amount of any unprovided deferred taxation in respect of the period should be disclosed in a note and analysed into its main component parts.
9. Under the liability method, the effect of a change in the basis or rate of taxation, or of a significant change in government fiscal policy, should be treated as an extraordinary item where such change is material.
10. The deferred tax balance and its main components should be disclosed in the balance sheet or in notes. Likewise, transfers to and from deferred tax should be disclosed in a note.
11. Where amounts of deferred tax arise resulting from the expected disposal of revalued assets, the amounts transferred to or from deferred tax should be shown separately as part of the movement on reserves.
12. The total amount of any unprovided deferred tax should be disclosed in a note and analysed into its chief parts.
13. When a company is a member of a group, it should, in accounting for deferred tax, take account of any group relief which, on reasonable evidence, is expected to be available and any charge which will be made for such relief.
14. Deferred tax in respect of the remittance of overseas earnings should be accounted for in accordance with these and the other provisions of SSAP 15. Where deferred tax is not provided on earnings retained overseas, this should be stated.

Principal areas of difference

The following are the principal areas of difference giving rise to deferred tax:

1. Timing differences
2. Permanent differences
3. Losses
4. Items not included in profit or loss on ordinary activities
5. Advance corporation tax

In attempting to assess whether or not a tax liability will crystallize, the combined effect of timing differences should be considered rather than an examination of each timing difference separately.

A number of timing differences arise from using a receipts and payments basis for tax purposes as well as the accruals basis in financial statements. Examples of these and other timing differences are:

(a) Interest receivable accrued in the accounting period but taxed when received.
(b) Dividends from foreign subsidiaries accrued in a period prior to that in which they arise for taxation purposes.
(c) Intra-group profits in stock deferred upon consolidation until realization to third parties.
(d) Interest or royalties payable and accrued in the accounting period but allowed when paid.
(e) Pension costs accrued in the accounts but allowed for taxation purposes when paid or contributed at some later date.
(f) Provisions for repairs and maintenance made in the accounts but not allowed for tax purposes until the expenditure is incurred.
(g) Bad debt provisions not allowed for taxation purposes unless and until they become 'specific'.
(h) Provisions for revenue losses on the closing down of plants or for costs of reorganisation upon which tax relief is not obtained until the costs or losses are incurred.
(i) Revenue expenditure deferred in the accounts, e.g. development costs or advertising, if it is allowed for tax purposes as it is incurred.

Some of these differences are short term in that they can be attributed to specific transactions and normally reverse in the accounting period following that in which they arose. Short term and other timing differences should be considered together when trying to assess whether or not a tax liability will crystallize.

Examples of permanent differences are fines (which are disallowed) and UK entertaining, regional development grants and interest on tax repayments. Stock relief in the Republic of Ireland is effectively a permanent difference. These are permanent in the sense that they will not reverse in future periods and thereby give rise to no tax effects in other periods.

Accordingly, as Holmes and Sugden point out, in companies' financial statements where only timing differences exist and where provision for the total of these differences is made in a deferred taxation account, the sum of the tax payable plus deferred tax should always be equal to the corporation tax rate percentage on adjusted taxable profits.

Accelerated capital allowances

Accelerated capital allowances are timing differences arising from the availability of capital allowances exceeding the related depreciation charges in financial statements. Depreciation charges in accounts can also exceed capital allowances available for tax computations, thereby reversing the effect.

In many companies, such as the high-tech example considered earlier, timing differences arising from accelerated capital allowances tend to be of a recurring nature. Reversing differences are themselves accordingly offset either in full or in part. These then give rise to continuing tax reductions or the indefinite deferral of any liability attributable to the tax benefit received. Accordingly, a company having a comparatively stable or increasing investment in depreciable assets can obtain tax relief year by year on its capital expenditure. Such tax relief may equal or exceed the additional tax which would otherwise have been payable due to the reversal of the original timing differences through depreciation.

When for financial, or other reasons, companies show a highly irregular or spasmodic incidence of capital expenditure, a substantial period of time will need to be considered in trying to assess whether a tax liability will crystallize.

Where there is a decreasing incidence of capital expenditure, any originating timing differences will generally reverse. Deferred tax in such cases should be provided for unless it is likely for other reasons that no tax liability will crystallize.

Deferred tax related to losses

SSAP 15, paragraph 30, requires that deferred tax assets, including those arising from losses, should be recognized only when they are expected to be recoverable. Recovery is understood to be without replacement by equivalent debit balances. Recovery can be affected by the period of time for which the losses are available to be carried forward for tax purposes.

Where a company sustains a loss, it is entitled to carry the loss back for up to two years in order to recover corporation tax previously paid. Deferred taxation provides for the carry forward already noted, where the loss can be carried forward indefinitely to offset against future profits.

Losses sustained by UK subsidiary companies, however, cannot be offset against profits arising from elsewhere within the group unless the subsidiary is at least 75 per cent owned by the parent company. Holmes and Sugden point out that when the loss-making subsidiary is less than 75 per cent owned, the group's tax liability will appear unduly high, but that the subsidiary's losses can be carried forward within the subsidiary itself. If and when this loss is subsequently matched against future profits, the net effect on the group's tax liability will, of course, be reversed.

The losses sustained by foreign subsidiaries cannot be offset against UK profits. They can, however, be carried forward in the same manner as losses made by UK subsidiaries. The tax effect is thus the same.

Losses sustained on the sale or disposal of investments cannot be offset against trading profits. Deferred tax relating to current trading losses may be treated as recoverable if:

1. The loss results from an identifiable and non-recurring cause.
2. The operation or previous operation has been consistently profitable over a consider-

able period, with any past losses being more than offset by income in subsequent periods.
3. It is assured beyond reasonable doubt that future taxable profits will be sufficient to offset the current loss during the carry-forward period prescribed by tax legislation.

These criteria of current trading loss recoverabilities can be contrasted with deferred tax treated as recoverable on capital losses.

1. When a potential chargeable gain not expected to be covered by rollover relief is present in assets which have not been revalued in the accounts to reflect that gain and which are not essential to the company's future operations.
2. When the business has decided to dispose of these assets and thereby realize the potential chargeable gain.
3. When the unrealized chargeable gain (after allowing for any possible loss in value before disposal) is sufficient to offset the loss in question, such that it is assured beyond reasonable doubt that a tax liability on the relevant portion of the chargeable gain will not crystallize.

Fixed asset revaluations

As noted earlier, when a fixed asset is revalued above its cost, a timing difference potentially arises in that, in the absence of rollover relief, tax on a chargeable gain may be payable if and when the asset is disposed of at revalued amount.

Where it is probable that a liability will crystallize, provision for the tax payable on disposal is required by SSAP 15 to be made from the revaluation surplus. This is based on the value at which the fixed asset is carried in the balance sheet.

Whether or not a liability will, in these circumstances, crystallize can normally be determined (in the absence of rollover relief) at the time the company decides to dispose of the asset.

Analysts should note that SSAP 15, paragraph 42, requires that where the value of an asset is not incorporated in the balance sheet, but is given elsewhere such as in a note, the tax effects, if any, which would arise were the asset realized at noted value should also be shown. This also applies where the value is given in the directors' report in lieu of in the notes to the accounts.

We have, several times, mentioned rollover relief. This is choosing to have the gain arising on the disposal of an asset deducted from the cost of the new or replacement asset rather than suffering tax on the gain itself.

Rollover relief

Rollover relief has the effect of postponing the reversal of the timing differences arising on the revaluation on an asset beyond the date of its disposal, or of creating a timing difference on the sale of an asset that has not been previously revalued, or relief can give rise to a combination of the two cases.

Where rollover relief has been obtained on the sale of an asset, with the base cost of the replacement asset for taxation purposes accordingly being reduced, and the potential deferred tax has not been disclosed, SSAP 15 requires disclosure of the fact that the revaluation does *not* constitute a timing difference and that tax has, therefore, not been quantified as it will not otherwise be evident from the financial statements.

Advance corporation taxation

Under the imputation system of taxation introduced in 1973, whenever a company pays dividends to shareholders, it is required to pay ACT. This is, in effect, the basic rate of income tax that would be payable on the dividends were they grossed up at that rate. Accordingly, if the basic rate of income tax equals x per cent, the amount of ACT payable is expressible by:

$$\frac{x}{(100-x)} \text{ of the dividend paid}$$

In other words, if the basic rate of income tax is 30 per cent, ACT will represent 30/70ths of the dividend actually paid shareholders.

The minimum tax charge in the profit and loss account in any accounting period will generaly be the amount payable as ACT (net of any recovery) plus any amounts charged in respect of overseas tax.

ACT which cannot be recovered from the corporation tax liability on the income for the year, but which is carried forward to be recovered from the corporation tax liability on the income for future years may, subject to certain limitations, be deducted from the deferred taxation account. Where no balance on the deferred tax account exists, or in those cases where the balance is insufficient for this purpose, consideration will need to be given as to whether ACT is recoverable from the corporation tax liability on the income from future periods.

In certain circumstances, it may be incorrect to carry forward an amount of ACT to offset an equal credit amount of deferred tax. This is for the reason that ACT may be carried forward at the basic rate of income tax only on the gross amount of any distribution, to be set off against corporation tax at the full or small companies' rates on the same gross amount of taxable income, excluding any chargeable gains.

The treatment of deferred tax in companies' accounts has already been noted. Corporation tax payable can be set out in two portions:

1. Current liabilities: Where the previous year's corporation tax is yet unpaid less any ACT on dividends paid in the previous year.
2. Creditors: Amounts falling due after more than one year: Where there is a liability for the year in question less any ACT on dividends paid in the year in question.

Analytical treatment of deferred taxation accounts

Having looked at the scope and structure of deferred taxation, we now should examine the treatment of deferred tax by credit analysts. While the fundamentals of this tax may be complex, its analytical treatment is straightforward.

It is clear that deferred tax is a postponement of a liability. Furthermore, in many cases, we have seen that the liability may not crystallize or that it may be reversed.

Accordingly, whilst analysts compute the difference in the deferred taxation account every two periods to arrive at the increase or decrease to add back to gross cashflow, the 'quality' of such an 'asset' (when it *is* such) is of the same abstract quality as that of depreciation. Simply, depreciation does not constitute a sum of cash in the tangible sense. Likewise, deferred tax represents, at its simplest, money that may have to be paid out by the company at some future period. In the meanwhile, the firm has had the use of that money. Thus in this sense, both depreciation and deferred tax represent abstract 'assets' when calculating cashflow.

If the deferred taxation difference in question is attributable to the purchase of fixed assets, it is plain that the company had to generate sufficient cash to make those purchases. It would, on the other hand, be overly simple to say that cash for the purchase of those fixed assets came from profits. The money may have been hived off from trading profits or from any number of profit measures. Between them, depreciation and the deferred tax account difference indicate the *use* of those fixed assets. From our foregoing account, we can see that deferred tax can also represent certain allowable income in addition to certain disallowable expenditures. Thus, for the reconstruction of cashflows, deferred tax and depreciation are schematic.

The salient consideration in computing and assessing cashflows is the quantitative contribution made by each item. Thus, in looking at a gross cash flow composed of 10 per cent profit after taxation, 50 per cent depreciation, and 40 per cent deferred taxation increase, we could argue that the contribution made by the generation of net profit was relatively low—relative that is to the other two accounts. The 'quality' for credit-granting purposes of such a cashflow cannot be high.

Likewise, a gross cashflow made up of the following items could also be held to be weak:

Profit after taxation	
But before extraordinary item	
(tax credit)	6,500
Extraordinary item	25,500
Depreciation	7,300
Deferred tax/increase	1,234
GROSS CASHFLOW:	40,534

An all-inclusive view of profit would cause the analyst to include the extraordinary item of 25,500. If so, analysis of the flow itself would show that this credit represents some 63 per cent of the total, whereas profits contributed only 16 per cent. As has been stated earlier, the company's health must be assessed on its ability to generate profits. The stages during a financial year at which distributions are made from those profits are of less account. The same sort of analysis can be performed with good effect on total funds generated by the operation in the funds flow statement. Plainly, credit decisions will be more favourable in direct proportion to the subject companies' abilities to earn profits. The composite gross cashflow made up of profit after tax, depreciation and increase/decrease in deferred taxation, provides a valuable indicator of a company's cover for priority debt and other current liability items. The telling point, however, is the composition of the total cashflow. Do profits contribute a proportionately high and increasing share of the total over several periods? If so, the total flows should show yearly increases given periodic replacement and purchase of fixed assets.

Two basic views can be taken on interpretation of the contribution to cashflow made by deferred tax. Either the analyst can argue that in all likelihood the deferred liability will not crystallize in the foreseeable future—which, of course, entails that the deferred tax contribution to gross cashflow will be of high quality; or he can hold that interim use of the deferred obligation, in effect, as cash, may crystallize at any time in the next or subsequent accounting periods—entailing that the quality of the 'asset' is low. While both analysts will add the deferred tax difference to their cashflows, the second will minimize its effects in assessing the debt-service quality and quantity of that cashflow. Where priority debt (current debt) is composed of fixed instalment term loan portions currently repayable, the analyst will not be sanguine about the ability of a gross cashflow made up of a proportionally high volume of deferred tax increases to service that priority debt in the next accounting period.

To a degree, continued increases in the deferred taxation account depend on continuing investment in fixed assets. If the contribution to flows made by profits is low, eventually, the company may not earn adequate money to make such investments. If this is so, eventually, the volume of deferred liabilities will decrease. Accordingly, the total gross cashflow will decrease.

In the balance sheet, the deferred taxation account must be treated as a long-term liability by analysts. It is normally posted in accounts under Creditors: Amounts falling due after more than one year.

As a long-term liability item that may or may not crystallize, deferred tax ranks as a constituent of capital employed in that the company has had the use of the funds deriving from the postponed obligation for one year or more. As the liability is not a current item, it is long-term and ranks as permanent capital in the same way as term loans and equity.

Again, analysts should assess the quality of any company's permanent capital. In the main, the bulk of permanent capital should be represented by shareholders' funds (equity) rather than by borrowings. In a significant sense, deferred liabilities are borrowings, though in the case of deferred taxation, timing differences may reverse the liability. The likelihood of this should be assessed from considerable knowledge and experience of particular industry sectors.

Likewise, in the computation of tangible net worth, net assets, and current worth, the deferred tax account should be deducted along with other liability items.

Sources

Deloitte, Haskins and Sells, *Taxation in Europe*, Oyez, London, 1980.
Holmes, G., and Sugden, A., *Interpreting Company Reports and Accounts*, Woodhead-Faulkner, Cambridge, 1983, Chapter 13.
Institute of Chartered Accountants of Scotland, *Accounting for Deferred Tax, Summary and Guide to SSAP 15*, Revised May 1985, passim.
Shock, J., *Capital Allowances*, Oyez, London, 1981.
Sumption, A., and Lawton, P., *Tax and Tax Planning*, 9th edn, Oyez, London, 1981.

8

THE RADICAL TREATMENT OF OFF-BALANCE-SHEET EXPOSURES

A distinction obtains between the accounting treatment and analytical treatment of off-balance-sheet exposures. Such commitments or exposures refer to a number of items:

Leases and hire purchase contracts
Guarantees and cross-guarantees
Capital contracts authorized and/or entered into
Legal actions and other contingent liabilities
Banks' off-balance-sheet business

Leasing commitments

Prior to July, 1984, UK companies had the option of capitalizing financial leases, or they could include under current liabilities portions of those leasing obligations due within the period. Where the balance of the leasing obligations was not capitalized, it could be posted in the notes to the accounts. In August 1984, SSAP 21 was published. This Statement distinguished between operating and finance leases and calls for separate accounting treatment for the two.

Finance leases are contracts which transfer substantially all the risks and benefits of ownership of an asset to the lessee. Operating leases are drawn up to cover periods substantially less than the expected useful life of an asset. This has the effect that the lessor retains most of the risks and benefits of ownership.

Before SSAP 21, companies could opt for finance leases in lieu of outright borrowing for the purchase of assets. There was no obligation to post either the asset itself or the commitment to the lease payments in the balance sheet, although many public companies set out their leasing commitments fully in the notes to the accounts.

This option produced off-balance-sheet financing which had the effect of minimizing apparent borrowing. Formal gearing, thus, appeared lower than it actually was since companies had, effectively, borrowed just as much, if not more, by having entered into the leasing commitment as if they had borrowed money to fund the assets. Instead of having to pay interest charges on borrowed money, the companies had to pay leasing charges as well as bearing depreciation charges on the assets in which they had effective ownership.

For private companies, in particular, small firms, these off-balance-sheet commitments (i.e. balances of finance lease payments not currently due) were not always given in the

184 PROBLEMS IN THE COMPUTATION AND INTERPRETATION OF DATA

notes to the accounts. Accordingly, because of the less stringent reporting requirements allowed private and small companies, true gearing is often considerably hidden. For the credit analyst, hidden gearing produces a distorted picture of a company's capacity to service debt and also, to contract further debt. Additionally, hidden gearing distorts the measurements of net worth.

Finance leases

Under SSAP 21, finance leases must be posted in balance sheets of the lessee as an asset *and* as an obligation to pay future rentals. The initial amount noted as an asset and as a liability should be the present value of the minimum lease payments. This is calculated by discounting both at the interest rate implicit in the lease. Figure 8.1 illustrates this accounting treatment.

An asset is acquired under a finance lease. The lease payments are £20,000 per annum for five years with an option to continue the lease for another five years at £3,000 per annum. Payments are to be made annually in advance with the first payment made on taking delivery of the asset.

1. The interest rate implicit in the lease is 15 per cent, or £3,000/£20,000.
2. The present value of the minimum lease payments discounted at 15 per cent per annum can be calculated by using figures from any present value tables.
3. Accordingly:

Rental payment date	*Present value*	*Present value of £20 k payment*
On delivery	1.0	£20,000
In 1 year	0.870	17,400
In 2 years	1.626	16,748
In 3 years	2.283	15,434
In 4 years	2.855	14,290
Present value of minimum Lease payments:		£83,872

4. The asset will accordingly be posted at £83,872 and the liability for future lease payments will similarly be posted at £83,872.

Figure 8.1 Treatment of finance leases

In this example, after the first year the asset will suffer depreciation over the shorter of the lease's life or the asset's expected useful life. The lease's term is ten years, and let us say that the asset's expected useful life is five years. On a straight-line depreciation basis, the present value of minimum lease payments of £83,872 would, therefore, be depreciated by one-fifth of £83,872 or £16,774 approximately. This lowers the asset value to £67,098.

The present value of the balance of the minimum lease payments is recalculated. There is no longer a minimum lease payment due in four years' time (£14,290 in Figure 8.1) and, accordingly, the present value of future lease payments is now £69,582 or £83,872 less

£14,290. £14,290 is deducted from the future liability and the balance of £5,710 of the initial payment of £20,000 on delivery of the asset is posted as interest paid. These computations would need to be repeated for every subsequent year where at the end of year 5, the asset's value would be nil and the remaining lease payments and interest charges would also be nil.

At this stage, it will be as well to summarize the disclosure requirements on lessees imposed by SSAP 21.

Disclosures by lessees

Gross amounts of assets held under finance leases including the equivalent information concerning hire purchase contracts which have similar characteristics, together with the related accumulated depreciation should be disclosed by each major class of asset. The total depreciation allocated for the period in respect of assets held under finance leases should be disclosed by each major class of asset. (Section 49)

The information required by Section 49 may, as an alternative, be integrated with it so that the totals of gross amount, accumulated depreciation, net amount, and depreciation allocated for the period for each major class of asset are included with similar amounts in respect of owned fixed assets. Where this alternate method is used, the net amount of assets held under finance leases included in the overall total should be disclosed. So should the amount of depreciation. (Section 50)

The amounts of obligations related to finance leases (net of finance charges allocated to future periods) should be disclosed separately from other obligations and liabilities, either on the face of the balance sheet or in the notes to the accounts. (Section 51)

These net obligations under finance leases should be analysed between amounts payable in the next year, amounts payable in the second to fifth year inclusive from the balance-sheet date, and the aggregate amounts payable thereafter. This analysis may be presented either:

(a) separately for obligations under finance leases and similar character hire purchase contracts, as noted earlier, or
(b) where the total of these items is combined on the balance sheet with other obligations and liabilities, by giving the equivalent analysis of the total in which it is included. If the analysis is presented according to (a) above, a lessee may, as an alternative to analysing the net obligations, analyse the gross obligations, with future finance charges being separately deducted from the total. (Section 52)

The aggregate finance charges allocated for the period in respect of finance leases should be disclosed. (Section 53)

Disclosure should be made of the amount of any commitments existing at the balance-sheet date in respect of finance leases which have been entered into but whose inception occurs *after* the year end. (Section 54)

Operating leases

Under operating leases, the lessor retains the bulk of risk and benefits of ownership. The accounting treatment under these leases charges rental payments to the profit and loss account of the lessee as those payments arise. Assets under operating leases, therefore, do not appear on the face of the balance sheet and nor do the liabilities for future rental payments. Figure 8.2 provides an example:

	£'ms	
Payments due during y/ending	*Operating leases*	*Finance leases*
31 March 1986	4.0	12.8
1987	3.4	12.2
1988	3.2	9.5
1989	2.9	7.2
1990	2.7	3.8
Payments due after 31 March 1990	22.7	11.5
	38.9	57.0
Less: Finance charges Allocated to future periods:	—	7.0
Obligations under leases:	38.9	50.0

Figure 8.2 Treatment of operating leases

The following sections of SSAP 21 summarize the disclosure requirements of lessees:

The total of operating lease rentals including the equivalent information in respect of hire purchase contracts which have characteristics similar to those of operating leases, should be charged as an expense in the profit and loss account. The expense itself must be disclosed and analysed between amounts payable in respect of hire of plant and machinery and in respect of other operating leases. (Section 55)

In respect of operating leases, the lessee should disclose the payments which he is committed to make during the next year, analysed between those in which the commitment expires within that year, in the second to fifth years inclusive and over five years from the balance-sheet date, showing separately the commitments in respect of leases of land and buildings and other operating leases. (Section 56)

Disclosure should be made of the policies adopted for accounting for operating leases and finance leases. (Section 57)

Implementation of SSAP 21

The chief effect of SSAP 21 on lessees' balance sheets is that where they have leased assets under a finance lease, they will now have to reflect the asset and the liability in their balance sheet. For companies already making full disclosures in notes, capitalizing or partially capitalizing such commitments, the impact of the Standard will be minimal from the analytical or assessment point of view as analysts will already take into net worth and other computations many, if not all, off-balance-sheet liabilities when these liabilities are noted.

The Standard's impact on lessees relying on the cosmetic effects of hidden gearing will be in many cases material once off-balance-sheet commitments have been properly accounted for. This will be particularly true for smaller firms where leasing commitments have tended not to be analysed in the notes to accounts.

The aforegoing accounting practices are mandatory for financial statements relating to periods beginning on or after 1 July 1987. Many firms may feel, accordingly, that the requirements under SSAP 21 can be effectively shelved. Note, however, that the disclosure requirements set forth in Sections 52 and 54 to 57 cited earlier apply to accounts relating to periods beginning on or after 1 July 1984. Accordingly, most firms with 30 June 1985 year-ends will have to comply. The effect of these provisions is that finance leases do not have to be capitalized during the period of transition. Accounts prepared before the end of 1988, are, therefore, likely to differ greatly in their treatment of finance leases until the Standard takes full effect, creating eventual uniformity.

Analytical treatment of leases

In credit analysis, all material assets and liabilities must be accounted for. Therefore, finance leases form contractual undertakings to observe a certain schedule of payments. To all intents and purposes, finance lease obligations are treated similarly to bank loans and other contractual borrowings. Analysts, Trade and Commercial Credit Corporation calculate current priority debt as follows:

Current debt items
Current portions of bank loans due for repayment and overdrafts
Current portions of mortgages due for repayment
Taxation currently payable including value added tax
Hire purchase commitments currently payable
Portions of all leases currently payable
Debenture interest currently payable
Insurance premiums currently payable
Bills of exchange and other documentary instruments currently payable

In the practical, if not in the legal sense, these obligations enjoy a seniority to non-contractual or unsecured and more easily postponable debt, e.g. the bulk of trade creditors.

The end effect of the disclosure requirement of SSAP 21 will, of course, be a lowering on net worth for many companies where full leasing obligations had not been previously noted. Gearing for these companies will show higher levels, and the credit-granting implications in these cases will be less favourable. Also, the capitalization of finance leases will tend to increase capital employed on the face of balance sheets at least after the first leasing period when the asset value and liability value of the commitment are self-cancelling. Against higher totals of capital employed, some performance indicators, e.g. prime ratio and profit margin may shrink.

The charging-off to profit and loss of operating leases is commonly practised, or should be, at present. However, future commitments under these leases has not generally been analysed in the accounts of smaller and private companies. SSAP 21 will eventually impose this analysis. Accordingly, a higher level of leasing commitments at future periods will be taken into various analytical calculations, e.g. total debt or tangible net worth.

Whilst the analytical treatment of leasing commitments will be the same when applied to

US companies, the differences between US and UK accounting practice with regard to finance and operating leases should be made clear.

US practice is covered by Financial Accounting Standards 13, 17, 22, 23, 26, 27 and 29 (L10). Leases are required to be capitalized in accounts and treated as either a direct financing lease or a sales-type lease depending upon circumstances. Lease transactions that meet any of the four specific criteria are to be capitalized:

1. When the lease transfers ownership to the lessee.
2. When the lease contains a bargain purchase option (hire purchase).
3. When the life of the lease (including bargain purchase renewal periods) covers 75 per cent or more of the remaining useful life of the asset (with the exception of certain used property).
4. When the present value of the minimum lease payments (including termination penalties) is 90 per cent or more of the asset's market value.

Leases that do not fulfil any of the four criteria above are taken as operating leases. Thus, in US accounts, capital leases refer to finance leases.

Contingent liabilities and their treatment in analysis

Contingent liabilities are a type of post-balance-sheet event. They represent events that might happen rather than events that have actually happened. The EEC Fourth Directive, the historical cost convention, and SSAP 18 require that provision be made for future losses arising from current transactions whilst future gains are not accounted for (under the prudence concept and on the grounds of non-realization). Yet where there may be uncertainty about the future and the size of any gain or loss, SSAP 18 requires that all contingencies material to an assessment of the business be noted in the accounts. The date on which the accounts were approved by the directors should also be noted. This extends the view of the 1967 Companies Act which refers to the need to disclose contingent liabilities but does not cite gains. From an accounting viewpoint, the question of what may be material by way of contingency is the source of some debate—in particular, when the disclosure of some possible event may cause that event to occur.

Examples of contingent liabilities are:

1. Guarantees to banks.
2. Guarantees to trade creditors and others.
3. Bills of exchange discounted with bankers.
4. Goods sold under guarantee or warranty.
5. Legal action pending.
6. Uncalled payments on partly paid shares.
7. Any potential liabilities on other claims.
8. Performance bonds.
9. Commitments under a revolving credit facility.
10. Uncalled liabilities under a capital market instrument (for investment and participating banks).
11. Cross-guarantee instruments for companies and banks.

Figure 8.3 gives an illustration of Ford Motor Company's notation of contingent liabilities in its 1971 accounts:

	£'000s	
	1971	1970
1. *Contingent liabilities*		
Debts contracted with third parties which give recourse to Ford Motor Company Ltd or its subsidiaries in case of default	8,796	5,107
Uncalled capital of a subsidiary	950	950
Guarantee of subsidiaries' and affiliates' borrowings	17,111	11,029
	£26,857	£17,086

Figure 8.3 Notation of contingent liabilities (1)

The notation of contingent liabilities can be more cryptic in detail. Here is Monsanto's note 19 on contingent liabilities from its 1983 accounts:

	£'000s	
	1983	1982
19. *Contingent liabilities*		
Contingent liabilities mainly represent guarantees entered into in the normal course of business		
Consolidated and company	2,946	1,952

Of concern to analysts will be largely unquantified notes covering contingent liabilities. Figure 8.4 from the 1983 accounts of London and Northern Group PLC furnishes a prime example:

28. *Contingent liabilities*
    Contingent liabilities, for which no provision has been made in the accounts, exist in respect of the following:
    1. Guarantees, indemnities and undertakings:
        (a) By the holding company in respect of borrowings of its subsidiaries and contract performance of its subsidiaries and, in certain cases, former subsidiaries.
        (b) By group companies in respect of borrowings, contract performance and other normal trading agreements of their own and of fellow subsidiaries and, in certain cases, former subsidiaries.
        (c) By a group company in respect of the bank overdraft of a related company
    2. Options in respect of shares in subsidiaries held by minority shareholders which can be sold to the holding company on terms generally related to the original purchase of the majority interests and the subsequent achievements of the subsidiaries concerned.
    3. Additional purchase consideration for shares in subsidiaries dependent upon profits realised in future years.
    4. Uncalled share capital of investments amounting to £50,000.

Figure 8.4 Notation of contingent liabilities (2)

Apart from the uncalled investment share capital of £50,000, such a setting-out of contingent liabilities tells the analyst (or the interested reader of the accounts for that matter) very little. It does, fairly or unfairly, appear to suggest that whatever the unquantified contingencies are, they are probably not inconsiderable.

For sheer obscurantism and non-compliance with at least the spirit of SSAP 18, the note on Hadson Petroleum International PLC's contingent liabilities is unbeatable (Figure 8.5):

---

17. *Contingent liabilities*
(a) Pursuant to the operating agreements governing the licence interests of the group, the various operators and, in certain instances, the other participants, have been granted charges over the relevant rights and interests in the licences, any production therefrom and over all equipment and materials relating to those licences as security for the payment of any sums due from time to time under the operating agreement.
(b) Pursuant to the farmout agreement covering licence P244, a subsidiary of the Company has granted to Bomin North Sea Limited a charge over all its assets both present and future, as security for amounts receivable by Bomin North Sea Limited under the farmout agreement.
(c) Under the terms of the various operating and farmout agreements the group may be liable in certain circumstances to bear increased costs as a result of, *inter alia*, the default or withdrawal of any other party to such agreements.
(d) The group is liable to pay certain royalties in respect of revenue from its share of petroleum produced from:
   (i) United Kingdom Production Licences 111, 114, 116A and B, 118, 119, 206, 207, 208 and 209 at the rate of 1 per cent on gross production;
   (ii) United Kingdom Mining Licences ML18 and ML21 at the rate of 10 per cent on gross production; and
   (iii) Spanish offshore licences Vizcaya-A and Santander-C at the rate of 1 per cent in respect of the group's interests in proceeds of sale production after the deduction of certain costs.

Figure 8.5 Notation of contingent liabilities (3)

As a note of Hadson's contingent liabilities, the 'information' contained in Figure 8.5 is worthless for analysts as it is totally unquantified. More interestingly, perhaps, it is also unquantifiable.

Holmes and Sugden point out that there is reticence in the UK on the part of companies to disclose potential liabilities arising from legal action still before the court, though such disclosure is accepted practice in the US. They hold that fuller disclosures are, however, being made in the UK and cite the following note from Turner & Newall's 1983 accounts as an example:

> The Company and certain subsidiaries are among more than 300 companies named as defendants in a large number of court actions concerned with alleged asbestos-related diseases in the USA and are among a number of defendants to claims in the UK from employees and former employees.

Because of the slow onset of these diseases the directors expect that similar claims will be made in future years but the expenditure which may arise from such claims cannot be determined. (Holmes and Sugden, p. 63)

Broadly speaking, analysts can take two views of contingent liabilities. Firstly, all quantified contingent liabilities can be added to total liabilities—current and long-term liabilities on the face of the balance sheet—and the restated total liabilities can be deducted from total assets in calculating net worth. It is imprecise and over-ambitious to try and work contingent liabilities into forecasts of current liabilities to be serviced from operational inflows unless very detailed information can be supplied. It is arguable that were this the case, the contingency would cease to be a contingent liability and become a long-term liability.

The cut-and-dried approach of this view affords the most prudent estimates, but often at the expense of common sense and always at the expense of timing of flows. This view does, however, give analysts a 'worst possible outcome' which can be especially useful in the assessment of ailing companies. It also provides a hard computation of tangible net worth.

The second view takes a more lenient approach and holds that in most cases, no actual liability arises from contingencies. Accordingly, potential liabilities not warranting a place on the balance sheet can be largely disregarded.

The difficulties in this view are evident. In striving after a prudent view, the analyst following such an approach will be in danger of painting too rosy a picture. Holmes and Sugden, who appear to espouse more of the second than the first view, point out that sometimes, contingent liabilities are extremely important. But how can analysts identify the important or material ones? Holmes and Sugden suggest watching for a sharp rise in the total amount of contingencies, and also, for any arising outside the normal course of business. They go on to suggest that any contingency, for instance, in the form of a guarantee, arising in respect of a subsidiary that has been disposed of can be particularly dangerous. They argue that here is the implication that either the new owners are not prepared to give their guarantee, or that such a guarantee is unacceptable to the other party. This, rightly, Holmes and Sugden view as an indication of weakness. They add that guaranteeing the liabilities of an entity over which the company now has no control must entail risk. Certainly, it entails greater risk than acting as guarantor for a subsidiary. Guaranteeing the obligations of associate companies or affiliates likewise entails greater risk as the level of control over these companies is less than the control exerted over subsidiaries.

Particularly for analysts taking the second and more lenient view of contingent liabilities, knowledge of subject companies' types of business and markets is invaluable. Otherwise, it will be difficult to spot contingent liabilities that are not part of companies' normal activities. This is complicated in volatile and innovative fields such as investment banking with its proliferation of new off-balance-sheet financing instruments.

Off-balance-sheet banking business

The non-bank credit analyst will, from time to time, be called upon to assess the financial resources of banks which are being considered for one-off financing deals, special projects, or permanent relationships. In the strict accounting sense, banks lag far behind commercial trading companies in depth of disclosure. Hidden reserves as well as the treatment of off-balance-sheet business serve as cases in point.

Very briefly, the reasons for the expansion of off-balance-sheet banking business are:

1. Narrowing profit margins on conventional business.
   This has been caused by increased competition and increasingly aggressive marketing of bank products.
2. Supervisory attempts to bolster banks' capital adequacy.
   When capital/assets ratios fall, many institutions will seek to remove risk calling for higher levels of capital from their balance sheets, as capital is inadequate for the conduct of on-balance-sheet business.
3. Deregulation.
   Many banks are entering new fields, e.g. clearing banks issuing debt securities, previously the work of investment banks. Where a banking group is not highly diversified in specialist subsidiaries, investment banking business may be carried out via the controlling or main operating company in the group. The investment banking business will thus entail off-balance-sheet exposures in some cases.
4. Technological advances.
   The administration and monitoring of new financial instruments as well as conventional bank products has made it easier and quicker for banks to design and service products more readily than to account for them in the traditional ways.
5. In many countries, banks are (to date) largely or totally free from realistic capital requirements.
   In countries where capital requirements exist in any significant sense, much off-balance-sheet business has, according to the Bank of England, been transacted to avoid the prudential guidelines or requirements.

As the banking system is, for better or for worse, international in its interdependence, the taking on of sizeable, unaccounted-for risk—in this case, off-balance sheet—by many major banks, provides the scenario for potential failures. Even one major bank failure could set off a domino effect, ultimately causing the whole system to collapse. Also, central bank supervisors tend to see the proliferation of off-balance-sheet business in its present state as the concentration of risks that were previously more widely dispersed. This applies especially to foreign exchange and interest rate risks in swaps business.

The most recent Bank of England discussion document argues for the view that the individual kinds of off-balance-sheet risk inherent in certain new capital market instruments are, in essence, no different from the other types of risks inherent in on-balance-sheet transactions. The Bank of England, accordingly, suggests that what we have come to think of as off-balance-sheet risks should be analysed and accounted for integrally with banks' overall risk profiles. Bank supervisors feel that it is particularly crucial for banks to adopt a co-ordinated approach to risk management, paying especial attention to the possible correlation of varying types of risk, both with respect to individual banks and banking groups as single entities. The Bank of England paper does not address itself to accounting issues, particularly, credit risk. The point is made clearly, however, that many supervisors consider that the information concerning off-balance-sheet exposures both in the UK and in other countries, e.g. the US, is generally inadequate to give depositors and shareholders reasonable pictures of banks' activities. The Bank of England paper examines off-balance-sheet risks from three aspects: market/position risk, operational/control risk, and credit risk.

Briefly, market/position risk refers to funding risk where banks may not be able to finance commitments under off-balance-sheet instruments as those commitments fall due. Operational/control risks centre around interest rate and foreign exchange risks which can give rise to losses due to movements in the respective markets. Credit risk, perceived by the paper as the most serious, refers to the risk of banks losing money should customers of the new instruments default.

The paper goes on to quantify the comparative credit risks inherent in the off-balance-sheet instruments. Three chief categories are identified:

Full risk: Equivalent to that of a direct credit carried on the face of the bank's balance sheet.
Medium risk: Significant risk but not so great as that of a direct credit.
Low risk: Where there is a small credit risk yet not one that can be ignored.

These categories of risk are intended to form the points of reference against which capital requirements will come to be imposed on off-balance-sheet business.

They are reported as according with the risk-asset system employed by the EEC for the measurement of capital requirements and due to be adopted by the US, Canada and Japan.

The Euromarket correspondent of the *Financial Times* judges that the Bank's paper furnishes only a modest beginning to the eventual solution of a complex and important problem in that the paper avoids prescribing precise capital requirements. It merely assigns different types of financing instrument to the general risk categories mentioned before. It is agreed, however, that the paper succeeds in arriving at a series of common definitions for the mass of new financing instruments as well as the degrees of risk they presuppose. With the capital markets as innovative and fashion-prone as they are, this is no mean achievement.

Attention is directed to the wholesale funding risk inherent in the extensive world-wide total of standby commitments stemming from the underwriting of Euronotes, standby letters of credit, loan commitments, and undrawn overdraft facilities. The paper holds that these should not be permitted to develop out of line with individual banks' ability to meet these commitments as they fall due.

Giving rise to especial worry are options under which banks buy or sell the right to trade a given financing instrument at a predetermined price at some time in the future. To limit and control such transactions, rigorous systems are vital. The paper also stresses that 'as with any dealing activity bank managements need a formal written policy for authorizing the activities of their traders'.

In debt swaps, banks exchange the debt of one borrower for another. The paper argues that in these cases the credit risk is limited to the cost of replacing the cashflows necessary for debt-service at current market rates should one party default. The difficulty here is that such cashflows will necessarily fluctuate, depending on the maturity of the contract outstanding and the interest and exchange rate levels at any one time. Notwithstanding, bankers need to provide for such risks to the best of their ability by estimating the potential credit exposure arising from swap transactions in order to comply with credit limit constraints. Such estimation will also be important for determining the optimal pricing of the deals.

'Banks are advised', says the paper, 'to build a cautious bias into their estimates and to revalue their portfolio of such instruments regularly to ensure that they are not underestimating counterparty credit exposure.'

The paper states that off-balance-sheet exposures should be included in the computation of credit limits set for individual customers. This is prudential to avoid excessive exposure to single customers.

Without installing effective risk control and measurement systems, banks can have no sound basis for the planning, monitoring, or control of off-balance-sheet business. The paper adds that 'without accounting systems which enable independent checking and reconciliation procedures to be carried out on a routine basis, the detection of potential losses will be very difficult and the risk of fraud will increase'.

By the end of 1986, the Bank of England expects to prescribe detailed capital requirements for banks conducting such off-balance-sheet business as swaps and the underwriting of note issuance facilities in the Euromarkets. In May 1985, the Bank imposed a capital requirement on Euronote underwriting facilities equivalent to 50 per cent of the capital requirements applying to straightforward loans.

Off-balance-sheet business has been categorized by the Bank as follows:

1. *Guarantees and similar contingent liabilities*
   Guarantees
   Acceptances
   Transactions with recourse
   Standby letters of credit
   Documentary letters of credit (in US: Commercial letter of credit)
   Warranties
   Indemnities
   Performance bonds
   Endorsements, e.g. Per Aval, or a bill of exchange already accepted by another bank.
2. *Commitments*
   Irrevocable commitments with certain exercise or draw-down
   Irrevocable commitments where draw-down is entirely at the discretion of the other party and where it is unclear whether or not and to what extent the credit risk will actually materialize
   Asset sale and repurchase agreements
   Forward forward deposits
   Partly-paid shares and securities
   Unconditional standby facilities and similar commitments
3. *Foreign exchange, interest rate and stock index related transactions*
   Hedging mechanisms for swaps
   Options, futures and similar contracts
4. *Advisory, management and underwriting functions*
   Fiduciary and agency functions forming part of the operational and control risks where a bank's standing and reputation may be at stake
   Securities underwriting

In 1985, the Bank for International Settlements reported for the first time figures for net lending in the international banking and capital markets combined. These showed that in the initial half of 1985, net new finance provided to non-bank borrowers totalled only $70 bn. Compare this with net borrowing for the same sector in 1981 where total net lending stood at $190 bn. Perhaps more than others, the syndicated loan market has suffered to a higher degree than the bond market. Syndications are still depressed at time of writing. According to the OECD as reported in the *Financial Times*, total international bank loans declined in 1985 to only $43.2 bn against the $56.8 bn of 1984.

In terms of net drawings, the fast expanding market in Euronote issuance facilities has not yet significantly compensated for this decline. Business in note facilities, however, rose in 1985 to $50.2 bn (1984: $28.8 bn), and even these figures represent a 'theoretical maximum of actual lending'. Accordingly, draw-downs under these facilities are actually far smaller. A recent estimate is not much in excess of $15 bn. At such a level, the actual size of the Euronote market is still less than a tenth of the commercial paper market in the US. That leaves a yet growing market in Eurocommercial paper which does not call for any underlying bank credit. Figure 8.6 shows the increasing borrowings in the international capital markets:

Borrowings on international capital markets
(US$ bn)

	1983	1984	1985*
Bonds	77.1	111.5	167.7
of which: at floating rate	(19.5)	(38.2)	(58.4)
Syndicated bank loans†	67.2	56.8	43.2
Note issuance facilities and other facilities‡	9.5	28.8	50.2
Total	153.8	197.1	261.1

*Provisional
†Excluding loan renegotiations ($5.2 bn in 1984 and $15.9 bn in 1985)
‡Excluding merger-related standbys ($26.5 bn in 1984 and $6.3 bn in 1985)

Figure 8.6 Borrowings on international capital markets. Source: OECD

Summary: Tradeable debt and banks' need to check the extent of off-balance-sheet commitments

Against the manifest growth of the international capital markets, the innovations in financing instruments in these markets, the expansion of credit in all sectors, and the erosion of profit margins, radical changes have swept through international banking. Central banks as well as those government agencies responsible for banking supervision have begun to show their concern.

At the heart of this concern is the securitization of debt—the process of making a debt a security and trading it. The growing tradeability of debt has tended to remove assessable risk from the balance sheet to disclosed or undisclosed positions off the balance sheet. If risk is off-balance sheet, it is difficult to analyse and assess.

For instance, under a note issuance facility (NIF), a bank may not necessarily provide funds to its customer. The bank, however, must be willing and able to provide funding if required under the conditions of the facility. Such an off-balance-sheet commitment is a potentially real commitment.

Given further economic downturns and the possible credit squeeze following from such downturns, higher degrees of commitment under note issuance facilities would result. Were a particularly large borrower in the Euronote market to become financially troubled, the same type of domino effect could be set off. In these circumstances, banks could be embarrassed in having to raise very sizeable amounts of money simultaneously. Were one or more major banks unable to meet their commitments, the international financial system might suffer considerable damage or even collapse.

At present, there is no reliable way of assessing whether or not banks would be able to raise such large amounts and still show profits. The present writer feels it is highly unlikely. With one crisis of confidence, the tradeability of such commitments can be totally extinguished. Whilst individual commitments might be met by underwriters as opposed to participating banks, a decline in debt tradeability would quickly contract underwriters' willingness and ability to provide ultimate backing for future securitized issues.

In its 1985 study, the Bank for International Settlements warned of five prime areas of risk in today's capital markets.

True to the perennial credit paradox (those companies that need cash the most are the worst credit risks), the BIS study identified a two-tier market in which the bulk of actual lending was to customers who did not qualify for securities issues. Lesser-quality credit risks extend as well to the second tier composed of various large debtors, for example, developing countries in Latin America. These lesser-quality borrowers are also dependent to a high degree on actual loans whereas they are excluded from the capital markets altogether. Debt-service in these cases is made harder because of lack of restructuring flexibility in the loan market compared with the capital markets. Also, without the capital market back-up, additional sources of finance have been closed off to them.

Thirdly, the BIS claims that the returns on off-balance-sheet business were too low to justify the attendant risks. Securitization had encouraged banks to stockpile marketable securities. This gave their accounts a misleading liquidity quotient because of the off-balance-sheet risks. Also, in the event of a credit squeeze, the value of these assets would fall sharply or evaporate.

Finally, new instruments are new instruments and not even the major players in the markets have much actual experience at monitoring and control. BIS and the 1986 Bank of England study pointed out that neither the central banks nor many market practitioners could easily understand the structures of many new instruments at the rate in which they were developed. Accordingly, no one was well prepared to solve problems as they arose.

The Federal Reserve Board's consultative document published in January, 1986, argued that whilst banks have improved (forcibly) their capital gearing in recent years, they have achieved this in part by shrinking their balance sheets rather than by injecting fresh capital. As high quality assets are easier to sell than poor quality loans, the 'assets' left on balance sheets have tended to be lower in quality and, therefore, less liquid. This indicates that the putative improvement in capital gearing has been inadequate.

The FDIC then proposed a system of measuring assets according to the actual risks they entailed. This type of risk-asset system is already used for banking supervision in the EEC and is soon due to be implemented in Japan. In the US it would be incorporated with the present system which relies upon the total volume of assets to arrive at an adequate capital size.

The new system would assign commitments under a note issuance facility a weighting of 0.3 when the risk asset ratio was calculated. Ordinary loans would have a weighting of 1. Banks would then have to calculate their overall risk asset ratio and those with particularly high risk business would then be obliged to raise new capital even were this to take them over the 5.5 per cent of assets currently required in the US. Alternately, they could decrease the risk profile of their activities.

Writing in the *Financial Times*' International Capital Markets Supplement of 17 March 1986, P. Montagnon argued that such a system was cumbersome and overly rigid in that it attemped to categorize different types of risk. He reported that the FDIC also admitted initial defeat in attempting to cover all types of off-balance-sheet risk admitting, for instance, that it did not know how to evaluate the risks inherent in the $200 bn interest rate swap market and simply looked for advice from public comment.

The Bank of England paper referred to earlier reflects many of the same difficulties. In sum, practical control, monitoring, and accounting systems to regulate off-balance-sheet instruments are still in their infancy. If and when such commitments are treated by the accounting profession in ways similar to quantified contingent liabilities—which seems to be the prudent way of treating such exposures and keeping them off the face of the balance sheet—non-bank credit analysts will better be able to assess the overall quality of banks' financial conditions. Without such quantification, accurate risk profile assessment of bank players in the international capital markets will remain highly speculative.

Sources

Bank of England, *The Management of Banks' Off-Balance-Sheet Exposures; A Supervisory Perspective*, Committee on Banking Regulations and Supervisory Practices, Basle, March 1986.

Holmes, G., and Sugden, A., *Interpreting Company Reports and Accounts*, Woodhead-Faulkner, Cambridge, 2nd edition, 1983, pp. 62–63, 3rd edition, 1986, pp. 64–65.

Hughes, M., 'Banking Supervision (White Paper on Banking Supervision)', *The Accountant's Magazine*, March 1986, Vol. 90, no. 956, pp. 29–30.

Montagnon, P., 'Bankers Agree on Hidden Risk Guidelines', *Financial Times*, 17 March 1986; 'Off-Balance-Sheet Risk', *International Capital Markets Supplement, Financial Times*, 17 March 1986, p. 8; 'Bank May Set Rules for Off-Balance Sheet Risks', *Financial Times*, 21 March 1986.

The Accountant's Magazine, 'SSAP 21—Its Impact on Lessees', *The Accountant's Magazine*, August 1985, Vol. LXXXIX, no. 950, pp. 364–367.

Part Three

THE CORRELATION AND TREATMENT OF COMPANY DATA

9

DATA SOURCES

In Chapter One, we listed some thirteen varying sources of company data. Briefly, these were:

1. Accounting statements (audited and unaudited)
2. Representations from managements.
3. Financial and other types of private investigations.
4. Economic and market reports.
5. Financial and general press information.
6. Special financial statements produced in support of particular credit applications.
7. Credit insurance audits/other audits, e.g. factoring company audits.
8. Intercompany/industry sector comparisons.
9. Intercompany intelligence.
10. Interbank intelligence.
11. Trade references.
12. Bankers' references.
13. Rating agencies.

With the possible exceptions of items 2, 6, and 7, the work of credit analysis can be made easier in that most of this data can be obtained from one source. Effective reporting companies' work is the providing and correlation of such data on either a disclosed or undisclosed basis. Good correlation entails the formation of an overall view of the information given by the data and the writing of an opinion or summary on these findings. This, in no way, obviates the need for credit analysis on the part of the lender or provider of trade credit. The provision and basic interpretation of data merely streamlines and reduces his time and costs in final analysis.

The point should be made here that intelligent credit analysis is not concerned only with the existing or potential debtor's willingness and ability to meet commitments on schedule. Good analysis must also take into account the financial condition and requirements of the provider of credit. In the case of banks, as we have seen, capital/assets guidelines must be observed. Sectoral risk must be kept diversified. In general, lending should not be overly concentrated in too few industry sectors. For banks, liquidity considerations always obtain. And of late, the tradeability of debt is important in certain off-balance-sheet transactions. For banks and trading companies, the terms of individual credits should, whenever possible and not without special reasons, fit in to the grantor's normal credit framework. Where individual credits fall outside the normal company policy or points of reference, financing costs and liquidity considerations must come into play. These types of considerations are, of course, highly idiosyncratic and must be treated summarily (if not definitively) by in-house credit analysts.

Thus, the data correlation and general interpretation obtainable from good reporting companies does not diminish the need for internal credit analysis in most instances. In the case of volume small credit limit determination, thorough reports from third-party companies may be treated as sufficient—although internal credit management of the accounts in question must still be carried out. The type of credit management in these cases centres around sales ledger work and effective collections. Because of the high volume of accounts and their individual low monetary values, exhaustive internal credit analysis is not cost-effective. In the end result, risk is often adequately diversified because of the high volume of small accounts in question. That having been said, most companies' sales ledgers do not consist solely of small accounts of roughly equivalent cash value. Pareto analysis shows continually that about 20 per cent of companies' sales ledgers are represented by certain concentrations of high value accounts. Sometimes these may be very few numerically. As such, it is important that adequate credit assessments be made on these accounts.

A central problem with effective credit analysis is its cost. A secondary, though still important problem, is the time required to carry out a thorough analysis. The background considerations to both problems which often fail to justify time or costs are the recency and the reliability of data. Whilst credit analysts must develop some forecasting ability, forecasting can never be regarded as accurate. In other words, the sanction of credit must never be made on the basis of a financial or market forecast alone. In general terms, the most accurate forecasts will come from the best quality data—always presupposing the analyst's skill at forecasting.

Database reporting companies

Still speaking in general terms, whilst the correlation and interpretation of data is handled easily and cheaply by reporting companies in particular, age of data and reliability, in many cases, greatly lessen the value of agency reports. In theory, the development of database reporting agencies should lessen these risks. In the practical sense, however, databases for all their speed and cost advantages, are only as good as the data put into them. Where data inputs are made by unskilled staff and where data itself is old, the results will be not only worthless but dangerous.

Examples of error in the inputting of data can occur chiefly in the extracting of accounting information from microfiche records when computer operatives do not have an adequate knowledge of company accounts and the significance of the various quantities that make them up. Error can also occur in the simple transmission of accounting numbers, for example, where the operative keys in a wrong digit.

For the maintenance of a high quality database, constant updating and checking are vital. A quality database, computerized or manual, must do more than parrot Companies' House information—all of which can be readily seen from microfiches or in hard copy print-outs. As the retrieval of company data from the Registries in London and Cardiff is absurdly laborious (for instance, no postal service is available on English and Welsh limited liability companies), most database reporting services have been marketed on the basis of saving time. In this, they succeed very well, especially in respect of computer link-ups with customers. From the standpoint of breadth of information, most current databases are distinctly lacking. The bulk of information in most cases is Companies' House data centring on registered information and audited accounts. Both registered and accounting data from Companies' House frequently suffer from age. Again, in general terms, data compiled from 1981 accounts is well-nigh worthless for current credit purposes.

When information is not antique, many databases still lack the ability to treat a mass of items synoptically. These databases have no overall assessment nor 'scoring' facilities. Supplementary data (when captured) such as trade or bank references are printed out textually. There is nothing wrong in that, but such extraneous data should still be incorporated within the overview of a company's performance. It is very simple to do this by assigning numerical values to the different types of bank or trade reference and building these values into an holistic model.

An important aspect gravely lacking in almost all databases is the ability to turn out synoptic interpretations based upon specific or estimated exposures. Accounting information, in these cases, is extracted and parroted back with no reference to safety margins should particular credits be granted. Again, from a computational or numerical point of view, this 'bespoke' work would be simple to do. The sad fact is that the building of synoptic scoring models in the credit field is still in its infancy. Also, not a great deal of significant work in this line has been done since Altman and Taffler. A crucial point obtains here. The construction of financial predictive or synoptic models has generally been seen as attractive and worth while. Taffler, among others, has always made the point that design or use of financial models by unskilled hands is highly dangerous. Models that have not been thoroughly debugged and tested for both significance and accuracy can lead to costly decision errors on the part of users. Also, and almost as important, the use of models whose accounting, statistical, or informational contents are 'unknown' is sheer idiocy—even when model findings are used merely as corroborative devices. In the course of this writing, we discovered a highly reputable database company, trading successfully in the market, whose management had no inkling of the statistical parameters of the holistic scoring model on which their reports are founded. In this case, the company's scoring model had been constructed by another firm. With hope, the other firm tested the model before having handed it over. Certainly, corroborative devices are important and highly useful. Notwithstanding, can it make sense to rely upon such devices when their fundamental or underlying principles may disagree radically with one's own? How significant will such touchstones actually be? Secondly, how should one view 'unknown' model findings when they materially disagree with one's own assessments? If model workings are 'unknown', how much credence can one put in them? The scope and quality of the financial models available on the market are highly varied. While a model's utility need not be contingent upon its users' professional brilliance in accounting, statistics, or forecasting, users should none the less know the leading assumptions that structure the models on which they rely for corroboration. In essence, users should see the force of these leading assumptions and agree with the view they tend to present. When this is not the case, or when users have no idea of what their models are operating on, how can the best decisions be taken either when the user is in the dark, or when model findings diverge sharply from his own analyses?

Updating and augmenting information

When credit risk is adequately diversified over a high volume of small value accounts, and when conventional database information is recent and of reliable quality, the material on which analysts can work can be obtained quickly and inexpensively. When exposures are low, say below £1,000 per month on credit sale accounts, reliance on conventional database reports by in-house analysts is justified in terms of time and cost-savings. Database reporting costs, for 'full' company reports range from about £11.00 per unit to £45.50. Within this range, the depth of reporting is not always in direct proportion to the price. The inexpensive Dun & Bradstreet reports, as we will see later, can be of considerable scope, correlating an impressive amount of discrete information and interpreting the same on a widely-used and respected rating system.

When credit risk is bunched in a number of small, high value accounts, it is important that managements do not cheese-pare in the matter of reporting or analytical costs. Whilst banks and commercial lawyers tend to have a realistic appreciation of the costs of financial intelligence, the bulk of the commercial public remains dim-witted. First of all, financial and market intelligence data is not and is not likely at some future time to be available from databases. By its very nature, financial intelligence is confidential. To obtain such information, the interested party must pay for it. The provision of confidential information often entails paying ultimate sources. The ethics or lack of them in such situations must be matters for consideration both by users and by reporting companies/investigators. In the legal profession and in the courts, two basic views seem to obtain. The first view is the purely commercial one that argues that the information counts. The provenance and cost of the information are matters directly decided by clients. Provided that such information is reliable and admissible in court, it is valuable and should be adduced. The second view holds that such confidential data as banking account balances are only obtainable in the first place by unlawful methods. Accordingly, such data should not be admissible. In actual practice, the first view far outweighs the second.

For sizeable credit exposures, as opposed to legal claims or attachment of assets, most database information will be patently insufficient. Banks, as well as many commercial credit managers, will require periodic personal interviews before credit decisions are reached. Many require such interviews before credit applications are processed. Certainly, much of this is done on the commonsense dictum having to do with instinct: 'If it were *my* money at stake, would I lend it?'

Bank credit applications and many large trade credit facilities require supporting documents such as budgets, cashflow projections, personal information on principal parties, and product-line data. Traditionally, applicants have been expected to produce such information themselves. With the growing sophistication both of borrowers and of lenders, intermediaries of various kinds are increasingly used by applicants in the preparation of such data.

Detailed supplementary data of this type cannot be prepared by undisclosed third parties. The full, open cooperation of management must be obtained. A few reporting companies provide such services on a disclosed basis. Trade and Commercial Credit Corporation will frequently, after having obtained a customer's authority, disclose their function to subject companies (debtors or potential debtors), requesting supplementary information. It is explained that the data is needed to help the customer company reach a favourable credit decision on the firm's recent application. In most cases, the data is willingly provided. When it is not provided, the fact is notified to the potential credit grantor and the subject's failure to provide information is weighed accordingly in the analysis.

The salient fact is that when approached courteously, helpfully, and with the full necessary permissions, credit applicants show a high level of cooperation. The data they provide is, in many instances, vital in updating and augmenting information available for public inspection. Credit and general financial reporting on a disclosed basis is, therefore, a straightforward and effective adjunct to database-type information.

Market and economic background information divides itself between the purely historical and the predictive. The most effective market/economic background information for use in credit analysis will, accordingly, be an amalgam of the two types. Few reporting companies and fewer database companies offer such information. But such information exists in abundance for most industry sectors in most countries. Lloyds Bank International Economic Unit's green booklets on different markets in different countries are an excellent example. Trade Indemnity's *Quarterly Economic Review* is another prerequisite for such market intelligence. The annual Industrial Performance Analysis tables published by ICC Information Group Ltd provide sectoral averages based on samples of up to 100 named leading companies.

Whilst the obtaining of this information is not costly, it can be time-consuming from the point of view of updating and also, from the standpoint of forming an overall view.

Trade references can be supplied directly by credit applicants and taken up by supplier companies or via reporting companies. The arguments against trade references are well known. Essentially, no one in his right mind would give a trade referee who was likely to say something adverse.

As with other bits of received wisdom, the point is commonsensible. It does not, however, rule out a trade reference's utility as part of a credit analysis, provided that the reference is taken up skilfully. In most cases, when trade references must be taken up by letter, the result is useless. Firstly, the delay in time taken up by correspondence works against quick decisions. Secondly, referees are quite properly wary of committing opinions as to the conduct of an account to paper. Thirdly, in written reference requests where referees are merely asked to fill in blanks, or to write a few lines, the important nuances of their opinions will be lost. Whenever possible, it is, accordingly, best to take up trade references over the telephone or in person. Much unsaid or implied information can thus be gathered. When including references in a credit report, they should be noted verbatim. They can also be assigned a numerical value and incorporated in any scoring system accordingly. In noting references, it is important to state the position of the referee. The 'significance' of the referee will sometimes vary inversely with his job status in the company. For example, a credit controller's opinion on the conduct of an account may be more valuable for analytical purposes than the more remote opinions of a financial director. The credit controller, after all, has a daily working knowledge or first-hand experience of the account in question. It goes without saying that for trade as well as bank references, specific figures—and always exposure—should be cited. In other words, the crux of a reference is: 'Can you speak for such and such an exposure?' If the reference speaks for figures significantly below those requested, that in itself will be telling. Trade references from a group of companies to which the applicant belongs should not be treated as valid in most circumstances.

As with trade references, there is widespread disbelief in the utility of bank references. Again, where the right questions are asked, much valuable information can be gained from bank references. In foreign trade transactions, bank references are vital and no credit sanction of any amount should be granted without a supporting bank opinion on the matter and the amount of exposure. In these cases, the bank reference helps to mitigate the often scrappy, out-of-date, or plain phoney accounting data from abroad. In many trade credit applications, audited accounting data even in extract form will not be available from foreign companies. This must always be regarded as highly adverse. In these instances, a bank reference speaking for specific figures will provide the only financial data obtainable. Against bank references, it is well known that banks are greatly limited in respect to the customer information they are at liberty to divulge without contravening banking confidentiality presupposed both by the laws of their jurisdictions and by their customers. Also, referencing is not a prime nor even profitable banking activity. Finally, the time-lag in correspondence between non-banks and banks is a source of perpetual annoyance to exporters and all those having foreign business. Obtaining a bank reference may take weeks. Such problems can be minimized by chanelling the reference through another bank—presumably one's own company's principal bankers. Banks will communicate more readily and rapidly on an interbank basis than with non-banking companies. Another solution to the time delay problem is to instruct reporting companies who are also financial intermediaries to take up the reference.

For large legal claims, sizeable foreign credits be they one time only or subject to extended contracts, detailed and highly particularized bankers' opinions can be obtained through financial intelligence sources. These opinions tend to be extremely valuable in that they summarize the conduct of the subject's banking as well as business affairs. They can also be informed with a high and on-the-spot knowledge of markets and likely developments in markets. In some cases, the opinions will contain useful personal assessments of management capability and probity. As these opinions contravene every known banking regulation relating to confidentiality, they are difficult to obtain. They are normally off-the-record; and they are costly. Obviously, when such information is called for, the intermediary working on an undisclosed basis can perform more effectively than principals.

An often neglected source of useful data can be provided by other supplier companies. The petroleum and meat-processing industries are examples where a high level of swapping of credit data takes place. In the meat and poultry industries, for instance, regular periodic credit exchange meetings are held where information can be gained and problems discussed. Notes and sources from such meetings can be kept and included with good effect in credit analyses for new or existing accounts.

In the case of large credits, it can be instructive for analysts (as well as loan officers in the case of banks) to visit applicants' premises. But in these cases, the possibility of assessment error is very great. How, for instance, does the numerical-oriented analyst assess either shabby premises or marbled halls? What ought one to say about the managing director's Rolls-Royce? Are the conclusions to be drawn from a messy desk loaded with paperwork generally to be adverse? Does the Queen's Award to Industry flag outside the factory give one a feeling of real confidence? As discussed earlier, all these so-called 'signs' can be interpreted in various ways. Persons such as liquidators interpret such signs from a background of financial stress. Trade creditors see the signs from a possibly wider body of prejudice. Reporting companies have the virtue of interpreting such information from a strictly impartial point of view. Most reporting companies, particularly the large database organizations, do not, however, offer such a service. In banks, such work is carried out by loan officers. In commerce, by credit managers. In both cases, credit analysts tend to be left at home. The on-site assessments brought back to them in these cases are, accordingly, second hand. As such, they are not easily quantifiable (if ever). They are, however, better than nothing, and should find their way into the full credit report.

In sum, much good quality financial and operational information is available on public companies and other large concerns. This type of information can be accessed through reporting agencies such as Extel Statistical Services. The quality of such data is high due to the stringent reporting requirements on quoted companies. When syndicating large credits, banks tend to issue information memoranda to participating banks. These memoranda, contain the very latest financial, economic, and forecast data. The memoranda, however, are always accompanied by disclaimers to the effect that members of the syndicates should always make their own enquiries as the information contained is not intended to give the basis of any credit or other evaluation. In our experience, bank information memoranda of this type are neither selling documents *per se* nor credit assessments. They are merely catalogues of financial information concerning certain uses in respect of certain borrowers. None the less, the depth and quality of the information contained are very high. As the majority of such issues are for major borrowers with high updated credit ratings from the main agencies, this quality is to be expected.

In the same quality league, but normally having to do with lesser quality and smaller sized borrowers, we have the reports available from the few firms of independent credit analysts and financial intermediaries. These reports can include all latest statutory and registered data, latest audited accounts in full, comprehensive credit analysis on the accounts and bespoke items of financial and other types of intelligence information including industrial sector and economic background. The detailed credit analysis in such work generally leads to the operation of one or more financial models. The workings and the holistic scores are explained as are all the key performance indicators. Supplementary documents such as the chairman's report or directors' report are included and commented on interpretively in relation to what is known and forecast for the subject company's market. Bank and trade references may be taken up and reported verbatim. In cases where security is advised for the credit, explanation and possible illustration of the recommended security will be given.

In the next tier, data can be summarized in reports from information companies. These are generally database organizations, the scope and quality of whose work has already been mentioned.

Finally, we have the supplementary information provided by specialist agencies or investigators. Occasionally, these services can be provided by firms of analysts and intermediaries.

None of these sources of data lessens the need of in-house credit analysis, especially in the case of sizeable exposures relative to turnover. Let us now look at some examples of data sources previously discussed.

Bank information memoranda

EXAMPLE 1

As we have already discussed off-balance-sheet exposures, let us first look at the informational content of a bank information memorandum used in the sale of short-term notes under a transferable revolving underwriting facility in the capital markets. The issuer is a large foreign corporation acting through a major international bank. At any one time, up to US$35m worth of notes may be outstanding.

The contents of the memorandum are as follow:

Summary of terms of the notes
Issuer
Amount
Form of notes
Denomination
Status of notes
Interest
Maturity
Withholding taxes
Placing agent
Principal paying agent and reference agent
Paying agent
Reference banks
Governing law
Summary of terms of the facility
Note format
Information on the borrower
Introduction
Capitalization:
   Long-term debt less current portion plus stockholders' equity
Notes on borrowings
Summary of financial data (six yrs)
   Sales
   Cost of sales
   Gross profit
   Selling, general and administrative expenses
   Operating income
   Other income deductions
   Earnings before taxes
   Taxation
     Current
     Deferred
   Earnings before minorities
   Minorities
   Net earnings
   Current assets
   Current liabilities
   Total assets
   Total indebtedness
   Shareholders' equity
   Merger notes

General trading information
Export performance
Quantified product line breakdown (3 yrs)
Quantified markets (turnover—3 yrs)
Import performance
Analysis of 3 main industrial activities
Note on competition in relation to general trading division
Backlog of contracts (4 yrs)
Overseas contract work by country
Domestic contract work (note)
Government regulations and Competition relating to one of the corporation's main activities
Significant operating policy
Domestic consumer business
Manufacturing business
Resources development and imports
Information on subsidiaries (consolidated/nonconsolidated)
Group history and principal businesses in terms of shareholding, sales, net profits, total assets (latest yr's opening and closing balances)
Brief descriptions of main members of the group
Note on share capital and shareholders
List of management
Note of employees
Financial statements of the corporation and consolidated subsidiaries in original currency and converted to US$ thousands
    Consolidated balance sheets
    Consolidated statement of earnings (profit and loss)
    Consolidated statements of stockholders' equity
    Consolidated statements of changes in financial position (funds flow statement)
    Notes to the accounts
    Opinion of independent accountants
Notes on the corporation's country of origin
Geography
Population
History
Government
Political parties
Foreign relations
Economic background of country of origin
General information
Government economic development plans
Table of approved foreign investments by industry
Gross national product
Agriculture
Industry

Foreign trade
  including table of exports by commodity
Balance of payments (5 yr tables)
Official foreign exchange reserves (5 yr table)
External debt service
Prices and wages
Money supply
Public finance
Table of consolidated government revenues and expenditures comprising general and special acounts (5 yrs)

This memorandum requires some 41 pages of information. The data, with regard to the issuer's country of origin, were obtained from published official statistics compiled by the ministries and agencies of that country. The borrower, its reporting accountants, and the bank compiled the balance. The memorandum is headed by the various usual disclaimers mentioned earlier. The disclaimers stipulate, 'This information memorandum is not intended to provide the sole basis of any credit or other evaluation. Each potential purchaser of the notes should determine for itself the relevance of the information contained in this Information Memorandum and its interest in purchasing notes should be based upon such investigation as it deems necessary.'

EXAMPLE 2

The second example of a bank information memorandum is shorter (22 pages) and sets forth data on a US$500m commercial paper programme. The facility is for a sovereign borrower and the memorandum was used as an adjunct to the sale of Eurocommercial paper. Six banks are mandated as dealers to sell Sovereign Euronotes.

The contents of this memorandum are as follows:

Summary of the terms of the notes
Issuer
Amount
Dealers
Issuing and reference agent
Paying agents
Reference banks
Form of the notes (bearer form on interest-bearing basis)
Maturity
Interest rate
Denominations
Taxes
Status of notes
Secondary market
Governing law
Note format (specimen)
Information on the sovereign borrower
Summary statistics

Summary (historical/trading/inflation/GDP/labour)
Political structure
Economic structure
Private sector development
Unemployment
Inflation
Prices and wages
Monetary policy
Money supply growth
Trade and trade balances (5 yrs)
Foreign reserves
International reserves (5 yrs)
Fiscal management
Statistical appendix
Tables in support of:
  Gross domestic product
  Prices and wages
  Employment
  Balance of payments
  International reserves
  Money supply
  Foreign exchange rates (yearly average per US$) (all other tables for 5 yrs)

The source cited for the financial and statistical information was the country's central bank. The disclaimers state that the borrower 'hereby convenants and agrees that whenever there shall occur any change to the financial condition of . . . (the country) that would be material to be brought to the attention of potential purchasers of the Notes, . . . (the country) will amend, update or supplement the then most recent Information Memorandum to reflect such change. . . .' The disclaimer also stipulates that 'none of the dealers makes any representation, express or implied, as to the accuracy or completeness of any of the information in this Information Memorandum.' The normal credit evaluation disclaimer then follows (see Example 1) The independent credit evaluations made in this case will certainly take into account country risk ratings prepared both by the banks considering purchasing the notes and by international rating agencies.

EXAMPLE 3

The third example is an information memorandum used for the syndication of a US$25m US commercial paper programme to be supported by a surety bond. The issuer is a foreign (non-UK) public utility, and the memorandum in question was used for syndication by the arranging bank. The memorandum is set out as follows:

The utility's industry in its country
Structure of the industry
Nationalization of areas affecting the industry
Energy policies
  National energy plan

    Consumption of the industry's product/s
    Installed capacity
    Production
    Power plants programme
    Other (competing) energy programmes
  Investment and financing
  Government incentives
  Pricing policy
    Tariffs
    Consumption tax
    Compensations
  Industry cooperation
  The utility
  History and ownership
  Management
  Manpower resources
  Participation in other companies
  Installed capacity and production
    Regional production and consumption
    Supply, production and consumption
    Installed capacity
  Capital investment programme
  Financial information
    Balance sheet
    Profit and loss account
    Financial projections 1983–1987
    General economic outlook
    Energy balance
    Sources and applications of funds
  The country
  Introduction
  Government
  International organization and foreign relations
  The economy
  Foreign trade
  Private foreign investment
  Monetary and banking system
  Public finance
  Public debt

Tables of figures in this memorandum are given for six years. The utility's accounting statements are extremely full (itemized and with copious notes). Throughout the memorandum, information is quantified whenever possible.

Revolving underwriting facilities

The above examples of information memoranda represent, despite the various disclaimers, data to be used by participants in credit assessment. Participants in syndicates may use these memoranda as bases of reference, but are expected to carry out whatever analyses they feel required using their own facilities. The memoranda, however, furnish up-to-date, reliable, and plentiful information in and of themseves. Paradoxically, the reams of data provided in such memoranda are for high-quality borrowers. The debt instruments available to these borrowers, be they public utilities, large corporations, or sovereign states, are not accessible to lesser-grade borrowers. Generally speaking, for lower-rated borrowers, the range of information available tends to decline both in quality and quantity. For this reason, we have placed bank information memoranda for capital market instruments in the front rank of data sources. How such data is treated by individual participating banks must be another question.

What of the capital market debt instruments giving rise to these memoranda? Chiefly, these have been 'revolving underwriting facilities'. According to N.W.F.-R. Dungan, Executive Director of investment bankers, Merrill Lynch Europe Limited, revolving underwriting facilities encompass all facilities where the main method of funding is intended to be the issuance of short-term Euronotes or certificates of deposit (CDs). Revolving facilities, or credits, as such, do not refer to the products of any individual investment bank or arranger of such facilities.

In the late 1970s, investors in the Euromarkets had a residual preference for placing short-term liquid balances on bank deposits. This preference accounted for the slow start of a Eurocommercial paper market even before the banking crises of the late 1970s. By the early 1980s, the emergence of the revolving underwriting facility (RUF) capitalized on investors' wishes to diversify their portfolios of short-term investments, and thus, move away from bank deposits alone. Also, RUFs furnished a liquid back-up to issuers giving those issuers an assurance of medium-term funds. Issuers were seen to be willing to pay a continuous fee in return for the assurance of such liquidity.

A RUF in its purest form is described by Dungan as a Eurocommercial paper programme backed in total or partly by a syndicated credit, with both sides of the deal generally combined into one operation.

Many RUFs (mainly but not exclusively stand-by facilities) have in-built options for underwriters to make unsecured advances to issuers at higher yields in the event that more than a nominal amount of commercial paper is allocated. Other facilities include utilization fees which accomplish the same purpose. These options guard the underwriters from inadequate return should market conditions decline or if the perceived creditworthiness of the issuer deteriorates during the term of the RUF.

Accordingly, issuers tend to use RUFs either for straightforward funding or as reserve sources of fundings; the latter being a standby credit or facility. As a stand-by, it is clear that the RUF serves as a back-up to such instruments as commercial paper programmes where it may exist only as a kind of insurance until such time as the need for use arises.

Dungan claims that short-term investors in the Euromarket are prepared to consider a far wider range of issuers than in the US commercial paper market. He argues that this is due chiefly to the absence in Europe of those credit ratings generated by independent agencies. These ratings, he adds, are crucial to the issuance of US commercial paper. Thus, US investors have come perhaps to rely unduly upon credit judgements made by the independent rating agencies, whilst in the UK and Europe, investors must assess the creditworthiness of a multitude of diverse and non-rated issuers.

There are moves afoot, prompted by one US rating agency to start rating short-term paper issued under RUFs. Dungan, however, doubts that credit ratings will in the near future become 'a pre-requisite to an issuer's establishing a RUF'.

Credit risk in RUFs

Earlier, we looked at the Bank of England's paper on off-balance-sheet exposures. It argued that in unconditional stand-by facilities and similar lending commitments, a credit risk is entailed but that this risk was variable depending upon amounts drawn-down *and* the overall condition (creditworthiness) of the borrower when utilizing the facilities. Credit risk for the arranging bank was seen as 'medium' when there was a 'reasonable probability that only a part of the commitment would ever be utilized. The Bank of England states that a similar type of credit risk arises in the underwriting of note issuance facilities (NIFs) and RUFs. Under these facilities, credit exposure for underwriters of the notes materializes when markets become reluctant to buy or accept an issuer's paper within the agreed price range. Here, the risk is held to be significantly greater than in conventional underwriting as the facility ordinarily supports continuous short-term issues over an extended period of years. Significantly, when the underwriting bank under the terms of the facility must fund, it may, under these circumstances, take on a credit risk already assessed as unacceptable by other banks.

The Bank of England states that in some countries, such commitments are regarded as the equivalents of guarantees. It argues that a balance should be struck between the possibility that only a comparatively small proportion of the aggregate commitments may be drawn, and the probability that any assets acquired under such commitments may well be sub-standard. At present, the Bank perceives the overall credit risk in such commitments as 'at least of a medium nature'. It also suggests that banks might now wish to set an overall limit on the total of such commitments they contract.

Dungan's view, on the other hand, appears more sanguine. He argues that the attraction of participating in a RUF as an underwriter is precisely the remoteness of credit risk. Perhaps, in no significant order, he also cites increased return on assets as well as the marketability of such short-term assets when compared with syndicated Euroloans. Certainly, apart from these attractions, freedom from on-balance-sheet capital constraints must also make RUFs attractive.

According to Dungan, credit risk is made remote for two reasons. Firstly, under a RUF, the probability of funding is, 'by definition, more remote than in a conventional revolving credit'. This point is fairly taken given that participants under a revolving credit facility must fund the borrower on demand when the borrower has complied in full to the conditions precedent to drawing. Dungan holds that under a RUF, funding requirements depend both on the borrower's 'decision to issue' and upon the placing agent bank's inability to sell the short-term paper. He adds, 'On the premise that the underwriter's ultimate risk is the banker's risk of non-repayment of principal and non-payment of interest, it is clear that a commitment in which the underwriter is two steps removed from funding, rather than only one step removed, presents a lower level of risk'. It is salient that many stand-by RUFs contain features discouraging use of the facility in any event. This further distances risk.

Dungan's second argument for the remoteness of credit risk suggests that as long as paper is held by third-party investors, 'the underwriters bear no risk of non-repayment of principal' or non-payment of interest for that space of time. He feels it is crucial for underwriters to develop the internal ability to account for the effective removal of credit risk from their books. In practice, underwriters receive 'both notice of intended issuance and notice of allocations of unsold paper: the difference represents the risk that has effectively been sold away from them for the period of issuance'.

The Bank of England's qualms on the deterioration of overall creditworthiness of borrowers using such facilities is answered by Dungan's assurance that any significant declension in an issuer's financial condition noted at such times when underwriters might be at risk (i.e. on rollover dates), would bring into effect the conditions precedent to drawing or the cancellation events for underwriters' commitments. In sum, the issuer's altered creditworthiness would invalidate the facility and thus prevent any funding.

Both the growing sophistication of borrowers and the proliferation of complex financing instruments have meant that the simple RUF described by Dungan under which use would be barred given a deterioration in the credit perception of the issuer may become less attractive. As high-quality borrowers continue to obtain increasingly advantageous terms from banks, the remote or lessened credit risk may also be effectively reversed. Dungan attests to this in speaking of multiple component facilities. Under such commitments, 'so long as paper is held by investors, the underwriters' risk is transferred to the investors for that period. But if a facility provides to the borrower the option of direct borrowings from underwriters, as a replacement for issuance of short-term paper, then the underwriters have been put back into being one step only removed from funding and the RUF becomes a revolving credit to be funded, perhaps but only perhaps, through short-term paper issuance'.

Dungan suggests that there is a 'widely agreed upon need' to try and standardize the structure of RUFs. He explains that the diversity of RUFs has largely been due to competitor investment banks attempting to differentiate themselves. He adds that in his view the 'development of the market as a whole will be most enhanced by greater standardization of the structure of the underwriting commitments and the structure of the placement of the short-term paper'. The Bank of England would most likely agree.

Currency and interest rate swaps

Currency and interest rate swaps were touched on earlier. Apart from commitments under RUFs, swaps are the most prevalent form of off-balance-sheet exposure. According to G.T.K. Hsu, Head of Swaps at Chemical Bank, New York, the world-wide swaps market now approaches US$150 bn in total volume. According to Hsu, much of the risk analysis performed to date is founded on untested assumptions as defaults have been rare. Defaults that have occurred to date tend, in the main, to be settled out of court. The losses from swaps thus remain undisclosed. The International Swap Dealers Association as well as some players in this market have accordingly argued for well-publicized default—involving parties other than themselves.

In a currency swap, two banks contract to exchange equal net present value cashflows stemming from specific assets or liabilities which are expressed in different currencies. The Bank of England defines the classic interest rate swap as two parties contracting to exchange interest service payments (and sometimes principal service payments) on the same amount of indebtedness of the same maturity and with the same payment dates—one providing fixed interest rate payments in return for variable rate payments from the other and vice versa. Basis swaps, in contrast, are floating rate exchanges based on different indices, for instance, prime rate against London interbank offered rate (LIBOR). Further 'refinements' include 'circus swaps', combining interest rate and currency exchanges. A wide range of variations giving rise to highly complex swaps have come into being. These can involve many counterparties and banks will often act as intermediaries between participants, either guaranteeing each principal party against default of the other, or themselves acting as principals between two parties. In these cases, the banks enter into matched deals with each party. In some instances, the banks may wish to transform the swap structure of their own book by entering into a swap transaction without a second offsetting transaction with another party.

The Bank of England sees the risks to banks arising from taking on positions by entering into such swaps and also, from the possibility that default by a counterparty will open up unexpected or unplanned-for foreign exchange or interest rate exposures during the life of the swap.

Hsu feels that only on the basis of actual experience can assumptions about swap risks be tested. He notes the commonly held, though implicit, supposition that the non-defaulting party in a swap can merely take its losses and walk away in the same way that a lender can write off an uncollectable loan. As a recent default case suggested, this may not be the limit of risk. In this, the non-defaulting party was faced with a continuing obligation to swap payments with an unwanted counterparty. Hsu points out that the counterparty was a government agency. He suggests fairly enough that other similar cases might involve a 'bankrupt company under insolvency laws which seeks rehabilitation of the bankrupt instead of liquidation'.

According to Hsu, the typical swap user is a corporation or financial institution which neither arranges nor intermediates swaps on a regular basis for profit. Users often swap solely in one direction—either to pay or receive a fixed rate.

Credit risk in swaps

Swaps are designed as risk management devices. From the aforegoing discussion, it is, however, plain that swaps entail risk by their very nature. Apart from market risks, credit risk must be regarded as ever-present. Credit risk here is simply the possibility that the swap user's counterparty may become insolvent. Should this happen, the counterparty will be unable to meet its obligations under the swap contract as those obligations fall due. Market risk, on the other hand, is perceived as the possibility that adverse market conditions prevail at default entailing that the swap user may have to find a replacement counterparty. Irrecoverable costs may attend both contingencies.

Hsu points out that for an actual loss to occur, two events must happen simultaneously. First, the counterparty must default; and second, an interest or currency rate movement counter to the interest of the non-defaulting party must take place. The 'exposure' in swaps is the simultaneity of both events.

It follows that to quantify exposure, probable losses must first be computed. Hsu describes three methods currently in use in the swap market:

1. The formula method.
2. The general damages method.
3. Agreement value or cost of swap replacement method.

The formula method projects the remaining flows of an aborted swap. To do this, imputed borrowing costs or investment returns are used. This method then determines the non-defaulting party's loss as the present value cost of this alternative transaction at the time of default.

The general damages method attempts to define the loss as all costs incurred and reasonably attributable to the counterparty's default.

The agreement value or cost of replacement swap at time of default has, according to Hsu, become the most widely accepted method of assessing exposure among major players in the US dollar interest rate swaps.

A swaps exposure has been seen to be a function both of the counterparty's overall financial condition (solvency) and a function of future market conditions. The majority of interest rate swaps are intermediated by banks and other financial institutions. In acting as intermediaries, these institutions effectively assume the inherent credit risk as they guarantee the swap payments. Hsu stresses that this assumption of credit risk by intermediaries is the reason why the assessment of counterparty credit standing by swap users tends to focus on the creditworthiness of the intermediary. He explains that when the creditworthiness of the intermediary is unknown, a published credit rating augmented by credit analysis and past experience of others with the same intermediary generally constitute an adequate evaulation.

Whilst it is not the greater of the two inherent swap risks, market risk is less familiar. Hsu reports that a method commonly used to evaluate market risk is the computation of replacement costs of hypothetical swaps in hypothetical defaults under various interest rate (and for currency swaps, currency exchange rate) possibilities. These, he says, can be either the rates taken over the last five to ten years, or a projection of future rates. 'In either case, one can assume a constant swap spread because, although unrealistic, its impact on ultimate replacement cost would be relatively minor.'

The pricing of a new swap is accordingly seen to depend wholly on the levels of interest rate assumptions. A more prudent approach is then to assume that the direction of rate movements always entails having to replace swaps at a loss. From these assumptions, the hypothetical replacement costs of any swap between origination and maturity date can be calculated. The computations would be done by calculating the present value of the swap at time of default in terms of the stream of periodic cashflows produced. This would be done by multiplying the difference between the hypothetical swap coupon and the original coupon by the notional principal amount for every payment period throughout the balance of the term. By computing this hypothetical cost at determined intervals through the life of any swap, the results can be aggregated, an average taken producing the number accepted as the exposure. This would be expressed as a fraction of the notional principal amount.

Exposure size in swaps

Currency swaps have tended to result in larger exposures than interest rate swaps. Hsu attributes this to the incremental foreign exchange risk and to the required exchange of principal amounts at maturity in typical currency swaps. Interest rate swaps do not call for an exchange of principal amounts. For these reasons, a slight fluctuation in the spot exchange rate (even assuming no movement in interest rates) can give rise to significantly high replacement costs.

Frailties in exposure evaluations

We have seen that the credit risk exposure in swaps can be measured—and is thought to be most acceptably measured—by the replacement cost method. This method measures the cost of replacing the stream of cashflows at current market rates. But it is also evident that the leading assumptions in such computations are riven with frailties. Costs will necessarily fluctuate contingent upon the maturity of the swap contract outstanding as well as the actual level of interest rates and exchange rates at any interval along the way. In conventional on-balance-sheet exposures, on the other hand, potential loss is comparatively simple to compute. It is principal plus overdue interest accrued. With swaps, however, the degree of accuracy with which potential losses are forecast must be seen as highly questionable.

The Bank of England's recent thinking on this subject advises banks to build a 'cautious bias into their estimates and to revalue their portfolio of such instruments regularly to ensure that they are not underestimating counterparty credit exposures'.

When swaps are used as hedging devices either on their own in respect of other deals or to hedge other swaps, a bank will be exposed only if one counterparty to the hedge defaults. We saw that it is regarded as highly unlikely that both counterparties would default simultaneously. Were they to do so, the bank intermediary would notionally have a flat position. The Bank of England makes the point, however, that the degree to which a swap claim of this type would be treated by liquidators or receivers is as yet insufficiently known due to lack of precedent. The Bank suggests, accordingly, that 'In considering the gross volume of a bank's swap book on a portfolio basis, this will need to be taken into account, along with any legally enforceable netting arrangements banks may have with particular counterparties'. It also adds that when banks use the 'cautious bias' approach to estimated exposures suggested earlier, the resulting total amount of replacement cost exposures can be regarded as 'subject to medium credit risk'.

Hsu sets out precautions along these lines in the attempt to reduce swap risks. These are:

1. More rigorous credit analysis and greater care in choosing swap counterparties.
2. The stipulation in master agreements that all swaps between two parties are cross-defaulted to each other. In this case, default on any one swap triggers suspension for payments on all others covered under the master agreement.
3. Collateralization with marketable securities as a feature of swaps with doubtful credits. Hsu points out, however, that many counterparties will resist posting collateral as they are often constrained by a negative pledge or *pari passu* clauses in credit agreements. Also, many market participants have grounds for doubting the legal efficacy of taking security in cases where US bankruptcy laws prevail. Accordingly, some financial institutions will not be of the opinion that collaterilization in these transactions reduces credit risk.
4. Better and more comprehensive documentation to trigger remedial action before

defaults occur. Hsu instances incorporation of the various tests of financial condition found in many other types of credit agreement.

Cross-default or cross-acceleration clauses can, if incorporated, afford users the benefits of such covenants even when they are not specifically set out in the swap contract. Although swap exposure is mutual, Hsu feels that a user 'can expect that its concession of a cross-default clause will not be reciprocated'.
5. Insistence on same-day, net settlements on the grounds that a payments' lag can leave a user vulnerable to loss of its counterparty defaults before the corresponding payments have been made.

Credit risk, remote or otherwise, under swaps and RUFs are, accordingly, seen as highly variable in amount and duration. Certainly, borrowers using RUFs tend to be of high credit standing. Swap users may or may not be of comparable creditworthiness. Credit analysis, in some form or other, is necessary for both types of borrower. Bank information memoranda seek to provide background information for analysis in the case of high-quality borrowers intending to issue debt in the capital markets. These memoranda are sources of information and not credit analyses as they do not, in and of themselves, offer any credit judgements. They do, on the other hand, furnish copious, reliable, and extremely detailed financial and financially-linked data on which to base credit opinions. With swap instruments, it appears that any credit analysis is, at present, carried out internally (if at all). The bulk of such analysis focuses on the financial condition of intermediaries who, in effect, guarantee the deal rather than on the counterparties. Also, analysis is carried out on the risk probabilities of the transactions themselves. Whilst both the major practitioners and the more responsible central banks would agree that such analytical estimations are greatly to be desired, it is also vital that the financial condition of counterparties be assessed and forecast using the latest acceptable analytical methods.

In the fast-moving financial markets as well as in the often slower-paced commercial credit sector similar quality data gathering must be encouraged for the assessment of significant exposures. As data sources, bank information memoranda are excellent. As interpreters of data, they fall very short. In the main, they are not intended either as 'selling documents' or as credit assessment reports.

Analytical treatment of data

Generally speaking, the purpose of credit reports is twofold:

1. To collect data.
2. To interpret the data in respect of overall surplus liquidity and solvency, and/or in respect of ability to support specific exposures.

The credit report is thus the medium or central vehicle of credit analysis. Credit reports can obviously be prepared by banks or companies for internal use as well as by independent or third-parties. Although the proliferation of reporting companies has tended to devalue the significance of credit reports (as there are so many out-of-date, cursory, and non-specific ready-made credit reports available cheaply), the fact remains that within a proper credit report, the whole of analysis and a reasonably grounded opinion can and should be encapsulated. In other words, the credit report is the end-product of analysis.

As an encapsulation of data and also an interpretation into one opinion formed from disparate information, the credit report, at its best, should represent the mirror of analysis. In this sense, the credit report will deal not only with known historical data, correlating and interpreting it in significant ways, but will forecast using assumptions drawn from the real world—in particular, markets, industries, and management. This argues for the fact that good credit reports are not merely tabulations of data (numerical or otherwise). Nor are they purely academic 'proofs' of certain suppositions or theses. While good credit reports will contain hard data from which 'proofs' can reasonably or with certainty be inferenced, the report will furnish the vital bridge between the past and the future. The bridge in question is, of course, the present. Optimal credit reports (in which all analysis is contained and interpreted) thus accomplish three things: they treat the past, predict the future, and in doing these things, give us a clearer and more representative understanding of the present.

We are speaking of the ideal credit report. In practice, only a minute sampling of credit reports written could hope to fulfil these criteria. The fact that more reports are not of better quality, whether prepared by internal analysts or computer-generated by database reporting companies, is not due so much to human error or stupidity as to lack of real data.

Whilst credit analysis as a discipline attempts, wherever possible, to quantify data, analysts have not always been either adequately selective in data gathering, or in their attempts to understand the significance of data itself.

Data collection is time-consuming and relatively expensive. The world of credit analysis to date has shown a quite staggering sterility of innovation in the collection of data. Bank analysts are possibly less guilty than commercial analysts of being truly investigative in spirit. But it appears to be a source of pride to many bank analysts to say that data by way of back-up to credit applications is obtained either direct from the applicants or from the banks' research departments alone. Where banks have a large spread of clients as well as banking 'products', such an attitude to data collection is imprudent. Data obtained directly from credit applicants may not always be reliable or cautious enough in bias to warrant even the most prudent extrapolations. Secondly, no bank either has access to or can build and run all the necessary financial modelling systems even currently on offer. Whilst most banks could afford to buy-in this type of technology, they tend to be prevented by an unmerited arrogance. Unmerited when one considers the volume and quantity of loans and other facilities that have either been written off as uncollectable, or that ought to be. Thirdly, for all but very large exposures, most banks' so-called assessment spreadsheets for treating financial accounts have not progressed beyong simple and often unintentionally obscure restatements of the balance sheet and profit and loss account. The list of performance and operational indicators drawn from these restatements tends to be sadly brief and naïve. Current ratio and acid-tests loom large. Fourth, how much economic background data is brought to bear on individual smaller credit applications? This, of course, is impossible to answer definitively, but one may suppose, relatively little or not enough. The investment banks tend to be more receptive to such information than the clearers. That having been said, most of the clearing banks, if not all, now have economics departments. Some, like Lloyds Bank, are extremely useful both to the banks concerned and to the general commercial public. In the main, most economics research tends to be macro rather than micro in its orientation. For optimal use in credit analysis, it ought to be both.

For many of the smaller exposures, the clearing banks will make the credit decision on the basis of an interview between the client and the loan officer and the applicant's latest audited accounts. Whilst this is better than nothing, it is not good enough.

Again, leasing companies tend to be even more slipshod in their approach to credit analysis. Whether or not to write an equipment lease frequently depends solely on a database-generated company report and the age of the company concerned. Rarely, if at all, are managements interviewed, and even more rarely are unaudited or management figures called for. Credit assessment in these cases is completely by remote control. In 'big ticket' leasing deals, more care is taken as the possible losses are greater. Most big ticket deals are done through the banks and through syndicating intermediaries. For participants in syndicates, however, more analytical focus is directed at the credit standing of the arranging intermediary than, generally speaking, is directed at the borrower. One can only hope that the arranger of a big ticket deal has carried out his own thorough credit analysis.

Thus, the basic collection of data by financial institutions for back-ups to smaller credit exposures is by no means so germane and so thorough as one is led to believe. The collection of data by commercial analysts for trade credit exposures, large or small, tends to be even worse. Economic background data is more or less unknown. There is total reliance in many instances on mere extracts of historically antique data, e.g. accounting statements. No thought is given to the cost of the credits. Credit managers and commercial managers tend to be largely unschooled in financial analysis in general, much less in credit analysis and its peculiar handling of dimensionality. Accordingly, 'analytical' assessment procedures are makeshift and largely untested. Increasingly, ready-made financial assessment models are being bought in by companies wishing to avoid the costs of maintaining in-house credit analysts. To date, however, there is not a system on the market that will warrant such a course of action. Worse yet, many companies buy in models (some of which may be perfectly excellent in what they do) of which they have no understanding—either of the models' basic premises or workings. Still other companies rely wholly upon computer-generated status reports of a third party to make their credit decisions for them. Of all the cases mentioned, this is perhaps the least fair and most absurd way of doing things. It is also the way leading to the highest level of bad debt write-offs.

Mega-models

It is a categorical fact that there is not one database company offering credit or status reports on the open market that operates an omni-sector, historico-predictive mega-model that will process and make sense of a deep range of past, present, and forecast information (financial, product, market, macro and micro-economic and management data). This, of course, would be the super model that could replace proper credit analysis as carried out by human beings. It is not beyond the realms of possibility that a mega-model encompassing most of these types and treatments of data could be developed as an expert system. It would lack, however, 'instinct' which, in the right quarter, should be one of the most valuable tools in credit assessment and in banking proper. Such a mega-model would, of course, require constant updating. Its reports could be only as good as the assumptive premises of the model and of the data inputs' scope and accuracy. Also, both in banking and in trade credit applications, the whole apparatus of granting credit must be seen against the grantor's own capital requirements and liquidity. The two basic questions still remain: (a) If this money were my own, would I advance it? and (b) Can I afford to advance it even if I am willing to do so?

The costs of developing and maintaining a mega-model of this type would be very considerable. The cost-efficiency of reports from such a model for use in the commercial sector would thus be prohibitive—at least initially. As the main consideration of credit managers tends to be assessment costs rather than analytical quality, cheapness of information has been the order of the day. In credit assessment, as in all other fields, you get what you pay for.

Three credit reporting companies and their products

We will now examine sample credit reports provided by permission of Dun & Bradstreet, Qui Credit Assessment, and Trade and Commercial Credit Corporation. (Examples of these are shown between pages 231 and 259.) On the basis of previous remarks concerning credit reports and the importance of data collection and interpretation, readers can form their own opinions of the three specimens. All are fictitious.

In selecting this work, the distinction was made between reporting companies and information companies. In the latter case, a company like Jordan's issues database information leaving readers to form their own assessments. Reporting companies aim to interpret collected data.

Analysis of the three sample reports

Bearing in mind the wide range of information and interpretive comment that is necessary for effective credit reporting, let us examine the various types of data displayed by the three sample reports.

Registered data

As it is a summary of company information, the good report will include and clarify companies' registered data. As the three sample reports are based on different fictitious companies, the registered data will, of course, vary. In the main, however, Companies' Registry's latest data should be summarized and set out in a demystified manner. This data should, wherever possible, include details that are likely to be of assistance to busy credit managers or loan officers. Such information includes the company's current trading address, address to which financial dealings including invoices should be addressed, telephone numbers, telex, facsimile, and registered office for legal communications. The specimen report from Dun & Bradstreet gives the corporate trading address and a mailing address. In 'live' Dun & Bradstreet reports, the trading address is placed at the top of the report and registered offices are included. The sample report also lists telephone numbers and telex. It also specifies that the subject is a subsidiary of Palmer Holdings International Ltd. The balance of registered data is then scattered through the text of the report with notes of the firm's principals, confirmation of a winding-up petition, record of county court judgements against the company, note of principal bankers and sorting code, note of ultimate company (United Kingdom Staple Removing Co. Ltd), notes on the directors' appointments and other interests charges over assets, information on registered indebtedness, branches and operations (which include data on price and product ranges). Taken as a whole, the body of registered information is detailed and useful. The reservation may be made, however, that it is not contained in one section, but interspersed throughout the report. Possibly, by setting out the registered data in this way, the report is made more easily readable. In particular, the interspersing of facts with figures may help to bring the figures alive.

Qui's specimen report gives the annual date on which the company makes its statutory returns, registered number, and date of incorporation. Dun & Bradstreet also gives date of incorporation, but notes it under a 'summary' section including financial information. Qui lists directors and company secretary, but does not give their private addresses. Issued and paid-up share capital are noted. Qui also supplies charges over assets information (registered mortgages), a note of main trading activities, and registered indebtedness at date of the latest annual return. At a later place in the report, directors' other interests are noted. Qui does not give the subject's telephone numbers, telex, nor trading address in this case. Major shareholders are cited with their holdings. In general, Qui's registered data is less interspersed than Dun & Bradstreet's, but it is also intended to be less copious.

Sample 3 from Trade and Commercial Credit Corporation gives a table of contents listing Registered and Statutory Information on the Companies in a section of its own. Other sections of their report give Charges Over Assets, including copies of the latest Mortgage Register and a List of Past and Present Members. (These last two sections, along with the specimen companies' accounts, have been omitted due to space constraints.)

The registered information supplied by Trade and Commercial Credit Corporation includes registered office, trading address, telephone, telex, registered number, date of incorporation, note of principal trading activities, registered indebtedness and charges over assets, dated and explained in the body of the credit analysis proper.

Also given is the subject's capital structure, full list of directors with private addresses and other interests, a list of shareholders, bankers with a note of the company's principal account's location, account number and sorting code. Post codes are given for all addresses. No note is provided as to invoicing address. The record of county court judgments is not usually given by Trade and Commercial Credit Corporation unless specifically requested.

The three reporting companies obviously view registered information in different ways. Qui treats it initially and briefly. Dun & Bradstreet interprets it most imaginatively both by interleaving it throughout its report, and also by commenting on it and amplifying it, especially in connection with information provided on the directors. Trade and Commercial Credit Corporation gives plentiful data but relegates it to the final sections of its report. Possibly, this treatment is not meant to minimize the importance of the data so much as to 'contain' it neatly and, at the same time, to give pride of place to the subject's accounting statements and the analysis of them.

Hard copy accounts

Hard copy accounting statements should accompany credit analyses. Readers of credit analyses may or may not agree with analysts' findings. Also, they may wish to verify data.

In any event, it is vital to be able to check on the accuracy of financial reporting, as well as on the overall tenor of information possibly not apprehended by analysts. This overall view can only be gathered from the subject's full accounting statements. In speaking of the provision of hard copy accounts, a distinction can be drawn between credit analyses and credit reports in terms of the fullness of data supplied. That having been said, it goes without saying that hard copy accounts should include directors' report, auditors' report, chairman's statement (if any) and full notes. The notes are particularly important for a correct reading of capital commitments, off-balance-sheet exposures, capital contracts entered into, and contingent liabilities. The main accounting statements themselves are profit and loss account, balance sheet, and funds flow statement—in that order. Where subjects are associates or subsidiaries of proximate or ultimate companies, individual company accounts plus consolidated figures must be supplied in analyses. When reporting companies do not supply such full accounts, it is more often the fault of the customer who begrudges the extra charges in ordering more reports or the hard copy statements themselves. This, in the case of sizeable credit exposures, is a false economy and, ultimately, short-sighted to a dangerous degree. Nowhere is this more true than in instances where cross-guarantees for borrowings exist. Somewhere along the line, financial strength adequate to meet these obligations must be discovered. The discovery can most reliably be made either by credit reports (if they are good ones), or by private financial investigations which will be many times more expensive and where quality varies extremely widely.

Of the three sample reports, Dun & Bradstreet provides under its 'finances' section, abstracts (consolidated in this case) from the latest published profit and loss account and balance sheet. Hard copy accounts will also be supplied on request. As abstracts go, these are very full. For instance, current assets and current liabilities are mercifully itemized. Profit and loss information also is set out fully. Information has been abstracted from the notes and we are told that in this case, no contingent liabilities have been indicated. Also, we have details on the subject's marketable securities and provisions for doubtful debts. However, in the case of stock, inventories are posted including work-in-progress and no itemization from the notes has been supplied. Lack of this information can lead to non-indicative assumptions about liquidity in that the nicest calculation of the acid-test ratio cannot be made. In providing full accounts and/or abstracts, Dun & Bradstreet, along with other reporting companies, can only supply what is available. Where modified statements only are lodged at the registries, neither hard copy statements nor abstracts will prove entirely satisfactory.

Dun & Bradstreet do not intersperse their accounting abstracts with analytical comment. Qui provides a highly abbreviated profit and loss account (sales, profit before and after taxation), balance sheet and no notes. Qui's subsequent section covers main financial ratios, liquidity, and various performance indictors. In Qui's sample, we see that the company has received a 'going concern' qualification. Dun & Bradstreet's example was not qualified, and nor was that of Trade and Commercial Credit Corporation. Full accounting statements were produced by Trade and Commercial Credit Corporation (omitted in the examples due to lack of space). These were print-outs of microfilmed latest audited accounts for the subjects on file at Companies' House. In this case, the accounts were for the year ending 28 February 1985. Subsidiary company and consolidated figures were provided. Interestingly, all three reporting companies quoted 1985 figures. When figures are older than 1985, at present time, some type of forecasting and augmentation from reliable sources should be supplied in order to update past history. Of the three samples, Dun & Bradstreet and Trade and Commercial Credit Corporation make forecasts in varying degrees and emphases. Qui does not provide a forecast but operates an holistic assessment model assigning a 'score', as do the other two companies.

Accounting and other financial analyses

Dun & Bradstreet gives three years' figures for their subject; Qui, two; and Trade and Commercial Credit Corporation, four. In fairness to the three companies, each casts its treatment of the subjects' accounts with different emphases. In this sample, Dun & Bradstreet does not provide detailed financial analysis and offers no financial and operational indicators, e.g. ratios. A newly launched product, 'Dun's Financial Profiles' (DFPs), one section of which gives 20 key ratios, is available on request. As part of this sample business report, Dun & Bradstreet does, however, present a unique 'Paying Record' section and a 'Payment Score'. After presentation of the subject's accounting abstract in some detail, Dun & Bradstreet focuses on the needs of a working commercial credit manager. The payments sections of their report is thus extremely valuable both as an extrapolation based on the company's latest accounts (for instance, if it is seen that the subject is highly illiquid, the payment information if recent and statistically significant might logically reflect this in a pattern of slow settlements and a resultingly low payment score), and as the most pragmatic 'credit score' for trade suppliers in particular. Interestingly, however, Dun & Bradstreet finds that payment performance sometimes is in direct opposition with such general indicators given by the latest lodged accounts. This is said to be true especially when the accounts are old; but Dun & Bradstreet points out that the converse can also apply. The typical trade supplier relying on Dun & Bradstreet's and other reporting companies' work, is not, by and large, overly concerned with the finer points of analysis. They want to know whether or not they are likely to have their invoices settled to terms. Continuing along these pragmatic lines, Dun & Bradstreet offers useful management information concernd with future expansion, product lines and the statement that in view of these developments and the company's poor performance, 'suppliers may wish to seek suitable assurances or guarantees'. In its treatment of the subject's accounts, Dun & Bradstreet leaves analysis to the reader.

With Qui, eight analytical ratios are supplied for both years' accounts and these are pertinently compared with the subject's industry sector averages. Qui cites the source of industrial averages as the latest figures published by the Department of Trade. Also, debt-turn and stock turnover are calculated. In the 'Quinotes' section that parallels the ratios, analytical readings of the accounts are given together with any registered and accounting data that are considered to be significant but are not included elsewhere in the report. They start with a note of the subject's going concern qualification and go on to treat turnover, profitability, debt and intercompany borrowings. Further data is provided on bankers' extension of facilities and new charges by way of security. Itemizations of fixed assets are given and a useful note on recent property revaluation. As mentioned earlier, Qui operates a proprietary financial scoring model. This assigns a 'QuiScore'. The subject's accounting and other data are supplied to the model, and the resulting scores are explained clearly and concisely. In this instance, the subject cannot support the £25,000 exposure notified and pro forma terms are recommended. As with Dun & Bradstreet, a pragmatic approach is taken by Qui. If the parent company is financially able to guarantee the £25,000 credit to its subsidiary, Qui implies that the facility can be sanctioned. Qui wisely advises that the assessment of the ultimate's financial capacity be the subject of a report on the parent. Qui provides the following indicators.

Profit margin
Profit/total assets
Profit/capital employed
Sales/total assets
Current ratio
Acid-test ratio
Debt-turn
Stock turnover

Interpretations of these indicators are summarized in the 'QuiNotes' referred to earlier. Usefully, Qui specifies what each of these ratios is meant to measure.

Trade and Commercial Credit Corporation's accounts analysis treats both the subject's statements and those of the Group to which it belongs. The analysis is set out in a complete section with a four-year financial summary following by way of resumé. This is then followed by economic background data on the subject's industry sector. Of the three sample reports, Trade and Commercial Credit Corporation's provides the most detailed and academic analysis. And this is justifiable on pragmatic grounds as the exposure notified is £$\frac{1}{4}$ m at any one time. As the report is long, pragmatism is also served by placing the credit opinion first, before concentrating on an exhaustive interpretation of all available figures. This treatment begins with a statement of leading assumptions including use of the all-inclusive view of profits mentioned earlier in this writing. It then discusses the parameters of the method to be used in analysis. Like Qui, it sets out to measure the accounting data from certain standpoints. In this case:

Liquidity
Debt and debt-service ability
Profitability
Capital adequacy
General trading performance
Solvency

Trade and Commercial Credit Corporation makes these measurements by using standard analytical procedures, e.g. ratios and performance indicators, and by corroborative holistic models. In the latter application, it is stated that the models analyse accounting information singly, severally, and simultaneously. The models' concepts are also briefly explained. Model workings are examined at length in a subsequent stage in the analysis.

Dun & Bradstreet does not mention a particular credit exposure in this specimen, but as a matter of policy and practice always responds to specific exposures. The exposures and responses are on a supplementary note. Qui cites £25,000 on no particular terms. Trade and Commercial Credit Corporation states that the exposure is £250,000 at any one time. The bulk of their analysis is geared around this exposure and its putative effects on the subject's financial condition. Also, the emphasis in this analysis is on the computation and interpretation of quantities not readily 'seen' from accounting statements in full or in abstract. Examples are gross cashflow, normalized profits, normalized working capital, debt-cover (actual and forecast), tangible net worth, total debt, and priority debt items ('current debt' extracted from current liabilities). The interaction of various key flows is stressed both under standard analysis and by the models. Group flows are contrasted with subsidiary companies' flows. Analysis here is done by combining narrative with tabulated figures set out in block paragraphs on A4 pages, rather than on computer stationery. Ratios and other indices are fully explained and all analytical terms are defined. From the sample, it is clear that Trade and Commercial Credit Corporation is not sparing with interpretive comment.

In the following Financial Summary section, accounting data is given for an understanding of debt-service, payment performance, liquidity, profitability, and capital adequacy. The treatment of payment performance is different from Dun & Bradstreet's, in which actual trade suppliers have been contacted. Trade and Commercial Credit Corporation calculates the more abstract difference between trade debtors' turnover (debt-turn) and trade creditors' turnover. The resulting 'monetary lag' indicates the time, in days, on which the company 'grinds on air', if suppliers are paid more quickly than trade debtors settle their accounts. In the financial summary and the previous analysis of the group's accounts sections, an extremely wide range of ratios and performance indices are used. Forecasting is provided by use of economic background data as well as by the company's synoptic scoring models, together with the computations for debt-cover and averaged free capital. All forecasting takes into account notified exposures.

Miscellaneous supplementary data

Is the following miscellaneous supplementary data provided by the three companies?

Economic information
D&B   No
Qui   No
TCCC   Yes

Trade references
D&B   Yes/part of payment performance
Qui   Not normally
TCCC   Yes/for large exposures/reported verbatim

Bank references
D&B   Yes/not reported verbatim
Qui   Not normally
TCCC   Yes/on all large UK exposures/all foreign trade and other credit exposures

Payment performance
D&B   Yes
Qui   Indirectly
TCCC   Indirectly

County court judgments
D&B   Yes
Qui   Not normally
TCCC   Not normally

Key employee/directors' histories
D&B	Yes
Qui	No
TCCC	Not normally

Directors' other interests
D&B	Yes
Qui	Yes
TCCC	Yes

Recommendations for securing credits
D&B	Yes/not detailed
Qui	Yes/not detailed
TCCC	Yes/detailed for all exposures

Holistic assessment routines including financial models
D&B	Yes
Qui	Yes
TCCC	Yes

Hard copy documentation including accounts
D&B	Yes/on request
Qui	No
TCCC	Yes

Citation of sources
D&B	Sometimes/depending on source and type of information
Qui	Yes
TCCC	Yes/economic data, bank, trade, and any specialist supplementary information if referees' permission not withheld

Credit opinions

Credit opinions are, of course, the most important feature of a report or the end product of analyses. All other data should be used as means for justifying the opinions reached. Good credit opinons need to be practical, as easy as possible to implement, and fair. Taking the last point first, fairness consists chiefly in not turning away trade summarily. Possibly, the full exposures notified will not be acceptable. In these cases, it may be viable to grant lesser exposures on different terms within acceptable degrees of risk. To arrive at fair opinions, data should be as full and as fresh as possible. Reporting companies offering credit opinions are, however, constrained in most instances, by their own databases and by the need to price reports competitively. Accordingly, most database operations and non-database, but highly computer-reliant firms, are limited to a correlation and treatment of whatever historical data happens to be lodged for public inspection. We have seen that in the case of Dun & Bradstreet, this is offset by their compilation of payment performance from supplier companies. Trade and Commercial Credit Corporation as well as Dun & Bradstreet include forecasts of varying kinds. Dun & Bradstreet's have been notified directly by the subject.

Trade and Commercial Credit Corporation relies upon statistical spreading and financial models, some of which are driven by economic sectoral inputs.

As for the organization or layout of credit opinions, Trade and Commercial Credit Corporation devotes the first section of it report to a four-page opinion and a specimen of the recommended securing instrument for the credit. In this case, only £90,000 of the £¼ m exposure was advised; and the £90,000 at any one time was to be backed by a strong letter of comfort. In layout and expression of its credit opinion, Trade and Commercial Credit Corporation uses the format most frequently used by banks.

Qui's credit opinion is placed last in its report following on logically from the previous accounts analysis. Qui stipulates that the subject cannot support the £25,000 credit and that pro forma terms are advised unless the parent company be proved financially sound enough to give a guarantee. This proof is contingent upon another report on the parent company. In making this recommendation, Qui is not merely looking for more business, but is acting with necessary professionalism. If the parent company can be proved to have adequate financial resources to guarantee the credit, trade is not being turned away out of hand. By contrast, if no further report is done and the parent company gives a guarantee, the guarantee may be worthless. This group situation is very common in the UK and thus Qui's recommendation is made in its customer's best interests.

With Dun & Bradstreet, various ratings are provided. The credit opinion, as such, is very brief and is to be found in this example after the forecasting section. The opinion reads, 'In view of the trading and balance sheet figures, suppliers may wish to seek suitable assurances or guarantees'.

Summary

The three companies' sample reports are interesting in that they cater for different markets despite some overlap. Respective charges vary accordingly. They range from about £16 for one-off orders to £45.50. All three companies offer prepaid account facilities which provide discounted unit charges.

Reporting language must be comprehensible to readers. Neither Qui nor Dun & Bradstreet can be faulted on this score. Trade and Commercial Credit Corporation's sample may be more difficult of access to non-financial readers. In mitigation, Trade and Commercial Credit Corporation is careful to define and interpret its reporting. When there are, as in the sample provided, many findings, the non-financially trained reader could lose his way through the detail.

In terms of user speed, the examples are more difficult to evaluate. Purely for speed of reading and concision, Qui's formats are excellent if less 'full' than Dun & Bradstreet's, with Qui assuming the responsibility for deciding which items of background information are not relevant, and so omissible. Some may, however, find Dun & Bradstreet's 'interspersed' format as quick and informative. The lengthy, detailed work of Trade and Commercial Credit Corporation is neither quick to read nor easy. Admittedly, the subject company, the parent company, and the consolidated figures make the analysis complex, and the size of the credit exposure also calls for the most thorough treatment possible in the customer's interests. The bulk of this report is made more workable by use of the table of contents which directs the reader to those sections with which he may be most immediately concerned. The credit opinion in this example comes first and a clear precis of the following sections of the report is provided by way of justification.

Sources

Bank of England, *The Management of Banks' Off-Balance-Sheet Exposures: A Supervisory Perspective*, Committee on Banking Regulations and Supervisory Practice, Basle, March 1986, pp. 12–13, 15.
Bathory, A., 'Credit Analysis: Sharpening the Blunt Sword', paper presented to The London International Corporate Finance Conference, 1985, passim.
Dun & Bradstreet Ltd, *Confidential Business Report* (sample), 1986.
Dungan, N.W.F.-R. 'Corporate Applications for Euronote Facilities', paper presented to The London International Corporate Finance Conference, 1985, passim.
Hsu, G.T.K., 'Assessing the Risks to Swap Users', *Euromoney, Supplement* January, 1986; 'Innovation in the International Capital Markets', pp. 106–107.
Merrill Lynch Europe Ltd, *Bank Information Memoranda Data*.
Trade and Commercial Credit Corporation Ltd, *Credit Report* (sample), 1986.
Qui Group (Qui Credit Assessment Ltd), *QUI Rating Report* (sample), 1986.

```
                                            DunsData  ©   L Dun & Bradstreet Ltd
                                                           a company of
                                                           Dun & Bradstreet International

Business Information Report
Comprehensive Report
Date Printed 26 February 1986

     CONFIDENTIAL ...... THIS REPORT IS FURNISHED BY DUN & BRADSTREET LTD.
     IN STRICT CONFIDENCE, AT YOUR REQUEST UNDER YOUR SUBSCRIPTION
     CONTRACT NO.  965-150001LCT, AND IS NOT TO BE DISCLOSED.

               ATTN:  MR P BRADLEY

         *IN DATE*

     DUNS:  21-456-7885          COMPREHENSIVE REPORT      DATE PRINTED 26 FEB 1986


     PALMER DISTRIBUTION LTD
     SUB OF:   PALMER HOLDINGS INTERNATIONAL
               LTD,                                   RATING --
               SUTTON
     ROMFORD STAPLE REMOVERS
     WYCOMBE REMOVERS

     14 STAPLE HO, 114 HIGH ST              MAILING ADDRESS:
     CHADWELL HEATH                         PO BOX 564 HIGH ST
     ROMFORD                                ROMFORD RM12 7XA
     ESSEX   RM12 7YH
     UK

     TEL.  0708-567879                      STAPLE REMOVER MFRS, EXPTRS &
     TELEX  4423791                         MFRS AGTS & CARDBOARD BOX MFRS
                                            SIC      3579     5112     2652

          ANY AMOUNTS HEREAFTER ARE IN POUNDS STERLING UNLESS OTHERWISE STATED

     SUMMARY

     STARTED           1948            SALES          18,074,325
     DATE INC          1952            NET WORTH       3,031,350
     LEGAL FORM        SEE BELOW       EMPLOYS         392
     REG NO            434567                         (330 HERE)
     CONDITION         UNBALANCED      NOM CAP         2,000,000
     TREND             DOWN            ISS CAP         1,500,000
     FINANCING         SECURED


     PRINCIPALS
               Frederick R Palmer, chairman.
               Joseph H Palmer, managing director.
               Alan Palmer, sales director.
               Henry Ralston-Smith, company secretary.


     SPECIAL
     EVENTS
               On 16.05.85 a petition for the Winding-up was made by Stickers Ltd
               of Throwley Way Sutton.  At a hearing on 17.06.85 the petition was
               dismissed by consent.
     PAYMENTS

Important  See Overleaf           Important  Voir au Verso              Belangrijk  Zie Ommezijde
```

Figure 9.1 Credit assessment (Dun & Bradstreet Ltd)

DunsData c   L
a company of Dun & Bradstreet International

```
PALMER DISTRIBUTION LTD        26 FEB 1986            PAGE 002
REPORTED
                         -----------------
                         PAYMENT SCORE 22
                         -----------------
                              ** KEY **
              SCORE    PAYMENT              SCORE    PAYMENT
              100      ANTICIPATE           50       SLOW TO 30
              90       DISCOUNT             40       SLOW TO 60
              80       PROMPT               30       SLOW TO 90
              70       SLOW TO 15           20       SLOW TO 120

       (Amounts may be rounded to nearest figure in prescribed ranges)
       PAYING           HIGH         AMOUNT       AMOUNT       SELLING
       RECORD           CREDIT       OWED         OVERDUE      TERMS

10.85  Slow 45          20000        20000        20000        N30
       Unsatisfactory.
       Slow 60          35000        35000        35000        N30
       First sale.
       Slow 60          500          500          500          N30
       Bad debt
       Slow 120         50000        50000        50000        2% 10 N60
       Cash own option.
       Slow 120         40000        40000        40000        N30

       In some instances, payments beyond terms can be the result of over-
       looked invoices or disputed accounts.
       Payment experiences may have been obtained from the same source on
       different days.

PUBLIC RECORD
INFORMATION
       Registered 15.1.84 a county court judgment for 345 against Palmer
       Distribution Ltd of R/O 14 Staple Ho 114 High St Romford.
       (Plaint number:  8754634    Court: Plaistow).
       Registered 20.9.85 a county court judgment for 2470 against Palmer
       Distribution Ltd of R/O 14 Staple Ho 114 High St Romford.
       (Plaint number:  8347135    Court: Walthamstow).

BANKERS
       National Westminster Bank PLC 1 Long Acre London WC2E 9LJ
       (50-30-21)

       Barclays Bank PLC PO Box 2 Town Square Stevenage Herts SG1 1BB
       (20-81-86)

FINANCES
                                   Fiscal       Fiscal       Fiscal
                                   Group        Group        Group
                                   30.6.83      30.6.84      30.6.85

Turnover                           23,752,400   19,730,485   18,074,325
```

Important See Overleaf   Important Voir au Verso   Belangrijk Zie Ommezijde

Figure 9.1 (*Continued*)

```
PALMER DISTRIBUTION LTD            26 FEB 1986                PAGE 003

Pre-tax profit(Loss)                  426,210          (21,073)         (894,770)
Net Worth                           3,827,193        3,806,120        3,031,350
Fixed Assets                        4,973,150        7,200,055        7,045,365
Total Assets                       18,520,000       18,173,434       17,177,147
Current Assets                     12,546,850       10,626,273        8,984,321
Current Liabs.                     11,782,290       11,730,153       12,012,255
Working Capital(Deficit)              764,560       (1,103,880)      (3,027,934)
Long Term Debt                      2,910,517        2,637,161        2,133,542
Employees                                 475              429              392
Intangibles                           163,725          163,725          163,725

              Abstract from consolidated fiscal balance sheet as at 30.6.85

Capital                   1,400,000   Land & Bldgs              4,071,000
Preference Capital          100,000   Fixtures & Equipment      2,974,365
Share Premium A/C           350,000   Goodwill/Intangibles        163,725
Revaluation Reserve         114,365   Investments                 422,461
Reserves                    127,500   Deposits                    725,000
Retained Earnings         1,103,210
Deferred Taxation            96,325
Mortgages/Loans           2,037,217

Current Liabilities:                  Current Assets:
Trade Creditors           9,100,373   Stock & Work in Prog      4,853,527
Bank Overdraft/Loans      2,641,709   Debtors                   3,571,142
Directors Accounts           47,376   Prepaid Expenses             94,850
Taxation                    213,470   Other                        34,170
Other Current Liabs.          9,327   Cash                         21,054
                                      Marketable Securities       210,505
                                      Due from Group Co's         137,320
                                      Other Current Assets         61,753

Total Current Liabs.     12,012,255   Total Current Assets      8,984,321
Total Liabilities        17,340,872   Total Assets             17,340,872

          Profit and Loss Account: Annual from 1.7.84 to 30.6.85.
     Sales                          18,074,325

     Cost of Goods Sold             14,003,721
     Gross Profit                    4,070,604
     Selling/Admin. Exp.             1,137,417
     Deprec./Amortisation              411,320
     Payroll                         3,217,500
     Operating Income (Loss)          (420,633)
     Other Income                      275,000
     Interest Expense                  474,137

     Income before Taxes              (894,770)
     Profit After Tax                 (894,770)
     Extraordinary Items               120,000
     Net Loss                          774,770
```

Figure 9.1 (*Continued*)

DunsData © L
a company of
Dun & Bradstreet International

PALMER DISTRIBUTION LTD   26 FEB 1986   PAGE 004

    Retained earnings at start   1,877,980
    Net Loss   774,770
    Dividends   0
    Retained earnings at end   1,103,210
    Balance sheet obtained from subject 23.09.85
    Contingent debt: None indicated.
    Stocks valued at lower of cost or market.
    Debtors shown as a net value, less 60,000 allowance for doubtful accounts.
    Fixed assets shown as a net value, less 3,943,270 accumulated depreciation.
    Tangible net worth is computed after deducting intagibles consisting of: trade patents - 163,725
    Investments consist of: trade investments in associated companies
    'Other current liabilities' consist of accruals - 9,327. 'Other current assets' consist of taxation recoverable. 'Extraordinary Items' consist of the profit derived from sale of property.
    Marketable securities consist of Listed Government securities - 173,200 & unlisted securities (USM) - 37,305.

    Charges have been registered including: Registered in 1983 a charge to Barclays Bank PLC.
    Registered in 1984 a general charge to National Westminster Bank PLC. The last charge was: Registered in 1985 a debenture to Barclays Bank PLC.
    Registered indebtedness at annual return date was shown as 623,000.
    On 23.9.85
    F R Palmer, Chairman submitted the following partial estimates.

    Projected annual turnover: 25,000,000

    He further stated that sales would increase in 1985-86 by 38% dueto the launching of a new range of products.
    In view of the trading and balance sheet figures, suppliers may wish to seek suitable assurances or guarantees.

HISTORY

    Frederick R Palmer (born 1920) - appointed: 01.11.52 (director) appointed 06.07.82 (chairman) - work history: over 40 yrs experience in the industry - also associated with Stevenage Staple Removers Ltd

    Joseph H Palmer (born 1922) - appointed: 01.11.85 (director) appointed: 06.07.82 (managing) - work history: over 40 yrs experience in the industry. Formerly managing director of Around the Corner Stores Ltd - also associated with Stevenage Staple Removers Ltd & Welwyn Staple Removers Ltd

    Alan Palmer - appointed 20.06.76. No other directorships recorded - work history: formerly a director of Hickory Investments PLC - also associated with Hillingdon Staple Removers Ltd, Welwyn Staple Removers Ltd & Around the Corner Stores Ltd. Business started 1948 by F R Palmer, under the style 'Romford Staple Removers'

Important See Overleaf   Important Voir au Verso   Belangrijk Zie Ommezijde

Figure 9.1 (*Continued*)

DunsData ©
a company of
Dun & Bradstreet International

```
PALMER DISTRIBUTION LTD          26 FEB 1986           PAGE 005
```

      40% of capital is owned by F R Palmer
      Registered as a private limited company 01.11.1952.
      Name changed from Romford Staple Removers Ltd on 31.12.71.
      Nominal Capital 2,000,000 in 4,000,000 shares of 50p each. Issued
      Capital 1,500,000.
      Search at Companies Registry 23.09.85 showed annual return made up
      to 04.07.85.

      The following are related through principal(s) and/or financial
      interest(s).
      Lime Regis Ltd (50%)
      Universal Contractors Ltd (25%)

PARENT/
SUBSIDIARIES
      The company is a subsidiary of PALMER HOLDINGS INTERNATIONAL LTD
      SUTTON RM12 7HH (Duns: 22-537-1442) , which holds 60% interest.
      year started 1971 - operates as: Holding company
      The ultimate parent is United Kingdom Staple Removing Co Ltd.

      Subject has 2 subsidiaries.
      Staple Removers (South East) Ltd, % of ownership: 100 - year
      started: 1971
      Aberdeen Staple Removers Ltd, % of ownership: 100 - year started
      1971

OPERATIONS
      Manufacturers, importers and exporters of staple removers and other
      stationary accessories, including cardboard boxes
      EMPLOYEES: 392 including 14 principals. 330 are employed here.
      Sells to: Wholesale/distribution companies principally. Price range:
      1.00 - 30.00. Terms are: Net 30 days (UK) & letter of credit
      (overseas). Number of accounts: 400. Territory: 70% National.
      Exports 30% of sales to Europe, Sweden & Norway.
      Imports 25% of sales from Far East & U S A
      Product Names: 'Easilift' & 'Coribox'.
      Seasonal business peaking Summer
      Owns offices, factory, warehouses covering 123000 sq.ft. Parent
      company also operates from these premises.
      Registered offices: at heading address.

BRANCHES
      15 High St High Wycombe Bucks HW3 5UT, branch. Operates as: Staple
      remover importers.

              - COMPREHENSIVE DISPLAY COMPLETE -

Important See Overleaf   Important Voir au Verso   Belangrijk Zie Ommezijde

Figure 9.1 (*Concluded*)

QUI RATING REPORT

QUI REFERENCE   : Q11077
YOUR REFERENCE : B/27/KY
SEARCH DATE   : 25/01/1986
CREDIT PROPOSED : £25,000

SUBJECT : Vicente Sales Limited
COMPANY

QUISCORE : 22.4

QUISCORE RANGE :

```
 0   10   20   30   40   50   60   70   80   90   100
 |----|----|----|----|----|----|----|----|----|----|
       -X-
<HIGH RISK>  <CAUTION>   <NORMAL RISK>   <CONFIDENCE>
```

QUIRATING : £ 0

** TO BE READ IN CONJUNCTION WITH QUINOTES ON PAGE 2 **

QUI CREDIT ASSESSMENT LIMITED
66 NORTH END
CROYDON CR0 1UJ
SURREY

COMPANY INFORMATION   ANNUAL RETURN DATE : 13/11/1985

REGISTERED NUMBR : 1411589   DATE OF INCORPORATION : 06/11/1967

REGISTERED OFFICE : Vicente House, Victoria Road, London

PREVIOUS STYLES :

None

DIRECTORS : Luigi Vercotti (Italian), Mario Vicente (Italian),
Carlo Alberto (Italian)

COMPANY SECRETARY :

H Branson

ISSUED SHARE CAPITAL :

510,000 ordinary £1 shares have been issued, for cash.

MAJOR SHARE HOLDERS :

S P L Holdings Limited - 510,000 ordinary shares

ULTIMATE HOLDING COMPANY :

S P L Holdings Limited

REGISTERED MORTGAGES :

23/08/85 - Debenture for all monies due, as fixed and floating
charges over all book and other debts in favour of Midland Bank.
14/08/85 - Debenture for all monies due, as a fixed and
floating charge over all assets in favour of Midland Bank.
28/12/84 - Mortgage for all monies due, by way of continuing
security on the company estate, in favour of Midland Bank.
There are two other charges also registered.

REGISTERED INDEBTEDNESS :

£2,732,922

PRINCIPAL ACTIVITIES :

Retailers of household goods, garden furniture and toys.

Figure 9.2 Credit assessment (Qui Credit Assessment Ltd)

QUI RATING REPORT

QUI REFERENCE : Q11077

FINANCIAL RATIOS	1985	1984	INDUSTRY AVERAGE
Profit Margin (%) (Profit/Sales)	1.5	3.5	4.2
Profitability (%) (Profit / Total Assets)	4.1	10.4	8.4
Return on Capital Employed (%) (Profit / Capital Employed)	23.9	72.3	15.8
Capital Usage (Ratio) (Sales / Total Assets)	2.8	3.0	2.0

LIQUIDITY :

	1985	1984	INDUSTRY AVERAGE
Current Ratio (Ratio) (Current Assets / Current Liabilities)	1.0	0.9	1.0
Acid Test (Ratio) (Current Assets minus Stock / Current Liabilities)	0.3	0.2	0.5
Credit Period (Days) (Debtors / Sales x 365)	2.5	1.5	28.0
Stock Turn (Ratio) (Sales / Stock)	4.8	4.7	8.5

A minus sign (-) in this position indicates a negative value

Industry Averages are obtained from the latest figures published by the Department of Trade

DIRECTORS' OTHER CONNECTIONS :

All are directors of Vicente Enterprises Ltd; Vicente (Import/ Export) Ltd; Italian Wine Import Co Ltd and L V Trading Co Ltd

QUINOTES :

The latest accounts filed by the company have received a "going concern" qualification from the Auditors. The accounts have been prepared on the basis that continued support will be provided by the trade creditors and the subject's holding company.

Sales for the year rose by 14%. Despite this increase, profits halved, and the company broke-even at the yearend. The company is increasingly dependent upon its trade creditors for short term funding, the figure having increased by 48%, and is more than two and a half times the amount of shareholders funds. Other current assets include an amount of £1.5 million owed by group companies (1983 £811,000).

You will note that the subject's bankers have considered it prudent to extend the security on their loans, by placing a charge on the company's book and other debts.

Fixed assets comprise : Land and Buildings (£515,000); Fixtures and Fittings, Plant and Equipment (£1.2 million). A total of £110,000 was invested in fixed assets during the year with freehold property being revalued adding a further £124,000.

Your subject's poor profitability and dependence upon its trade creditors have contributed to a QuiScore that falls in the High Risk Band. The QuiRating has been zeroised. Proforma terms are therefore recommended, unless the parent company is of sufficient capacity to provide a guarantee. Should you wish to pursue this further, a report on S P L Holdings Limited is suggested.

Credit ratings and limits, together with other opinions and information are given to clients in strict confidence and are not to be passed to a third party. They are given as guides and should be used in conjunction with information from other sources. All information and opinions are given in good faith and without engaging any responsibility of Qui Credit Assessment Limited, its directors, employees, agents or informants in any way. Full Terms of Trade are given on Qui order forms.

PAGE 2 of 3

Figure 9.2 (*Continued*)

QUI RATING REPORT

QUI REFERENCE : Q11077   12 MONTHS ENDED 31/03/1985   12 MONTHS ENDED 31/03/1984

	CONSOLIDATED £'000	CONSOLIDATED £'000
PROFIT AND LOSS ACCOUNT		
Sales	27,043	23,740
Profit before Tax	395	821
Profit after Tax	395	821
	=========	=========
BALANCE SHEET		
Assets :		
Fixed Assets	1,739	1,616
Investments	0	0
Goodwill	0	0
Other	0	0
Total	1,739	1,616
Current Assets :		
Stock and Work in Progress	5,515	4,874
Debtors	188	99
Cash at Bank and in Hand	45	13
Other Current Assets	2,253	1,306
Total Current Assets	8,001	6,292
Current Liabilities :		
Creditors	4,283	2,894
Bank Overdraft	293	570
Other Short Term Loans	0	0
Owed to Associates	1,803	1,761
Other Current Liabilities	1,707	1,548
Total Current Liabilities	8,086	6,773
Working Capital	85-	481-
TOTAL NET ASSETS	1,654	1,135
	=========	=========
Issued Share Capital	510	510
Share Premium	0	0
Capital Reserves	225	101
Revenue Reserves	919	524
Total Shareholders Funds	1,654	1,135
Deferred Taxation	0	0
Long Term Liabilities	0	0
Minority Interests	0	0
CAPITAL EMPLOYED	1,654	1,135
	=========	=========

A minus sign (-) in this position indicates a negative value

Figure 9.2 (*Concluded*)

TRADE AND COMMERCIAL CREDIT CORPORATION LIMITED

CREDIT REPORT

Metal Engineering Limited

Metal Engineering Holdings Limited

CONTENTS

ITEM		PAGES
I	Credit Opinion	1 - 4
II	Analysis of the Group's Consolidated Accounts	5 - 11
III	Financial Summary - The Holding Company	12
IV	Trend Key to Financial Summary	13
V	Economic Background on the Industry Sector	14 - 16
VI	Industry Sector Bad Debts and Business Failures Notified to Trade Indemnity PLC	17
VII	Commentary on the 1985 Chairman's Report	18 - 19
VIII	Audited Accounting Statements and Notes: 1982 - 1985	20 - 72
IX	Registered and Statutory Information on the Companies	73 - 76
X	Trade References	77
XI	Banker's Reference	78
XII	Charges Over Assets: Copies/Mortgage Register	79
XIII	List of Past and Present Members	80

****

Figure 9.3 Credit assessment (Trade and Commercial Credit Corporation Limited)

240 THE CORRELATION AND TREATMENT OF COMPANY DATA

STRICTLY PRIVATE AND CONFIDENTIAL DATE 30, May, 1986

<u>CREDIT REPORT</u> Page 1

The following information is given in strict confidence and must not be passed to any unauthorised person upon any pretext whatever. It must equally be understood that in this and the following attachments, if any, and in any further reports that no responsibility can be accepted for any inaccuracy transmitted therein, and that whilst the greatest care is given to obtain reports of a reliable character, it is advisable that you make further enquiries through your own channels before arriving at final credit decisions.

<u>I</u>

<u>OPINION</u>

SUBJECT COMPANY: Metal Engineering Limited and parent company Metal Engineering Holdings Limited

BRIEF: To examine Metal Engineering Ltd with a view to the sanction of a domestic trade credit exposure of £250,000 at any one time.

SUMMARY: From the data following this Opinion Section, the following points can be made:

1) The potential credit exposure of £¼m at any one time is disproportionately large to the Group's latest audited financial resources.

2) The Group's historical record of net profitability over the last four financial years is poor.

3) The Group's industry sector has suffered over the last five years from economic stagnation. Historic output in the mechanical engineering sector has fallen, until recently, below that of electrical/electronic engineering. A significantly high number of corporate failures and bad debts have been recorded for both sub-sectors.

4) Sub-sector's economic performance has improved over 1985 and a steady return to earlier levels of prosperity are forecast, though our sources doubt whether mechanical engineering will return to its record 1980 output levels within this decade.

5) Your subject (in this case, both companies) has implemented wholesale management/procedural changes. It has also sought to increase its market share particularly in respect of export orders. Previously, exports represented only approximately 10% of total sales.

6) The companies' chairman has forecast sustained and increased profitability based on the management and systems changes noted above and also on generally improved market conditions. Immediate benefits from both gave the Group a considerably stronger second half-year, although significant net losses were still sustained.

CREDIT PERSPECTIVE: The potential £¼m exposure represents 64% of the Group's latest Working Capital and 94% of its Normalised Working Capital. It is also 10% of 1985 (latest) Turnover and 42% of Equity. First, these proportions are outsized and, in our view, imprudently high. Second, the existence of a bank's

Figure 9.3 (*Continued*)

STRICTLY PRIVATE AND CONFIDENTIAL   DATE 30, May, 1986

<u>**CREDIT REPORT**</u>   Page 2

The following information is given in strict confidence and must not be passed to any unauthorised person upon any pretext whatever. It must equally be understood that in this and the following attachments, if any, and in any further reports that no responsibility can be accepted for any inaccuracy transmitted therein, and that whilst the greatest care is given to obtain reports of a reliable character, it is advisable that you make further enquiries through your own channels before arriving at final credit decisions.

Continued/-

prior charges over the undertaking makes the securing of such an exposure effectively impossible as the bank is not likely to subordinate its claims. Third, both standard credit analysis and the use of synoptic models and forecasting routines return weak and, in some cases, worsening figures. Strict measures of liquidity were shown to be weak. Profitability seen historically was very low to non-existent. Both accounting and industrial information suggest that the Group has been suffering from depressed market conditions, lack of dynamic management, lax credit control, and, possibly, want of strategic or directional planning. Whilst much of this may have already been corrected in the second half of 1985, the financial impact of these corrections will not begin to be seen until the Group's 1986 results become available.

Credit grantors (when security is not available) can view this Group in two ways. Either a strict apportionment of credit can be made on an historical basis using what have become standard guidelines in many industries. An example of such a guideline is: "do not grant unsecured credit exceeding 15% of Net Current Assets as at latest accounting date." The percentage amounts, of course, vary from industry to industry. The weak point in this method is that it takes no account of trend; and nor does its take any account of forecast performance - internally generated or from third parties. Accordingly, when applied to more or less volatile industrial sectors, the strict apportionment method is demonstrably faulty. It is also potentially unfair.

The second method entails greater risk to the credit grantor. It assumes a view based both on past performance over a representative period of financial years. Of almost equal importance, it takes a risk based upon informed forecasts of future performance, adjusting the prudential guidelines (limits) accordingly.

In your subject's case, we feel that the latter method is preferable. Our view can be justified on the bases of the industry sector's historic depressed conditions and on its present and long-range return to higher, more profitable output levels. It is also justified by your subject's historical accounting statements.

These show significant problem areas: profit-making, adequate financial resources for further capital investment, narrow market with increasing competition, an high degree of product specialisation, and a fairly steady shedding of workforce with attendent redundancy and related payments costs. All of these appear to have contributed to the Group's flat past performance.

On the plus side, the Group has stayed in business through it all. That is a not inconsiderable feat given the industry sector. It has won the full support of its bankers in the form of a term loan. It has rid itself of superfluous staff and also, of non-productive directors and managers. It has introduced radical procedural improvements and systems. It is busy trying to open up new markets both in the UK and abroad. Finally, it appears - from the remoteness at which we stand to the operation - to be working as a team to attempt and right the company, making it stronger and more profitable. "Spirit", therefore, seems good.

Figure 9.3 (*Continued*)

STRICTLY PRIVATE AND CONFIDENTIAL   DATE 30, May, 1986

<u>CREDIT REPORT</u>   Page 3

The following information is given in strict confidence and must not be passed to any unauthorised person upon any pretext whatever. It must equally be understood that in this and the following attachments, if any, and in any further reports that no responsibility can be accepted for any inaccuracy transmitted therein, and that whilst the greatest care is given to obtain reports of a reliable character, it is advisable that you make further enquiries through your own channels before arriving at final credit decisions.

Continued/-

From the credit viewpoint, the Group has published excellently full accounts. These statements are both up-to-date and detailed in respect of on and off-Balance Sheet commitments/events. Nor are these accounts qualified. It is obvious that such accounts are made available by dint of conscious policy and not by happenstance. The Chairman's Reports furnish much trading and policy information. This indicates responsible reporting and accountability. Not least, it also suggests a will to survive and grow stronger.

The qualifications and apparent management acumen of the main board directors and chief operating subsidiary's (your subject proper) are strong and relevant. We see a rational and, to our thinking, correct division of labour between the selling, engineering (technical) and financial functions of the Group. This disposition of management should tell favourably should the Group seek further injections of permanent capital.

For all these reasons, we advise that an unsecured exposure of £90,000 at any one time be granted Metal Engineering Ltd (the subsidiary) to be reviewed at six months' intervals after examination of unaudited management accounts to be supplied direct to ourselves and held in confidence. Interim figures will be examined along with the Group's latest audited accounts and supplementary data as advised. We make this recommendation of a £90,000 cap also conditional upon Metal engineering Holdings Ltd (the parent company) providing you with a Strong Letter of Comfort indicating its support of this credit.

The £90,000 exposure represents some 31% of the average last six months' order book totals (Group), 23% of working Capital, 34% of Normalised working Capital (WOrking Capital less WIP in this case). Gross Cash Flow in 1985 having been negative does not, of course, cover this exposure. Gross Cash Flow, however, was largely affected by Extraordinary Items commented on later in this Report. The proposed £90,000 also represents some 34% of Total Funds Generated by the Operations including the term loan of £280,000. It also accounts for some 13% of Tangible Net Worth (TNW). TNW ex-loan would stand at £428,537, and the proposed £90,000 exposure would thus represent 21% of re-stated TNW.

Subject to concurrence from your Legal Department, the suggested Letter of Comfort should take the following form:

    To: Yourselves   Date:

    Gentlemen,

    We understand that you have agreed subject to the production of certain documentation to provide £90,000 trade credit facility at any one time to our subsidiary, Metal Engineering Ltd. We appreciate your willingness to extend this facility and assure you that it is our company's intention to maintain its 100% ownership of Metal Engineering Ltd unless this company notifies you to the contrary.

Figure 9.3 *(Continued)*

STRICTLY PRIVATE AND CONFIDENTIAL   DATE 30, May, 1986

                        CREDIT REPORT   Page 4

The following information is given in strict confidence and must not be passed to any unauthorised person upon any pretext whatever. It must equally be understood that in this and the following attachments, if any, and in any further reports that no responsibility can be accepted for any inaccuracy transmitted therein, and that whilst the greatest care is given to obtain reports of a reliable character, it is advisable that you make further enquiries through your own channels before arriving at final credit decisions.

Continued/-

    It is the policy of Metal Engineering Holdings Ltd to manage its subsidiaries so that they are able to meet their obligations and to honour any mutually agreed schedules attaching thereto.

    Please contact us should you have any queries in connection with this matter.

    Yours faithfully,

    Chairman
    And/Or
    Financial Director

NOTE: The following attachments form integral parts of this Report.

            TRADE AND COMMERCIAL CREDIT CORPORATION LIMITED

FOR FURTHER INFORMATION: The analysts who have compiled this Report are listed below should points of discussion arise or you further information be required:

        M J P Figs MA, FCA, MICM
        P T Pears MBA, MICM
        I A Apple, Solicitor, MA

Figure 9.3 (*Continued*)

STRICTLY PRIVATE AND CONFIDENTIAL   DATE 30, May, 1986

CREDIT REPORT

Page 5

The following information is given in strict confidence and must not be passed to any unauthorised person upon any pretext whatever. It must equally be understood that in this and the following attachments, if any, and in any further reports that no responsibility can be accepted for any inaccuracy transmitted therein, and that whilst the greatest care is given to obtain reports of a reliable character, it is advisable that you make further enquiries through your own channels before arriving at final credit decisions.

II

ANALYSIS OF THE GROUP'S CONSOLIDATED ACCOUNTS

ASSUMPTIONS: For the sake of prudence and indicativeness we have examined four years audited figures for both companies, parent and subisidiary. The results of this work are noted in Item III (Financial Summary). In the following analysis, we direct our remarks mainly to the companies' 1984 and 1985 results as being the most relevant for trade credit purposes.

In examining profitability, we take an all-inclusive view of profits as opposed to a current operating performance concept. The all-inclusive view holds that the Profit & Loss Account should include all transactions that bring about a net increase/decrease in net tangible assets during the current period, apart from dividend distributions (not applicable for your subject).

As the credit exposure notified to us is sizeable in relation to the subsidiary, Metal Engineering Ltd, we considered it essential to examine the parent company's figures with a view both to supporting the exposure and also, to providing adequate financial support to the subsidiary in general terms and with respect to this credit.

As per accounting date, 28th February, 1985, the Group's subsidiaries were:

Company	Nature of Business	Shareholding
Metal Engineering Ltd	manufacturers of differential gears/ engineers of differential gears and casings	100%
Metal Trade Investment Company Ltd	investment company/ non-trading since 28/2/81	100%

Shares at cost in Metal Engineering Ltd totalled £160,490 and shares at valuation in Metal Trade Investment Company Ltd totalled £3,000 giving the Group a total interest of £163,490.

We have not examined the accounts (non-consolidated) for Metal Trade Investment Company Ltd as they are immaterial to this enquiry.

AUDITORS' QUALIFICATIONS: None of the accounts examined was qualified.

Figure 9.3 (*Continued*)

6

Analysis of the Group's Audited Accounts
Continued-

METHOD: In the following analysis we will examine the Group from the standpoints of:

    Liquidity
    Debt & Debt-Service Ability
    Profitability
    Capital Adequacy
    General Trading Performance Indicators
    Solvency

These indicators will be examined both singly, severally, and finally, simultaneously by the use of two synoptic models.

The models used in this examination are multiple sector hybrid ratio-based, weighted, discriminant models, one forecasting the possibility of collapse within two accounting years due to insolvency; and the other, forecasting debt cover (free and liquid capital including your credit exposure of £250K forecast over the next accounting period from which settlement is to be expected).

The parent company reduced its negative Gross cash Flow from £24,659 in 1984 to £7,476 in the latest period. Notwithstanding the 70% improvement, the flows were still negative. Profit After Taxation was effectively demolished by the £71,818 Extraordinary Item of redundancy and related payments. Depreciation, on the other hand, contributed only £48,177 to Gross Cash Flow against the sharp £55,653 loss after taxation. As progress appears to be upward, this might not appear too grave but for the amount of priority debt (Current Debt) that must be serviced from operational inflows. Neither in 1984 nor in 1985 could the Group's priority debt of £241,988 and £140,512 be discharged purely from Gross inflows. Note, however, the 42% reduction in this priority debt in the last year. We computed Current Debt in this case as:

    Current Loans/portions payable in the year
    Borrowings on Overdraft
    Taxation
    Leasing Payments Due & Any Other Financial Creditors

We netted-out the Group's Accruals liabilities.

By contrast, Metal Engineering Ltd showed a negative Gross Cash Flow of £39,403 for 1984 against a 47% improved but still deficient flow of £20,756 for 1985. Against these flows, we saw Current Debt of £241,108 and £108,111 respectively. Here, priority debt was reduced by 55.2%. Nonetheless, it is clear that neither parent nor subsidiary could service its priority obligations purely from latest operational inflows.

This inability will, of course, have effects on liquidity, anticipated debt cover, and scope for further borrowings. Superficially, the balance of Current Assets with Current Liabilities looks strong. We calculated a Current Ratio for the parent of 1.270 for 1984 rising to 1.504 for 1985. The subsidiary's Current Ratios stood at 1.145 against 1.316 for the same periods. The question is, however, what proportion of the Current Assets for both companies are liquid?

Figure 9.3 (*Continued*)

Analysis of the Group's Audited Accounts
Continued-

First, we simply deducted Stock from Current Assets in order to give the Acid-Test or Liquid Ratio. The results were:

Parent	1985	1984
Acid-Test/Parent	0.869	0.726
Subsidiary		
Acid-Test/Subsidiary	0.761	0.649

Both sets of indicators show the heavy dependence upon quick turnover of Stock in this operation in order to maintain liquidity at satisfactory levels. This is true, generally speaking, of the whole manufacturing sector. Stock-Turnover was then computed at 73 days for 1984 shortening to 72 days for 1985 for both companies. We have seen quicker manufacturing Stock-Turns. The Chairman's remarks on implementation of new and improved processing systems may allude to a longish turnaround of Stock suggested by these figures. If so, a shorter Stock-Turn will have beneficial effects on liquidity in the next set of accounts.

We also computed Normalised as well as Net Current Assets. Net Current Assets represents Working Capital for the everyday use of the business. Normalised Working Capital represents available Working Capital from which only some Stock and other slower-moving items have been netted-out. In this case, we deducted only Work-In-Progress (WIP). The figures were:

Company	1985	1984
Parent/Working Capital	392,202	221,696
Subsidiary/Working Capital	281,171	123,945
Parent/Norm Working Capital	264,770	144,304

Group Working Capital rose by 77% whilst Normalised Working Capital rose by 83.5% This shows the result of a slightly quicker Stock-Turn and/or the possible holding of less obsolete inventories.

In summing up liquidity and debt-service ability at this stage, it is fair to argue that the Group's superficially healthy trading balance between Current Assets and Current Liabilities is due in large part to bank participation in the forms of a term loan and overdraft facilities. These are, expectedly, fully secured by fixed and floating charges over the undertaking in its entirety. It should also be pointed out that the subsidiary showed a reasonable trading balance of Debtors (Trade) £654,407 against Trade Creditors totalling £504,420. This allows for some £149,987 worth of surplus inflow. Again, while the balance is in the right direction, it is, in our view, insufficient to meet with adequate liquidity, most of the other Current Liability items posted.

With only about 10% of Turnover represented by export orders, the Group still showed a Trade Debtors' Turnover (Debt-Turn) of 94 days rising to 96 days for 1985. Both figures are long for the sector, representing as they do, the credit periods allowed customers. Accordingly, in 1985, the company had to wait an

Figure 9.3 (*Continued*)

8

Analysis of the Group's Audited Accounts
Continued-

averaged 96 days for its customers to settle while Trade Creditors were paid (or had to be paid) on average in 76 days. This left an overhang of 20 ostensible cash-starved days. While this is less grim that at first appears due to the postponement of debt to the parent company, various creditors, and the existence of bank finance already noted, it does show that on a strict trading basis and, indeed, on a credit management basis, the Group could sharpen its performance quite apart from sales. Tighter credit control could, in this case, contribute a great deal to liquidity and, by consequence, to debt-service ability. As suggested earlier, if the Group pushes export orders, it will have to ensure that sharp payments are agreed and kept - either with the customers direct or with whatever banks, factors, or confirming houses that are providing documentary back-up.

Profitability can be examined in various ways. We discuss herewith what we see as its leading indicators. Basically, the Group's profits performance over the last four years has been very poor and very erratic. Poor - in the sense of being comparatively modest when profits after tax have been achieved (one year out of four/ 1983 with a Net Profit of £18,297). Pre-Tax Profits look marginally better with the Group turning in Profits Before Taxation of £16,165 in 1985 and £46,090 in 1983, and the rest, losses both pre and post-tax.

Accordingly, the Prime Ratio (measuring Profit Before Tax and Interest as a function of Capital Employed) reads very feebly:

Company	1985	1984	1983	1982
Parent	1.8%	Nil	6.3%	Nil

This gives an arithmetic average Prime Ratio of only 2.03% and it itself is not truly indicative of the Group's performance as it ignores those years of losses, 1984 and 1982.

Profit Margins (Pre-Tax Profits/Sales) read similarly:

	0.65	Nil	1.91	Nil

Even in the company's industrial sector, these margins are viewable as very low. This is especially apparent when these margins are looked at against levels of Turnover. The Sales levels themselves indicate something of a chronic stagnation in activity - that currently promises to improve according to the Chairman's forecasts.

Company	1985	1984	1983	1982
Parent				
Turnover:	£2.5M	£2.2M	£2.4M	£1.8M
Net Profit/(Loss)	£(55.7K)	£53.5K	£18.3K	£(186.1K)

As a trend, the losses are more consistent than increases in sales. The latest trend for 1985 looks grim with sales up by 11% and losses up by 4%.

Figure 9.3   (*Continued*)

Analysis of the Group's Audited Accounts 9
Continued-

It is, of course, from profits - indeed, profits after all extraordinary items - that the company will be able to continue trading. Its historic indebtedness on overdraft (since, switched to a term loan and overdraft) has kept it afloat. Its sales record has hardly been aggressive. Its internal credit control performance has not been tight. Its real liquidity level has not been high, and a look at the relation of Trade Debtors to Trade Creditors betrays the slim operating inflows behind the bank financing and other debt in the main operating subsidiary.

Profitability, therefore, more than all those other indicators discussed so far, causes us the most concern in trying to justify a £250K credit at any one time to this Group - and it must be clear at this stage that in no way could such a credit facility be sanctioned solely to the subsidiary without guarantee of some kind from the parent. Relative size of the credit exposure necessarily leads us on to a consideration of the Group's capital adequacy.

We have already seen that debt-service ability is tenuous - or at least has been so over the last periods. We have likewise seen that the Group's profits record is very weak to non-existent. Those years of losses (none of them small in relation to the Group's Capital Employed and Reserves) necessarily diminished reserves. These depletions have been counter-balanced by higher borrowings. Equity represents the shareholders' stake (investment in cash) in their own business. Here are the Group's Equity figures:

Company	1985	1984	1983	1982
Parent				
Equity:	591,300	661,953	715,467	698,270
Capital Employed:	884,758	720,995	735,710	698,270
Proprietorship Ratio: (Equity/Capital Employed)	66.8%	91.8%	97.2%	100.0%

Bankers often worry when borrowings exceed 50% of Capital Employed. The Group thus has not too much leeway for further borrowings purely on the basis of these figures. Clearly, the Equity stake in the business is falling each year and this must be viewed as an adverse trend. It is due, as noted before, to the inability of the company to generate profits to top up the level of reserves.

Of even more concern is the annual reduction in the Group's Tangible Net Worth. We calculate Tangible Net Worth as Total Assets less Intangible Assets less all liabilities including capital commitments contracted/entered into, and off-Balance Sheet financings including guarantees. Because these accounts are so clear and detailed, the Group's TNW matches in each year its Net Assets figures:

Company	1985	1984	1983	1982
Parent/consolidated (Tangible Net Worth)	591,300	661,953	708,537	698,270
Total Assets:	£1.7M	£1.5M	£1.4M	£1.3M
Priority Debt	£140.5K	£242K	£313.7K	£262.3K
Priority Debt as a % of TNW:	24%	37%	44%	38%

Figure 9.3 (*Continued*)

10

Analysis of the Group's Audited Accounts
Continued-

Lest Current or priority debt in the last figures when seen as a percentage of TNW lead one to suppose that debt has actually been reduced, that is not the case. Current Debt is calculated by us solely from Current Assets items. Here, the conversion of large overdrafts into term loans effectively places £240,770 worth of bank finance away from Current Assets into Long-Term Creditors where only £59K worth of Government Grants exists previously.

Bank debt, therefore stands in these accounts at £348,670 whilst Total Debt equals £1,071,699. Were the bank borrowings all Current Debt items, the restated priority debt would be £554,422.

We applied the Group's accounting data to our financial models mentioned before. The insolvency forecasting model provides a range of scores. Scores of +20 and below to 0 indicate companies at risk within a range of two accounting periods of collapse due to insolvency. Negative scores indicate insolvent firms, technically insolvent and otherwise. In arriving at its scores, the model examines debt-service ability, capital adequacy, annual and cumulative profitability, and liquidity. Here are the model scores for parent and subsidiary companies:

Company	1985	1984	1983	1982
Parent Model Score:	+30.2	+30.5	+54.5	+34.5

Interestingly, the holistic model score is lowest in the latest year, thus assuming that despite the various improvements set in motion, the Group's overall solvency quotient is at an all-time nadir. Nor does the +30.2 score look at all strong - even for the sector.

Here are the subsidiary's scores:

	1985	1984	1983	1982
Metal Engineering Ltd:	+9.5	+8.0	+28.9	+6.5

Only for 1983 did the company realise a fairly riskless score, which was, in itself, very weak. These scores show the absolute dependence on parent company financing as well as the precarious nature of the subsidiary's trading performance.

The second model to which we applied the Group's accounting data is designed to forecast Debt Cover where this available free or surplus capital is also meant to service a potential credit exposure - in this instance, £250,000. As it is plain that only the consolidated figures would be relevant given this amount of exposure, we operated the model over the Group's accounting data for four years. On this basis, the model returned a score of -67%. Again, this is hardly promising.

At this stage, the point should be clearly made that financial models, and in particular, forecasting models, are meant to be indicative only. Their accuracy assumes the non-supervention of extraordinary events that may grossly affect a company's normal performance.

Figure 9.3 (*Continued*)

250 THE CORRELATION AND TREATMENT OF COMPANY DATA

11

Analysis of the Group's Audited Accounts
Continued-

The Group may currently be reaping the benefits of its wholesale management changes and planning. It may be currently broadening its export markets. It may currently be trading at all-time profitable levels. Not much of these outturns, however, are apparent from its last four years' results. The models base their findings upon these results, and, therefore, return a conservative and pessimistic view.

The sensible analysis should seek, wherever possible, to mitigate such findings from whatever may be known of the company, its markets, and the economy at large - domestic as well as international.

In another section of this report, we have given analyses of the macro and micro-economic background. We have also given a commentary and analysis of the Chairman's Report - which we feel indicates reasonable optimism for the group's trading performance and market share. Both these analyses and our acquaintance with the subject's industrial sector along with the aforegoing accounts analysis have been taken into account when arriving at our credit opinion.

TRADE AND COMMERCIAL CREDIT CORPORATION LIMITED

LONDON,
30th May, 1986

IV

13

FINANCIAL SUMMARY - TREND KEY

AD = Adverse/Declining
FS = Favourable/Strengthening
VW = Variable to Worse
VB = Variable to Better (Stronger)

FOUR-YEAR AVERAGES

The four-year averages given in the Financial Summary are computed on a strictly arithmetic mean basis, including those items, eg Prime Ratios and Profit Margins, making no numerical contribution in a given year. All sums have, therefore, been divided by 4.

Figure 9.3 (*Continued*)

FINANCIAL SUMMARY III — THE HOLDING COMPANY

Item	Trend	1985	1984	1983	1982	4-Year Averages
Debt-Service						
Gross Cash Flow:	VB	(7,476)	(24,659)	50,861	(164,740)	(36,504)
Priority Debt:	FS	140,512	241,988	313,652	263,292	239,861
Payment Performance						
Debt-Turn: (days)	VW	96	94	88	119	99
Trade Creditors' Turnover (days)	VW	76	80	53	66	69
Differential (days):	VB	20	14	35	53	30
Liquidity						
Acid-Test Ratio:	VW	0.869	0.726	0.909	0.987	0.893
Working Capital:	VB	392,202	221,696	360,410	385,932	340,060
Normalised Working Capital:	VB	264,770	144,304	267,628	255,020	232,931
Stock Turnover (days):	VB	72	73	64	79	72
Working Capital as a % of Total Assets:	VB	23.6	14.4	26.0	29.3	23.3
Profitability						
Prime Ratio (%):	VW	1.8	/	6.3	/	2.03
Profit Margin (%):	VW	0.65	/	1.91	/	0.64
Pre-Tax Profit:	VW	16,165	(53,571)	46,090	(138,497)	(32,453)
Post-Tax Profit:	VW	(55,653)	(53,514)	18,297	(186,104)	(69,244)
Sales:	VB	2,489,778	2,241,270	2,413,896	1,828,293	2,243,309
Capital Adequacy						
Equity:	AD	591,300	661,953	715,467	698,270	666,748
Proprietorship Ratio: %	AD	66.8	91.8	97.2	100	88.95
Tangible Net Worth:	VW	591,300	661,953	708,537	698,270	665,015
Tangible Net Worth as a % of Total Liabilities:	AD	55.2	75.2	104.8	112.8	87.0
Post-Tax Profit/(Loss) as a % of Equity:	VW	(9.4)	(8.1)	2.6	(26.7)	(10.4)

Figure 9.3 (*Continued*)

<u>V</u>   14

BACKGROUND DATA ON THE MECHANICAL ENGINEERING SECTOR

Both the Group's financial results to date and sectoral analysis should be commented upon against the following macroeconomic background:

> "In our judgement, the world economy is now in a period of disinflation, from which the UK can benefit provided that the exchange rate does not fall too rapidly. The economy continues to grow steadily, but in this, our most probable scenario, there seems little likelihood that genuine unemployment will fall appreciably.
>
> A high exchange rate policy - necessary if inflation is to be brought down rapidly - would be compatible with a more buoyant labour market only if the rate of growth of wages and salaries moderated quickly or productivity growth in the non-oil sectors of the UK economy was sufficient to make good some of the shortfall which exists at present in comparison with major competitors. Unless the UK enjoys differential productivity growth, some depreciation of the real exchange rate can hardly be avoided, as the balance-of-payments benefit from North Sea oil diminishes. Productivity growth, therefore, remains the key to the future performance of the UK economy. "
>
> Source: The Midland Bank Review,
> 4th November, 1985,
> p 6

Firstly, it should be noted that the Group places great emphasis on improved productivity - a significant portion of which will be channeled into export sales. According to the Chairman's Report and the half-year figures cited therein, the company's productivity appears to have picked up sharply in the second six months of 1985 - notwithstanding the overall loss for the year. As suggested earlier, greater volumes of export sales are bound, without fairly sophisticated financing mechanisms, to lengthen Debt-Turn, that is, the length of time the company allows before payment is received, or credit period. Debt-Turn is already long and appears sluggish. Export sales, therefore, could without the proper documentary instruments, cause greater payment delays not to mention possible higher incidences of bad debt levels in some cases. Nonetheless, truly improved productivity coupled with the right pricing and distribution will make these credit risks worth taking. Turnover, under the Group's improved productivity schemes already noted, should increase and profit margins should widen. They are spotty to poor at present and have been so historically as the Financial Summary makes clear.

The Group should also be considered against the microeconomic background of its particular industry sector. How do the company's prospects stack up against what we know about mechanical engineering?

> "Since 1982, the fortunes of the two main engineering sectors have differed markedly. The downturn in the electrical sector .... stopped in 1982 and, by 1984, output had grown by 25.5%. By contrast, mechanical engineering declined both in 1983 and in 1984 when output was 3.4% below its 1982 level. The popular images of a vibrant sunrise electrical sector and a moribund smokestack mechanical sector seemed to be bo rne out by the statistics."

Figure 9.3 (*Continued*)

15

Background Data on the Mechanical Engineering Sector
Continued-

>"However, last year saw an end to the long decline of mechanical engineering and a significant deceleration in the growth rate of the electrical sector. Both sectors contributed toward the 2.4% increase in total output in the first quarter. In the subsequent three months, the 1.3% total improvement depended entirely upon the mechanical side, while electrical engineering stagnated. Then, in the third quarter of 1985, both main sectors suffered declines in output of around 2.5%."
>
>Source: Economics Department,
>   Trade Indemnity PLC,
>   Quarterly Economic Review,
>   February, 1986,
>   pp 5-6

It is instructive to try and match the Group's figures and forecasts with the general level of activity in the sector. Trade Indemnity report that mechanical engineering output in the first nine months of 1985 was nearly 4% increased on the prior period's level. Interestingly, they note that the greatest contributors to the 9-month growth were metal working machine tools (+22%), mechanical power transmission equipment (+21%) and construction and earth moving equipment (+15%).

If total engineering sales lifted by some 6.3% in the initial nine months of 1985, the Group's recovery beginning in the third quarter appears to have followed suit. Also, both electrical and engineering sectors saw a 12.5% rise in export orders. Again, strong export experience of your subject company bears out this finding. Notably, mechanical engineering orders increased by some 2.8%, boosted by a significant 18.9% jump in export sales. Trade Indemnity report, however, that domestic orders fell by 5%. Possibly, your subject has been experiencing weak domestic demand and is pushing export sales as a corrective until home trade picks up.

The increase in mechanical engineering output is expected by most sources to continue during 1986. Trade Indemnity forecasts modest growth as characterising the last part of the decade. It is, however, doubtful whether the sector will regain its 1980 level of output.

>"Exports will have to play a major role in this improvement, so much will depend on the exchange rate, especially vis-à-vis European currencies."
>
>"Import competition affects almost every area of mechanical engineering, with developing countries and Comecon undercutting the simpler end of the product range, whilst advanced countries threaten the future of the more complex end of the market. Although the effects of earlier rationalisation still continue, their benefits are already on a declining path. To compete, the sector will have to place more emphasis on sophisticated production methods and materials."
>
>Sources: Trade Indemnity PLC,
>   Op Cit.

Figure 9.3 (*Continued*)

Background Data on the Mechanical Engineering Sector
Continued-

From the accounting point of view, we have not yet seen the main effect of
those management plans and changes referred to by the Group's Chairman in his
1985 Report. Admittedly, the company's second half-year results pulled it out
of the financial hole resulting from weak and unprofitable trading in the first
half.

To recapitulate, the Chairman referred to "substantial changes" taking place
in   the main operating company in the Group, in the areas
of "management, procedures and systems, the UK sales force, and labour relations."
Also, the new productivity bonus scheme for shop-floor workers is forecast by
the Chairman to continue to lift productivity. A 20% plus increase was claimed
for the period under review.

The Group is currently turning its attention to a wholesale review of the
export market. Only 10% of its Turnover has been represented by foreign orders.
The new export marketing thrust is planned to increase the volume of both direct
and inderect export orders.

During 1985, the Group purchased £15,000 of the spares, repairs and replacement
business of B Jones   & Co. By anyone's standards, this is a cheap acquistion.
The Chairman claims that "in relation to its cost, the business has already
contributed handsomely to your company's performance."

It is evident that the revival, financial and otherwise, at the Group appears to
progress pari passu with that of its industry sector. This is by no means always
the case.

If, as forecast, the sector continues to strengthen in terms of output and
profits, the Group seems already well-poised to take every advantage of the
improved situation. To take advantage of the waiting export market, however,
a coherent and flexible financing programme will be needed. From its audited
figures, the Group is not particularly managing well its existing credit control.
If customer credit periods are not shortened and if creditors are not paid
at later intervals, further strains on the Group's liquidity will result.
A high level of exporting with its attendant risks of poor credit assessment,
control, and long payment periods, will be a major determinanat in this. The
Group's liquidity is not so buoyant as to withstand such a strain placed on it.

The Group's main source of financing is the £280,000 term loan from Harris Bank PLC
Both this and the overdraft (at accounting date: £67,900) are secured on a Fixed
and Floating Charge over the assets. Repayment of the loan began in August, 1985,
with equal instalments of £40,000 and interest at 3% over Harris's Base Rate.
The fact that Lloyd's has obviously converted a running overdraft into a term
loan (with all the usual security) demonstrates a certain confidence in the Group.
The bank could, after all, have merely ordered a reduction or total pay-back of
borrowings on overdraft. Ostensibly, then, it will be to their bankers that the
Group will turn in seeking financing for its intended foreign trade. Because of
the apparent confidence reposed in the company by its bankers, it can reasonably
be assumed that the necessary documentary credits facilities will be provided the
company. Trade creditors, however, should note the existence of prior charges
which rule out effectively any hope of securing trading debts with the Group.
Documentary credits will, in such a case, prove the most effective payment
guaranteeing mechanism both for inland and foreign trade when applicable.

Figure 9.3 (*Continued*)

17

VI

BAD DEBTS AND BUSINESS FAILURES NOTIFIED TO TRADE INDEMNITY

Extract from Annual & Quarterly Totals

Year & Quarter	Engineering & Metals Sector
1984	
I	229
II	252
III	217
IV	<u>213</u>
Total:	911
1985	
I	217
II	192
III	202
IV	<u>160</u>
Total:	771

Decrease in Total Bad Debts & Business Failures over two years: 15.4%

Source:

Trade Indemnity PLC
Quarterly Economic Review, February, 1986
p 11

Analysis: Failures among metal manufacturers fell by 22.6% and equipment manufacturers by 46.3%. Metal manufacturers and processors accounted for 190 failures in 1984 down to 147 in 1985, whilst equipment manufacturers and distributors turned in 78 failures in 1984 against 58 in 1985.

Figure 9.3 (*Continued*)

STRICTLY PRIVATE AND CONFIDENTIAL   DATE 30, May, 1986

CREDIT REPORT   Page 18

The following information is given in strict confidence and must not be passed to any unauthorised person upon any pretext whatever. It must equally be understood that in this and the following attachments, if any, and in any further reports that no responsibility can be accepted for any inaccuracy transmitted therein, and that whilst the greatest care is given to obtain reports of a reliable character, it is advisable that you make further enquiries through your own channels before arriving at final credit decisions.

VII

COMMENTARY ON THE 1985 CHAIRMAN'S REPORT

(Chairman's Report Precedes Accounts-qv)

I. £71,818 in redundancy costs, severance pay, and compensation for loss of office was paid out in the latest year. Also, £44,812 in bank interest was payable. These payments helped account for the Net Loss of £55,653 sustained in 1985.

The Chairman stresses the extraordinary nature of the redundancy and related payments (we feel, unduly). Note the following figures:

	1985	1984	1983	1982
Redundancy/Related Payments:	71,818	-	27,793	47,498
Average Employees per Week:	106	123	140	158

The trends are self-evident.

II. The Group's subsidiary company under the leadership of T W E Smith attempted a management buyout for 51% of the Issued Share Capital. The controlling directors/shareholders turned this down, and Smith was given a seat on the holding company board - without shareholding.

Despite the sanguine tone of the Chairman's Report, these events may indicate a certain degree of management and staff unrest or dissatisfaction. Further redundancies might exacerbate this.

III. During 1985, the Group was awarded a £200,000 order from an Iranian company. This order represents some 12% of Turnover in the latest period. Were this project to turn sour, could the Group's already tenuous profitability be seriously affected? Without documentary credits assistance, payment/s for this contract may be slow and/or irregular. This will further lengthen Debt-Turn and put a greater squeeze on liquidity.

IV. The Chairman takes an optimistic tone, extrapolating from the "latest months". He implies that the directors' confidence and activity in the Group are high. Accordingly, he forecasts "a coming year of profits and prosperity".

The poor profits performance, less than aggressive trends in sales levels, sluggish Debt-Turn, and grim cashflows suggest that little short of radical management planning and alterations to the system will justify these predictions.

Substantial changes have already been made according to the Chairman. These are in the areas of management, procedures and systems, UK sales force, and labour relations.

Figure 9.3 (*Continued*)

Continued/- Page 19

V. The Chairman sketches the impact of some of these changes. "... the benefits of these changes have had an immediate and dramatic effect, to the extent that in the last six months of financial 1985, Metal Engineering Holdings Ltd showed a profit of £118,000."

This profit is before the deduction of £23,000 bank interest payable. According to the Chairman, this represents the highest half-yearly profit for almost a decade. This, surely, begs the question. The year-end figures are important, not the interims as such.

The Chairman also mentions the introduction of a new productivity-based bonus scheme for shop-floor workers. This has apparently increased productivity by 36%. . From the aforegoing remarks, it is not totally clear whether the reference is to a 6 or 12 month period.

Nevertheless, the year-end results are poor. It must remain to be seen whether or not profitability can be pushed to higher levels in order to restore eroded reserves, service priority and other species of debt, and finance the continuing capital investment programme vital to this type of business.

Figure 9.3 (*Continued*)

20

NOTE

VIII, IX, XII & XIII

For reasons of limited space, the fifty-five pages of accounting statements and registered information on the companies have been omitted. Also, the copies of the Mortgage Register (Charges over Assets) and List of Past and Present Members have been omitted.

77

X

TRADE REFERENCES

I. <u>PVT Limited</u>: Mrs B James, Credit Manager, reports, " ... and we have traded with Metal Engineering for about five years. They have conducted the account pretty well even during the difficult times in '81 and '82." When asked about credit limit allowed Metal Engineering, she reported, " ... about £1,600 per month."

Analysis:

PVT Ltd supply drinks for vending machines. They are thus not a vital supplier to your subject. Also, note that the amount of credit sanctioned (£1,600 pcm) is very small. It cannot be significantly related to the exposure under analysis.

II. <u>TNE International Ltd</u>: Mr A M J Miller-Jones, Group Credit Controller, stated, " The company is a reasonable sized account for us but they tend to try and take about fifteen days over the top each month. They do about £30,000 worth of business with TNE over the year." When questioned about the average level of business per month, Mr Miller-Jones said that " it's not at all even. It's quite up and down in fact with the bulk of orders from them coming in after the beginning of Autumn." When asked about credit limit on this account, he replied, " ... if it weren't for their late payments which are pretty chronic now, we'd give them more than the £3,000 a month limit they've got." TNE has had this account for 2 years.

Analysis:

TNE provides solder to your subject. It is, therefore, a fairly important supplier. Again, the credit limit is not significant against the figures we are examining. Interestingly, the referee speaks of delayed payments of about a half month. On such a small account, this possibly suggests the effects of illiquidity and slow debt-turn on the part of Metal Engineering Ltd. Note too that orders are sporadic. Were your subject's productivity increased more evenly over the year, orders to suppliers of this kind might show a steadily increasing volume. Also, the referee mentions greater volumes of orders in the last half of the year. this bears out the Chairman's claims of improved sales in the second half.

General: While these trade references are of interest in themselves, the figures for which they speak are not material to this enquiry.

Figure 9.3 (*Continued*)

STRICTLY PRIVATE AND CONFIDENTIAL   DATE 30, May, 1986

CREDIT REPORT

The following information is given in strict confidence and must not be passed to any unauthorised person upon any pretext whatever. It must equally be understood that in this and the following attachments, if any, and in any further reports that no responsibility can be accepted for any inaccuracy transmitted therein, and that whilst the greatest care is given to obtain reports of a reliable character, it is advisable that you make further enquiries through your own channels before arriving at final credit decisions.

XI

BANKER'S REFERENCE

Harris Bank PLC: "We are informed: Private limited company considered good for their normal trading obligations (£50,000 on 60 day terms). Bank holds fixed and floating charge. We cannot speak for your figures of £250,000."

Analysis: Despite the bank being unable to speak for £½m exposure - which after examining the group's figures will hardly be a surprise - the reference is quite reasonable. We requested references on the parent and subsidiary companies. The bank reference does not appear to distinguish between the two. In view of the £50,000 limit seen as normal, it would appear that Group credit facilities are intended. These would amount to about £100,000 over one year. Sixty day terms could be viewed as too long by some suppliers. Note too that neither of the trade suppliers maintained accounts of this volume, although one trade reference was not from a major supplier.

The bank's mention of its charges over the undertaking rule out any security for trade credits.

If trade credit from say £50,000 to £100,000 were to be sanctioned, how could the payment terms be shortened enough to make the credit attractive to yourselves and afford the nearest thing to security? (cf- Opinion/Section I)

The bank reference plus the historic accounts and forecasts carried out corroborate the view that the £½m exposure is effectively out of the question. (cf- Opinion/Section I)

END

TRADE AND COMMERCIAL CREDIT CORPORATION LIMITED

Figure 9.3 (*Concluded*)

10

VARIED CORPORATE CREDIT ASSESSMENTS

Credit insurance

Optimal credit analyses must differ in format, focus, and final interpretation according to:

1. The function of the credit-grantor.
2. The capital requirements of the credit-grantor.
3. The specific purpose of the credit.
4. The disclosure or degree of non-disclosure of data between credit-grantor and credit applicant.
5. The exposure and terms of the exposure.
6. The depth and quality of supplementary or back-up data from third-party sources or from the market.
7. The degree of risk (full or partial) to be borne by the credit-grantor.

Accordingly, what might be deemed an optimal analysis for a clearing bank considering a large secured exposure might not be either cost-efficient or particularly informative for unsecured trade credit purposes. The assessment behind the design and placement of debt securities in the capital markets by investment banks will necessarily differ from those procedures used by other banking companies in providing overdraft facilities, term loans, or participations. Still different approaches will be used by factoring companies whose business is the provision of cash against agreed proportions of book debts. Possibly, the most complete and sophisticated assessments are currently carried out by the major credit insurance companies.

Their function is the underwriting of clients' buyer insolvency and delayed payment risks. Credit insurers' assessment routines are necessarily wide as they are particularly remotely placed in relation to clients' sales and credit management operations and even more remote from those risks attendant on their clients' debtors. The credit insurance company is therefore assessing risk on the following fronts:

1. The quality of clients' sales.
2. The quality of clients' internal credit management, including assessment.
3. The financial ability of clients' debtors to meet their obligations.
4. Their own prudential guidelines and capital requirements.
5. The interpretation of failure trends in multiple industry sectors.
6. The risk of inability to reinsure.
7. In some cases, the assessment of political risk.

As credit insurance covers such a wide range of risk assessment, and as credit insurance is becoming more generally used by the commercial public, we shall examine the services and assessment procedures of the UK's principal underwriter of credit risk, Trade Indemnity PLC.

Trade Indemnity offers nine main policies:

1. Whole Turnover Policy.
2. Principal Accounts Policy.
3. The Specific Account Policy.
4. The Anticipatory Credit Policy.
5. The Smaller Business Policy.
6. Whole Turnover Export Credit Policy.
7. Export Credit Policy (Whole Turnover Including Work In Progress).
8. Credit and Political Risks Policy (Whole Turnover) Political Risks Endorsement.
9. Excess of Loss Catastrophe Policy.

A nicer appreciation of the types of risks entailed can be gained by examining these policies in greater detail.

The Whole Turnover Policy insures a company's entire UK domestic sales within the terms and credit limits agreed with Trade Indemnity at the policy's issuance date or as subsequently agreed at the time of the policy's approved amendment. This policy is written to offer clients discretionary limits in taking on new business without the requirement to apply formally to Trade Indemnity for additional cover. Apart from the on site audit Trade Indemnity carries out to assess the potential insured's credit management capabilities, specific buyers' accounts information is required for analysis. This information includes the following data to be updated within a period of 12 months previous to granting the credit, by the insured's experience of the buyer's account during that time, or where both information and experience exist. These data consist of:

Limit of discretion
Terms of payment
Approved sources of information

The Principal Accounts Datum Policy covers a specifically agreed portion of a company's UK sales: its larger accounts only.

Trade Indemnity explains that typically, the larger company which is prepared to absorb losses on smaller accounts, but looks to insure against the financial risks it might face in the event of principal customers' failure, is the client profile for this policy. Trade Indemnity requires, in its schedule for the policy, information on the period for delivery of goods, notes as to specific buyers, terms of payment and permitted limits.

The Specific Account Policy is structured to guard a company from the financial failure of an individually named customer or group of customers representing a special credit risk. Additionally, the policy is designed to protect a company where a special one-off contract with a specific customer is proposed. Trade Indemnity gears this policy toward those companies whose sales are dominated by one large account or a specific grouping of large accounts; or to a company looking for credit protection for a specific one time only contract. Apart from assessment carried out on the proposed insured, Trade Indemnity requires a note of insured buyer/s, payment terms and permitted limit/s, as well as dates for the delivery of goods.

The Anticipatory Credit Policy is structured for companies who have prepaid for work done or goods to be supplied and who wish protection against their suppliers' default or insolvency. The client profile here is a company laying out substantial deposits on major capital items or on large-scale sub-contract work. In addition to assessment of the insured, Trade Indemnity requires the following buyer data:

Country
Discretionary limits
Payment terms
Approved sources of information

The Smaller Business Policy is intended to provide the benefits of Trade Indemnity's Whole Turnover cover to the smaller, growing company. The terms of this policy are generally standard and the fact that only two returns of information are required by Trade Indemnity ensures that the paperwork involved is kept to a minimum. The two types of return here are a monthly list of accounts seriously in arrears and a statement of total annual sales. This policy's customer profile is a company with total annual sales under £1 m supplying goods or services to UK customers. As with its other policies, a statement of buyers' country, limit of discretion, payment terms and approved information sources are required. The general objectives of Trade Indemnity's Export Credit Policies are choices of protection to allow maximum flexibility to meet exporters' specific needs. These needs will vary according to what is being exported and the nature of the risk. The range of protection includes:

(a) Whole turnover for exporters whose sales in one or more markets or in total exceed £1 m.
(b) Specific account cover for credit given to one or more specified export customers.
(c) Catastrophe cover for exporters able to budget for 'normal' risk but who require cover against abnormally large, unexpected potential losses.
(d) Smaller Exporters' Policy for companies whose annual export sales are under £1 m.
(e) Anticipatory policy to insure exporters from the results of supplier default.
(f) Political risk cover issued in conjunction with policies (a) to (e) above.

The client profile for these policies shows typically UK export companies and foreign companies shipping goods and engaged in the provision of services to overseas markets.

The Catastrophe Policy noted above is designed for companies prepared to accept an initial share of credit risk. Payments to the insured are made only when their losses exceed an agreed amount. This sum is expressible either as a percentage of sales, or as a fixed amount. Trade Indemnity gives the client profile for this policy as large companies whose level of turnover and spread of accounts enable them to accept an initial credit exposure. This presupposes that the credit management in the client companies is 'dynamic, efficient, and successful'.

Trade Indemnity also identifies an important and increasing market for tailor-made or special cover in the areas of financial and contingency risk. The company sees this area as 'the single biggest untapped potential market in the whole field of trade insurance.' A Special Underwriting Unit exists at Trade Indemnity to offer terms and operate policies in this field. The company, however, does not cover financial guarantees, preferring to capitalize in the area of insolvency risk where it has long experience. The Special

Underwriting Unit will write policies on a one-time-only, individual basis over most forms of insolvency.

It makes the proviso that the risks covered should not be 'trivial' or on a premium basis, less than around £5,000. Trade Indemnity claims to be able to make informed initial decisions on good quality risk proposals within 24 hours. The second stage in underwriting in these cases requires data from the potential insured. These data include up-to-date financial information and, when available, a copy of the contract involved. The policy is then written and forwarded for discussion between broker and client. On approval and prepayment of the premium, the special policy is activated. These policies can provide cover against insolvency or contingency risk for up to five years. In some instances, 100 per cent protection is obtainable. As Trade Indemnity's financial standing and general reputation are high, its credit cover in such sensitive areas can prove a sizeable benefit in reducing the potential impact of risk on clients' balance sheets.

The gathering of information for credit risk underwriting

Figures 10.1 and 10.2 illustrate Trade Indemnity's specimen proposal form for credit cover on a whole turnover basis. Figure 10.2 shows the company's Credit Management Questionnaire as an addendum to the proposal form for a whole turnover policy. The credit management questionnaire is completed by the potential insured in addition to Trade Indemnity's own assessment of the administration of the sales ledger and related areas.

Trade Indemnity operates a rating of wide-ranging proportions for the evaluation of buyers' creditworthiness. D.L. Howson, General Manager and Underwriter at Trade Indemnity stresses that the rating system in question is only one way of approaching the assessment of credit standing. He feels it is 'most important to understand this philosophy as any kind of point-scoring evaluation is an evaluation taken in a vacuum and may bear no relationship at all to either its position in its own environment, or to commercial realities.' With this caveat, Howson acknowledges the utility of every aspect of information that might be used in making a credit assessment fairly. He cites industrial data, trade information, industrial and trade forecasts, agency credit reports, bankers' opinions, balance-sheet analysis including the use of discriminant analyical techniques, along with the analysis of all types of confidential financial data obtained direct from companies.

In addition to this body of data, Howson singles out adverse corporate information as the most valuable data of all. Such information can be gathered from gazettes, e.g. Stubbs', the insured, the underwriters' continual relationships with the trades in which they specialize, and from Trade Indemnity's own Collection Department.

The rating system referred to above is seen by Howson as 'useful particularly in cases of buyers who are being looked at for the first time and where it is necessary to make a very quick assessment in order to take an initial (provisional) decision'.

This system operates on similar ultimate codings to Dun & Bradstreet's, but with different values. Trade Indemnity preface their system guidelines by saying that, 'there is no precise mathematical formula for assessing creditworthiness. We have established, by long experience, however, that there are four main variable factors involved in the assessment.' In this framework, the four factors are given arithmetic values and the sum of them yields a

Trade Indemnity
Trade Indemnity plc
Trade Indemnity House
12-34 Great Eastern Street, London EC2A 3AX
Telephone 01-739 4311, Telex 21227

MODEL PROPOSAL FORM

PROPOSAL FOR CREDIT POLICY WHOLE TURNOVER

FOR OFFICE USE ONLY		

Please inform us of the terms on which you are prepared to issue a policy to indemnify us against losses we may sustain through the insolvency or protracted default of our buyers in the countries named below. To enable you to do this we give you, in the strictest confidence, the following information.

1. COUNTRIES

Countries NOTE: If insufficient space please attach schedule	Estimated Annual Turnover	Approximate Number of Accounts	Normal Terms of Payment
U.K.	£5m	100	MONTHLY A/C (PAYMENT DUE END OF MONTH FOLLOWING MONTH OF DELIVERY)
Totals	£5m		

2. APPROXIMATE NUMBER AND SIZE OF ACTIVE ACCOUNTS

Number	Size	Number	Size
4	Over £50,000 outstanding at one time	20	£1,001-£2,500 outstanding at one time
10	£10,001-£50,000 Do.	15	£501-£1,000 Do.
20	£5,001-£10,000 Do.	16	£251-£500 Do.
15	£2,501-£5,000 Do.	–	Up to £250 Do.

3. TOTAL OF DEBTORS' BALANCES

At last 31st Mar.	£ 800,000	At last 30th Sep.	£ 500,000
At last 30th Jun.	£ 992,000	At last 31st Dec.	£ 498,000

4. PAST EXPERIENCE

Financial Year Ending	Turnover	Relative Net Bad Debt Losses	Largest Individual Net Loss	Number of Losses
31.12.1980	2,350,000			
31.12.1981	3,610,000	11560	11200	2
31.12.1982	3,812,750	1750	1750	1
31.12.1983	3,830,000	30,000	30,000	1
31.12 1984	4,840,000	–	–	
Current year to date 28.2	882,000	6000	6000	1

Notes: (i) Turnover figures should exclude sales to associated and subsidiary companies, Government Departments, Public Authorities and Nationalised Undertakings which cannot be covered under the Policy.
(ii) In the event of an abnormally heavy loss in any year, an explanation of the circumstances should be attached.

Form No. 83-2 Swan Registered Office 12-34 Great Eastern Street London EC2A 3AX. Registered in England. Registered No. 149786.

Figure 10.1 Trade Indemnity PLC: Proposal for credit policy (whole turnover)

2. QUESTIONS

To be answered by the Applicant.

5. NATURE OF BUSINESS

(a)	Kind of goods sold?	*DOORS & WOODEN FRAMES*
(b)	To what trade (or section of trade) are they sold?	*40% BUILDERS MERCHANTS* *60% FURNITURE MANUFACTURERS*

6. CREDIT CONTROL

How do you investigate the standing of your buyers? (Give particulars of enquiry agents and/or other sources of information employed.)	*1, OBTAIN BALANCE SHEETS FOR LARGE ACCOUNTS.* *2, DUNN & BRADSTREET REPORTS, BANK REPORTS.*

7. SPECIAL TERMS

Have you any accounts where special terms of payment, differing from the normal terms of payment stated in Section 1, have been agreed to?	*YES* *JOHN BROWN FURNITURE LTD.* *90 DAY BILL OF EXCHANGE FROM DATE OF DELIVERY.*
NOTE: If the answer is "Yes", the Applicant should attach details, viz. names and addresses, special terms and amounts involved.	

8. OVERDUE ACCOUNTS

Have you any accounts on your books which are seriously overdue or otherwise causing you anxiety at the present time? If so please, give names, addresses, dates and amounts involved. If not please state "None".	*NO.*

9. POLICIES, GUARANTEES AND/OR SECURITIES HELD OR APPLIED FOR

Do you at present hold any Policy of Insurance or guarantee or any security in connection with the credit risk on any of your buyers? If so, give particulars.	*YES.*

We declare that the information given above is to the best of our knowledge and belief correct, and we are not aware of any circumstances which we have not disclosed to you which might influence your acceptance of the risk.

Address

Signature of Applicant and Company stamp

Date

Trade

Figure 10.1 (*Continued*)

3.
PRINCIPAL BUYERS

Notes—(i) The object of this list is to assist the Company to appreciate the quality and size of the larger accounts.

(ii) Please ensure that names and addresses are given accurately and in full.

	Names and Addresses of Principal Buyers	Maximum Credit Limit Required £	For Office Use Only
1	A.M. LTD, 120. BROOM LANE, CHELMSFORD, ESSEX.	45,000	
2	G.H. WILKINS LTD, UNIT 2, MANOR ESTATE, DISS, SUFFOLK.	75,000	
3	UNITED BUILDERS LTD, 198-204, DOCKSIDE, IPSWICH, SUFFOLK.	80,000	
4			
5			
6			
7			
8			
9			
10			
11			
12			
13			
14			
15			

Please continue overleaf, if necessary.

Figure 10.1 (*Concluded*)

Trade Indemnity
Trade Indemnity plc
Trade Indemnity House
12-34 Great Eastern Street, London EC2A 3AX
Telephone 01-739 4311, Telex 21227

CREDIT MANAGEMENT QUESTIONNAIRE
ADDENDUM TO PROPOSAL FOR CREDIT POLICY WHOLE TURNOVER

Please complete the questions listed below and return together with the completed proposal form.

1. **GENERAL**
   Please state name and position of person responsible for operating credit management.   ....
   ....

2. **EXISTING ACCOUNTS**
   (a) Is reference made to the state of an account:
      (i) On receipt of an order?   Yes ☐   No ☐

      (ii) Before despatch or completion of work?   Yes ☐   No ☐

   (b) Are credit limits set and operated?   Yes ☐   No ☐

3. **FOLLOW UP PROCEDURE**
   (a) How soon after despatch of goods are invoices sent out?   Same day ☐

      No. of days [   ]

   (b) Up to what date are statements prepared?   [   ]

   (c) How soon after this date are they sent out?   [   ] days

   (d) What is the procedure for following up overdue accounts?
      Telephone ☐
      Letter ☐
      Visits ☐

   (e) After how many days beyond due date do you approach your customers?
      1st approach [   ] days
      2nd approach [   ] days
      3rd approach [   ] days
      4th approach [   ] days

   (f) After how many days beyond due date is an account put on stop?   No. of days [   ]

   (g) After how many days beyond due date is an account put out for collection?   No. of days [   ]

We declare that the information is to the best of our knowledge and belief correct and will form part of any policy that may be issued.

Signature of Applicant .... Position ....
Company ....
Address ....
Date ....

Form No. 83A   Registered Office 12-34 Great Eastern Street London EC2A 3AX. Registered in England. Registered No. 149786.

Figure 10.2 Trade Indemnity PLC: Credit management questionnaire

Trade Indemnity's buyers' credit rating system

FACTOR 1—GENERAL STANDING

To assess the general standing of a company, Trade Indemnity uses the net worth of the subject as a guideline.

By net worth the analyst computes the company's value after deduction of current and long-term liabilities. Apparently, off-balance-sheet exposures, including capital contractual commitments and contingent liabilities, are not taken into the calculation. Neither is it apparent whether or not intangible assets are deducted at the outset. Trade Indemnity states that its net worth figure is sometimes shown as net assets on the balance sheet.

Where no balance sheet is available, the underwriter or analyst must make a 'reasoned assessment based on his general knowledge of the buyer and the trade involved and taking account of the paid-up capital in the case of companies'.

Under general standing as a factor, the following weighting-groups and definitions follow:

Weightings	Groupings	Definition
1	Highest	Net worth over £25 m/companies of very high standing
2	High	Net worth over £10 m/companies of high standing
3	Very good	Net Worth over £5 m/companies and partnerships of good standing
4	Good and substantial	Net worth over £2 m
5	Good	Net worth over £½ m
6	Fair	Net worth over £¼ m
7	Moderate	Net worth over £100,000
8	Reasonable	Net worth over £50,000
9	Small	Net worth over £25,000
10	Very small	Net worth under £25,000
11	Speculative concerns with only nominal capital	

FACTOR 2—HISTORY

Here, values are assigned to the length of time a buyer has been established as well as his reputation. There is an apparent overlap to some degree between the buyers' reputation as an historical datum and his 'general standing' assessed in the first factor. The evaluation in this second factor is set out as follows:

Weightings	Groupings	Definitions
1	Old established	Over 20 years with a good reputation
2	Well established	10 to 20 years with a good reputation

3	Established	5 to 10 years with a good reputation
4	Established	2 to 5 years with a good reputation
5	Concerns which:	

      (a) do not have good reputations, or
      (b) have not had a trouble-free financial history, or
      (c) have been established within the last 2 years only

FACTOR 3—LIQUIDITY

By liquidity, Trade Indemnity understands the ability of a buyer to meet current liabilities from its current assets. It is stressed that assessment of liquidity on this measure is not 'a mere arithmetical exercise; regard must be paid to the nature of the current assets and liabilities; and in particular, to stock and work-in-progress'. The examination is made as follows:

Weightings	Definitions
1	Current assets substantially in excess of current liabilities
2	Current assets adequately covering current liabilities
3	Current assets and current liabilities broadly in balance
4	Current assets moderately less than current liabilities
5	Current assets substantially less than current liabilities

Trade Indemnity appreciate that this type of assessment requires use of balance sheets. Where none is available, 'a reasoned assessment' is claimed possible based upon the buyer's 'payment record'. When the buyer has a satisfactory payment record but no balance sheet is available, Trade Indemnity in the absence of information to the contrary would 'reasonably assume' that current assets adequately cover current liabilities. By contra, where payment records are poor, 'it would be reasonable to assume that current assets did not cover liabilities, whether moderately or substantially being a matter of opinion'. Finally, a very good payment record should not, according to Trade Indemnity, be taken to 'assume that current assets are substantially in excess of current liabilities. It would be safer to assume that current assets are merely adequately covered.'

It is intended that the evaluation of liquidity and payment record be considered as integral. *Factor 4—Payment Record* assesses the settlement experience of suppliers as disclosed by overdue account returns, ledger experience, and status reports among other sources. The assessment is made on the following lines:

Weightings	Groupings	Definitions
1	Very good	Confirmed prompt payers generally
2	Satisfactory	Most engagements on or about due date
3	Fair	Some delays reported
4	Poor	Takes extended credit generally/some collections reported
5	Very poor	Takes extended credit generally/frequent collections including County Court Judgments and/or writs

The rating system based on the sum of the four factors above gives rise to 20 or more possible sum totals and yields 18 Trade Indemnity codings.

As noted earlier, this system forms part of the company's credit rating system only. The system is simple in concept and straightforward in operation. It is of particular interest in the pragmatic way in which numerical values are assigned to evaluative judgements. For instance, particular knowledge of industry sectors must obtain before users of the system can evaluate whether current assets are *substantially* in excess of current liabilities. The system could be seen as potentially biased following on from this. In the absence of any 'pro' payment data for example, one collection notified Trade Indemnity on a disputed invoice might lead to a non-indicative evaluation of the buyer's overall payment performance. Then what of the equation of age with standing? To some degree, it must be held to be perfectly reasonable. For a company to have survived for a considerable time does argue for capital adequacy. Nevertheless, it would be unfortunate were a well-capitalized and well-managed company's general standing to be downgraded due to its 'youth'. There are also various types of businesses that could not have been in existence twenty years ago. These include companies both in the manufacturing and service industries. How well will this system cope with assessing them?

Whilst it is self-evident that the system's framework is commonsensible, it is also clear that users at Trade Indemnity must make their initial value judgements from a highly informed position. Without detailed sectoral knowledge, the system's utility must be questioned. On the purely computational side, the implied equation of net worth with net assets is open to argument and ought to be open to argument since the invention of leasing as an off-balance-sheet financing mechanism. In other words, Trade Indemnity's balance-sheet analysis will be only as good as its analysts. Accordingly, we are not examining an 'expert system' in the sense that the skill of an expert (in this case, a credit analyst) is not captured *within* the system to make that skill available to non-experts when they require it. With the system we have examined, the real experts remain outside the system.

As part of its assessment work, Trade Indemnity maintains an Economics Department. This helps to provide the various levels of industrial background data that seem so sadly lacking in most reporting companies, financial institutions, and even some large banks. Trade Indemnity publishes a *Quarterly Economic Review* focusing on the UK economy as a whole, major industry sectoral analyses, annual and quarterly totals of bad debts and business failures and analyses of failure trends.

In addition to its already formidable array of assessment techniques, Trade Indemnity has always been ready to buy-in outside expertise. This may take the form of computerized financial models to augment its other systems' assessment routines, on-line data links with information companies, and a wide range of status and credit reports from approved agencies. The 'approved sources of information' items referred to in the various policy schedules discussed earlier call for the insured in some cases to order reports on buyers from agencies approved by Trade Indemnity for underwriting purposes. Trade Indemnity will also, as noted before, use reports from external sources as integral parts of the credit assessment both of the insured and of some buyers.

Factoring—data collection and analysis

Factoring and its related invoice discounting are financial mechanisms to provide cash against credit sales invoices. Factoring has a different focus than invoice discounting because factors buy total sales volume and continual volume debt from their client companies. Full factoring facilities also provide additional service elements in that the factor becomes responsible for the collection of the debts. Accordingly, the sales ledger is administered by the factoring company. Factoring facilities can also be provided on a non-recourse basis with 100 per cent credit protection or on a recourse basis whereby the credit risk on the credit sales to the debtors remains with the client, i.e. the selling company.

Invoice discounting furnishes cash against debts. Invoice discount finance can be provided against debts on a whole turnover basis or as cash against specific debts.

Factoring companies usually wish to provide their facilities to established companies, that is, to those which have been trading for some two or three years. Invoice discounters also look for businesses with a well-established track record.

In both cases, either factoring or invoice discounting, the proposed clients' businesses do need to show accounting statements which would indicate basic financial soundness, an expanding sales ledger and an annual turnover in excess of £100,000. Because of its focus, factoring may not be suitable to a range of companies such as small or new businesses in particular.

The cash against credit sales invoices in factoring is normally applied at a maximum 80 per cent of a company's sales ledger.

Invoice discount finance can match this at its upper range and can be as particularized or concentrated as required. Generally, however, the discount finance is in the region of 70 per cent of the discounted debts.

Traditionally the two services differ as well in the fact that under an invoice discount contract, clients are left to manage their own collection and credit control. On the other hand, with factoring, the client is provided with total sales ledger administration. Invoice discount finance is thus a confidential service which does not reveal the facilities to the customers (debtors), whereas factoring services are disclosed to the client's range of debtors.

Business expansion entails its own problems. Foremost among these can be the financing of increased turnover. Borrowing on the required scale is not normally easy to organize, particularly when there is a lack of track record or of asset backing. Often, borrowing, when possible, will carry with it onerous terms. Attracting external capital also generally entails some loss of control. Factoring, by releasing cashflow with its advances against book debts, can provide cost-effective finance for an increasingly wider range of companies. Factoring is now much better understood than in the past for the useful tool it is, and major factoring houses are growing more willing to offer flexible and imaginative finance to more types of companies in addition to younger businesses.

In brief, factoring provides a determinable cashflow which grows in line with expanding turnover. It can also afford 100 per cent credit cover if required (non-recourse factoring). Credit assessment experience of the factor has the effect of minimizing bad debt risk. By assumption of sales ledger administration by the factor a client's administration overheads can be reduced as well as his staff costs. This is true especially in the sales ledger/credit investigation and collection departments, and also, in the overhead costs of postage, telephone collection and the not inconsiderable expenses of credit investigation. The effective removal of the burden of sales ledger management can free companies to devote more time to product development, marketing and sales.

The injection of liquidity provided by factoring will also enable companies to take advantage of cash discounts and bulk purchase discounts. Higher levels of liquidity additionally allow companies to accept larger orders whilst permitting sales to be made to customers on credit terms.

Taken at its best, factoring should, therefore, increase a company's competitiveness and productivity on a sound financial footing.

As in the case of credit insurance underwriting, factoring companies are underwriting their contracts on a continuum of multiple risks. These are perceived as:

1. Client solvency/temporary insolvency.
2. Client's terminal insolvency leading to liquidation.
3. Buyer insolvency or protracted or non-settlement of account.
4. Internal capital requirements.

Item 1 can destroy fine margins for the factor. Item 2 can cause irrecoverable loss in the form of factoring advances. Item 3 can also erode margins on a cost of money basis in the case of delayed settlement, or in the event of non-collectible debts, the factor under a non-recourse contract will bear the loss. Item 4 may restrict the finance available to certain clients who may have need for more liquidity than the factor is able to provide. This might apply in the case of a company in increasing financial distress *despite* the assistance of factors. Such a company may show a decreasing turnover and eroded or non-existent profit margins. Like banks, factoring houses must spread their risk. Their assistance in such cases will necessarily need to be finite.

Because the factor is concerned with a comparatively wide range of risks, data collection and holistic analysis of the information gathered is vital. Data is normally gathered from a variety of sources. These include:

Agency reports on buyers
Internal database information
Inspection and analysis of accounting statements
Bank opinions
Trade references
On-line rating and information services
Trade and economic data

Whilst factors' databases will include information gathered and stored from this representative spectrum of sources, the initial and most valuable client data is gathered, as in the case of other credit-grantors, direct from the client. Figure 10.3 illustrates client information forms provided by permission of Arbuthnot Factors Limited.

The format for data collection shown in Figure 10.3 is far fuller than most application forms for credit sale accounts—and necessarily so. The factor is supplying not trade credit but a banking product of a specialized nature—trade finance in its widest sense secured on book debts of the company. The first page of the form calls for the type of information found in better agency reports but in a concise, easy to read layout. Page two contributes data not normally to be had in most agency reports; notably, details of principal current account balance and overdraft limit. Also, a breakdown of sales profile is requested including terms of trading, sales ledger latest monthly balance, debtors in the ledger with current balances and total number of debtors. A valuable addition here is the request for projected sales for the next year and an estimate of export sales within that figure. Finally, Arbuthnot asks for a breakdown in percentages of sales per export country as at latest

COMPANY INFORMATION

Company name/Business name (including trading style)		
ANY COMPANY LIMITED		
Telephone	Telex	Contact
01-000-6906	49416294	J. SMITH - M.D.
Business address		
UNIT X, NORTH LONDON BUSINESS PARK		Postcode N4 N4
Registered office (if different from above)		
HOLDSWORTH CHAMBERS W1.		
Registered no.	Date established	Date trading commenced
2969428246	1983	1983
Type of business		
LINGERIE MNFRS & COSTUME JEWELLERY		
Nominal share capital		Issued share capital
£1,000		£1,000

Directors/Partners

Full name & position	Address	No. of shares held
J. SMITH	ACACIA AVENUE, LONDON SUBURB	900
MRS A SMITH	- do -	100
Other shareholders		
-	-	-

Associated Companies

i.e. companies in which Directors have an interest or which are parents or subsidiaries of this company

Total shares issued

Name	Address
-	-

Figure 10.3   Arbuthnot Factors Ltd: Client information form

274 THE CORRELATION AND TREATMENT OF COMPANY DATA

Finance & Advisers

Bankers	MAINLINE
Address	HIGH STREET, ANYTOWN

Overdraft limit £ 30,000   Current balance £ 28,600   debit / credit

Secured by DIRECTORS P.G.'s SUPPORTED BY 2ND CHARGE ON PRIVATE HOUSE

Auditors	ACCOUNTS & CO.
Address	HIGH STREET, ANYTOWN

Financial year end   APRIL 30th   Date next accounts expected (if not current)   JULY/AUG '86

Loans to the Company since last accounts £   -

Loans from the Company since last accounts £   -

Where did you first see/hear about Arbuthnot Factors   TRADE PUBLICATION ADVERT

SALES INFORMATION

Types of customer	% sales
Exporters	10
Manufacturers	
Public Bodies	
Retailers	70
Wholesalers	
Other	20

Terms of trade (including any settlement discounts)

UK Sales   20th-19th payable 10th following month, less 2.5% discount

Export sales (including shipping terms)
30 days less 2.5%, 60 days NET

Special terms (give details of any offered)
-

Total of sales ledger balances at end of last month £ 49,375

Number of debtors in ledger   259   Number of debtors with balances   98

Projected turnover for next 12 months
UK £360,000   Export   £60,000

Export countries (give % of sales per country and invoice currency)   1984/85 Sales

USA	£8,404	Invoiced in dollars
W. Germany	£4,573	Invoiced in DM
France	£2,023	Invoiced in F.FRS
Others	£1,371	Invoiced in £

Figure 10.3 *(Continued)*

CUSTOMER INFORMATION

Please give details of your larger accounts. Include a full current aged analysis where available

Name	Address	Telephone	Amount outstanding £	Approx. annual sales £
Fenwicks	New Bond St. London W1	01-629-9161		7,662
Bradleys	83 Knightsbridge, London SW1	01-235-2902		4,298
Butchers Dept. Store	Swan Lane, Norwich	0603-617621		3,157
Beales	Old Christchurch Rd. Bournemth	0202-22022		1,897
Carole Molyneux	2 Francis St. Stoneygate, Leics	0533-709252		1,927
The Chiffonier	98 Morningside Rd. Edinburgh	031-447-6715		2,579
Edna Cornwell	186 Ashley Rd. Hale, Altrincham, Cheshire	061-928-1072		2,272
Feathers	110 Derborough Road, High Wycombe, Bucks	446529		7,630
Gillian Ellen	49 West St. Alresford, Hants	096273-4253		1,954
Halls	3 Bridge St. Bost, Lincs	0205-67168		1,602
Frasers (N.Div)	109 Berkeley St. Glasgow	041-204-2711		4,870
Keddies	High St. Southend-on-Sea	0206-41311		1,560
La Donna Elegante	35 Bloomsbury Way, London WC1	01-405-5564		1,529
Pretty Things (IOM)	15 Ouchey Shopping Precinct Oldham	0624-3774		5,012
Silks	2 McClaren Place, Glasgow	041-633-0442		1,613
Something Special	2 Mancet St. Southport	0704-32204		1,724
After Eight	12 Belmont St. Aberdeen	0224-645645		4,675
Nouvelle	Bleibtreustr. 24, 1000 Berlin 15	8814737		2,503
Bloomingdales	New York 10022			2,705
Le Sac	3222 M Street, NW, Washington DC	202-333-0405		1,735

Details of Credit Insurance Policies held

UK   —

Export   —

Details of bad debts over last 2 years

1. Nicholls
   1984 — £204

2. Frillies Ltd. Leeds
   1983 — £550

Figure 10.3 (*Continued*)

Analysis of sales – last 12 months

Month	Year	UK sales (inc. VAT) £	Export sales £	Value of credits £	Number of UK invoices	Number of Export invoices	Number of credit notes
MAY	1984	8,524	2,081	104	56	7	6
JUNE	1984	9,708	2,136	143	56	3	4
JULY	1984	5,708	281	31	40	3	2
AUG	1984	15,351	651	182	55	2	4
SEPT	1984	20,475	-	-	66	-	-
OCT	1984	22,511	333	788	79	2	8
NOV	1984	34,375	2,128	530	98	9	7
DEC	1984	11,949	228	241	56	1	5
JAN	1985	3,541	1,465	322	24	1	1
FEB	1985	17,440	-	545	68	-	5
MAR	1985	13,764	157	380	75	2	3
APR	1985	6,759	6,911	119	42	13	1
Totals		170,105	16,371	3,385	715	43	46

We understand that the completed questionnaire will be treated in the very *strictest confidence*. To the best of our knowledge and belief the information we have given is correct, and we are not aware of anything materially significant in the business or financial position of the company, we have not disclosed which might affect your decision.

Signature ....

Position ....

Date........... 10th July 1984

When returning this questionnaire please enclose a copy of the last two years' accounts together with a sample invoice and credit note.

Figure 10.3 (*Concluded*)

accounting date and a note of the currencies in which invoices were uttered. This last can give valuable insight into potential foreign exchange exposures involved in delayed collections, whilst the 'types of customer' sales analysis noted before gives another indication of the spread of buyer risk. In the example given, we see that only 10 per cent of turnover was represented by export orders. This can signify to the factor that total volume of exports involved should not materially lengthen debt-turn when calculated over the whole turnover. In practice, this would be favourable from the factor's point of view.

Again, this breakdown of customer types shows that 70 per cent (the bulk) of orders were accounted for by retailers. Depending upon the industry sector, this might imply a further shortening of debt-turn—for instance if the retailers in this example were predominantly in the food and drinks industry where debt-turns tend to be short due to high volumes of cash purchases.

We see that 20 per cent of sales were accounted for by unspecified buyers. This might cause some concern to the factor were credit information not available on the major buyers within that grouping. In this example, the 'other' customers constitute a significant share of total sales.

On the third page of Arbuthnot's form, details of larger customer accounts are required, including a current aged debtor analysis where available. This will be of considerable help to the factor in assessing the spread of debt the quality and quantity of which is his prime assessment consideration. Note that Arbuthnot asks for details of any credit insurance policies held for UK and/or export sales. Presumably, it will be heartened in its client and debt-spread assessment if it sees that a credit insurer has already assessed the range of risks as well as the client's internal credit management and has written a policy underwriting whole or partial turnover.

Next, we find details for bad debts over the last two years. The factor will be interested to compare the size both of individual and aggregate bad debts with total annual sales and with individual as well as averaged larger account values. This kind of analysis will give the factor important historical risk data in addition to an insight into the quality of past sales against present or latest turnover. Note that in this example, both bad debts appear to be quite small. They are well below the average value of the client's turnover for larger accounts and represent only 0.2 per cent of forecast turnover for the next twelve months. The customer (debtor) information on large accounts requires addresses and telephone numbers. This will prove helpful both for referencing/validating purposes and possibly for collection work.

The final page of the form calls for an analysis of turnover for the last year. Where audited accounts are available, this analysis can be read in conjunction to give the factor a full picture taken directly off the sales ledger of the client's cashflow. Naturally, the sales analysis should marry up with the audited turnover figure without addition or deduction of extraordinary items and asset disposals. The seasonality important to a factor's own capital requirements will also be made apparent from the monthly sales analysis. Again, an important distinction is made between export and domestic orders. Further detail is supplied by requests for the number and value of credit notes. This will also indicate efficiency and order-fulfilment. Both domestic and export sales expressed in numbers of respective invoices will help apprise the factor of administrative work required in taking over management of the client's sales ledger. Finally, Arbuthnot requires copies of the client's last two years' accounts along with a sample invoice and credit note.

Figure 10.4 shows how Arbuthnot spreads the accounting information: Arbuthnot's spreadsheet for account analysis is straightforward and simple to complete. The first and last sections are possibly the most interesting as in the initial section factored or factorable sales are directly compared with total turnover. A proper attention is then paid to gross profit which, in turn, is compared with profit after deduction of indirect costs but before taxation and extraordinaries. It is also telling that directors' remuneration is given such prominence (it is the fifth item in the spreadsheet). Presumably, the factor, or indeed any other provider of capital, will not be happy about funding an operation which is being milked of liquidity by its own greedy directors. Next in the apparent priorities comes a notation for bad debts (the provision can come either from the profit and loss account or the balance sheet). This is followed by retentions for the year only. New capital refers to surplus on the funds flow statement or to additional long-term liabilities plus latest profit added to form the latest capital employed increase.

Arbuthnot's computation for tangible net worth is normally taken as capital and reserves. Opening net tangible worth refers to the prior year's figure whilst closing net tangible worth is the latest year's total.

The middle sections of the spreadsheet are self-explanatory and are simply slight restatements of the balance sheet.

The final section of the spread is interesting in that capital employed is calculated using only the sum of called-up capital and reserves. It is also interesting that the company does not add deferred long-term liabilities along with long-term borrowings to the sum total of capital employed. The spreadsheet itself looks unclear in this computation. Capital employed is normally calculated as:

> Shareholders' funds
> +
> Creditors: Amounts falling due after one year
> +
> Deferred taxation

A prime ratio as an indicator of profitability is then calculated both by the standard profit before taxation/capital employed, and by the unusual profit after taxation/capital employed.

Strictly speaking, true profit-earning capacity will be distorted by this second measurement. On the other hand, something about the company's tax-minimization ability may be inferred. Further distortions could enter as profit after taxation might include gains or losses on various asset disposals and/or extraordinary items none of which could be held to form integral parts of a company's normal business activities. The amount of distortion here will, of course, be dependent upon where in the profit and loss account the analyst takes his profit after taxation figure. If he takes profit after taxation but before extraordinary items, a more indicative reading will result.

Next, debt-turn is called for followed by creditors' turnover ('credit taken'). Note that there is no place in this spread for the difference between the two turns. The difference here is important as this represents the surplus or deficiency of cashflow available for ordinary trading (monetary lag). Finally, stock-turn is called for in times of complete turnover of inventories instead of the more common measurement in days.

If the cost of sales figure is available in the profit and loss account, it can be employed

FINANCIAL SUMMARY £'000

Client:	ANY COMPANY LIMITED						
Date and period covered:							
Audited/Qualified/Draft & Date:	30.4.84.						
		%		%		%	
Total Sales	236	(100)		(100)		(100)	
Factored Sales		( )		( )		( )	
Gross Profit		( )		( )		( )	
Pre-tax Net Profit	98	( )		( )		( )	
Directors Remuneration	29						
Bad Debts							
Retained Profit	29	( )		( )		( )	
New Capital							
Opening Net Tangible Worth	1						
Closing Net Tangible Worth	30	30					
CURRENT ASSETS							
Cash	4						
Trade Debtors	29						
Other Debtors							
Stock & WIP	56						
Loans							
		89					
CURRENT LIABILITIES							
Bank Overdraft (Sec/Unsec)	48						
Trade Creditors & Bills	32						
Other Creditors							
Current Tax							
Dividend							
Other Loans							
		80					
Net Current Assets		9					
Associated Companies							
Debit Balance							
Credit Balance							
FIXED ASSETS							
Land & Buildings							
Other	21						
Less H.P. Commitments		21					
INVESTMENTS							
Subsidiary Company							
Other							
DEFERRED & LONG TERM L'TIES							
Mortgages & Loans							
Future Tax							
Other							
		30					
SHAREHOLDERS' FUNDS							
Issued Capital	1						
P & L A/c & Reserves	29						
Capital Reserves							
Loans from Directors							
Loans to Directors							
Less: Intangibles		30					
Capital Employed							
Return on Cap. Emp— Pretax		%		%		%	
„ „ „ „ — After tax		%		%		%	
Debt turn		days		days		days	
Credit Taken		days		days		days	
Stock turnover		times		times		times	

Figure 10.4 Arbuthnot Factors Ltd: Financial summary

instead of the turnover figure and, assuming stocks are represented mainly by goods for resale (as with a retail or distribution operation), the ratio stock/cost of sales can be expressed in days of stock or as stock turned over so many times per year. Holmes and Sugden point out that greater accuracy can be gained by taking the average of the opening and closing stock balances. Thus Arbuthnot probably intends its analysts to divide the cost of sales by an averaged stocks figure.

Arbuthnot uses a combination of on-line information facilities, its own database, agency reports, customer information forms, accounting statements, internal spreading, and on-site 'audits' in its data collection. It does not currently use in-house scoring systems, as its chief concern is not with insolvency prediction but with the quick roll-over of debt against which it will advance cash.

The assessment of the data gathered by Arbuthnot is carried out at two levels: at departmental level and by the Credit Committee. This arrangement is similar to most banks. Exposures over the £100,000 level are forwarded to the Credit Committee. The Committee is composed of the company's Managing Director and other directors, particularly those with credit and collection responsibilities. Also present is the Credit Manager who will present the various applications.

For exposures around £$\frac{1}{2}$ m and above, Arbuthnot will carry out extremely detailed analysis both at departmental level and in committee. For sizeable business, the company will require sensitivity analysis to be presented to the Credit Committee. In most instances, this work is carried out by a New Business Manager who has a dual sales and analytical function.

Arbuthnot, like Trade Indemnity, for all its computerized information systems, still relies to a high degree on its employees' knowledge of certain industry sectors. The company is, accordingly, selective in the new business it contracts. For instance, some businesses are highly attractive to factors in general. Examples are: the garment industry when proper attention is paid to product ranges (i.e. how fashionable and thus quickly saleable are they?) and the seasonality of sales; the office cleaning and general labour hire industry where factoring covers the short cash gaps between payment of wages and settlement of buyers' accounts. Also, some franchise operations, service industries and distributorships are particularly attractive. Hotel turnovers can be factorable if the bills are raised on limited company invoices. On the other hand, Arbuthnot along with other factoring houses does not find the construction industry viable with its routine stage payments.

Credit analysis at Arbuthnot is then an amalgam of computational and data collection routines coupled with informed opinion based on knowledge of the behaviour of various business sectors. In this knowledge, account is taken of individual companies and how they fit into their particular industry sectors, margins, seasonality, the speed at which debt can be rolled over, the spread of debt, management information and management figures, product and sales data, an assessment of clients' ethical behaviour, and the relationship between client and debtor companies.

Sources

Arbuthnot Factors Ltd, Company Information Form and Spreadsheet (samples).

Bathory, A., 'New Invoice-Discounting for Credit Management', *Credit Management*, 1982, passim.

Holmes, G., and Sugden, A., *Interpreting Company Reports and Accounts*, Woodhead-Faulkner, Cambridge, 1983, p. 166, example 23.10.

Mathieson, R., 'Tomorrow's Accountant—Expert Aided? (Expert Systems)', *The Accountant's Magazine*, April 1986, Vol. 90, no. 957, pp. 22–24.

Trade Indemnity PLC, *Information on Policies, Proposal Forms (samples) and Buyers' Rating System Guidelines.*

11

DATA COLLECTION AND ASSESSMENT IN A LARGE CORPORATE

The collection and assessment of data on customer accounts presents organizational as well as intellectual problems. In the main, these problems centre around speed and accuracy. In this Chapter, we examine organizational procedures in a major oil company with a total turnover of about £650 m. Roughly 10 per cent of these sales are export orders. The company's UK operation requires some twenty-five distributorships. In general, the company's UK business has shifted from lower to higher risk sales—that is, a movement from sales of heating oils (supplied to firms with relatively high investment levels in fixed assets) to firms with fewer fixed assets, e.g. hauliers. Fixed assets tend to be important as a means of securing some of the company's credit facilities or as a base for recourse or even attachment in the event of customers' financial trouble when such distress materially affects credit standing.

The company's credit policy is geared around the maximizing of cashflows. This emphasis is required by the need to maintain certain levels of turnover and profit margins demanded by the economies of scale implicit in the company's refining, distribution and marketing operations. Potentially, sales falling below these implicit economic levels could result in more serious losses for the company than individual bad debts. These considerations shape the company's data collection and credit assessment routines.

In common with most other firms in the industry, this company's terms are the 20th of the month following delivery. For non-compliance with these terms, supplies are normally stopped four days thereafter. In about seven days, a final demand is sent to the customer. If payment is not received subsequently, the debt is generally placed in the hands of a collection agency. The company will seldom accept such problem accounts back on the books even when settlement has been made as a result of formal collection.

Because of the high volumes of transactions as well as the high monetary values involved, the streamlining of credit operations is viewed as an important priority. Accordingly, whenever applicable, payment by direct debit is encouraged. The company is installing a new direct debiting system. This is to be backed by sophisticated software that will allow increased flexibility of terms for settlement of accounts. This system will have obvious cashflow and procedural advantages for the company as well as proving attractive to many of its customers.

The system of payment on one specific day of the month cannot suit all customers. Traditionally, this stood in the way of the favoured direct debit payment method. The new flexible system will be conditional on customers agreeing to direct debits on the dates they nominate. The software will permit the company's field locations to communicate directly to the London-based computer to obtain credit status information, account balances and other details. This direct communications link provides current information more quickly and inexpensively than the usual method of telephone enquiries. The higher level of computerization sharply reduces man-hours and paperwork.

Flexible direct debiting, improved communications links, and ultra-modern internal sales accounting systems still require input. The collection and interpretation of credit data will remain a vital consideration in the company's database operations. Input is accordingly developed on a highly organized and well-defined set of procedures both for data gathering and for analysis. These procedures, which will be subsequently described, have worked well for the company. Total write-offs in the last financial year represented only 0.019 per cent of turnover. These write-offs were mainly small accounts. Such losses are given proper perspective when seen against the price of one load of diesel oil—at time of writing, about £8,000. On a larger perspective, the company has historically maintained very low averaged days sales outstanding in respect of its industrial accounts and the oil industry sector.

Data gathering and assessment procedures

From information supplied by sales representatives, the company's credit staff complete an enquiry listing sheet shown in Figure 11.1. As a summary document, this form is highly effective, condensing registered, status, departmental, general financial, payment performance, and supplementary credit information concisely. Sales representatives are required to obtain name and address of the customers' banks and further bank details, e.g. sorting codes. Postal codes can be obtained direct or taken from Dun & Bradstreet publications. The company uses Dun & Bradstreet for a range of services. Note the space given prominence in the upper right-hand corner of the form for the Dun & Bradstreet rating. If a direct debit mandate is attached to the credit application, it is passed to the analyst responsible for processing the application. Staff completing the Enquiry Listing sheet must then order the following status information:

1. Agency report from Dun & Bradstreet's on-line facility or reports from other approved agencies.
2. One bank reference.
3. One set of the customer's latest accounts.
4. Trade references are taken up.

This body of information is then passed to the company's internal credit analysts. Managers and analysts are active and visible, visiting sales divisions, customers and bankers as part of their financial assessment work. The chief concerns in the assessment area are accuracy, speed and practical application. To these ends formal credit analysis is kept to a minimum. Credit-granting is rightly viewed as a commercial rather than an academic discipline. Accordingly, the credit department works closely with the company's sales department to maximize profitable turnover in a market that is demonstrably increasingly competitive and one in which margins become finer daily.

When the credit analysts have received the Enquiry Listing sheet (Figure 11.1), agency report, balance sheet, bank and trade references, the data are reviewed and the terms of

284 THE CORRELATION AND TREATMENT OF COMPANY DATA

```
┌─────────┐
│ U/S     │           STATUS ENQUIRY LISTING/APPRAISAL SUMMARY
│ NEW A/C │
└─────────┘
```

Name.. Division.............
Address... D&B Rating...........
....

Agents for Enquiry	Bank for Reference	Exposure Required	Date Requested
....	....	....	....
....	....	Existing Credit Limit	
....	....	Type of Account	

Date Started	Nominal Capital	Issued Capital	Years with Company	County Court Judgments
....	....	....	....	....

Payment Performance - Direct Debit/Good/Fair/Poor ....

FINANCIAL PERFORMANCE MONTH YEAR ENDED .... GENERAL OBSERVATIONS AND COMMENTS

	19	19	19	
Turnover				....
Pre-Tax Profit				....
Profit Margin	%	%	%	....
Return on Cap. Emp.	%	%	%	....
Net Worth				....
Working Capital				....
Current Ratio	:	:	:	....
Quick Ratio	:	:	:	....
Long Debt/Equity	:	:	:	....
Short Debt/Equity	:	:	:	....
				....

Customer Number .... Division Code ...... Account Class ......   SPECIAL INSTRUCTIONS

Credit Limit .... Terms . C'worthiness .. Review Date ../../...   ....
                                                                      ....

Recommended	Recommended	Approved/Rejected	....
....	....	....	....
Date	Date	Date	....
....	....	....	....

Figure 11.1 Enquiry listing sheet

trading are decided. The internal analysts have discretionary limits beyond which decisions must be referred.

The company's system of referrals involves executives, directors, and occasionally, committees. The credit department, however, is responsible for decisions concerning payment terms and credit levels. In practice, very few credit department decisions have been referred.

The company does not generally view accounts of £20,000 and below as cost-effective to review annually. Problem accounts of any size are reviewed by analysts and managers at will. This flexibility has contributed significantly to the company's extremely small bad debt write-offs. Because of the low level of bad debt losses, the company covers none of its turnover by credit insurance as the premiums would greatly exceed historical losses. Credit insurance costs and cover are, however, reviewed periodically.

Decision

Once documents have been examined by the credit analyst and terms of trading are set, if the credit limit is within his authority, the analyst can approve the Enquiry Listing sheet; otherwise, the file with the analyst's recommendation is passed to one of the senior analysts for approval or recommendation to the Assistant Credit Manager or Credit Manager. The approval or rejection is noted at the base of the Enquiry Listing sheet.

If the account is approved, the following information will be inserted under the relevant headings:

Customer Number
Division Code
Account Class
Credit Limit
Terms
Creditworthiness code
Review Date
Special Instructions (any comments)

If the account is rejected on the grounds of poor creditworthiness or other reasons, the analyst initials and inserts the date under the heading 'Rejected' and a code number below the heading 'Terms', passing the file to a senior credit analyst for a second opinion. Where an account is rejected by the senior analyst, the file should be passed to the Assistant/Credit Manager for an opinion.

For rejections, a comment is always deemed necessary under the 'Special Instructions' heading noted earlier. The Credit Manager must approve all rejections of existing accounts.

Reviewing unallocated cash

The company's analysts review credit that cannot be allocated in any other way, taking action to make sure that these accounts are cleared each month. They also review miscellaneous claims, chiefly in respect of haulage issued monthly by the distribution department.

An analysis is generated. This is a list of customers with balances outstanding at the end of the month. It is divided by Sales Division, market, and further sub-divided by customers who pay or do not pay by direct debit.

Remitance advices are received daily from the Accounts Section who in turn receive them from the Banking Department Financial Services who are responsible for banking the cheques and sorting the remittance advices by Division.

Cash received is marked off the analysis daily by the Credit Department and the date of receipt noted.

Suspense accounts

On expiry of the seven day final demand letter mentioned earlier, a delinquent account is transferred by the Credit Department to 'Suspense'. This is a separate section of the accounts receivables aged debtors analysis. The following accounts are transferred to this section:

1. Delinquent accounts subject to legal action.
2. Accounts under moratorium agreement.
3. Accounts in the hands of a receiver.
4. Accounts in liquidation.
5. Accounts for collection by agents.

A memorandum is then sent informing the Division that (a) legal action is about to be taken; (b) that sales representatives should cease contacting the customer; and (c) that any subsequent approach by the debtor company should be directed to the Credit Department.

If an account is to be passed to collection agents, the following are prepared:

1. Statement of account.
2. Copies of all outstanding invoices (one copy for internal file and three copies to agents).
3. Copies of all relevant correspondence.
4. Letter to the agent describing circumstances and requesting immediate action.

Receiverships, liquidations, and moratoria are handled internally. In the absence of regular reports from liquidators or receivers, accounts are noted for follow-up on a quarterly basis.

Uncollectable balances are subsequently combined in a list of recommended writeoffs along with small items from the Direct Division accounts. This list is prepared quarterly in sufficient time to allow for the issuance of credit/debit notes for inclusion in the accounts receivable prior to the financial quarter-end.

'Merge and purge': Updating information and control

Every month with the final aged debtors analysis and associated data, a tape is run listing all accounts with current balances by customer number, name, division, account, classification, credit limit, registration number, review and update intervals. The tape is then sent to a specialist agency for re-sorting by division and review date and then passed to a database reporting company to extract those status review reports that will be due during the following month. These reports are generated automatically and sent to the company. Receipt of the reports generates the annual/periodic review similar to the review of a new enquiry—namely, report, accounts, and bank reference. Within a maximum of six days after issue, a report is produced and returned from the specialist agency. These reports are then used by the internal credit analysts in reviewing the position of customers in respect of overdue accounts. The records are then annotated and passed with reports to the Assistant Credit Manager.

Every week a typed list is produced by Companies' House detailing those companies which have filed annual returns and accounts and changed registered offices, this list by company registration number is run by the specialist software agency mentioned earlier against the company's own list. Where a coincidence occurs, the information is automatically sent to the internal analysts. The analysts then endeavour to move review dates to be consistent with companies' expected accounts filing dates in order to reduce the number of file reviews.

Each quarter, Dun & Bradstreet sends the company a tape for recording selected sales ledger details. The tape enables Dun & Bradstreet to gather commercial statistics, trade reference data, and offer a name-matched service. Each day the company's computer generates a Credit Violation Report. This shows on a divisional basis any customer whose drawings exceed the approved credit limit. The excess drawings may be due to a number of reasons:

1. A new customer's credit limit may not yet have been input.
2. A customer may be exceeding the credit limit by higher than expected sales. In this event, a new credit application form is required from the Division giving details and justification from the analysts for the proposed increase in credit limit.

   In some instances, an increased credit limit can be sanctioned by analysts without the generation of a new credit application.
3. An unapproved prospect has ordered from the company but does not have at date of order a credit limit. Here, the analysts contact the Terminal and Division to ensure that no further supplies are delivered without reference to the Credit Department.

   Divisional managers have the authority to release one load *only* to new prospects on receipt of a satisfactory bank reference. None the less, the analysts should be informed that the reference has been taken and asked for advice concerning terms.

A copy of the complete Credit Violation Report with comments by the appropriate analysts is supplied to the Assistant Credit Manager weekly. Once a month on the nearest workday to the 20th, a complete violation report is reviewed and annotated by each analyst and passed to the Assistant Credit Manager.

Annual review of smaller accounts

For accounts with credit limits up to and including £20,000, the company's annual review requires no status report, bank references nor automatically produced accounting statements. Customer accounts with limits up to and including £20,000 will not be reviewed unless there is reason for concern. Reasons for concerns tend to be:

(a) Slow payment.
(b) County Court judgments and legal actions.
(c) The credit limit requires increasing to the next category (above £20,000).

Where there is concern, but not necessarily when limits need increasing, analysts are able to act quickly by withholding supplies at the terminal and/or by rejecting the problem account. All such reviews are dated 01.12.90 to ensure that no reports are produced. Likewise, they can be dated the 25th of the month of review where no report is required but the latest filings of balance sheets are recorded.

These procedures apply solely to the updating of existing accounts. The company handles all new enquiries in both categories in the manner initially described—ordering full status reports, bank and trade references, and provision of latest accounting statements for assessment by the analysts.

Both the highly organized data gathering and review procedures and the computerization of the credit department function are designed to supply decision criteria to managers and analysts as quickly as possible. The assessment of customers' accounts and accounting statements by the company's analysts remains a human function. This financial assessment is held to be as important in credit sanction and control as trading/payment performance. If the credit analysts in this company are more visible than their counterparts in financial institutions or reporting companies, they rightly feel that first-hand experience and knowledge of particular industry sectors are vital in making effective credit assessments.

In this way, the company frequently advises customers on their own credit procedures and systems. The company regards their distributors' cashflows as important determinants of their own cashflow. Accordingly, a spirit of cooperation and partnership is cultivated actively.

For the assessment of customers' financial statements, the company may require unaudited management figures when the latest audited accounts are old. In the main, computer-generated management data are regarded more favourably than manually prepared accounts. With computer-generated accounts, inputs are made direct from customers' internal records and the scope for computational error and other irregularities is perceived to be lower.

Security for credit

In some instances the company will take charges over authorized distributors' assets in order to secure credit facilities.

These charges can take the following forms:

1. Debentures.
2. Floating charges (The Company sometimes must negotiate with banks for the subordination of their prior claims. In the company's experience, banks have tended to prefer taking the fixed charge, leaving the floating charge to the company).
3. Charges ranking pari passu with banks' charges. Such charge instruments are extremely varied in structure.
4. Personal guarantees.
5. Parent company guarantees.
6. In Scotland, the assignment of receivables in the case of non-limited liability entities.

Summary assessment indicators

From the aforegoing, it is clear that the company relies both upon manual and computerized data collection and credit assessment techniques. Included in data gathering, the company employs a full range of agency reports, database retrievals, updates, and 'merge and purge' operations for review and corroboration of customer information.

The company's Enquiry Listing sheet (Figure 11.1) alone is superior in format and classes of information summarized than most commercially obtainable status reports. The accounting data abstract in this form provides for six important ratio indicators:

1. Profit margin.
2. Prime ratio (return on capital employed).
3. Current ratio.
4. Liquid ratio (quick ratio).
5. Gearing (long-term debt to equity).
6. Borrowing (current) as a multiple of shareholders' funds (short-term debt to equity).

These indicators are interspersed with key financial quantities:

1. Sales
2. Profit before taxation
3. Net worth
4. Working capital

Ratios and key quantities are required for three years' minimum when subject companies have traded for that length of time or more. Compared with some other spreadsheets illustrated in this writing, this oil company's spread manages to extract crucial items in the simplest form. A place for analytical comments is provided beside the columns of figures. Whilst the company would not regard this abstract as a credit analysis proper, it finds the Enquiry Listing sheet a quick and effective summary for reference purposes and for detailed examination of points emerging for overall review.

As analysis must be thoroughly practical in orientation, this company necessarily widens the scope of traditional credit analysis. Credit analysis in this case entails careful data collection from a range of sources, continual updating, and close liaison with the sales function.

As a major supplier to most of its customers (and certainly to its distributors), the company enjoys a special niche midway between a bank and a normal trade creditor. Accordingly, when circumstances warrant, the company can look to some customers for security and expect to receive it. Apart from a handful or major suppliers in similar positions, the taking of charges by trade creditors is as yet rare in the UK.

The interplay of credit analysis and control is justified by the company's excellent results in respect of liquidity, credit periods allowed customers, flexibility of credit and settlement terms, and very low levels of bad debt write-offs.

Sources

The contributor of source material for this chapter has requested that identity be withheld. Author.

Part Four

TOWARDS THE PERFECT CREDIT ANALYSIS

12

CREDIT ANALYSIS IN LENDING OPERATIONS

Modern bankers deal with a wide range of lending applications. Essentially, lending is based on three premises: investment of bank funds profitably for the shareholders and the protection of depositors; the servicing of legitimate credit demands; and the making of advances on a sound and collectable basis. Some of these loans will have extended or 'term' maturities; others will be short-term accommodations. Loans can be based on the security of real property and other forms of collateral, whilst other loans can be unsecured. Briefly, we shall take lending to include any financial facilities involving credit risk. For this chapter, we will not deal with off-balance-sheet facilities. Loan and facilities operations appearing on the face of a bank's balance sheet will, therefore, be termed conventional lending. Also, we intend examining secured lending in its most general form with respect to analytical precedures and concepts that underpin it. Consumer lending and its associated analytical procedures will not be covered. Nor is it our purpose to discuss various types of loan. Of greater value for this writing will be the fundamental analytical principles that lie behind the assessment of conventional lending.

The quality of conventional loan portfolios

The quality of loans is necessarily of prime importance to the health and survival of banks. Low quality loan assets are more likely to lead to provisions for loan losses, reduced levels of liquidity, and the need for increased and often expensive capital. It is the job of credit analysis both to assess loan applications and to monitor the performance of loans. In these ways, credit analysis can be thought of as quality control functions in banking.

Banking sector analysts at Scrimgeour Vickers & Co, T. Clarke and W. Vincent, recently published a research report on the quality of the respective loan portfolios of the UK's four major clearing banks. This study concludes that rapid economic growth and the effects of inflation have tended to disguise much poor quality lending in the past. The economic environment has, however, changed sharply with specific reference to collapses in particular markets, e.g. tin, oil, and certain agricultural products; and also, debt crises in various developing countries. These, according to Clarke and Vincent, have 'already produced sharp dislocations in individual countries and in the banking industry'.

Clarke and Vincent's study is concerned with the four major clearers' control and lending procedures. The authors argue that whilst all of the 'big 4' have essentially competent lending controls and employ reasonably prudent loan granting criteria, only one of the banks examined has, in their opinion, a 'unique checking system to help ensure good quality lending'. This bank makes two independent assessments for all save the smallest loans. One assessment is made by the loan officer dealing direct with the customer. The loan officer assesses the going rate for the loan. The second assessment is made by a representative from the Advances Department. This department enjoys an independent status within the bank and has special responsibilities for risk assessment and loan monitoring.

The other three clearing banks, according to Clarke and Vincent, all provide guidance on risk assessment but 'allow the lending officers to make their own decisions as to whether the potential reward in a particular loan compensates for the risk which the bank takes'. The authors note that in cases of sizeable exposures, the lending decision is referred higher up in the banks' management structure.

Loan quality implies highest rates of return on capital at the lowest risks. According to Clarke and Vincent, loan quality is achieved and maintained in three ways:

1. General management controls imposed on aggregate lending growth.
2. Lending criteria.
3. The quality of bank staff training and management.

Of these, the first two will be of particular interest in this examination.

Lending controls

Currently, the Bank of England imposes only the most general controls on UK banks. However, following on from the collapse and rescue of Johnson Matthey Bankers Ltd, the Bank of England now requires banks to 'set out their policies, including exposure to individual customers, banks, countries and economic sectors in writing and that this statement should be formally adopted by the bank's board of directors. The necessary control system to give effect to those policies must also be clearly defined and put in place by the board.' There is, as yet, no obligation for the banks concerned to publish this information for public inspection.

Clarke and Vincent point out that these obligations refer only to the exposures of banks in particular areas and the control systems under which they fall rather than the credit policy judgements underpinning lending policies. These exposures are normally known as 'risk concentration' and as such, form only a portion of banks' overall loan quality. Briefly, lending policies should at best contain an overall outline of the scope and allocation of a bank's credit facilities, the manner in which loans are made, serviced, and collected. This synopsis presupposes organizational structures ensuring compliance with the lending guidelines and procedures determined by the board of directors. The US Comptroller's Handbook for National Bank Examiners advises that this can best be achieved by the establishment of an internal review and reporting system 'which adequately informs the directorate and senior management of how policies are being carried out and provides them with sufficient information to evaluate the performance of lower echelon officers and the condition of the loan portfolio'.

Clarke and Vincent point out that whilst the four major clearers' traditional banking business has been generally well controlled due to these banks' essentially prudent character, in some areas of new business as well as in lending areas where changes in attitude have taken place over the past years, some of the 'big four' appear to have failed to keep pace. Clarke and Vincent adduce three examples of the kind of lending controls which can assist in ensuring prudent banking:

1. The presence of finance directors.
2. The establishment of an internal audit committee.
3. Use of bad debts as a training technique.

A bank finance director

Whilst banks would, in the main, tend to view with suspicion corporate customers whose boards had no qualified director responsible for overall financial policy and decision, banks themselves have been slow to appoint finance directors. The chairman of TSB group, Sir John Read, was recently quoted as stating, 'Financial institutions are of course skilled in managing money and knowing how to look after other people's money. Often, however, the work of the finance director seems to be either carried out, piecemeal, by all the board members or not at all.' Despite the Bank of England's recommendation that banks should appoint a finance director, a number of clearing banks do not yet have one. Clarke and Vincent argue that: 'The prime reason for having a finance director is that it is his responsibility to control group finances and provide an independent view on them at board level.' They further argue that this responsibility includes the important area of management controls. They finally recommend that the finance director's work should be distinct from the normal commercial line responsibilities of senior bankers.

Internal audit committees

The latest Government White Paper on banking supervision strongly endorses 'the desirability of banks having audit committees'. Clarke and Vincent found that all the 'big four' have audit committees in operation with non-executive directors serving. Additionally, they saw that all the clearers placed great reliance on their own in-house bank inspectorates. Both help ensure the active function and revision of comprehensive control systems. The audit and inspection teams 'report problems up through their own structures as well as to the head of the relevant department to ensure that any necessary corrective measures are taken'.

Bad debts as a training technique

The adequacy of lending controls originates in the 'competence and attitudes of management'. Despite the systematic and detailed training of lending bankers, Clarke and Vincent conclude that in the UK clearers, 'debt work out' could usefully be added to their 'prudential armoury'. The authors found that in each of the four clearing banks, larger loans are 'worked out' on a centralized basis by a special department having particular expertise in this area. Managers, however, were not normally made to pursue any non-performing or poorly performing loans to a conclusion when they change branch. Clarke and Vincent argue that 'a banker learns more about lending cautiously from doing his own bad loan workouts than from any other experience'. The clearing banks in their study did, however, take managers' bad debt incidence into account in assessing their performance.

The general credit expansion has given rise to more aggressive lending. When banks lend aggressively (more widely and on generally finer margins), it follows that higher numbers of distressed loans will develop. Accordingly, in today's environment, the importance of learning from past mistakes is crucial. For bankers, the choice of remedies in distressed loans can be threefold:

1. Workout.
2. Liquidation.
3. Sell the loan.

Numbers 2 and 3 may often be unattractive or effectively impossible. In liquidation the bank is attempting to withdraw the funds it has committed to a company or as large a portion of those funds as it can extract. The general slowness, expense, and difficulties (financial and self-promotional) in liquidating a customer company should make this choice the least appetising in most circumstances.

Transferability or the sale of a loan to another bank depends upon the legal status and covenants governing individual loans. Thus, it may or may not be possible to sell off distressed loans to third parties. If the loan is structurally saleable, a buyer must still be found and terms negotiated.

Under a workout, the bank elects to continue with a customer. Workout implies extension of credit. Is a portion of the credit with the remainder to be repaid? Is there to be an extension of the full amount of the credit? Is there the possibility of having to supplement the credit with further funds?

If the borrower can repay a sizeable part but not the total of the loan, an extension of credit might be in order. But should this level of repayment involve draining off so much of the borrower's liquid capital as to impair his normal business operations and prevent necessary expansion, extending the credit will be a poor choice. In this type of case, outright liquidation might prevent loss for the lender. The basic principle here is that the longer liquidation is postponed, the less will be the amount that can be realized from it.

Particularly when banks are lending unsecured, they cannot afford to be generous if merely to keep other creditors paid, leaving themselves with 'the tag ends of the business'. On the other hand, overly harsh collection techniques on the part of the bank may precipitate a restriction of credit by the other creditors so that the debtor company is forced into liquidation.

Given that a bank can find a satisfactory argument for workout which includes other creditors, the workout will resemble the granting of a new credit. The bank will probably insist upon the budgeting of all further activities with an especial emphasis on cashflow budgeting. Additionally, the bank might insist that all capital outlay ceases. Establishment expenses may be sharply pruned whilst purchase budgets may be adjusted to only the most pessimistic estimates of future turnover.

Most workouts demand a high degree of supervision. For this reason, they tend to be expensive even when the amounts concerned are fully collected. An important consideration in workout decisions must always be that if a bank deals sympathetically with a competent borrower who is distressed as a result of temporary troubles or bad luck, a loyal customer of improved creditworthiness can result.

Depth of management controls

General management controls on lending will shape banks' credit policies at every level. Basically, banks are concerned with loan maturities, concentration of risk, country risk, and latterly, with off-balance-sheet risk.

Loan maturity, according to Clarke and Vincent, has become increasingly 'tightly controlled in recent years as the volatility of interest rate movements' has affected profitability. Clarke and Vincent find that 'Given the nature of clearing banks' operations and the demands of the customer base, it is unrealistic to expect any bank to run a totally matched book. In the circumstances, therefore, it seems that the clearers tackle this problem in a workmanlike way. Such differences as one can detect in their approach to the subject do not seem to be of fundamental importance.'

The recent increase in bank failures points out the importance of spreading risk and avoiding too great a concentration in the loan book. Clarke and Vincent describe risk concentration as lending to one individual or connected group as well as over-exposure to one commodity or industry. Better spreading of risk can be achieved through effective sectoral controls. The recent Banking Supervision White Paper requires that any individual exposure exceeding 10 per cent of a bank's capital base must be notified to the Bank of England. Exposures above 25 per cent of capital base are permissible only with the Bank's prior approval and would entail lenders maintaining 'significantly greater capital resources'. Clarke and Vincent find that 'These controls compare reasonably prudently with those in force in Europe (which has been relatively slow in introducing consolidated accounts, making it difficult to identify concentration within the groups). . . .' They point out furthermore that in the US, 'the Comptroller's Handbook for National Bank Examiners imposes a 10 per cent limit on connected lending and the limit for federally chartered banks is 15 per cent, both of which look more conservative than our own proposed regulations.'

Risk concentration within industries, Clarke and Vincent find subject to added considerations: external economic conditions as well as 'market acceptance which might equally affect all members of the group'. They cite the UK example of the collapse of property prices in the mid-seventies as an example. In the US, the incidence of distressed industry sectors appears higher. Clarke and Vincent mention railroads, electronic data processing, real estate investment trusts (REITS) and aerospace. Problems in industry sectors have tended to become global in recent years. Tin, agriculture, and energy (notably oil) serve as good examples.

The Bank of England sets the limit of a bank's industry concentration at 25 per cent of its capital base in all save the most exceptional cases. The US Comptroller's Handbook's limit is more conservative at 20 per cent.

Clarke and Vincent mention that therefore 'similar restrictions in the UK on lending more than 10 per cent of a bank's capital base to individual countries (except, in the Bank's words, to the most credit worthy, whatever that means). Only 5 years ago it would probably have included much of Latin America! It should, however, be noted that there are no prudential restrictions on the amount of personal lending the banks undertake either in the UK or the USA.' Possibly, the clearing banks comply more easily and more completely with the Bank of England's limits on risk concentration than the non-clearers and more specialized banks. Clarke and Vincent found that all the clearing banks in their study operated detailed monitoring systems to ensure that risk concentrations were identified and limited before they reached the Bank's set levels.

Lending criteria

Clarke and Vincent rightly maintain as the central thesis to their study that 'the control systems used to monitor lending, combined with the criteria on which loans are granted, determine the quality of bank lending'. The bulk of clearing banks' financial resources take the form of short-term deposits from private and corporate customers wishing to keep their funds safe. This type of depositor base works against and in most cases precludes long-term, equity lending. As they need to pay depositors interest rates in direct proportion to inherent degrees of risk, the UK clearing banks avoid providing venture capital funding as we have seen. Again, because of their overall depositor bases, the UK clearers must be especially careful in assessing loan applications. In general, lending officers and managers look at the following criteria:

1. Term of the loan.
2. Amount of the loan.
3. Purpose of the loan.
4. Customer's debt-service ability.
5. Course of repayment of principal and payment of interest.
6. Available security.
7. Central bank guidelines on industry sector lending.
8. National Interest government guidance.
9. Customer's own financial participation.
10. If an existing customer, conduct of the account/s.
11. Any third-party intelligence or assessment reports.
12. Internal risk, capital, and structural requirements.
13. Source of repayment.
14. Subjective assessment of management capability.
15. Instinctive assessment subject to documentation, formal interview, and prior knowledge.

At this stage, it is interesting to compare the overlap between the banker's lending criteria with the criteria of a commercial credit manager for the sanction of trade credit facilities:

Comparison of credit sanction criteria

1. Term of the credit: Banks and credit managers.
2. Amount of the credit: Banks and credit managers.
3. Purpose of the credit: Banks and credit managers.
4. Debt-service ability: Banks and credit managers.
5. Course of repayment: Mainly banks but also credit managers when arrears develop.
6. Security: Banks though not in all cases and credit managers (major suppliers) in some cases.
7. Central bank guidelines on sectoral lending: Banks.

8. National interest/government guidelines: Banks and credit managers only in the most exceptional cases, e.g. to primary industries in times of war or other national crises.
 9. Customer's own financial participation: Banks and credit managers—start-ups.
10. If an existing customer, conduct of account: Banks and credit managers.
11. Third-party intelligence/assessment reports: Banks and credit managers.
12. Internal risk, capital and structural requirements: Banks and credit managers.
13. Source of repayment: Banks and credit managers in cases of overall poor financial assessment/experience and/or small/new companies.
14. Subjective assessment of management capability: Banks and credit managers.
15. Instinctive assessment: Banks and credit managers.

Apart from item 7, there is a striking overlap of credit-granting criteria. It is this overlap and similarity which justifies treating bank and trade credit analysis as essentially the same discipline—particularly in the cases of medium to large exposures.

Banks' data collection

As discussed earlier, banks have the same sources of information as providers of trade credit with several important additions. These are:

1. Economic intelligence and forecasting units.
2. Inter-bank intelligence sources.
3. Access to full audited accounting statements direct from customers.
4. Access to financial updates including various budgets direct from customers/applicants and data from loan application forms.
5. Information from debenture and other charge forms.

Of these, we have already examined the first four. Item 5 bears closer study. Generally speaking, the taking of security implies compensation for a higher degree of risk than is the case in unsecured lending. In this way, all commercial lending can be secured if required, though as Clarke and Vincent point out in their recent study, all advances are by no means secured as many are made simply on the creditworthiness of borrowers. Obviously, the reason for security is to provide the bank with an asset which could be utilized or sold off to repay the credit should the customer fail to do so.

In taking security from a company, banks adopt the following procedure:

1. The company's borrowing and charging powers are verified.
2. The articles of association are studied to discover:
(a) whether any special authority is needed for the giving of security and, if not,
(b) what the directors' borrowing powers are.
(c) whether the charge need be executed under seal. If the charge requires execution under seal, as in the case of a legal mortgage of land, then the sealing must be witnessed by company officials.
3. Before security is accepted and the advance taken, a search is made on the company at the Registry of Companies to ensure that the property or assets are not charged elsewhere, e.g. under a floating charge.
4. The security, if registrable, is then registered at the Companies' Registry within 21 days of execution.

Debenture and other charge forms as data sources

Debentures are written acknowledgements of indebtedness by a company. These are generally given under seal. The debenture deed sets out the terms for interest and repayment. Debentures are normally long-term debt instruments. Companies may issue a single debenture to a bank or a series of debentures to groups of debenture holders. Debentures may be redeemable at a fixed date or on demand. They can also be irredeemable. When a business is wound up, debenture-holders have a first claim on assets charged. Thus, generally, but not in all cases, debenture-holders in law rank as preferred creditors.

In the case of a bank debenture, a single debenture is issued by the company in favour of the bank. The instrument normally incorporates a fixed charge over the company's existing permanent property as specified, e.g. land and buildings, and/or a floating charge over the company's other assets and the general undertaking both present and future, e.g. stock and work-in-progress. Debtors are covered under the fixed charge and not under floating charges.

As the debenture is given to secure all moneys owing at any time by a company, it is important for the bank holding a debenture to monitor the company's assets and liabilities carefully as well as attempting to maintain an accurate picture of the borrower's overall financial condition. Such information can be gained from the bank's usual range of information sources, but a particularly fertile source of numerical data will be the debenture forms or cards. Their formats will vary from bank to bank; so will the required frequency of reporting. In most cases, debenture statistics can be obtained on a monthly basis. Notwithstanding, the taking of a debenture coupled with monthly statistics cannot eliminate risk.

Debenture formulas

In his study, 'The Interpretation of Debenture Statistics', F. R. P. Curzon states: 'There are no rules governing what a formula should be in any individual case or for any particular type of industry.' He adds that optimal formulas should be related as much to a bank's perception of risk in a specific case as to the interpretation of its historic balance sheets.

The bank's scope in laying down the ideal terms or debenture formulas are theoretically unlimited. In practice, however, they must be limited to the practical and attainable. Also, some thought must be given to what stringencies customers will bear. Curzon perceives the risk to be considered in debenture formulas as:

1. The ability of the company to report figures accurately and reliably.
2. The potential realizability of security at reported levels.
3. The possible extent of prior claims, e.g. preferential creditors.
4. Trading risk.

Concerning trading risk, Curzon suggests that the formula for a well-established, highly profitable company might reasonably be less stringent than that laid down for a struggling, loss-making operation. For an average company between these extremes, he proposes the following formulas for consideration:

1. Three times cover by current assets, including twice cover by debtors. He sees this as appropriate to a profitable manufacturing entity with a good spread of trade debtors.

2. Three times cover by debtors. This is viewed as appropriate to a less successful service company; a firm not dealing with first-class names; or a company whose debtors are few in number.
3. Three times cover by stock. This cover is seen as suitable to successful retailers where inventories are quickly turned over for cash. Curzon specifies that this type of formula should not be laid down unless the bank is satisfied that adequate stock insurance cover is in place and the premiums paid up to date.

As a minimum, Curzon advises $1\frac{1}{2}$ times good trade debtor cover for bank advances. In the absence of adequate debtor cover, twice cover by stock/work-in-progress. Formulas can be made more stringent by relating terms to the company's book balance or even borrowing limit in lieu of specifying cover related to the bank's ledger balance. Also, there may be cases in which cover is stipulated against the total of ledger balance and preferential creditors. In the laying down of terms, Curzon stresses, 'It cannot be over emphasised, however, that there are no standard formulae which can be applied to our customers regardless of circumstances. Considerable managerial judgement is needed to analyse each proposition on its merits and to tailor the formula appropriately.'

The treatment of debenture and other charge statistics

Figure 12.1 (a) and (b) illustrate typical bank monitoring spreadsheets for debenture statistics. Curzon gives the following guidelines for the notation of assets and liabilities on debenture reporting forms:

Assets

Debtors (trade debtors) are taken to include all invoiced amounts owing to the company inclusive of VAT, but exclusive of any amounts regarded as bad debts. He advises the omission of intergroup debts from this total and suggests separate notation. This follows the normalizing principle of credit analysis in which any items likely to cause distortion to a precise quantity being measured are netted-out and noted. An example is normalized profit.

Care is recommended in the treatment of debts against which payments may have been advanced under a factoring or invoice discount contract or ECGD facility. Curzon advises

Debenture formula agreed (state which facility(ies) the formula covers)		Credit given			
		Credit taken			
Date formula agreed	Regularity of figures	Company's year end			
Date of figures					
Date received					
Tick box (✓) if formula is met					
State whether figures are audited, customer's or estimated					
Sales less returns (indicate period)					

Figure 12.1(a) Specimen bank monitoring form

302 TOWARDS THE PERFECT CREDIT ANALYSIS

Debtors (excluding prepayments)	— Normal trade						
	— Overseas						
	— Inter-company						
STOCK (unencumbered)	— Raw materials						
	— Finished goods						
Stock, which may be encumbered							
Work in progress							
Bank in company's books (CR)							
Short term deposits/quoted investments							
Due from group companies							
TOTAL 1							
BANK IN COMPANY'S BOOKS (DR)							
Preferential creditors							
Trade creditors							
Other creditors							
H.P. debts							
Due to group companies/ directors loans							
TOTAL 2							
Liquid surplus (deficit) 1–2							
Variation in liquid surplus (deficit)							
Capital expenditure since last report							
BALANCE IN OUR BOOKS							
DEBTOR ANALYSIS (excluding covered by E.C.G.D. prepayments and inter-company)	Up to 1 month						
	1+ to 3 months						
	Over 3 months						
	TOTAL						
CREDITOR ANALYSIS (ecluding inter-company)	Up to 1 month						
	1+ to 3 months						
	Over 3 months						
	TOTAL						
PREFERENTIAL CREDITOR ANALYSIS*	Corporation tax						
	V.A.T.						
	P.A.Y.E.						
	Rates						
	Other preferential creditors						
	TOTAL						

*Analysis format will necessarily be changed in respect of preferential claims when the Insolvency Act, 1985 provisions come into force (December, 1986) Preferential debts will be limited to employees' wages, "holiday pay", and collector taxes (qv).

Figure 12.1(b) Specimen bank monitoring form

that only the portion of the debt which has *not* been advanced should be included. As in the earlier example of factoring companies' concern with the spread of debts rather than simply the total, Curzon recommends awareness of the 'spread of debtors, not simply the amount, if we are to assess our debenture cover properly'. Again, the need for separate specification may arise when risk is perceived of a Crown set-off, e.g. VAT refunds.

For stock data, the accounting principle of stock valuation is applied: the lower of cost or net realizable value. Stock should not be included at invoice value, and obsolete stock items should be excluded along with VAT. Care must be taken to see that no stock items that have been invoiced and are simply waiting to be despatched are included. Again, good general analytical practices are called for by requests for stock breakdowns on occasion. These would show stock divided into raw materials and finished goods.

Stock information for such forms may be taken from cards, physical stock counts, or estimations. The exclusion of obsolete items in particular may be something of a pious hope. In calling for data on inventories, banks may also require to know approximately how many lines of stock are carried and whether the valuation includes several high-cost items.

The gathering of work-in-progress data must normally be done on a best estimate basis when job cards are not maintained. Curzon suggests that where accurate figures are not available, WIP can be estimated by companies assessing a job according to the number of days needed to complete the work from start to finish; computing the number of days already spent; and multiplying the resulting fraction by the estimated total cost of the job or the net realizable value, which ever is lower. Clearly, this calculation applies to sizeable pieces of work. When many small jobs exist, this type of computation is made harder. He points out that in these cases, the best the bank can reasonably hope to receive is a conservative 'stab' at a valuation. As with stock, VAT should not be included in the WIP computation. Neither should 'any element of profit, except in cases of very long term contracts, e.g. boat building, in which case this should be made clear.' In deduction of costs from WIP to give the required net figure, only materials and production overheads (which include direct labour) should be included.

Stock on which there is reservation of title should be the subject of a separate note. As mentioned before, legal precedent for a definitive ruling on this subject is still unclear. Curzon suggests that for bank purposes, reservation of title occurs either 'when it is specifically allowed for on an invoice or contract, or when the underlying nature of the stockholding presupposes it', and he cites an example of a motor dealer whose stock of new vehicles often remains the property of the supplier until such time as the stock is actually sold.

Hire purchase debt is often mistaken by analysts for hire purchase agreements in which case HP debt will appear inflated. Curzon suggests that where HP agreements exist in favour of the company,

1. Proper systems should exist to record and update HP balances on a monthly basis, and,
2. The amount of interest incorporated in the outstanding balance is clearly understood or specified. The amount of interest here is taken to mean interest calculated retrospectively or in advance over the entire term of the contract.

Liabilities

The monitoring form calls for a balance termed 'Bank in Company's Books'. This is computed by deducting the month's receipts from the month's payments in the cash books and adding the result to the total brought forward from the previous month. Bank-generated debits such as interest and standing orders should be included before the balance is struck.

In cases where other security such as charged property is relied on, loan balances are generally excluded. Where loans exist, Curzon recommends that the debenture formula indicate whether or not the balance is relevant to the debenture assessment of cover.

Concerning preferential creditors, the Insolvency Act, 1985, abolishes the right of preferential payment for rates and assessed taxes, and when these changes came into force in December 1986, preferential debts were limited to employees' wages, holiday pay, and 'collector taxes'. These last are comprised of VAT for the six months prior to insolvency, PAYE deductions for the twelve months before insolvency, National Insurance Contributions (also called Social Security Contributions), sums owing to occupational pension schemes and state pension schemes, as well as certain duties in relation to gaming and betting. Value Added Tax bad debt relief has been available in receiverships from 1 April 1986. Accordingly, the debenture forms would require statement of any corporation tax arrears as opposed to assessments; and where any refunds of tax were due, those amounts would be included under current assets.

Value added tax liabilities, arising from monthly or quarterly returns, which have not been paid together with any VAT liabilities arising since the date of the last return should be included. It is important that these liabilities not be ignored as failure of inclusion will distort the eventual surplus or deficit, 'bearing in mind that debtors and creditors will include VAT which has been incurred since the last return'. When the VAT balance is in the company's favour, it should be added to current assets.

Other creditors should include all invoiced day-to-day purchases and expenses as yet unpaid including VAT. Care should be taken as companies may incur a trade debt for which they have not yet been invoiced, that is, an accrual. A significant distortion can result from the omission of such a liability, especially where it applies to stock purchases when the stock has been included under current assets. All significant accruals must therefore be added to the total of creditors. Curzon suggests that accrued telephone, electricity and gas charges can normally be disregarded, though that must depend upon the nature of a business. For example, a telephone marketing company would need to add back substantial telephone accrual charges to avoid distortion; likewise, an operation dependent on gas turbines would have to account for gas accrual expenses.

Contrasted with HP agreements, HP debt required by the debenture forms will consist of all outstanding payments on current hire purchase contracts over the balance of their term.

'Balance in our books' can be completed either by the bank or by the borrower. Curzon states that 'the figure has absolutely no importance, other than in the context of a debenture formula'.

The ageing of debtors and creditors should best be done in a manner causing the least time and bother. Curzon suggests taking 'over three months' as meaning debts dating back to the month before last or before. Accordingly, this entails that 'one month' signifies debts invoiced during the last month. In this way, were figures submitted as per 31 December, 'one month' would apply to invoices issued between 1 and 31 December and not yet settled, whilst 'two months' would apply to November invoices, and 'over three months' to invoices for October and previous months.

The alternative, possibly favoured by credit managers more than bankers, would be to use the blank line for invoices reckoned to be 'current', that is issued within the last 30 days, and let 'one month' refer to debts between 30 and 60 days old.

The form shown in Figure 11.2 calls for an analysis of preferential creditors. As noted earlier, the Insolvency Act, 1985, has altered preferential claims. Concerning accrued salaries and wages, assuming that wages are paid weekly and that salaries are paid toward the end of each month (i.e. the reporting date for this form), the amounts should not be very significant. Holiday pay entitlements, on the other hand, could be sizeable at certain times when they remain 'substantially unutilized, e.g. May/June'.) Curzon points out that calculation of this liability need not normally be required of the borrower unless there is thought to be a distinct risk of a receiving order.

Capital Gains Tax (CGT) arrears (not assessments, as previously) will be included under corporation tax arrears (not assessments, as previously). Although CGT assessments will not now enjoy preferential status, banks will still wish to be informed of the possibility of future liabilities of this type arising from the disposal of fixed assets. In general, the main rate of corporation tax from 1 April 1986 is 35 per cent. The small companies' rate of corporation tax, applying to profits up to £100,000, is reduced to 29 per cent. The lower and upper limits for marginal relief, currently £100,000 and £500,000 respectively, have not changed, and the marginal relief has now become 3/200ths. The rate of advance corporation tax (ACT) is currently 29/71sts (since 6 April 1986). The rate of ACT will, in future, be automatically linked to the basic rate of income tax. CGT relief for small disposals of land now applies to disposals of up to 20 per cent of a holding. The relief remains subject to the upper limit of £20,000 proceeds.

Hidden preferential claims may arise when companies are in financial distress. Banks should be alive to such possibilities. Curzon points out that such claims may stem from rights of subrogation, for example, loans made by a director or facilities extended by other banks for the purpose of paying salaries and wages. For the fullest analysis of debenture statistics, Curzon proposes computations of capital outflows and inflows. The data contributing to these calculations would need to be provided to banks as supplementary figures to the debenture statistics already required on most forms. As with the other statistics on the debenture cards, capital outflow and inflow can be computed monthly.

Curzon suggests a typical capital outflow as comprising:

Loan repayments
Withdrawal of director's loan
Purchase of fixed assets (net of VAT for items other than motor cars)
Deposits (part-purchases of fixed assets)
Purchase of investments (placing of deposits)
Dividend payments

A typical capital inflow might be:

Sale proceeds of fixed assets (net of VAT)
Draw-down of loans

Additional loans from directors
New share capital
Sales of investments/withdrawal of deposits

Any new HP commitments contracted since the last reporting month should also be noted.

Curzon admits that the completion of a typical debenture card form by customers can sometimes be fraught with difficulties. Obviously, customers' numeracy and accounting skills will vary widely. Also, when the bank completes the cards from handwritten draft accounts, cashflows, and budgets, as opposed to computer print-outs, the possibilities for error, over-optimism, or false accounting multiply. Banks will, therefore, depend on advice from branch managers as to the accuracy and reliability of customers' statistics. Further checks can be done by comparing audited figures with twelve months' debenture statistics. Any major discrepancies between them should be explained. This, Curzon argues, 'can often throw a useful light on the customer's ability to report figures accurately'.

In the collection of debenture and other charge instrument statistics, banks are in a highly privileged position by virtue of their integral and 'permanent' relationships with customers. Reporting in such a detailed and frequent manner to trade creditors, apart from major suppliers holding charges, is neither possible nor desirable for commercial credit applications. Reporting of this kind requires efficient and accurate accounting systems on the part of the customer. These systems, Curzon states, should at the very least include:

1. Cash receipts book
2. Cash payments book
3. Comprehensive pay-roll records

Ideally, the system should also include:

4. Sales day book
5. Purchases day book
6. Sales ledger
7. Purchases ledger
8. Stock records
9. Job cards (for calculation of WIP)

According to Curzon, most companies keep day books and cash books, but the absence of sales and purchase ledgers is commonplace, whereas stock cards are even rarer. Concerning the provision of monthly statistics, Curzon feels, 'Whatever the sophistication of a company's bookkeeping system, there ought to be no reason why debenture statistics should not be produced promptly, within two to three weeks of the month-end'.

Interpreting the debenture statistics

Having amassed monthly or periodic statistics of this kind, what will bankers do with them? How are they interpreted? Curzon lists:

(a) Debenture cover
(b) Trends
(c) Profits

Firstly, as debenture cover is laid down in whatever formula is used, cover is the most readily calculated. 'We have a formula laying down a pre-determined margin of cover—over ledger balance, company book balance or borrowing limit—and it is a simple matter to see whether or not it is met.'

Trends and profits can be more open to interpretation according to Curzon. He advises checking the reported figures against what the bank expects the reported figures to be. As in the reading of all management figures, analysts will expect the most optimistic picture to be presented. Sales, stock, and WIP are all areas of particular cosmetology. Provision for bad debts forms another possible distorting element. Given what a bank may know of a customer's previous experience of bad debtors, the analyst of debenture statistics will want to be satisfied that the customer's potential bad debts have been deducted from trade debtor balances. In general, the worse the bank considers the customer's position to be, the less credence it should place on the unaudited reported figures.

Curzon provides a good example: 'As cash becomes tighter and debtors are more and more vigorously collected, those debtors which remain uncollected will tend to be "low quality". (As a rule of thumb, divide the reported figures by 2).' He also instances stocks of finished goods which will tend to be sold off in troubled times at only a fraction of their inventory value. Unless stock is composed of non-perishable, raw materials, it is not normally saleable even at cost price. As for WIP, it is of little or no value if an operation ceases trading.

Curzon holds that these considerations underpin the whole notion of margin of cover. 'The extent of this margin as embodied in the formula should reflect, in part, the risk we attach to accepting debenture figures at face value.'

The matching of figures with formulas is thus seen as almost purely mechanistic. The interpretation given to the figures, on the other hand, is viewed as highly subjective with the subjective criteria being:

1. Reading of the customer's past financial history.
2. Opinions arising from the comparison of the reported figures with informed expectations concerning financial performance.
3. Subjective resolution of any discrepancies between audited year-end figures and twelve months' reported, unaudited figures.
4. Discounts applied to reported figures, e.g. trade debtor balances divided by two to account for the presence of irrecoverable debts.

In our view, the presence of subjective as well as objective criteria enhances general analysis—provided that subjectivity is informed and experienced. Such subjectivity, of course, depends largely upon up to date supplementary data apart from the customer's monthly reports, e.g. economic background information on the customer's industry, and line knowledge of, in this case, commercial lending. Again, banks are in a favoured position in respect of the most effective mix of objective and subjective-based analysis simply from the point of view of data collection and bespoke interpretative formats, e.g. their range of specialized spreadsheets and reporting forms. Interestingly, the division usually made in banks between lending officers and credit analysts possibly reduces the scope for the effective mixing of subjective and objective analyses. With commercial credit managers becoming more interested in risk assessment and taking a more active role in customer accounts' management, the necessary mix of objective and subjective analysis appears to be developing quickly. A good case in point examined earlier were the guidelines laid down for analysts at the oil company.

Without experience and knowledge of the sort hinted at above, bankers cannot judge whether reported figures look right or not. Let us consider the typical banker's interpretations of the key quantities reported on charge forms.

Debtors

Curzon asks, 'Is the company's turnover seasonal?' When it is, the bank may be able to compare the reported figure with the same month's total in the prior year. Do any patterns of peaks and troughs emerge? In the case of a young company, both turnover and trade debtors' levels may have increased dramatically over those of the previous year either on a strict monthly or aggregate basis (where the build-up is not evenly spread monthly). Will the bank look askance at greatly increased sales and debtor levels in these cases? Also, when wise managements become aware of trading peaks and troughs, they generally attempt in some manner to 'smooth them out'. This could mean diversifying into complementary product lines or services by way of compensating for downturns in other products or services. How will the bank cope with a trading trough in one year followed by no trough, a pro rata increase, or peak in the next year? Such problems can only be got over by reliable information as to what the company is doing apart from what its figures may be.

What portion of the customer's sales is invoiced on credit terms? When there are no cash sales or few of them, will the bank expect fewer sharp fluctuations in debtors on a monthly basis than if there were a more even mix of cash and credit sales? Credit given and credit taken figures (see Figure 11.2) will help to clarify this, but again, information direct from the company as to its credit and credit management policies will be useful. Presumably, when the bank perceives its customer's credit management abilities as poor, it may welcome the presence of fewer credit sales in reported turnover and debtors.

If a sudden drop in debtors is observed, the bank may interpret this to a tightening of credit. It will accordingly ask why credit terms have been altered in this way. It will also want to see how the cash released by the tightening of credit has been used. What, in other words, has it been used to finance? Again, it is possible that the reduction in debtors has been caused by the writing-off of a sizeable debt. Curzon remarks that this is infrequent, and that normally, a drop in debtors is due to a fall in turnover and/or a reduction in credit terms. He adds, 'From background information, we ought to be able to tell which of these applies.'

Stock and work-in-progress

With stock totals, seasonality and manufacturing cycles are important in the interpretation of reported figures. In this way, a bank might look very suspiciously at a toy manufacturer with high reported stock levels for December. Also, stock turnover chronically longer than known manufacturing cycles would look unhealthy as the implication is that the goods are not being sold quickly enough.

In that event, the bank may see static or reduced debtor totals and increased stock levels.

Sudden, upward movements in stock and WIP can suggest, however, that the customer is taking advantage of liquidity to buy in stocks at bulk discounts.

In all these comparisons and readings, trend is important. Does stock turnover in December of this year compare favourably (i.e. is it quicker?) than December last year? Are monthly sales rising and stock-turns quickening? If so, the movements looks favourable. If sales are rising but stock-turn is lengthening, how will this affect liquidity? Debtors may not show *pari passu* increases as manufacturing cycles become longer. Possibly, the company needs help in reducing manufacturing times. Will this require further bank assistance?

If we see a drop in stock levels, accompanied by a reduction in overdraft or in creditors, is the company running-down inventories to 'finance payment of pressing debts'? If so, how will the resulting depletions in stock affect future production and how, in turn, will cashflow suffer significant reductions?

Stock and WIP levels remaining fairly static can suggest two things: production inefficiency particularly when turnover remains largely unchanged; and what Curzon terms 'an inadequacy in the company's stock recording system'. Static stock levels in notably seasonal businesses should also be looked at carefully.

A drop in stock levels can, when accompanied by higher debtor totals, indicate tighter stock control. Even if debtors show a reduction, liquidity may be high depending upon what the company has been purchasing with cash released from the paid invoices. All this can be the result of better management rather than mere *laissez-faire*.

Hire purchase agreements

Hire purchase and leasing agreements can be treated together for these purposes. Curzon argues that these should be treated as assets in the balance sheet. Accordingly, when an operation is heavily dependent upon HP or leasing, the bank will obviously expect reported balances to fluctuate monthly as new agreements are entered into whilst others are gradually discharged. When monthly sales figures are not included in the charge statistics, a steady decrease in HP and leasing balances could serve as an early warning sign that sales volume is decreasing.

Bank in the company's books

The probability that all cheques and credits posted in the company's cash books during the month will also have been registered in the bank account by the end of the month is remote. Normally, only a cessation of trading midway during the month could account for an identity between the company's ledger balance and the bank's. When the reported balances are identical, doubt must be cast on the efficiency of the company's bookkeeping. When the bank account has deteriorated sharply, the following questions should be asked:

1. Is there a corresponding reduction in creditors? If so, part of the fall in bank balance is accounted for by the company settling with trade and other creditors. What is the normal monthly conduct of the account? Are credit periods taken by the customer long? Why have creditors been paid off in such a sizeable lump at this time?
2. Is the company giving longer credit? Is this a conscious policy decision of the company or does it appear to be due to feeble credit management? If the latter, why are debts

proving difficult to collect? Is the company merely not doing anything about collection or is the quality of the debtors poor? If it is poor, is the longer debt-turn due to an outsized, uncollected or uncollectable debt?
3. Are stock levels excessive? If too much cash is tied up in stocks, have we seen any evidence to date of illiquidity? Is the stock level moving upwards with stock turnover? If not, production efficiency may be deteriorating.
4. Do we notice any capital expenditures? Have any of these had an immediate impact on turnover and debtors? For example, a new printing press might enable a printing company to lift sales and debtors significantly and quickly, but the purchase of the new equipment could easily dent the bank account. Does the capital outlay follow the pattern of previous capital purchases? For instance, did the company buy a new piece of equipment outright instead of leasing it as it has done with most of its other equipment purchases? If so, why?
5. Less commonly, what portion of the deterioration in bank balance is due to redundancy payments and related costs? Is this level of staff turnover unusual? Were key managers or directors included? How is this expected to affect the company's future productivity?

Because of the lag to be expected in figures applied to the bank's balance for the company at the end of each month, the ledger balance at the bank is not of prime importance. Rather, the bank balance in the company's books provides the significant figure in the context of all the other reported statistics.

Value added tax

Curzon adduces the case of a firm buying and selling zero-rated goods. There will still be VAT recoverable by the company on some purchases. Because of the timing of VAT returns and payments, running balances will never be zero. Also, VAT account balances necessarily change from month to month. When the bank sees abnormally low VAT liabilities, it may ask whether the liability has been distorted by:

1. Bulk purchases of stock.
2. Capital expenditure.
3. Sudden drop in turnover not accompanied by a proportionate fall in purchases.

For companies completing quarterly VAT returns, the bank would not expect to see less than two months' worth of VAT liabilities and conversely, never more than four, assuming that settlement is made from one month to six weeks after the end of the quarter.

For companies completing monthly VAT returns, the bank would expect reported balances to be positive, 'with seldom more than two months' worth of VAT outstanding at any one time'. Curzon adds that monthly returns are beneficial for companies with zero-rated sales as VAT on purchases (creating a positive balance) can be reclaimed more speedily.

PAYE

PAYE liabilities should be settled around the 19th of the month. Accordingly, the bank will worry if more than three to four weeks' PAYE should ever be reported as outstanding. PAYE includes, for these purposes, income tax as well as employers' and employees' National Insurance (Social Security) Contributions. These liabilities average around 40 to 45 per cent of most companies' total payroll costs.

Curzon suggests that a rough idea of the accuracy of the reported total can be obtained by:

1. Adding up salaries, wages and directors' remuneration from the last audited accounts,
2. Adjusting this total for any known or expected increases/decreases in staff or rates of pay, and,
3. Dividing the total by 12, then,
4. Dividing this total by $2\frac{1}{2}$.

If the reported PAYE figure is substantially higher than the above figure, enquiries should be set afoot.

Rates

The bank will expect to see a nil or positive figure as this is very often a prepayment. If the rates figure is negative, questions should be asked. Curzon suggests relating the size of the reported balance outstanding to the total rates expenditure taken from the last profit and loss account.

Trade and other creditors

For analytical purposes, the breakdown of creditors into trade and other, or 'expense' creditors is obviously useful. Expense creditors here are taken to mean unpaid overheads.

When the bank sees an increase in trade creditors, it will naturally look for a corresponding increase in reported stock levels or one-month aged debtors. This follows the accounting principle of a corresponding credit to every debit. When neither stock nor debtors have increased in this way, has the bank credit balance risen proportionally? Whilst this may be favourable in itself, Curzon points out that the build-up in creditors may only herald future pressure on the bank account.

How does the increase in creditors compare with the reported level of turnover? From what the bank knows of the customer's seasonal trading pattern, is the movement of creditors' total more or less predictable?

The breakdown of trade and expense creditors enables the bank to relate the movements of trade creditors more accurately to the movements in stock and sales. Also, when there is a trend either up or down for expense creditors, the reported figure can be viewed against the total of overheads taken from the last audited profit and loss account. Curzon suggests taking this total, excluding depreciation, all expense items on which credit is never taken (e.g. salaries and wages), all items recorded elsewhere on the debenture card (rates, HP interest), and all bank charges (unless an interest accrual has been allowed for); and adding VAT where appropriate to the resulting figure; and finally, dividing this into the total of outstanding expense creditors. By multiplying this fraction by 365, the approximate number of days' credit taken on overheads can be computed.

Hire purchase debt

Curzon's view here is that the HP debt figure should normally be a steadily declining one over most months unless there are continual changes in vehicle fleets or similar disruptions. He advises that when a marked increase in HP debt is seen, enquiries should be made at branch level to discover what purchases the new debt financed. The new debt may also materially affect cashflow. He finally recommends ascertaining how the amount of the new debt has been calculated as this may affect reported profits. On the other hand, static HP debt figures appearing month after month indicate that the company is not addressing itself to careful reporting procedures. If this is the case, then other debenture statistics may become suspect.

Ageing of debtors

The terms of trade should be obtainable direct from customers. Curzon writes, 'If prompt payment discounts are the norm, this will obviously colour our assessment of the ageing split and should be noted.' In interpreting the aged debtor analysis, seasonality should be borne in mind. If, for instance, a balance sheet were struck immediately following a firm's peak trading season (as in many companies is the practice), credit periods both given and taken will appear longer than is actually the case. Accordingly, debt-turn, trade creditors' turnover, and monetary lag will be distorted.

A preliminary cross-check is advised at this stage. A reporting error will have been made if the figure for two month debtors in the current period is greater than the one month total reported for the last period. Thirty-day debtors could only have been reduced as accounts were settled. Even were no accounts settled, the figure would have remained unchanged.

Curzon now advises converting the split of debtors into an average of days credit given. This can be done only when sales have been reported on a monthly basis. His computation is as follows:

$$\frac{\text{Debtors ex-VAT}}{\text{Total sales for last 3 months}} \times 90 = \text{Number of average days}$$

When only one or two months' sales figures are given, the computation can be performed using 30 or 60 as the multiplier.

It is pointed out that such calculations can be deceptive, and the following illustration is given:

	Company A		Company B	
Ageing	Debtors	Sales	Debtors	Sales
Over 3 months:	5,000	5,000	2,500	5,000
2 months:	2,500	5,000	2,500	5,000
1 month:	2,500	5,000	5,000	5,000
	10,000	15,000	10,000	15,000

Accordingly, Curzon advises relating each of the debtor sub-totals to the sales for the appropriate months to see how much of each month's sales totals are still awaiting collection. Generally, he holds that 90 to 100 per cent of the last month's sales might be expected to be outstanding; possibly 40 to 50 per cent of the previous month's; and 10 to 15 per cent of the month prior to that. He stresses that these percentages are rules of thumb only and cites the example of a company where turnover is predominantly in cash (a petrol station), where obviously, the percentage proportions will be far sharper across the board. Likewise, where companies' sales are mainly export on, say, 90-day bills of exchange, the percentages could be 100 per cent over the whole analysis.

Apart from the type of companies described above, Curzon suggests 'it is reasonable to take the following percentages as being healthy for the average company giving 30–60 day credit to its customers':

> Over 3 months: 10–15% of total debtors figure
> Over 2 months: 25–30% of total debtors figure
> Over 1 month: 50–60% of total debtors figure

It is felt that these percentages calculated monthly and noted on the debenture forms can often serve as better indicators of trend than the debtors' sub-totals.

According to Curzon, two-month debtors comprising 40 per cent to 45 per cent of the total from time to time should not necessarily cause worry. He suggests, however, that warnings signals might arise if:

(a) Three-month and over debtors steadily increase to over 30 per cent of the total. This could indicate an incipient bad debt or, at the least, feeble credit control. It does not matter greatly to the bank to know whether a debt has been outstanding for 90 or for 120 days. Both are equally undesirable as very few companies should have sizeable debts outstanding for more than 60 days according to Curzon. This, of course, entirely depends upon individual industries and the nature of specific contracts, e.g. agreements involving stage payments.

(b) One-month debtors falling below 30 per cent of the total might indicate a sharply reduced turnover for the month. Curzon suggests examining WIP to check on partly-finished jobs and keep a watching brief on subsequent months to see whether or not there is an upturn in debtors.

Banks are, of course, alive to the dangers of outsized projects to liquidity and solvency. Curzon observes, 'what is important is that we are advised by the company of any individual debtor where the amount exceeds 20 per cent of the total (aged debtor balance), and *how long this has been outstanding*. There is no need to highlight the dangers inherent in a single large debt which remains unpaid beyond 60 days.'

Ageing of creditors

The ageing of creditors is carried out on essentially the same principles as those outlined above for debtor ageing. As in commercial credit analysis, where debt-turn is taken to refer to trade debtors and not sundry debtors, here, creditors' turnover and aged creditor analysis refers to trade creditors.

Commercial analysts working mainly from audited accounts will experience difficulty in isolating trade from sundry and expense creditors when breakdowns are not given—as is often the case in modified statements. When reporting periods are monthly, the breakdown of different classes of creditor should be simple, though Curzon mentions that 'all too often ... expense creditors creep in to distort the picture'.

If we take the percentages suggested for ageing in the previous section on debtors, Curzon reckons that the same type of distribution will apply for the analysis of creditors—with the difference that here, the bank will not usually be informed of the total purchases for the months in question, where sales were given monthly for the debtors' computations. In the absense of total purchases figures, there is nothing against which the creditors' totals can be compared. Accordingly, he suggests the following computation:

1. When known, use the latest quarter's sales figure.
2. Multiply 1 by the average cost of sales percentage on the last profit and loss account taking care to include material purchases only and excluding wages and other direct costs.
3. Add any increase (deduct any decrease) in stock reported from the previous quarter.
4. The resultant figure should approximate the quarter's purchases. Calculate the average period of credit taken (creditors' turnover) in the way prescribed for debtors. When this varies significantly from previously noted ratios, enquiries should be made.

Curzon's computation differs from the more familiar calculation of creditors' turnover in that he is isolating purchases whereas in calculating creditors' turnover, all direct costs and sales are used including portions of salaries and wages when relevant in order to arrive at an approximate figure for days credit given.

He advises noting the distribution of debt and the comparison of monthly trends. Accordingly, the following questions can be asked:

Are monthly creditors abnormally high?
Is there an increasing trend in creditors' levels?
Can we note a build-up in three month creditors? If so,
Has it already resulted in a deterioration of overdraft?
Is there a corresponding increase in preferential creditors?
Can we see an increase in creditors accompanied by a build-up in stock *and* a drop in sales/one month debtors?

Each, Curzon states, is a warning sign in its own right. When observed severally or all together, they will almost certainly signal serious distress.

Liquidity surplus/deficit

Indications of liquidity can be distorted by HP debt some of which may be medium to long-term and HP agreements some of which are capitalized long-term. Also, stock valuation can easily be carried out inaccurately. Distortions can occur with other creditors which, 'in a particular month, happen to include a substantial debt in respect of a capital item to be funded eventually by long-term means'. When the resulting figures do look abnormal, the bank can simply ask its customer the right questions. Curzon adds that HP commitments can be assessed more realistically if the bank asks itself how much of it should be considered short-term. He suggests that for practical purposes, the view can be taken that three months' worth of HP contributions can be regarded as short-term and that the balance should not be permitted to distort the liquidity figure. When reporting terms are monthly, we see this suggestion as possibly overly stringent and would, in the absence of accurate data, divide quarterly HP debt by three to arrive at the monthly total. Curzon holds that there is a good case for disregarding such commitments entirely from liquidity computations as they relate normally to the financing of a fixed asset. Again, we would take an all-inclusive view of liquidity and make little or no distinction between the purposes of financial outflows.

Curzon advises that monthly surplus or deficit should be regarded as part of a trend and that the customer's liquidity norm taken from the last balance sheets should be contrasted with the monthly figures. He is rightly concerned with the quality of liquidity and asks, 'How readily realizable are the assets?' citing as an example WIP being less readily realizable than debtors. Also, many debtors are a healthier proposition for these purposes than few. He advises looking at stock. Does it contain many fast or slow-moving items? What it the character of liabilities? How pressing are they? Is there a creditors' build-up of three-months or more? How many of these are preferential? Does an apparently healthy acid-test ratio mask a possible cashflow problem which could lower the bank account to unacceptable levels?

Assessment of profitability from debenture statistics

The extraction of monthly profit approximations from debenture statistics is possible. In broad terms. Figure 12.1 provides the lineaments of a balance sheet less fixed assets and long-term liabilities. From a balance sheet as we have seen in previous chapters, surplus (profit) can be calculated by summing fixed and current assets and deducting the total of long and short-term liabilities. When this is done for two consecutive periods, the difference between the surpluses for the two periods equals profit after taxation for the second period. On the debenture forms, it follows that the variation in liquid surplus from one period to the next precisely reflects the profit or loss for the second period, except as Curzon points out, to the extent that current assets and liabilities have been distorted by capital movements.

The entry for variation in surplus/deficit is accordingly adjusted to allow for the inclusion of any receipts or payments *not* related to trading. Once depreciation is allowed for, the result is an approximation of pre-tax profit for the reporting period in question. Curzon offers the following computation:

> Favourable/(adverse) variation in surplus/deficit:
> *Less*
> Capital inflows during the period
>   Sale proceeds of fixed assets (net of VAT):
>   Draw-downs of loans:
>   Additional loans from directors:
>   New share capital:
>   Sales of investments/withdrawals of deposits:
> Prepayments by debtors during period (if not already allowed for):
> Depreciation for the period:
> HP interest for the period:
> Loan and mortgage interest for the period (where interest goes to principal):
> Accruals for the period (if not already allowed for):
> Plus

Capital outflows during the period
  Loan repayments:
  Withdrawal of directors' loans:
  Purchase of fixed assets (net of VAT for items other than motors):
  Deposits toward the purchase of fixed assets:
  Purchase of investments:
  Payment of dividends:
  New HP commitments:
  Prepayments to creditors during period (if not already allowed for):
  Indicated Profit/(Loss) for the period:

Curzon assumes that accruals will not already have been allowed for. He states, 'The only ones normally worth worrying about (other than major accruals relating to stock purchases) are overdraft interest and the audit fee. If figures are submitted monthly, divide the likely annual cost of the audit fee by twelve; if quarterly, by four and so on.'

For interest computations, the interest accrual will be nil when the reporting date is at the end of a month in which interest has been debited. For other cases, allow for a month's undebited interest, or for one to two month's interest where reporting is done on a quarterly basis.

Other accruals like electricity and telephone charges could be estimated from past periods or from the last audited profit and loss account's relevant accruals divided by twelve for monthly reporting or four for quarterly plus a conservative figure to allow for price increases/inflation and higher usage. Notwithstanding, the full measure of accruals can only be approximate on these calculations and nor is it likely that total prepayments will have been taken into account.

Distortions may enter the calculation from inaccurate stock and WIP reporting. Curzon remarks that, '... nine times out of ten, the reported figures under these headings (stock and WIP) will be gross approximations by the customer and should be treated with extreme caution.'

Accordingly, the profit or loss figure obtained from the debenture statistics will be only approximate. It can, nevertheless, serve as a significant indicator especially when trend is noted rather than monthly figures in isolation.

Curzon uses breakeven levels of sales taken from the last set of audited accounts to assess the 'credibility of the indicated profit and loss figures we have just calculated'. His computation is:

$$\left(\frac{\text{Fixed costs} \times \text{sales}}{\text{Sales less directly variable costs}}\right) \div 12$$

The caveats are that margins and prices may have changed. For instance, fixed costs can alter in the medium to long-term. It it likely then that some may have increased since the audited figures were made up. Seasonality may also account for trading losses observed in certain periods.

More cause for concern will be when profits indicated on the debenture forms appear consistently but where the reported turnover is below notional breakeven level. Curzon recommends asking the customer whether and how his circumstances have changed 'or—more to the point—whether the figures he has given us are accurate.'

Bank action

Curzon concludes his study with a summary of practical steps a bank can take when debenture statistics throw up warning signs. He observes that in most cases, statistics will be submitted and analysed monthly—that is two to three weeks after the reporting date. The statistics and inferences drawn from them need to be treated with caution as in many types of business financial condition varies rapidly. In such business particularly, fresh statistical data will be expected. Also, Curzon admits that it is possibly unjustifiable to take decisive action on the basis of a single month's figures—and these not probably presenting the truest and fairest view. However, warning signals given by two or more successive months' figures do, in his opinion, merit immediate and detailed enquiry.

To the bank, the most readily dangerous warning is the company's failure to meet the laid-down debenture formula. This often precedes a liquidity crisis either within the reporting period or very quickly. In such a case, the monitoring of debenture figures against cashflow forecasts and budgets can assist in bringing the data into a more revealing picture.

It is felt that whatever the warning sign, 'it is essential to question the customer'. Curzon suggests that a typical enquiry could include the following questions:

1. Are the figures either inaccurate or falsely pessimistic in some way? If not,
2. What has happened to cause the deterioration?

If individual figures stand out, ask about them.

If monthly management accounts exist, they should be requested and compared with the data already in the bank's hands.

Is the debenture formula unrealistic?

3. If the explanations and answers are not reassuring, can the bank forecast whether the company's position will improve or deteriorate further?

Ask about the order book; possible cost-cutting; pricing policy. Can excessive stock be reduced? Can better credit control be implemented? Are all the discounts possible from suppliers being taken? Would the company benefit by selling off under-utilized fixed assets to raise cash?

Has a budget or cashflow forecast been produced?

If the bank feels, according to all the evidence, that the customer's situation is deteriorating and that borrowing limits may be exceeded, there is an obvious case for reviewing limits and deciding upon what level of support the bank is prepared to offer the company.

From the analytical point of view, debenture statistics are interesting in that they bridge the very often considerable gap between quarterly management accounts. They also enable banks to take more prompt and decisive action in coping with problems than sole reliance on audited figures could justify. If debenture figures are seen to be lacking in holistic detail, they have the merit of frequency. Curzon summarizes, 'What is useful in the process as a whole ... is the promptness with which debenture figures enable us to identify problems before, rather than after, they happen, and the fact that by being closer to a company's performance in this way, we are very much better placed to take decisions about our lending than if we had to rely merely on out of date audited accounts.'

Sources

Bathory, A., *Predicting Corporate Collapse*, Financial Times Business Information, 1984, Chapter 2, p. 24
Clark, M., 'Recent Developments in Insolvency/Address to the National Conference/Institute of Credit Management, 1986', quoted in *Credit Management*, Institute of Credit Management, May 1986, p. 31.
Clarke T., and Vincent, W., The Quality of the Clearers, Scrimgeour Vickers & Co, United Kingdom Research Series, April 1986, passim and permission to reproduce Appendices III & IV.
Curzon, F. R. P., 'The Interpretation of Debenture Statistics', printed for a clearing bank's managerial training programme, 1983 passim.
Doyle, E. P., *Practice of Banking*, 2nd edn, Macdonald & Evans, London, 1972, pp. 184–191.
Robinson, R. I., *The Management of Bank Funds*, McGraw-Hill, New York, 1962, Chapter 12 passim.

13

BANK ANALYTICAL AND FORECASTING ROUTINES FOR MEDIUM TO LARGE CORPORATE CREDIT APPLICATIONS

Irrespective of the size of exposures, analysts' approaches to lending propositions should be grounded on seven basic canons. These are:

1. Character
2. Ability
3. Margin
4. Purpose
5. Amount
6. Repayment
7. Insurance

Character

Here, the banker and analyst are concerned with a company's history and product/services background. As the assessment is bound to be subjective, care is taken to form opinions on character from as wide a range of sources as possible. Such sources could include economic intelligence reports of a general or particular nature, newspapers (financial and otherwise), brokers' reports, journals, e.g. *The Economist*, and cannily, as one bank suggested, *Private Eye*. Also, the general operating environment of a company can be important in a bank's assessment of character. For instance, does staff appear happy and efficient? Is plant well-kept and up to date for the purposes required? Are there any instances of unwarranted extravagance? Are systems and procedures orderly?

Ability

Ability to repay principal and pay interest on the requested advance is a central concern. This is the function of financial analysis centring on interpretation of accounting statements, unaudited accounts, budgets, cashflows, quantified management information, and where the bank's facilities are extensions of existing credits, e.g. additional support for a distressed company, debenture statistics or data from other charge forms.

Margin

Margin in this context generally applies to the monetary return a bank will achieve for advancing funds. In practical terms, market forces tend considerably to dictate the margins and fees banks can command for particular advances. Margin can also apply to safety or comfort margins for loans and other facilities (Figure 13.1 illustrates the type of questions asked by a major bank in its attempt to assess risk). But as noted earlier, margin is generally understood to refer to monetary return.

Purpose

Why is the advance required? Does it fall within the current policy guidelines of the bank? These, of course, change from time to time. It is also important to ascertain the legal and ethical correctness of the company in using moneys for whatever the particular purpose may be. Could the moneys be needed for a particular change of direction (possibly radical)? Has the company's new policy (or altered policy) and the funds application been thought through? What, in other words, are the strategic implications for the company and for the bank?

Amount

Banks will always wish to determine whether or not the amount sought is realistic. This implies, is the amount enough? Is it too much? From the bank's point of view, it may not be realistic, depending upon a range of factors, for a very sizeable advance to be sanctioned within 24 hours. Banks will, accordingly, look at when the funds are needed. Also, can the proposed advance be supported by a realistic cashflow forecast? To answer this question, analysts will have to examine the cashflow projection in detail, compare it with the company's previous, historic cashflow performance. They will also need to know the assumptions behind the projection. Vital assumptions of this kind would be any particular changes in the terms of trading or in product-mix.

Repayment

How does the applicant propose to repay the advance? Is his proposition overly optimistic? Analysts will look at the company's profitability, funds flow along with the cashflow forecast in assessing whether the proposed repayment schedule looks realistic. Additionally, the timing and manner of repayment will be considered. Is there to be a grace period for payment of principal and interest? Are capital repayments to begin at once? Is the proposed term of the advance reasonable in light of anticipated cashflow and historic profitability?

Insurance

Is security required? What is the quality of the security offered? If the bank is lending on the security of a debenture, is the formula fair—both to the company and to the bank? What type of monitoring over the life of the loan is required? If frequent submissions are required from the customer, how reliable are these figures likely to be?

If lending is to be to a subsidiary of a parent company, how good is the parent company's letter of comfort. Has any security at all been offered by the parent or ultimate company?

Appendix IV

An example of the key questions asked by a major bank in its effort to classify risk

RISK CLASSIFICATION CRITERIA	RISK CLASSIFICATION MODIFERS
Principal Factors	
I. Industry	I. Agreement
A. Structure and Economics	II. Collateral
B. Maturity	III. Guarantees
C. Stability	
II. Company	
A. General Characteristics	
B. Management	
C. Financial Condition	
D. Capital Sources	
E. Financial Reporting	

Criteria

I.   Industry
   A.   Structure and Economics
      1.   Competition (monopoly, oligopoly, etc.)
      2.   Role of regulation and legislation
      3.   Importance and stature of industry in the economy
      4.   Degree of control exercised by industry participants over demand and selling prices
      5.   Industry's economic dependency on other industries or governments
   B.   Maturity
      1.   Stage of industry's life cycle
      2.   Ease of entry
      3.   Rate of capacity additions
   C.   Stability
      1.   Sensitivity to business cycles
      2.   Sensitivity to credit cycles
      3.   Supply/demand balance
      4.   Vulnerability to technological innovation
      5.   Vulnerability to production and distribution changes
      6.   Susceptibility to changes in consumption patterns
      7.   Mortality rate

II.   Company
   A.   General Characteristics
      1.   Position and role in industry hierarchy (e.g., leader)
      2.   Absolute size and size relative to industry standards by sales, assets, profits
      3.   Market share
      4.   Scope, in terms of both markets and products
      5.   Diversification of revenue sources
      6.   Reputation and record of accomplishment
      7.   Control over availability and price of supplies and raw materials
      8.   Vulnerability to uncontrollable or unpredictable events (e.g., acts of God)
      9.   Product characteristics: differentiation, substitutues, patents, brand loyalty, etc.
   B.   Management
      1.   Industry experience
      2.   Managerial breadth and qualifications
      3.   Managerial depth and turnover rate
      4.   Calibre and structure of Board
      5.   Management controls and forward planning
      6.   Management reputation
   C.   Financial Condition
      1.   Debt and capitalisation ratios
      2.   Liquidity ratios
      3.   Cash flow and coverage ratios
      4.   Profitability ratios
      5.   Quality of assets
      6.   Quality of earnings

Figure 13.1 Key questions in risk classification

Reproduced by permission of Scrimgeour Vickers & Co.

- D. Capital Sources
  1. Equity
     - Access to both public and private markets or just private
     - Degree of public ownership
     - Breadth of ownership
     - Liquidity and stability of market for equity securities
     - Market demand for company's stock
  2. Long-term debt
     - Access to both public and pirvate markets or just private
     - Bond rating(s)
     - Investment demand for company's issues
  3. Commercial paper
     - Commercial paper rating
     - Existence of back-up lines
     - Investment receptivity and secondary market liquidity
  4. Commercial bank relationships
     - Size and stature of lead bank
     - Dependence on single or few banks
     - Strength of relationships
  5. Investment banker
     - Stature and size of investment banking firm
     - Scope, size and financial condition
- E. Financial Reporting
  1. Acceptability and soundness of accounting practices
  2. Reputation and stature of audit firm
  3. Quality of audit opinion

Modifiers

I. Agreement
  - A. Type
    1. Current line
    2. Revolving credit
    3. Term loan
    4. Other
  - B. Security provisions
  - C. Repayment or amortization provisions
  - D. Restrictive covenants
  - E. FNBC position in credit (lead bank, uninfluential position)
  - F. Quality and reputation of other lenders

II. Collateral
  - A. Type
    1. Certificates of Deposit
       - FNBC
       - Other bank
    2. Short-term governments
    3. Long-term governments
    4. Municipals
    5. Corporate Bonds
    6. Equity securities
       - Common stock
       - Preferred stock
    7. Accounts receivable
    8. Inventories
       - Finished goods
       - In-process
       - Raw materials
       - Commodities
    9. Fixed assets
       - Real property
       - Plant
       - Equipment
  - B. Valuation considerations
    1. Securities
       - Marketability: national exchange, OTC, market demand
       - Price stability
       - Registration
       - Quality of obligor
       - Transaction costs
    2. Accounts receivable
       - Type of receivables (corporate, government, individual)
       - Quality of debtors
       - Warranties, contingencies
       - Audit
    3. Inventories
       - Marketability
       - Conversion costs and sales commissions
       - Obsolescence risk
       - Perishability risk
       - Physical location
       - Audit
    4. Fixed assets
       - Physical condition
       - Marketability
       - Sales commissions
       - Movement expenses
       - Conversion costs
       - Transferability of title (legally, practically)
       - Physical location
       - Liens or assignments
       - Obsolesence risk
  - C. Legal considerations
    1. UCC filings versus dominion over collateral
    2. Perfection of liens
    3. Conflicting liens

III. Guaranties
  - A. Collateralized or uncollateralized
  - B. Enforceability

Figure 13.1 (*Concluded*)

The requirement for security depends upon the size of the advance as well as the credit standing of the applicant. There should, accordingly, be no hard and fast rules for all applications.

Overall 'feel' for the operation

For sizeable credit applications, most clearing banks provide for a dual checks assessment function between branch lending bankers and credit analysts. In this way, analysts will need to consider the information provided from branch level.

This information can take account of the character and history of the applicant company from a working knowledge. For instance, the branch officer can supply details on the company's past usage of borrowing facilities if an existing customer. Much personal and subjective data can be offered. Also, if the applicant is not an existing customer of the bank, lending officers can supply valuable notes of interviews and correspondence. In his normal remove, the analyst is trying, in these cases, to get a 'feel' for the way in which a company operates and the direction in which it intends to go.

This entails looking closely at the operation and evaluating where it fits into a particular industry. How do its figures stack up with the industrial averages? Allowances must be made for size and age of the applicant—particularly in the case of young companies. Such allowances can work both to the favour or to the detriment of particular applications.

If the sector in which the applicant company operates has proved troublesome in the past, e.g. heavy engineering, electronics, or computers, most banks will take specialist advice concerning the viability of a large credit exposure. Most banks maintain specialist sections or departments which have day-to-day contact with particular sectors.

In the case of advances to an existing customer, the length of time the company has been with the bank will be material along with the size of the credit. For better or worse, the credit perception of any company must take into account the age of its operations. How long has the company been in existence. Statistically, the incidence of failure due to insolvency is highest in companies from one to eight years old.

At branch level normally, the company's management would be assessed. Are directors and key managers appropriately qualified? Are responsibilities for key functions adequately delegated and covered? What is the banker's personal assessment of the company's chief members? Do they seem reliable, active, intelligent, and trustworthy? What does the management style appear to be? Is it old-fashioned, aggressive and pioneering, expansionist, responsible? Of especial interest must be the quality and ability of the company's financial management. This extends to any external advisors. Attention is paid to professional advisers such as auditors, solicitors, and reporting accountants.

Manual analytical spreadsheet

Figures 13.2(a) to (d) illustrate a bank's manual analytical spreadsheet. This follows the format of accounts provided under the latest Companies Act. Following on from previous observations, the first page of the spread (Figure 13.2(a)) calls for a note of the branch for further reference and the name of the company's auditors. Further information is required on any significant accounting policies, e.g. treatment of WIP, fixed assets valuation, basis of consolidation, and so forth.

324 TOWARDS THE PERFECT CREDIT ANALYSIS

BRANCH_____

BALANCE SHEET ANALYSIS SPREAD SHEET

NAME *(State sole or consolidated)*_____

OCCUPATION_____ _____

AUDITOR *(State date of appointment, if known)*_____

SIGNIFICANT ACCOUNTING POLICIES AND OTHER INFORMATION *(See instructions for completion)*

265 (SPECIAL)/ADV10A (11/84)

Figure 13.2 Bank Manual analytical Spreadsheet (example 1)

DATE OF BALANCE SHEET 1				
Date of Auditors Certificate 2				
(State if qualified) 3				
Currency (in _____). 4				
QUICK ASSETS				
Cash and Bank 5				
Quoted Investments 6				
Debtors/Accounts Receivable/Bills Receivable 7				
SUB TOTAL *8				
OTHER CURRENT ASSETS				
Stock — Finished Goods 9				
— Work-in-Progress 10				
— Raw Materials 11				
12				
13				
Others 14				
TOTAL *15				
CURRENT LIABILITIES				
Creditors/Accounts Payable/Bills Payable 16				
Hire Purchase/Leasing — less than one year 17				
Bank/Short Term Loans/Acceptance Credits 18				
Current Portion Long Term Debt 19				
(Secured Debt — memo item) 20				
Due to Group Companies 21				
Due to Directors 22				
Dividends 23				
Taxation - Current 24				
25				
26				
27				
Other Current Liabilities 28				
TOTAL *29				
LIQUID SURPLUS/(DEFICIT) 15 - 29 = *30				
QUICK ASSET SURPLUS/(DEFICIT) 8 - 29 = *31				
FIXED AND OTHER ASSETS				
Land and Buildings (Net of Depreciation) 32				
(Market Value, if known) 33				
Machinery, Plant, Fixtures etc. (Net of Depreciation) ... 34				
Capitalised Leases 35				
Investments — Subsidiaries 36				
— Associates 37				
— Others 38				
Due from Group Companies 39				
40				
Other Fixed and Term Assets 41				
TOTAL *42				
TERM AND OTHER LIABILITIES				
Future Taxation 43				
Deferred Taxation 44				
Hire Purchase/Leasing — beyond one year 45				
Loans Due for Repayment — one to five years 46				
Loans Due for Repayment beyond five years 47				
(Secured Debt over one year — memo item) 48				
49				
Other Term Liabilities 50				
SUB TOTAL *51				
Minority Interests 52				
TOTAL *53				
NET TANGIBLE ASSETS — SURPLUS/(DEFICIT) 30 + 42 − 53 = *54				
Financed by:				
Share Capital — Issued 55				
Capital Reserves 56				
Distributable Reserves 57				
Less: (Goodwill and Intangibles) 58				
(Treasury Stock) 59				
SHAREHOLDERS FUNDS — SURPLUS/(DEFICIT) (= 54) *60				

Figure 13.2 *(Continued)*

	DATE				
PROFIT SUMMARY					
Profit Before Interest and Tax (**PBIT**)	71				
Associates	72				
Investment Income and Interest Receivable	73				
Profit Before Interest Paid	*74				
(Interest Paid)	75				
Profit Before Tax (**PBT**)	*76				
(Taxation)	77				
(Minority Interests)	78				
Extraordinary Items	79				
Attributable Profit/Loss After Tax (**APAT**)	*80				
(Dividends)	81				
Residual Profit/(Loss)	*82				
Additional Capital and Reserve Movements	83				
	84				
	85				
	86				
NET VARIATION IN SURPLUS/(DEFICIT)	*87				

KEY FIGURES AND RATIOS					
Sales	101				
Cost of Goods Sold	102				
Gross Profit	*103				
Depreciation	104				
Capital Employed	*105				
INFLATION ADJUSTED (*Where CCA Not Available*)					
Inflation Index	106				
Sales at Constant Prices	*107				
PBT at Constant Prices	*108				
PROFITABILITY					
Gross Profit Margin					
(*Gross Profit ÷ Sales × 100*)	%*109				
Net Profit Margin					
(*PBIT ÷ Sales × 100*)	%*110				
Return on Capital Employed					
(*Profit Before Interest Paid ÷ Average Capital Employed × 100*)	%*111				
CONTROL/LIQUIDITY					
Average Credit Given					
(*Average Debtors ÷ Sales × 365*)......DAYS	*112				
Average Credit Taken					
(*Average Creditors ÷ Cost of Goods Sold × 365*)......DAYS	*113				
Stock Turnover					
(*Average Stock ÷ Cost of Goods Sold × 365*)......DAYS	*114				
Working Capital Turnover					
(*Sales ÷ Average of Liquid Surplus/(Deficit)*)......TIMES	*115				
Current Ratio					
(*Current Assets ÷ Current Liabilities*)......RATIO	*116				
Liquid Ratio					
(*Quick Assets ÷ Current Liabilities*)......RATIO	*117				
GEARING AND SOLVENCY					
Gross Gearing (*Total Borrowings ÷ Surplus*)......RATIO	*118				
Net Gearing (*Net Borrowings ÷ Surplus*)......RATIO	*119				
Gearing (*Total Liabilities*)......RATIO	*120				
Interest Cover — Historic Profit Basis......TIMES	*121				
— Cash Flow Basis......TIMES	122				
— Sustainable Funds Flow Basis......TIMES	*123				
Dividend Cover — CCA Basis......TIMES	124				
Term Debt ÷ Operating Cash Flow......YEARS	*125				
Total Borrowings ÷ Sustainable Funds Flow......YEARS	*126				

Figure 13.2 (*Continued*)

OTHER KEY FIGURES	DATE				
Capital Expenditure	131				
Capital Commitments: Contracted	132				
Authorised	133				
Contingent Liabilities: Guarantees	134				
Other	135				
Leasing Obligations	136				
Directors Remuneration	137				

SOURCE AND APPLICATION OF FUNDS					
Profit Before Interest Paid *(per line 74)*	*151				
Depreciation	*152				
Adjustment for other items not involving the movement of funds	153				
Working Capital Variation *(See line 185)*	*154				
OPERATING CASH FLOW (BEFORE INTEREST & TAX)	*155				
(Interest Paid)	*156				
(Taxation Paid)/Taxation Refunded	157				
OPERATING CASH FLOW	*158				
Disposal of Fixed Assets	159				
(Capital Expenditure)	*160				
Extraordinary Items	161				
Miscellaneous Items	162				
CASH AVAILABLE FOR DIVIDENDS	*163				
(Dividends Paid)	*164				
CASH AVAILABLE FOR INVESTMENT	*165				
Investments	166				
Acquisitions	167				
CASH SURPLUS/(DEFICIT) BEFORE EXTERNAL FINANCE	*168				
FINANCED BY:					
Capital Issues	169				
Increase/(Decrease) in Long/Medium Term Debt	170				
Increase/(Decrease) in Short Term Debt	171				
(Increase)/Decrease in Cash Balances	172				
NET FINANCIAL REQUIREMENT/(SURPLUS)	*173				

WORKING CAPITAL VARIATION					
Stocks (Increase)/Decrease	181				
Debtors (Increase)/Decrease	182				
Creditors Increase/(Decrease)	183				
Other Variations	184				
WORKING CAPITAL SURPLUS/(REQUIREMENT)	*185				

SUSTAINABLE FUNDS FLOW STATEMENT *(Where CCA Available)*					
Profit Before Tax (PBT)	*191				
Plus: Depreciation	*192				
Less: (Taxation) *(per line 157)*	*193				
BASIC FUNDS FLOW	*194				
LESS: CAPITAL MAINTENANCE REQUIREMENT					
(Historic Cost Depreciation)	*195				
(Additional CCA Depreciation)	196				
(Cost of Sales Adjustment)	197				
(Monetary Working Capital Adjustment)	198				
SUSTAINABLE FUNDS FLOW	*199				

Figure 13.2 *(Concluded)*

Other information might also include amount, purpose and term of the credit to be borne in mind during the spreading and assessment of the company's latest audited statements.

Figure 13.2(b) immediately separates liquid from other current assets indicating the importance of liquidity (in this case, historic) to the bank. Stock is divided into finished goods, WIP, and raw materials as a further check on liquidity and also, to lend greater dimension to performance indicators involving stock, e.g. stock turnover or stock as a percentage of total assets.

Current liabilities are carefully broken down showing, among other items, current portion of long-term debt, secured debt, and short-term/bank loans/acceptance credits obligations. Overdraft borrowing will be included here. Current liabilities are then deducted from current assets to provide a working capital figure noted as liquid surplus/(deficit). Additionally, a quick asset surplus/deficit is obtained by deducting total current liabilities from total quick (liquid) assets. These indicators will be expressed subsequently (Figure 13.2(c)) in ratio form as current and acid-test (liquid) ratios.

Note that in this spreadsheet, current assets and liabilities precede fixed assets (the usual format of balance sheets). This helps to emphasize the bank's concern with trading position and liquidity. Fixed assets are now posted and note the line calling for capitalized leases following SSAP 21. Long-term liabilities with detailed schedules are now required. Note the inclusion of HP and leasing commitments. The analyst may take these direct from some balance sheets or from balance sheet and notes. Ideally, the balance sheet should provide totals of all long-term commitments and schedules should be found in the notes to the accounts. On these spreads, asterisks indicate totals and sub-totals. Minorities are then deducted from term and other liabilities. An interesting reconstruction of the normal balance sheet follows in calling for net tangible assets less liquid surplus/deficit. This, of course, gives net assets. Again, the financing of net assets is calculated by shareholders' funds comprised of the usual items, less liquid surplus/deficit. Presumably, in calling for these computations, the bank is attempting to highlight liquidity.

Figure 13.2(c) analyses the changes in the variation of liquid surplus/deficit with sub-headings itemizing profit in different stages. Profit before interest and tax (PBIT) is separated from profits earned by associate companies and from investment income and interest receivable. Of interest to the bank will be profit before interest paid. Immediately after, the spread calls for a note of interest paid, which deducted, will yield the figure for profit before taxation (PBT). Minority interests and extraordinary items are spread separately following accepted accounting practice. After these and taxation have been added or subtracted from PBT, we are given APAT (attributable profit/(loss) after tax. Dividends are deducted from this to give residual profit/(loss)—from which and to which new capital and reserve movements are added/subtracted to provide net variation in surplus/(deficit). To this point, the spreads manage, through careful restatement of the accounts, to give a dynamic rather than a static picture of a company's financial movements from period to period.

Under the heading key figures and ratios (Figure 13.2(c)), the analysis proper starts with sales, working through cost of goods sold, gross profit, inflation-adjusted figures where applicable, profitability, control/liquidity, gearing, and solvency. 'CCA' refers to current cost accounts (accounts adjusted for the effects of inflation). Of interest are the adjustments for sales at constant prices and PBT at constant prices. These are forecasting measures, as well as indicators of the effects current rates of inflation had on the figures to hand. Thus, it would be possible for PBT to be a positive number whilst PBT at constant prices to be a negative number indicating that a real loss was or will be sustained all things being equal. Both, of course, are sensitivity analytical measures.

The profitability indicators called for are two measurements of margin, gross and net, computed in the ordinary way. In speaking of computations, note that a virtue of this spreadsheet is that computational routines are specified, minimizing the possibility of error and standardizing analysis.

Some innovative ratios follow. To obtain the most representative picture possible of performance, the prime ratio computation is altered from PBIT/capital employed to PBIT over the average capital employed—or the mean between opening and closing balances. This will give a particularly indicative measurement of return on capital.

Moving to control/liquidity, we see an improved debt-turn ratio using average debtors as the numerator. Average credit taken calls ideally for trade creditors, although this figure may not be available in modified statements. Note that on Figure 13.2(b), current liabilities provide merely for creditors/accounts payable/bills payable. Likewise, debt-turn requires trade debtors. Where trade creditors and debtors are itemized, they can on this spreadsheet be noted as above and sundry creditors/debtors can be noted in the respective 'Other' boxes.

There is no provision here for the cashflow difference (monetary lag) between average credit given and average credit taken. The spreadsheet continues the control/liquidity section with a computation of stock-turn, again using the mean between opening and closing stock balances. The averaging process is particularly suitable for a calculation of working capital turnover as this is highly indicative of liquidity and of the efficiency with which net current assets are being utilized. Finally, we have the standard current ratio and acid-test mentioned before. As stock, in particular, and other current assets and liabilities are well itemized, the analyst could give normalized as well as standard ratios at this point.

The following section is concerned with gearing and solvency. Firstly, note the three computations for interest cover—i.e. how many times profit can decline before the company is unable to meet current interest charges from current profits. The standard computation is, of course, PBIT/interest. Here, the bank calls for this calculation plus cashflow/interest together with the CCA-applicable inflation-adjusted funds flow less capital maintenance requirement/interest.

Also, we see hybrid forms of the standard gearing measurements. Gearing, the ratio of loan capital to capital employed, is commonly used. Also, bankers are fond of shareholders' funds to capital employed. A nicer approximation is achieved by this bank's gross gearing ratio which takes total borrowings over surplus and a secondary net gearing of net borrowings over surplus—echoing the current and acid-test ratios. After this, a third gearing measure, total liabilities to capital employed is used.

A CCA variant on standard dividend cover is required. Dividend cover is the maximum dividend a company can pay from profits divided by the dividend actually paid. The computation is: Earnings per share/net dividend per share.

Term debt is then divided by operational cashflow. This measurement expressed in years indicates the length of time it will take given the operational cash inflow as at accounting date to extinguish term debt. Of course, the measurement is artificial in that cashflow will vary up or down in coming years and term borrowings will vary according to repayments made, interest rates, and the effects of inflation. The final measurement in this section is total borrowings over inflation-adjusted funds flow (CCA-applicable), again to indicate the defrayment of debt in years.

The bank will naturally interpret gearing indicators in varying ways. For example, a company financing vehicle leasing may have a gearing ratio of 8:1. Superficially, this may look overly high. Given, however, that the firm is heavily asset-backed and providing the bank can see a good spread of good leases over good quality assets, the abnormally high gearing may be acceptable.

Building companies may have a potential gearing as high as 2:1 and in some instances, as high as 4:1 has been seen for very well-managed and proven firms. In general, however, it would be unusual to see a gearing ratio of more than 1:1 or 50 per cent for the manufacturing and electronics sectors. For these and most other sectors, gearing in excess of 1:1 would prompt thorough investigation by the bank of both management and product.

This spreadsheet is very thorough. Accordingly, information from the notes to the accounts is included under the heading 'other key figures' in Figure 13.2(d). These quantities are: Capital expenditure, forward capital commitments e.g. a contract entered into, contingent liabilities and leasing obligations—this last, giving an added perspective to the leasing commitments already noted in the balance-sheet section in the event that full obligations were not noted previously or fully capitalized by the auditors. Also, the current interest in off-balance-sheet finance gives the leasing obligations column a particular importance. Equally, contingent liabilities, especially when they are substantial and properly reported in the notes, are seen by this bank as worthy of investigation. Directors' remuneration is included at this point, purely as an extracted figure with a view to establishing a notion of trend.

The bank's restatement of the source and application of funds section of accounts provides them with a particular format which indicates concisely where the funds have come from, how they are being applied, and how the resulting surplus/deficit is financed. It is particularly germane to note the division between capital issues, long/medium-term debt and short-term debt, and increase/decrease in cash balances.

The working capital variation follows from this as a funds flow concept. It is shown separately to highlight the company's ability to manage its working capital. It will be seen that a company which is very 'cash-hungry' due to its terms of trading will be pointed up at this stage. Equally, a retail business with a strong, positive cashflow will be highlighted by this arrangement.

The final section, sustainable funds flow statement, is only really applicable where CCA accounts are available. In the late seventies and early eighties when the UK experienced double-digit inflation, this section would have been completed for those companies producing inflation-adjusted accounts. However, with declining inflation rates as well as the apparent inability of the accounting profession to agree with the Inland Revenue on the format and relevance of current cost accounts, this section will have fallen largely into disuse.

After having examined this bank spreadsheet in some detail and seen its obvious strengths in respect of innovative restatement of figures, improved computations for the sake of greater indicativeness, and comprehensive detail covering all parts of a company's accounts, it will be interesting to compare the less impressive specimen bank spreads given in Figures 13.3(a) and (b).

BANK ANALYTICAL AND FORECASTING ROUTINES

Date of Balance Sheet					
Date of Auditors Certificate *(State if qualified)*	( )	( )	( )	( )	( )
Cash and Bank					
Quoted investments.					
(Market Value)					
Debtors – Trade					
Debtors – Other					
QUICK ASSETS SUB TOTAL 1					
Stock.					
Work in Progress					
CURRENT ASSETS TOTAL 2					
Creditors – Trade					
Other creditors, accruals, etc.					
Hire Purchase – less than one year					
Bank.					
Loans for repayment within 12 months					
Due to Group Companies					
Due to Directors					
Proposed Dividends.					
Taxation: Current					
Future					
CURRENT LIABILITIES TOTAL 3					
LIQUID SURPLUS/(DEFICIT) 2–3=4					
QUICK ASSET SURPLUS/(DEFICIT) 1–3=5					
Land and Buildings.					
(Market Value if known)					
Machinery, Plant, Fixtures and Fittings.					
Motor Vehicles					
Other fixed and Term Assets					
Investments – Unquoted/Trade/Associated					
– Shares in Subsidiaries					
– *(Market Value if quoted)*					
– Due from Group Companies					
FIXED AND OTHER ASSETS TOTAL 6					
Deferred Tax.					
Mortgages					
Debentures					
Hire Purchase – beyond one year					
Loans not due for repayment within 12 months					
TERMS AND OTHER LIABILITIES SUB TOTAL					
Minority Interests					
TOTAL 7					
SURPLUS/(DEFICIT) (4+6)–7=8					
Financed by: Share Capital.					
Capital Reserves					
Reserves					
Profit and Loss					
SUB TOTAL					
Less: Goodwill/Intangibles					
Deficit Profit and Loss					
NET TANGIBLE ASSETS – SURPLUS/(DEFICIT) TOTAL=8					

CUSTOMER:

Figure 13.3 Bank manual analytical spreadsheet (example 2)

332 TOWARDS THE PERFECT CREDIT ANALYSIS

	DATE				
9 Net/Profit(Loss)					
after Depreciation					
Tax					
Directors Remuneration					
Interest Receivable					
Interest Paid					
but before Dividends/Drawings					
10 Contingent Liabilities:					
11 Capital Commitments:					
Contracted					
Authorised but not contracted					
12 Sales:					
(including exports)					
Cost of goods sold					
Gross Profit					
Gross Profit Margin		%	%	%	%
Credit given in days: Debtors—Sales×365		days	days	days	days
Credit take in days: Creditors—Purchases×365		days	days	days	days
Stock Turnover in days: Stock—Sales×365		days	days	days	days
Current Ratio: Current Assets (2): Current Liabilities (3)		:1	:1	:1	:1
Quick Asset Ratio: Quick Assets (1): Current Liabilities (3)		:1	:1	:1	:1

Gearing:
      Total borrowings as at date of Balance Sheet
      Summary: Net Tangible Assets (8)
		:1	:1	:1	:1

Potential Gearing:
      Total lines of available Credit:
      Net Tangible Assets (B)
		:1	:1	:1	:1

13 Movement in Net Tangible Assets:					
Opening Balance (Total 8 brought forward from previous year)					
Add: Net Profit (above)					
Other Credits					
	SUB TOTAL				
Less: Net Loss (above)					
Dividends					
Other Debits					
Closing Balance (8 opposite)					

Figure 13.3 (*Concluded*)

Figure 13.4 Printout of manual spreadsheet

Company

		31 Aug 72	31 Aug 73 16 Jan 74	31 Aug 74 16 Jan 75	31 Aug 75 15 Jan 76	31 Aug 76 06 Jan 77	31 Aug 77 12 Jan 78	31 Aug 78 11 Jan 79
Date of balance sheet	1	31 Aug 72						
Date of auditors' cert.	2	NA						
(State if qualified)	3							
Currency (in ....)	4	1000	1000	1000	1000	1000	1000	1000
Cash & Bank	5	18	269	160	557	71	128	170
Quoted investments	6	16	77	72	51	51	50	57
Debtors/Accs/Bills rec.	7	1274	1659	2240	2658	3592	4190	4355
S. tot. quick assets	8	1308	2005	2472	3266	3714	4368	4582
Stock—Finished goods	9	1198	1556	2264	3011	3362	2241	2905
—Work-in-prog.	10	NA	NA	NA	NA	NA	664	674
—Raw materials	11	NA	NA	NA	NA	NA	1529	1576
	12	0	0	0	0	0	0	0
	13	0	0	0	0	0	0	0
Others	14	73	95	0	0	0	0	0
Tot. current assets	15	2579	3656	4736	6277	7076	8802	9737
Creds/Accs/Bills pay	16	688	1104	1147	1594	1768	2439	2350
H.P./Leasing <1 year	17	0	0	0	0	0	0	0
Bank/St. loans/Acc. crs	18	672	1495	1989	2042	3031	3564	4609
Current port. lt. debt	19	0	0	0	0	0	0	0
(Secured debt—memo)	20	0	0	0	0	0	0	0
Due to grp companies	21	0	0	0	0	0	0	0
Due to directors	22	0	0	0	0	0	0	0
Dividends	23	82	124	97	177	200	208	240
Taxation—Current	24	74	94	107	194	269	190	229
	25	0	0	0	0	0	0	0
	26	0	0	0	0	0	0	0
	27	0	0	0	0	0	0	0
Oth. current liabils	28	0	0	0	0	0	0	0
Tot. current liabs	29	1516	2817	3340	4007	5268	6401	7428

Figure 13.4 (*continued*)

Company

		31 Aug 72	31 Aug 73	31 Aug 74	31 Aug 75	31 Aug 76	31 Aug 77	31 Aug 78
Date of balance sheet	1	31 Aug 72	31 Aug 73	31 Aug 74	31 Aug 75	31 Aug 76	31 Aug 77	31 Aug 78
Date of auditors' cert.	2	NA	16 Jan 74	16 Jan 75	15 Jan 76	06 Jan 77	12 Jan 78	11 Jan 79
(State if qualified)	3							
Currency (in ....)	4	1000	1000	1000	1000	1000	1000	1000
Liq. surplus/(deficit)	30	1063	839	1396	2270	1808	2401	2309
Quick asset surp./(def.)	31	−208	−812	−868	−741	−1554	−2033	−2846
Land & bldgs (net of dep.)	32	859	1084	1236	1538	1782	1981	2011
(Market val., if known)	33	NA	NA	NA	NA	NA	NA	NA
Mac., plt., fix. (net dep.)	34	666	973	755	1226	1744	1701	2072
Capitalised leases	35	0	0	0	0	0	0	0
Investment—Subsids	36	0	48	0	0	0	0	0
—Associates	37	17	26	57	63	74	90	194
—Others	38	9	9	9	9	9	15	0
Due from group comps	39	0	0	0	0	0	0	0
	40	0	0	0	0	0	0	0
Oth. fixed & term assets	41	0	0	71	127	318	305	456
Tot. fix. & oth. assets	42	1551	2140	2128	2963	3927	4092	4733
Future taxation	43	0	0	0	0	0	0	0
Deferred taxation	44	250	364	722	1240	1284	271	318
H.P./Leasing >1 year	45	0	0	0	0	0	0	0
Loans due 1–5 years	46	0	0	0	0	0	0	0
Loans due >5 years	47	0	0	0	0	0	0	0
(Sec. debt >1 year-memo)	48	0	0	0	0	0	0	0
	49	0	0	0	0	0	0	0
Other term liabils	50	0	0	0	0	0	0	0
S. tot. term & O. liabs	51	250	364	722	1240	1284	271	318
Minority interests	52	0	0	0	0	0	0	0
Tot. term & oth. liabs	53	250	364	722	1240	1284	271	318
Net tang. ass.—Surp./def.	54	2364	2615	2802	3993	4451	6222	6724

Share capital issued	55	1262	1262	1262	1736	1736	1736	1736
Capital reserves	56	229	229	229	706	706	706	706
Distr'able reserves	57	982	1235	1422	1662	2120	3780	4282
Goodwill & intangibles	58	109	111	111	111	111	0	0
Treasury stock	59	0	0	0	0	0	0	0
S. holders—Surp./(def.)	60	2364	2615	2802	3993	4451	6222	6724
Check: line 54–Line 60 =		0	0	0	0	0	0	0
Prof. bef. int. & tax	71	433	581	1072	1460	1080	1582	1495
Associates	72	5	9	31	20	10	30	23
Invest. inc. & interest	73	3	3	13	12	26	4	5
Profit bef. int. paid	74	441	593	1116	1492	1116	1616	1523
(Interest paid)	75	−92	−133	−252	−291	−302	−391	−422
Profit bef. tax (PBT)	76	349	460	864	1201	814	1225	1101
(Taxation)	77	−134	−169	−465	−637	−117	−132	−100
(Minority interests)	78	0	0	0	0	0	0	0
Extraordinary items	79	−4	0	−33	38	9	−141	−189
Attr. prof./los. aft. tax	80	211	291	366	602	706	952	812
(Dividends)	81	−113	−124	−132	−212	−248	−277	−310
Resid. profit/(loss)	82	98	167	234	390	458	675	502
Addit. cap. & res. moves	83	NA	0	0	477	0	0	0
	84	NA	84	−47	−150	0	985	0
	85	NA	0	0	474	0	111	0
	86	NA	0	0	0	0	0	0
Net var. in surp./(def.)	87	NA	251	187	1191	458	1771	502
Sales	101	5712	6556	9187	12047	13400	17647	19084
Cost of goods sold	102	4637	5190	7153	9737	11134	14834	16118
Gross profit	103	1075	1366	2034	2310	2266	2804	2966
Depreciation	104	131	151	529	298	288	389	481
Capital employed	105	3286	4474	5513	7275	8766	10057	11651

Figure 13.4 (*continued*)

Company		31 Aug 72	31 Aug 73 16 Jan 74	31 Aug 74 16 Jan 75	31 Aug 75 15 Jan 76	31 Aug 76 06 Jan 77	31 Aug 77 12 Jan 78	31 Aug 78 11 Jan 79
Date of balance sheet	1	31 Aug 72	31 Aug 73	31 Aug 74	31 Aug 75	31 Aug 76	31 Aug 77	31 Aug 78
Date of auditors' cert.	2	NA	16 Jan 74	16 Jan 75	15 Jan 76	06 Jan 77	12 Jan 78	11 Jan 79
(State if qualified)	3							
Currency (in ....)	4	1000	1000	1000	1000	1000	1000	1000
Inflation index	106	100.00	112.80	143.00	173.90	202.99	238.82	257.39
Sales at const. price	107	5712	5812	6424	6928	6601	7389	7414
PBT at const. prices	108	349	408	604	691	491	513	428
Gross profit margin	109	18.82	20.84	22.14	19.17	16.91	15.89	15.54
Net profit margin	110	7.58	8.86	11.67	12.12	8.06	8.96	7.83
Return of cap. employ.	111	NA	15.28	22.35	23.33	13.91	17.17	14.03
Av. credit given days	112	NA	81.65	77.45	74.20	85.12	80.48	81.72
Av. credit taken days	113	NA	63.01	57.43	51.37	55.11	51.73	54.22
Stock turnover days	114	NA	96.84	97.46	98.87	104.46	95.85	108.57
Work. cap. turnov. times	115	NA	6.89	8.22	6.57	6.57	8.39	8.10
Current ratio	116	1.70	1.30	1.42	1.57	1.34	1.38	1.31
Liquid ratio	117	0.86	0.71	0.74	0.82	0.71	0.68	0.62
Gross gearing ratio	118	0.28	0.57	0.71	0.51	0.68	0.57	0.69
Net gearing ratio	119	0.27	0.44	0.63	0.36	0.65	0.54	0.65
Gearing ratio	120	0.75	1.22	1.45	1.31	1.47	1.07	1.15
I. Cov.—His. prof. times	121	4.79	4.46	4.43	5.13	3.70	4.13	3.61
—Cash flow times	122	NA	NA	NA	−0.02	−0.90	−0.09	−0.30
—Sust. funds times	123	NA	NA	NA	NA	0.34	1.54	1.82
Divi. cover (CCA) times	124	NA	NA	NA	NA	−0.47	0.59	0.72
T. debt/Op. cash fl. yrs	125	NA	0.00	0.00	0.00	0.00	0.00	0.00
Tot. Bor/Sus. funds yrs	126	NA	NA	NA	NA	−15.31	16.97	13.24
Capital expenditure	131	0	895	548	1075	1211	613	1400
Cap. commits—Contract.	132	195	424	656	576	88	0	137
—Auth.	133	75	27	227	0	0	144	465

Cont. liabs: Guarantees	134	0	0	0	0	0	0	0	0
Other	135	0	0	0	0	0	0	1765	2241
Leasing obligations	136	0	0	0	0	0	0	0	0
Directors' remun.	137	59	68	93	108	110	132	174
Profit bef. int. paid	151	441	593	1116	1492	1116	1616	1523
Depreciation	152	131	151	529	298	288	389	481
Not involv. fund move	153	0	26	−53	−4	47	−14	−20
Work. cap. variation	154	NA	−210	−1219	−469	−1013	−999	−975
Op. cash bef. int., tax	155	NA	560	373	1317	438	992	1009
(Interest paid)	156	−92	−133	−252	−291	−302	−391	−422
(Tax paid)/Tax refun.	157	NA	−35	−165	−88	−189	−226	−165
Operating cash flow	158	NA	392	−44	938	−53	375	422
Dispos. fixed assets	159	0	78	130	155	165	56	351
(Capital expenditure)	160	0	−895	−548	−1075	−1211	−613	−1400
Extraordinary items	161	0	0	0	0	−26	0	0
Miscellaneous items	162	0	7	50	−168	−90	0	0
Cash avail. for divis	163	NA	−418	−412	−150	−1215	−182	−627
(Dividends paid)	164	NA	−82	−159	−132	−225	−269	−278
Cash avail. for inves.	165	NA	−500	−571	−282	−1440	−451	−905
Investments	166	0	−72	−32	−29	−11	−22	−111
Acquisitions	167	0	0	0	−295	−24	−3	13
Cash +/− Bef. ext. fin.	168	NA	−572	−603	−606	−1475	−476	−1003
Capital issues	169	NA	0	0	950	0	0	0
+/− in long/med. debt	170	NA	0	0	0	0	0	0
+/− in short debt	171	NA	823	494	53	989	533	1045
+/− in cash balances	172	NA	−251	109	−397	486	−57	−42
Net financ. req./(surp)	173	NA	572	603	606	1475	476	1003
Check: Line 168 + 173 =		NA	0	0	0	0	0	0

Figure 13.4 (*continued*)

Company

		31 Aug 72	31 Aug 73	31 Aug 74	31 Aug 75	31 Aug 76	31 Aug 77	31 Aug 78
Date of balance sheet	1							
Date of auditors' cert.	2	NA	16 Jan 74	16 Jan 75	15 Jan 76	06 Jan 77	12 Jan 78	11 Jan 79
(State if qualified)	3							
Currency (in ……..)	4	1000	1000	1000	1000	1000	1000	1000
Stock (incr.)/decr.	181	NA	−314	−669	−299	−351	−1072	−721
Debtors (incr.)/decr.	182	NA	−343	−534	−220	−934	−598	−165
Creditors incr./(decr.)	183	NA	447	−16	50	272	671	−89
Other variations	184	NA	0	0	0	0	0	0
Work. cap. surp./(req.)	185	NA	−210	−1219	−469	−1013	−999	−975
Profit bef. tax (PBT)	191	349	460	864	1201	814	1225	1101
Plus: Depreciation	192	131	151	529	298	288	389	481
Less: (Taxation)	193	NA	−35	−165	−88	−189	−226	−165
Basic funds flow	194	NA	576	1228	1411	913	1388	1417
Less—Hist. cost depr.	195	−131	−151	−529	−298	−288	−389	−481
—Addit. CCA dep.	196	0	0	0	0	−312	−284	−314
—Cost sales adj.	197	NA	NA	NA	NA	−511	−505	−274
—Monet. Work. cap.	198	NA	NA	NA	NA	0	0	0
Sustain. funds flow	199	NA	NA	NA	NA	−198	210	348

Computerized bank spreadsheet analysis

Figure 13.4 illustrates the first bank's manual spreadsheet in computer print-out form completed for seven years' figures. The rationale behind analysis from such a format, apart from significant reduction in man-hours, is the ease with which it is made possible to determine basic trends in such key areas as profitability, borrowing levels, and the movement of funds.

Forecasting programmes

Figure 13.5 shows a simple forecasting programme based on ten considerations. Basically, the considerations are assumptions analysts take on the movement of interest rates, gross profit margins, net profit margins, changes in terms of trade, external inflation rate, constant sales price growth and net capital expenditure. Assumptions are also made concerning credit periods given and taken, and expected dividend payments.

In part, these views will be formed from a study of the company's past performance, and partly, by reaction to press comment, annual reports, and a range of supplementary data.

In this example, the analyst applied factors he thought might have appertained in 1979. This was a period of high inflation. Accordingly, this is reflected by the figures in the forecast column. The net effect on the balance sheet is a marginal increase in net tangible assets but at the expense of greater borrowing and reduced liquidity. The effect on profitability can be seen with additional interest required by the higher borrowing levels. This, in turn, caused the adverse change in gearing and interest cover.

The impact on funds flow is particularly marked. Note the substantial reduction in working capital requirement from £975,000 to £158,000. This is reflected throughout the company's financial flows but, based on the assumptions used, the company will still have to borrow moneys to fund its dividend payment. After the dividend payment, the external financing requirement will be in the order of £566,000.

Applying current cost figures to the basic funds flow, sustainable funds flow lurches heavily into deficit. This indicates that the company will not be able to repay existing debt from its current ability to generate funds.

This programme is not intended as a predictive model for corporate collapse. It is used simply to suggest further questions and to show probable outcomes of reasoned assumptions. It is also able to highlight trends that require investigation should the bank be approached for additional facilities or if existing facilities merit review.

In this bank's spreadsheets and in others' generally, emphases are placed throughout analysis on growth of turnover, the relationship between turnover and working capital, levels of investment in fixed assets, profitability, and the source and application of funds.

Growth of turnover

The salient questions concerning sales must be:

1. Are sales increasing year by year?
2. If so, are sales increasing over and above inflation rates?
3. If turnover has fallen, what are seen to be the causes?
4. Has the reduction in sales caused adverse effects on profitability?

```
COMPANY

DATE OF BALANCE SHEET      1    31AUG78        FORECAST
DATE OF AUDITORS CERT      2    11JAN79        ::::::
(STATE IF QUALIFIED)       3                   ::::::
CURRENCY (IN .......)      4    1000           ::::::
-----------------------------------------------------------
CASH & BANK                5         170          69.70
QUOTED INVESTMENTS         6          57          57.00
DEBTORS/ACCS/BILLS REC     7        4355        4819.96
    S.TOT.QUICK ASSETS     8     4582.00        4946.66
-----------------------------------------------------------
STOCK-FINISHED GOODS       9        2905        2862.17
     -WORK-IN-PROG        10         674         664.06
     -RAW MATERIALS       11        1576        1552.76
                          12           0           0.00
                          13           0           0.00
OTHERS                    14           0           0.00
    TOT.CURRENT ASSETS    15     9737.00       10025.66
-----------------------------------------------------------
CREDS/ACCS/BILLS PAY      16        2350        2580.93
H.P./LEASING< 1 YEAR      17           0           0.00
BANK/ST.LOANS/ACC.CRS     18        4609        5075.00
CURRENT PORT.LT.DEBT      19           0           0.00
(SECURED DEBT - MEMO)     20           0        ::::::
DUE TO GRP.COMPANIES      21           0           0.00
DUE TO DIRECTORS          22           0           0.00
DIVIDENDS                 23         240         200.00
TAXATION - CURRENT        24         229         -28.57
                          25           0           0.00
                          26           0           0.00
                          27           0           0.00
OTH.CURRENT LIABILS.      28           0           0.00
    TOT.CURRENT LIABS.    29     7428.00        7827.35
-----------------------------------------------------------
LIQ.SURPLUS/(DEFICIT)     30     2309.00        2198.30
-----------------------------------------------------------
QUICK ASSET SURP/(DEF)    31    -2846.00       -2880.69
-----------------------------------------------------------
LAND&BLDGS(NET OF DEP)    32        2011        2235.76
(MARKET VAL,IF KNOWN)     33          NA        ::::::
MAC,PLT,FIX(NET DEP)      34        2072        2072.00
CAPITALISED LEASES        35           0           0.00
INVESTMENT-SUBSIDS        36           0           0.00
          -ASSOCIATES     37         194         194.00
          -OTHERS         38           0           0.00
DUE FROM GROUP COMPS.     39           0           0.00
                          40           0           0.00
OTH.FIXED&TERM ASSETS     41         456         456.00
    TOT.FIX&OTH.ASSETS    42     4733.00        4957.76
-----------------------------------------------------------
FUTURE TAXATION           43           0           0.00
DEFERRED TAXATION         44         318         318.00
H.P./LEASING > 1 YEAR     45           0           0.00
LOANS DUE 1-5 YEARS       46           0           0.00
LOANS DUE > 5 YEARS       47           0           0.00
(SEC.DEBT>1 YEAR-MEMO)    48           0        ::::::
                          49           0           0.00
OTHER TERM LIABILS.       50           0           0.00
    S.TOT.TERM&O.LIABS    51      318.00         318.00
MINORITY INTERESTS        52           0           0.00
    TOT.TERM&OTH.LIABS.   53      318.00         318.00
-----------------------------------------------------------
NET TANG.ASS-SURP/DEF     54     6724.00        6838.06
```

Figure 13.5 Simple forecasting programme based on ten assumptions

```
SHARE CAPITAL-ISSUED      55        1736       1736.00
CAPITAL RESERVES          56         706        706.00
DISTR'ABLE RESERVES       57        4282       4396.05
GOODWILL&INTANGIBLES      58           0          0.00
TREASURY STOCK            59           0          0.00

S'HOLDERS-SURP/(DEF)      60     6724.00       6838.05
CHECK:LINE 54-LINE 60=               0.00          .00

                                              FORECAST
PROF.BEF.INT.& TAX        71        1495       1143.51
ASSOCIATES                72          23          0.00
INVEST.INC&INTEREST       73           5          0.00

PROFIT BEF.INT.PAID       74     1523.00       1143.51
(INTEREST PAID)           75        -422       -629.46

PROFIT BEF.TAX (PBT)      76     1101.00        514.05
(TAXATION)                77        -100       -100.00
(MINORITY INTERESTS)      78           0          0.00
EXTRAORDINARY ITEMS       79        -189          0.00

ATTR.PROF/LOS.AFT.TAX     80      812.00        414.05
(DIVIDENDS)               81        -310       -300.00

RESID.PROFIT/(LOSS)       82      502.00        114.05
ADDIT.CAP&RES.MOVES       83           0           .00
                          84           0          0.00
                          85           0          0.00
                          86           0          0.00

NET VAR.IN SURP/(DEF)     87      502.00        114.05

SALES                    101       19084      20419.88
COST OF GOODS SOLD       102       16118      16979.13
GROSS PROFIT             103     2966.00       3440.75
DEPRECIATION             104         481        575.24
CAPITAL EMPLOYED         105    11651.00      12231.06

INFLATION INDEX          106      257.39        301.15
SALES AT CONST.PRICE     107     7414.43       6780.72
PBT AT CONST.PRICES      108      427.76        170.70

GROSS PROFIT MARGIN      109       15.54         16.85
NET PROFIT MARGIN        110        7.83          5.60
RETURN ON CAP.EMPLOY     111       14.03          9.58

AV.CREDIT GIVEN DAYS     112       81.72         82.00
AV.CREDIT TAKEN DAYS     113       54.22         53.00
STOCK TURNOVER DAYS      114      108.57        110.00
WORK.CAP.TURNOV.TIMES    115        8.10          9.06
CURRENT RATIO            116        1.31          1.28
LIQUID RATIO             117        0.62          0.63

GROSS GEARING   RATIO    118        0.69          0.74
NET GEARING     RATIO    119        0.65          0.72
GEARING         RATIO    120        1.15          1.19
I.COV-HIS.PROF  TIMES    121        3.61          1.82
 - CASH FLOW    TIMES    122       -0.30        ::::::
 - SUST FUNDS   TIMES    123        1.82         -1.04
DIVI COVER(CCA) TIMES    124        0.72            NA
T.DEBT/OP.CASH FL.YRS    125        0.00          0.00
TOT.BOR/SUS.FUNDS YRS    126       13.24         -3.96

CAPITAL EXPENDITURE      131        1400        800.00
```

Figure 13.5 (*Continued*)

CAP.COMMITS-CONTRACT.	132	137	::::::
-AUTH.	133	465	::::::
CONT.LIABS:GUARANTEES	134	0	::::::
:OTHER	135	2241	::::::
LEASING OBLIGATIONS	136	0	::::::
DIRECTORS REMUN.	137	174	::::::

			FORECAST
PROFIT BEF.INT.PAID	151	1523.00	1143.51
DEPRECIATION	152	481.00	575.24
NOT INVOLV.FUND MOVE	153	-20	0.00
WORK.CAP.VARIATION	154	-975.00	-158.03
OP.CASH BEF.INT,TAX	155	1009.00	1560.73
(INTEREST PAID)	156	-422.00	-629.46
(TAX PAID)/TAX REFUN.	157	-165	-357.57
OPERATING CASH FLOW	158	422.00	573.70
DISPOS.FIXED ASSETS	159	351	0.00
(CAPITAL EXPENDITURE)	160	-1400.00	-800.00
EXTRAORDINARY ITEMS	161	0	0.00
MISCELLANEOUS ITEMS	162	0	0.00
CASH AVAIL.FOR DIVIS	163	-627.00	-226.30
(DIVIDENDS PAID)	164	-278	-340.00
CASH AVAIL.FOR INVES.	165	-905.00	-566.30
INVESTMENTS	166	-111	0.00
ACQUISITIONS	167	13	0.00
CASH +/- BEF.EXT.FIN.	168	-1003.00	-566.30
CAPITAL ISSUES	169	0	0.00
+/- IN LONG/MED.DEBT	170	0	0.00
+/- IN SHORT DEBT	171	1045	466.00
+/- IN CASH BALANCES	172	-42	100.30
NET FINANC REQ/(SURP)	173	1003.00	566.30
CHECK:LINE 168 + 173=		0.00	.00
STOCK (INCR)/DECR	181	-721	76.00
DEBTORS (INCR)/DECR	182	-165	-464.96
CREDITORS INCR/(DECR)	183	-89	230.93
OTHER VARIATIONS	184	0	0.00
WORK.CAP.SURP/(REQ)	185	-975.00	-158.03
PROFIT BEF.TAX (PBT)	191	1101.00	514.05
PLUS: DEPRECIATION	192	481.00	575.24
LESS: (TAXATION)	193	-165.00	-357.57
BASIC FUNDS FLOW	194	1417.00	731.73
LESS-HIST COST DEPR.	195	-481.00	-575.24
-ADDIT.CCA DEP.	196	-314	-375.52
-COST SALES ADJ.	197	-274	0.00
-MONET.WORK.CAP.	198	0	-1063.30
SUSTAIN.FUNDS FLOW	199	348.00	-1282.35

Figure 13.5 (*Concluded*)

Relationship between turnover and working capital

Analysts will wish to see:

1. Whether increases in sales are adversely affecting liquidity.
2. How efficiently working capital is being used.
3. If the relationship caused radical changes in credit periods given and taken. If so, are these changes necessarily adverse?

Levels of investment in fixed assets

Fixed assets tie up cash. They are also necessary to continuation (and normally, the expansion) of the business. Analysts, therefore, want to question:

1. How the company has financed its fixed assets.
2. Whether any changes in fixed assets financing are visible, e.g. sales and leaseback.
3. Unusual movements in fixed assets replacement expenditure.
4. How efficiently is the company using its fixed assets?
5. The inflation-adjusted replacement value of fixed assets.
6. Whether the company may be diversifying into areas requiring lower levels of fixed asset investment.
7. The contribution made by depreciation to gross cashflow, e.g. is depreciation greater than profit after taxation? If so, ought fixed assets to be financed differently to tie up less cash?

Profitability

Analysts will want to examine the effects of growth of turnover on profitability. In turn, has greater profitability been achieved at the expense of liquidity? What measures of profit are being considered? Is an all-inclusive or a current operating concept of profit being considered? Is profit being achieved at the greater borrowing costs? Have poor investment decisions or a long-term investment decision taken undue time to produce profits? If profitability varies in an apparently random fashion, analysts will want to ask why.

Source and application of funds

For bank purposes, the way in which a company generates and utilizes its funds is highly significant. Emphasis on funds flow statements will highlight a company's net financing requirement. Is this being funded by increases in short-term debt? The composition of whatever debt is funding the requirement is important. Is the correct form of debt being used for funding?

Sources

Barclays Bank PLC Management Training Centre, Interviews, general information, documentation.
Clarke, T., and Vincent, W., Bank Risk Classification Criteria.
Corns, M. C., *The Practical Operations and Management of a Bank*, 2nd edn, Bankers' Publishing Co, Boston, Mass., USA, 1968, Chapters XXIV, XXV.
Holmes, G., and Sugden, A., *Interpreting Company Reports and Accounts*, Woodhead-Faulkner, Cambridge, 1983, pp. 81, 175.

14

THE PERFECT CREDIT ANALYSIS

There is, of course, no such thing as the perfect credit analysis. This is true for the following reasons:

(a) Analyses necessarily vary in all respects with different types of credit applications. In this respect, credit analysis may be compared with bespoke tailoring in which every garment is made for one and only one customer. Rarely, then, will one man's suit be ideal for another.
(b) Credit analysis is a comparatively new discipline. Accordingly, more effective assessment routines are continually being developed. What we may, therefore, view as sophisticated today, may well be seen as crude and outmoded tomorrow.
(c) In large part due to the protracted world recessionary climate and because of the relatively slow economic recovery in most developed countries, the underlying interpretation of credit is shifting slowly. It is moving from 'borrowers' expecting credit to lenders looking more carefully at credit propositions. Accordingly, we are seeing a more urgent demand for good quality credit information, operation and management, and analytical assessment methods.
(d) Despite item c, credit analysis has previously been carried out largely by staff anxious to learn what they have been led to believe is only a rudimentary skill in order to progress into more supposedly glamorous fields, e.g. marketing or financial controllership. Credit analysis at banks has rarely attracted and kept first-rate and wide-ranging minds as these have tended until lately to be siphoned off by the marketing and corporate finance functions particularly.

In banks and in commercial credit departments, analysts are not usually professionally trained and qualified apart from in-house experience. Whilst first-hand training and line experience should not in any sense be minimized, credit analysis as a discipline has not yet had the formal and planned benefits of a curriculum of study and examination offered by a professionl body. Whether or not one may like it, formal courses of study both shape and sharpen the mind.

As credit analysis finds itself in orientation between accounting, banking, commerce, computer science, statistics, and treasury functions, the establishment of a professional examining and regulatory body appears difficult.

A distinction seems proper between credit analysis and financial analysis; credit analysis being concerned with particular applications over particular periods for particular monetary exposures; whereas financial analysis may include the analysis of credit but also includes a considerably wider range of concrete as well as speculative applications.

Of the previous list, perhaps the last two items, c and d, are the most interesting. The gradual shift away from more or less automatic trade credit facilities to more rigorous credit assessment and control must be perceived as something of a compensating mechanism for the virtual credit explosion we have seen over the last decade.

As the accountancy profession grew to its present pre-eminence on the back of complicated taxation legislation (and not from the commercial public's sudden appreciation of bookkeeping and the utility of company accounts), so is the credit management profession growing with the importance of trade credit to the conduct of all business. Credit analysis is normally seen as a function of general credit management in companies, and as a back-up procedure for marketing of financial products in banks.

We would suggest that both views of credit analysis are dangerously misconceived. As banks come to conventional lending business and new forms of financing more with their minds and less with their balance sheets, the relegation of credit analysis as a poor relation of marketing will be automatically corrected. The largest money market banks have, arguably, done more bad business than smaller banks. Certainly, the poor quality South American loans, as a case in point, are conspicuous both for size and for remoteness of collectability. In many cases, the lenders have been forced to extend and augment the loans. In few cases have the banks made sensible provisions reflecting the essential hopelessness of these deals on their books.

The awarding of greater importance to credit analysis in the banking sector thus stems from regulatory authorities and central banks who perceive from a slightly more detached viewpoint the increasing fragility and interdependence of international banking. Also, despite the obvious unwillingness of some major banks to take the necessary write-offs, the interbank market cannot help perceiving many such banks as poorer credit risks than before. Tighter terms for interbank business will ultimately have an adverse knock-on effect on all banks' balance sheets.

As banking margins grow finer and as much new off-balance-sheet business has already been deemed as unprofitable by the regulatory authorities in several key countries (UK, USA, and Switzerland), conventional and new forms of business will necessarily be 'costed' with more care. Credit analysis examines chiefly the applications themselves. Are they self-liquidating? More attention, however, will also have to be paid to how well credit propositions will fit into banks' overall portfolios. These considerations, of course, will ultimately need to be judged against banks' capital requirements and liquidity levels.

As far as credit analysis being perceived as a mere function of commercial credit management, that view must change as well for the following reasons:

(a) The legal position covering recovery of goods in the event of non-payment/receivership/liquidation is as yet unsettled. Retention of title increasingly bedevils the granting of trade credit, and no speedy solutions appear to be in sight.
(b) Volatility in the value of money. The irrational and highly erratic fluctuations in the comparative value of money inclines companies toward shorter credit terms in order to lessen the risk of uncollected cash being devalued. The haphazard movements of the money and capital markets also make the prospect of eventual partial recovery of money in certain legal situations, e.g. liquidations and receiverships, even more

worrisome than before. In other words, during the length of time needed to settle with unsecured creditors in these situations, the value of any eventual payments will very possibly be further eroded.

(c) Credit volume for most companies has increased dramatically over the last ten years. In other words, more credit sales and larger ones are taking place. This development is merely in line with the general credit expansion already noted. With higher amounts of money outstanding, companies will have to pay greater attention not only to the initial assessment of credit propositions, but also, to the conduct of credit sale accounts. This entails greater expenditure in man-hours and technology. The development of better monitoring systems alone has superseded any developments in the areas of collection, the financing of foreign trade, or the bringing together of credit management as a cohesive discipline in the eyes of the commercial public.

Briefly, the real technological strides in credit management are being made in assessment and monitoring systems. Both are the concerns of credit analysis.

(d) While company failures due to mismanagement and insolvency fluctuate, UK corporate failures have been running at record levels over the last three years.

These collapses have made the commercial public more aware of the fragility of an overblown credit expansion grounded on a shaky economic base. Paradoxically, credit management as a profession has not suffered loss of prestige from those monetary losses stemming from buyer failures. Pragmatically, greater attention has been paid to gearing-up credit management. The gearing-up has centred around improving credit assessment in the more progressive companies and less on sharper collections.

(e) As part and parcel of improving credit assessment and risk monitoring, progressive companies have accorded new importance to the utility of accounting data and analytical methods. The most exciting developments in methodology have followed on from Altman's insolvency prediction work in 1968, and include:
  (i) Other insolvency forecasting methods
  (ii) Treasury management risk monitoring
  (iii) Financial models including what if-type models
  (iv) Sensitivity analyses and models
  (v) Statistical-based computational routines and forecasting
  (vi) Assessment focus away from static to dynamic accounting analyses
  (vii) Current development of mega-models based on expert systems

Item e (ii) is beyond the purview of this book. The other items have already been discussed at some length. Item e (vii), however, bears comment. Earlier, we touched on expert systems in considering the development of multi-purpose financial and economic assessment models.

Expert systems

Previously, we noted that the purpose of an expert system is to capture the most relevant skills needed for problem solving, reaching conclusions, making judgements, answering questions, and giving advice, in one computer programme that can be operated by a non-expert. Where dependence upon human minds and time—particularly in mechanical or routine applications—can be reduced, but reproduced in a more accurate, more readily accessible, and more cost-efficient manner, the potentialities are very great.

In the case of credit analysis, the potentials of such expert assessment systems are striking. These include:

1. Reduction of credit risk
2. Reduction of credit assessment overheads including professional staff
3. Reduction of time in the credit assessment process
4. Time and ability to develop business more fully as potential business can be more readily assessed
5. Fairer credit opinions and sanctions

In all these, credit analysis moves closer as a business development function and further from its traditional role as the arch-inhibitor of aggressive business. The overall shift from an inhibitive discipline to a developmental function is useful for all concerned.

Expert systems are not intended to replace human beings. They are, however, intended to replace some human experts. Such systems merely make expert knowledge available to non-experts, allowing them to arrive at solutions to problems at much quicker rates and thus, far higher volumes, than any expert. In basic conception, the expert system is simplicity itself. It provides the same kind of service on computer that specialist books provide the expert and other practitioners. In this way, logarithms are codified in reference books. No one is expected to calculate individual logs although a better appreciation of their function can be gained by learning the principles of their calculation at some stage. Likewise, what, for the numerate, is the sense of calculating the many trends and percentage increases and decreases needed for good credit analyses if these can be done with perfect accuracy and in lightning time by computer?

The expert system structuring a credit assessment mega-model would, accordingly, encapsulate the specialist skills of a statistician, a mathematician, and an accountant, relating these skills to make them relevant to credit managers in such a way that the model can:

1. Set out in significant form historical data and interpret it.
2. Select and interpret macro- and microeconomic information having a bearing on the particular credit application and subject.
3. Produce forecasts according to accepted methods taking into account items 1 and 2 along with supplementary data inputs, e.g. references or assessments of management capability.
4. Offer all the previous items as justifications for giving users synoptic interpretations and:
5. Give intelligent advice contingent on the interpretations.

It has been suggested by R. Mathieson, a computer audit partner in KMG Thomson McLintock, Edinburgh, that the following characteristics can be particularly suitable for expert systems:

1. A narrow but deep domain—or an area well defined in scope but where a very broad base of knowledge is not needed. Mathieson suggests that if too broad a knowledge base is required, problems are more likely to result. In that event, he recommends the building of two small systems rather than one large one. He mentions that a small system is likely to operate on about 50 'rules'.
2. Where there are varied problems to be solved—he argues that a principal strength of an expert system is its ability to react to different problem conditions.

3. Tasks which nearly always receive the same answer logically from a human expert. This logical solution can be used by the expert system as a corroborative mechanism.
4. Tasks requiring objectivity and systems accepting many inputs with few outputs.
5. Tasks where humans might be subject to cognitive overload.
6. The readiness of potential users of such systems.

Credit analysis presents a different problem in every application. Credit analysis tends wherever possible to express findings in quantities and contrasting quantities, e.g. ratios. Exposures against calculated quantities present certain logical possibilities as 'answers'. The basis of credit analysis is the striving after objectivity based on many inputs and one credit opinion (the output). Without doubt, a computer system can replace all of the computational routines and process extraneous data more quickly and more holistically than any human being. It cannot, however, invent those routines nor originate the data on which they will be operated. Finally, the development of credit analysis since Altman has tended toward expert, holistic assessment methods, beginning with hybrid ratios, to multiple-ratio formulas, and carrying on to financial models of varying sophistication. The emergence of credit analysis as the axis and no longer the adjunct of credit management both in banks and in companies further leads the discipline to the creation of expert systems. The most useful expert systems are likely to be built by companies with existing analytical expertise and specialist information sources rather than by purely large database companies. Because of cost constraints, the most viable expert systems will most likely be designed to run on microcomputers. Software will need to be IBM-compatible if these systems are to become marketable. A major financial company is currently developing a mega-model based on several expert systems. The project, however, is to remain within the company for its own assessment purposes.

The expert system should incorporate the nearest approximation to the 'perfect credit analysis'. Both as an overview of previous information in this writing and as a summary of what data might best be included in the knowledge base of an expert assessment system, let us list the ingredients of an ideal analysis.

Collected data

1. Comparative registered/statutory information, e.g. present and past directors/directors' management/other relevant histories. Where no changes have occurred, accept latest data.
   Registered data should include:
   (a) Correct style
   (b) Correct address
   (c) Registered indebtedness
   (d) Parent and/or ultimate company
   (e) Registered office.
   This body of data can be input and printed out in the most suitable format for the finished credit analysis.
2. Comparative accounting statements' abstracts for the computer program and hard-copy statements in full by way of an attachment to the finished analysis.
3. Comparative management accounting statements' abstracts for the computer and hard-copy statements in full as an update and appendix to the finished analysis.

4. The same for interim figures issued by public companies in abstract and hard-copy by way of update.
5. The quantification of extraneous data for the computer program:
    (a) Bank and trade references scored numerically.
    (b) Directors' or Chairman's Report scored numerically.
    (c) Any management assessment from personal interviews/meetings scored numerically.
    (d) Industrial sector scored numerically with regard to:
        (i) Incidence of corporate collapse due to insolvency.
        (ii) Historical and forecast economic prospects, notably
            productivity
            demand
    (e) Industrial sector averages.
    (f) External agency ratings, e.g. QuiScore or Dun & Bradstreet rating.
    (g) Assessment of premises/overheads/working conditions numerically scored.
    (h) Age of the company numerically scored.
6. Auditors' report numerically scored

Spread data

1. Accounting data (comparative: audited, interim, management, debenture figures, budgets, projections) spread to highlight:
    (a) Key quantities, e.g. working capital or profit before taxation
    (b) Key quantities not immediately visible from hard-copies or abstracts:
        (i) Gross cashflow
        (ii) Priority debt
        (iii) Off-balance-sheet exposures
        (iv) Total liabilities
        (v) Normalized working capital
        (vi) Sustainable cashflow
        (vii) Capital employed
        (viii) Normalized working worth
        (ix) Tangible net worth
        (x) Monetary lag
        (xi) Averaged free capital.
    (c) Leading performance indicators from accounts and extraneous data, highlighting:
        (i) Financial indices, e.g. ratios
        (ii) Operational indices, e.g. ratios and quantities, e.g. debt-turn or stock turnover.
    (d) Comfort margins for the specific exposure against key flows and quantities.

Model data

1. Collected and Spreadsheet data transferred in whole or in part as required for the operation of financial synoptic models which should optimally include holistic assessment of:

(a) Liquidity
(b) Capital adequacy
(c) Debt-service ability
(d) Profitability
(e) Historical and forecast debt-cover
(f) Risk description for particular exposure/transaction
(g) Insolvency risk/historical and predictive:
   As discussed before, solvency is predicated on the holistic treatment of items (a), (b), (c) and (d). One model may therefore be used provided that the final print-out gives single and several model workings in addition to simultaneous or synoptic findings.
(h) Synopsis of extraneous data not included in the previous models but treated herewith and scored
(i) Previous model data treated holistically with the credit-grantor's key capital and liquidity requirements and numerically scored.

Secondary and comparative spread data

1. Model findings compared with accounting data for corroboration/variance.
2. Model findings compared with holistically treated extraneous scored data for corroboration/variance/further illustration.
3. Trend spreads for:
   (a) Historical accounting data
   (b) Forecast accounting quantities
   (c) Model scores and constituent workings
   (d) Economic indicators for the sector.

Print-out of leading assumptions

Print-out of report abstract including model findings

Print-out of credit opinion

(The operation of the computer program ends here.)

Attachments to the computer report for maximum utility

1. Provisions for updating the report and note of recommended frequency.
2. Note of security mechanism recommended if necessary.
3. If a bank credit application, the following attachments, when relevant, should be added:
   (a) Debt priority schedule differentiating between secured and unsecured debt separated between subsidiary companies and parent. Any debt ranking prior to the proposed debt must be noted
   (b) In cases where subordinated debt is in question, the type of subordination together with other provisions including acceleration should be set out

(c) Indenture review, i.e. a statement of the comfort or safety margin on ratio-based covenants, interim loans, and any perceptions that may affect the decision to grant or to extend the credit
(d) Legal commitments: It is essential that a complete synopsis of proposed terms, conditions, and covenants be included. Hale states that the credit analysis proper should contain a review of the salient controlling financial covenants as well as an evaluation of the effectiveness of the covenants in relation to past performance (if an existing credit) and/or projected performance.

Perfection, whether in credit analysis or elsewhere, carries the implicit notion of fullness or completeness. The so-called perfect credit analysis would, therefore, seem to have that type of completeness normally unseen in commercial credit reporting. Completeness on this scale— and completeness in every case over an almost infinite number of applications— can only be *approximated* with the help of computers. Bank credit analysis, if properly done, tends necessarily to be long and detailed. These analyses include not only registered and statutory data (and any necessary comments on it), but accounts analysis, interpretation, and the same for any supplementary financial documents forming material parts of the particular application. Additionally, sectoral information is brought to bear and contrasted with findings from the financial statements' analyses. An opinion with recommendations is, of course, required, followed by often voluminous legal and banking documentation. Banks, as well as commercial companies, must be able to respond quickly to lending propositions. It is, therefore, evident that the routine computational work and the complicated synthesizing of these masses of data (often disparate) can be best performed electronically. Computerizing many of these functions in no way diminishes accuracy. Rather, it can enhance accuracy provided that inputs come from informed and experienced staff working off the latest and best possible data.

For trade credit purposes, on the other hand, the potential benefits of computerized analysis—and in particular, expert systems—are possibly less superficially attractive. This may be for development cost reasons as well as from a deep and widespread lack of understanding about the scope, worth, and purpose of credit analysis.

In general, both banks and companies have not yet devoted much attention to the development of better credit analytical systems, expert or other. This, as we mentioned before, is now changing as the urgent need for better analysis becomes increasingly manifest.

The importance of dimensionality in credit analysis

Part of the completeness understood by the phrase 'perfect credit analysis' is dimensionality—or the examination of main financial flows from a variety of positions, times, and requirements. Again, few commercially available credit reports or so-called analyses provide such depth. Synoptic analytical methods and notably some financial models, e.g. Taffler's, Bathory's or Altman's, attempt multi-dimensional views. These attempts succeed, in the main, to a higher degree than anything before. None the less, as encapsulations of companies' total financial condition and that condition related directly to specific exposures, they err on the side of being too summary. In other words, not enough factors are being taken into account. In fairness to those model-builders mentioned, new credit exposures were not in question. Only one outcome, or probable outcome, of financial condition was being assessed—solvency.

But as these models show us, solvency as well as its constituent 'conditions' such as liquidity or debt-service ability are interconnected and interdependent. At this remove, such a statement appears self-evident, though within recent memory, such a thesis was more of a vague apprehension than a positive assertion. The models cited above are, in point of detail, very crude. Detail, its correlation, and interpretation are the fundamentals of credit analysis. The development of more detailed, dimensional models and their synthesis into an expert system that drives the so-called mega-model is the next stage of credit analysis.

Whilst data has long been collected, and in many establishments, very thoroughly, it has not generally been synthesized either logically, quantitatively, or truly informatively. This is not due to want of technical skill, but rather, to what Mathieson termed 'cognitive overload'. Just as true synopsis of a set of financial accounts cannot and has not taken place in any significant sense in the human mind (although we may know *how* to do it), it would be nonsense to argue that the human mind unaided by synthesizing weapons could 'process' and significantly evaluate the total data inherent in a normal credit analysis. All the available data may be considered and evaluated in due course and painstakingly, but rarely in the ordinary course of business, would this be quick enough. For these reasons, credit managers have, by and large, contented themselves with ordering 'status reports' of normally indifferent to appalling quality. The business of data collection and synthesis is, therefore, done for them. It is unfortunate that 'status reports' have come to be confused with analyses. They are generally nothing of the sort. Given that the data amassed is not antique, where is the dimensionality in an 'analysis' of the following kind?

	1985	1984
Current ratio:	1.5	1.3
Prime ratio:	23%	25%
Acid-test ratio:	0.9	0.8
Gearing ratio:	61%	57%

This is the sort of collection of supposed analytical indicators found in such reports. (a) The list is too brief. (b) Significant trend cannot be seen over two years only. In the case of a new or two-year-old company, there *is* no significant annual trend in the real meaning of the term. (c) And most importantly, there is no completeness in any resulting judgement made on liquidity, profitability, debt-equity mix, or any other significant corporate condition.

In the fictitious example above, it is not at all clear what the current ratio is intended to measure. Is it liquidity? Is it solvency? Is it trading balance? It is included, one must suppose, merely because credit managers like to see it computed. If it is intended to measure trading balance, i.e. the relationship between current assets and current liabilities as being the heart of the balance sheet and the 'outcome' of the profit and loss account, it provides only the crudest schematic representation. If it is to be used to indicate how the one lot stands in respect of the other lot, further indicators of trading balance are required to give the full picture. These might include debt-turn, stock turnover, monetary lag, acid-test, working capital, normalized working capital, and even the much broader picture given by totals generated from operations over total liabilities.

From this, it is clear that in analysis, some overlap of measurement devices will be common. The acid-test ratio can and is generally used to measure liquidity. But then liquidity is a function of trading balance.

Similarly, profitability should be measured from various angles. In the example, it is measured only by the prime ratio. The same lack of dimension applies to gearing.

In the example it is measured only once, and then in an unspecified way. The credit analysis worthy of its name will specify (when speaking to non-financial readers) exactly what the ratios and other performance indicators are supposed to be measuring. The resulting measurements themselves will be interpreted possibly in light of sectoral averages, trend, or forecasts. In this sense, 'simple' concepts such as liquidity will be measured using several devices. For instance:

Acid-test ratio
Current ratio
Working capital
Normalized working capital
Debt-turn
Stock turnover
Trade creditors' turnover
Monetary lag
Working capital/total assets
Normalized working capital/total assets
Working capital/current assets
Normalized working capital/total assets
Averaged free capital
Gross cashflow less current debt
Cash balances/current assets
Debt-cover
Exposure comfort margins
Forecast debt-cover
Totals generated from operations/total borrowings
Liquid assets/total assets
Sustainable cashflow
Sustainable cashflow/priority debt

The physical computation of such a collection of indicators would be exhausting. Some of them, in any case, may be unnecessary in particular cases. But assuming for a moment that to give one the most complete picture of a company's liquidity all should be calculated, we are still left with the problem of relating one to the other and forming a coherent and all-inclusive judgement based on the whole. In our opinion, this cannot be done by the human mind. The problem is cognitive overload. The computer can accomplish such a synthesis. The program needed for the synthesis is merely a large financial model that relates, rerelates, and interrelates the data, sums, and statistically 'interprets' the final 'score'. Whilst the program can be constructed by the human mind, it is absurd to expect human minds to *perform* the cognitive functions with sufficient accuracy and speed to make analysis the commercial tool it should be.

The dependence of credit analysis on good accounting

The heart of credit analysis is and will remain companies' accounting statements. As we commented earlier, good accounts must be synonymous with full accounts. Full, in this sense, understands accounting statements in which all key quantities or accounting numbers are disclosed. A set of accounts which does not disclose sales, for instance, is crippled at the outset. Truly accurate and informative credit analysis cannot be done off such statements. Full accounts presuppose full notes to the accounts in which all material information is disclosed, including off-balance-sheet exposures of all kinds. The current modifications allowed 'small companies' in accounts to be filed for public inspection must, therefore, be regarded by analysts as baneful. Often, they give rise to unnecessary and counterproductive suspicion on the part of readers. These readers are, of course, credit analysts and the credit-grantors who employ them.

Good accounting, for our purposes, also implies common-sense treatment of items or events that may be innovative, rare, contingent, and complex. Like credit analysis, final accounts must to some degree summarize as well as itemize. In this way, liabilities, whether on the face of the balance sheet or off it, are still liabilities. They should therefore be shown clearly. It goes without saying that off-balance-sheet liabilities, e.g. contingent liabilities and guarantees, should be quantified. Unquantified liabilities of this kind do more harm than good, particularly in the case of cross-guarantees.

Depreciation should be shown clearly in the accounts. It can appear either in the profit and loss account, balance sheet, funds flow statement, or in the notes. Modified accounts give no figure for depreciation. Our earlier suggestions for calculating backward to approximate depreciation are, therefore, only stop-gaps.

Stock should be noted according to class: Finished goods, goods for resale, raw materials, consumables, and so forth. Modified and many 'full' accounts do not currently give such breakdowns. They are necessary in measuring liquidity among other indicators.

Profit and loss accounts should be detailed. In particular, direct costs of sales should follow turnover; and indirect costs (establishment expenses) should follow gross profit. Extraordinary items and asset disposals should be posted separately as should interest account and any earnings not in the ordinary course of the company's business.

Especially in the case of large exposures, applicants' reluctance or inability to provide up-to-date audited full accounts should result in an immediate rejection of the application. As noted before, banks are better placed to demand such up-to-date information than grantors of trade credit. With hope, however, grantors of trade credit facilities will begin to demand best quality data as the importance of credit analysis for effective risk assessment is brought home to them.

The need for disclosure

The best quality credit analysis has traditionally been the preserve of banks as banking companies were locked into client relationships, business lending was more important as an external financing mechanism than it is presently, and also, because banks tended to have greater data collection facilities and sources than commercial companies. Finally, credit analysis originated as a banking discipline and was always discrete from financial reporting.

Commercial paper, securitized debt, factoring, invoice-discounting, collateralized bonding, trade creditor financing have all lessened the pre-eminence of straight commercial lending. The re-establishment of commercial lending as we have known it is not in sight. The banks themselves are rearranging their services in order to enter more profitable areas in financial services. The faults lie not in some inherent weakness of conventional loans but in the stodginess, short-sightedness, and Byzantine quality of so many banks. Borrowers are turning elsewhere for simpler, quicker, and cheaper facilities.

Credit analysis is the paramount weapon in assessing the viability of a loan. In recent years, credit analysis has been offered by several companies to the general commercial public with good effect. But the work is by no means complete. Just as banks require full disclosure of all information material to a credit application, good credit analysis requires that seekers after trade credit make full disclosures on the same lines. As commercial lending grows less and less important in company financing, the requirement for full disclosure will, in a significant sense, be transferred to the corporate credit sector. The lead in insisting upon full disclosures, accounting and other, will come both from credit managers and from credit analysts (whether internal or agency) as analysts become more visible in commerce.

Some amount of disclosure will be made unwittingly by subject companies when analysts carry out field-work and periodic review visits. Disclosures will be made during the course of meetings and interviews. Credit managers as well as analysts are tending to be more active in their contact with customers as the general credit function becomes more closely linked with marketing and sales.

The better observed the convention of fuller disclosures becomes, the less effective and more obsolete many databases will become when they rely on public sources for their inputs.

Summary

The perfect credit analysis will be complete in itself and synoptic. The information that forms it will be full and up to date. The analysis will be multi-dimensional and will treat a range of historic data as well as extrapolations and forecasts following from audited fact.

The analytical content will necessarily be ample, but the synthesis will be short.

The perfect credit analysis will assign numerical values or weights to non-numerical data, such as principal trading activities, in order to include extraneous but important information in quantified analytical routines and final judgements.

Spreading of data will present not merely restatements of accounting numbers but computations of non-immediately visible quantities, e.g. cashflows. Because spreading will be largely computer-aided, analysis of many more years' worth of figures will be carried out.

Holistic or synoptic analysis will be the keynote of the perfect credit analysis. The ideal analysis will provide data for a nest of models which will, in turn, power a mega-model. It is this last that will synthesize the whole, bringing its various parts into a simultaneous and comprehensive summary.

The computer programs needed to drive such models must be flexible and easy to update—especially where economic and sectoral data are concerned.

And what of the famous 'gut feeling' or much touted 'instinct' that appears to be the prerogative of bankers and credit managers? Of course, expert systems and mega-models will vary. Some will be designed to print out an opinion derived from their synopsis of data. Others will stop short of the opinion and give only a summary. In the latter event, gut feeling and instinct will have more to go on than vague apprehensions or incomplete understanding of facts. In these cases, gut feeling should be better informed and less at variance with the real world.

Of all the possible caveats that may apply to the construction and operation of such credit analysis, arguably the most important is that in any analysis, the quality and recency of the financial accounting statements is paramount. No model will work miracles with bad data or incomplete data. No model will train its operators in the meaning and reading of accounting statements. No model will go out and gather the data in the first place. In other words, the best credit analyses will be done by the best people. The computer only synthesizes and speeds up the process.

In these ways, the perfect credit analysis has yet to be performed by a totally complementary combination of machine and human mind.

Sources

Marsh, P., 'How Computers Tap Human Knowledge', *Financial Times*, 1 February 1985.
Mathieson, R., 'Tomorrow's Accountant—Expert Aided?', *The Accountant's Magazine*, April 1986, Vol. 90, no. 957, pp. 22–24.

BIBLIOGRAPHY

Argenti, J., *Corporate Collapse—The Cause and Symptoms*, McGraw-Hill, New York, 1976.
Bank of England, *The Management of Banks' Off-Balance Sheet Exposures: A Supervisory Perspective*, Committee on Banking Regulations and Supervisory Practices, Basle, 1986.
Bathory, A., 'Companies' House—Falling Down?', *Credit Management*, Institute of Credit Management, Vol. 34, mid-August 1983.
Bathory, A., 'Credit Analysis: Sharpening the Blunt Sword', Address and Paper presented to The London International Corporate Finance Conference, 1985.
Bathory, A., 'Departure from Fact: The Restatement of Accounting Numbers in Standard Credit Analysis', *Credit Management*, Institute of Credit Management, mid-October, 1984.
Bathory, A., 'Idiocy in High Places/The Department of Trade and Industry's Proposals for the Abolition or Further Modification of Accounting and Audit Requirements for Small firms—A Consultative Document', *Credit Management*, Institute of Credit Management, August 1985.
Bathory, A., 'New Invoice-Discounting for Credit Management', *Credit Management*, Institute of Credit Management, December 1982.
Bathory, A., 'Predicting Corporate Collapse: Credit Analysis in the Determination and Forecasting of Insolvent Companies', *Financial Times Business Information*, 1984.
Bierman, H. J., 'Measuring Financial Liquidity', *Accounting Review*, October 1960, pp. 628–632.
Clark, M., 'Recent Developments in Insolvency, Address to the National Conference of the Institute of Credit Management', *Credit Management*, May 1986, p. 31.
Clarke, T., and W. Vincent, 'The quality of the Clearers', *United Kingdom Research Series*, Scrimgeour Vickers, London, April 1986.
Cohen, K. J., and F. S. Hammer (eds), *Analytical Methods in Banking*, Irwin, Homewood, Ill., 1966, Chapter 6, pp. 124–127.
Coleshaw, J., 'A Simple Approach to Balance Sheet Rating', *Credit Management*, mid-June 1984, pp. 21–23.
Corns, M. C., *The Practical Operations and Management of a Bank*, 2nd edn, Bankers' Publishing Company, Boston, Mass., 1968, Chapters XXIV, XXV.
Curzon, F. R. P., *The Interpretation of Debenture Statistics: A Guide for Managers*, privately printed, 1983.
Deloitte, Haskins and Sells, *Raising Venture Capital*, Deloitte Haskins and Sells, UK, December 1983.
Deloitte, Haskins and Sells, *Taxation in Europe*, Oyez, London, December 1980.
Doyle, E. P., *Practice of Banking*, 2nd edn, Macdonald & Evans, London, 1972.
Dungan, N. W. F-R. 'Corporate Applications for Euronote Facilities', Address and Paper presented to The London International Corporate Finance Conference, 1985.
Edwards, H., *Export Credit, The Effective and Profitable Management of Export Credit and Finance*, Shaws Linton, Wantage, 1980.

Euromoney, 'Syndicated Loans/Data Supplied by the Euromoney Capital Markets Guide/Loans Recently Signed', October 1985, pp. 404, 410.
Fadel, H., and J. M. Parkinson, 'Liquidity Evaluation by Means of Ratio Analysis', *Accounting and Business Research*, Vol. 8, no. 30, Spring 1978.
Finanz, A. G., Zurich, 'Forfaiting', *Credit Suisse Special Publications*, Vol. 47, II, February 1982.
Hale, R. H., *Credit Analysis—A Complete Guide*, Wiley, New York, 1983.
Holmes, G., and A. Sugden, *Interpreting Company Reports and Accounts*, 2nd and 3rd edns, Woodhead-Faulkner, Cambridge, 1983 and 1986.
Horrigan, J. O., 'A Short History of Financial Ratio Analysis', *Accounting Review*, April 1968.
Hsu, G. T. K., 'Assessing the Risks to Swap Users', *Euromoney, Supplement*, January 1986. Innovation in the International Capital Markets, pp. 106–107.
Hughes, M., 'Banking Supervision' (White Paper on Banking Supervision), *The Accountant's Magazine*, March 1986, Vol. 90, no. 956, pp. 29–30.
ICC Business Ratios, *Industrial Performance Analysis (a Financial Analysis of UK Industry and Commerce)*, 8th edn, ICC Information Group, London, 1983.
ICFC (Industrial and Commercial Finance Corporation), 'Profit and Cash Flow Forecasting', *Management Series*, undated.
Institute of Chartered Accountants of Scotland, *Accounting for Deferred Tax, Summary and Guide to SSAP 15*, revised May 1985.
Marsh, P., 'How Computers Tap Human Knowledge', *Financial Times*, 1 February 1985.
Mathieson, R., 'Tomorrow's Accountant—Expert Aided?', *The Accountant's Magazine*, April 1986, Vol. 90, no. 957, pp. 22–24.
De Mesquita, A. G., *Questions and Answers/Business Mathematics and Statistics*, Longman Group, London, 1978.
Monsanto PLC, *Reports and Accounts*, 1980–1984.
Montagnon, P., 'Bank May Set Rules for Off-Balance Sheet Risks', *Financial Times*, 21 March 1986.
Montagnon, P., 'Bankers Agree on Hidden Risk Guidelines', *Financial Times*, 17 March 1986.
Montagnon, P., 'Off-Balance Sheet Risk', International Capital Markets Supplement, *Financial Times*, 17 March 1986, p. 8.
Myers, H., and E. W. Forgy, 'Development of Numerical Credit Evaluation Systems', *Journal of American Statistical Association*, Vol. 50, September 1963, pp. 797–806.
Phillips Petroleum Company Europe-Africa, 'Performance' (*Newspaper* for employees of Phillips Petroleum in Europe and Africa), no. 75, January 1986, p. 3.
Robinson, R. I., *The Management of Bank Funds*, 2nd edn, McGraw-Hill, New York, 1962.
Shock, J., *Capital Allowances*, Oyez, London, 1981, pp. 37–96 (general summary of provisions).
Smith, G., 'Added Value—The Key to Profitability', *Accountancy*, August 1983, pp. 56–58.
Smith, G., 'Analysing Financial Balance', *Annual Lecture Series*, 1986, Institute of Credit Management, *Lecture Notes*, 17 February 1986, available from G. & B. Smith Advisors Ltd, Halford House, Copse Hill Road, Lower Slaughter, Nr Cheltenham, Glos. GL54 2HY.
Sumption, A., *Sumption and Lawton's Tax and Tax Planning*, 9th edn, Oyez, London, 1981.
Swiss Bank Corporation, 'Documentary Operations', Swiss Bank Corporation, London, April 1979.
Taffler, R. J., 'The Empirical Models for the Monitoring of UK Corporations: The State of the Art', The City University Business School, London, *Working Paper Series*, no. 51, 1983.
Taffler, R. J., 'The Z-Score Approach to Measuring Company Solvency', *The Accountant's Magazine*, March, 1983.
Townsley, J., and R. Jones, *Numeracy and Accounting*, Polytech Publishers, Stockport, 1979.
Whittington, G., *The Prediction of Profitability and Other Studies of Company Behaviour*, Cambridge University Press, 1971.

APPENDIX I

Table of computations and formulas

Arithmetic mean: the sum of all numbers in a group divided by the number of numbers in the group; expressed as:

$$\frac{\Sigma x}{n}$$

Statisticians use the symbol $\bar{x}$ to stand for arithmetic mean.

Asset turnover: This ratio indicates how fully a company is using its capital. Normally, the more intensively the capital is used, the better. The computation is:

$$\frac{\text{Sales}}{\text{Capital employed}}$$

Averaged capital cover: This computation shows the extent to which averaged measures of surplus capital can decline before a company is unable to meet its obligations including a proposed credit exposure. The formula is:

$$\text{AVC} = \frac{(a+b+c+d)/4}{x}$$

Where a = Net cashflow
b = Net current assets
c = Normalized working capital
d = Net totals generated from operations
x = Credit exposure

Averaged ratios: These ratios attempt to present more indicative measurements than the standard computations for the same measurements—e.g. debt-turn. The standard debt-turn computation is:

$$\frac{\text{Trade debtors}}{\text{Sales}} \times 365$$

The averaged variant takes the opening and closing Trade Debtors' balances and divides them by 2 to obtain an arithmetic average, for instance, for yearly audited figures:

$$\frac{\text{Last year's trade debtors + this year's}/2}{\text{Sales}}$$

Banker's ratio: Also, proprietorship ratio: An indicator of gearing—the measure of equity to total funds used to run the operation:

$$\frac{\text{Shareholders' funds}}{\text{Capital employed}}$$

Base index: Used in trend computation for over two years' figures, using the earliest year's figure as the base 100 and scaling subsequent figures by dividing each year's figure by that for the first year and multiplying the result by 100.

Bathory's Model: A multiple ratio corporate insolvency classification model expressed by the formula:

$$Y = 0.20 \left(\sum x_{1-5} \right)$$

Where X_1 = Gross cashflow/current debt
X_2 = Pre-tax profit/capital employed
X_3 = Equity/current liabilities
X_4 = Tangible net worth/total liabilities
X_5 = Working capital/total assets

Capital adequacy ratio: There are many. A simple indicator is:

$$\frac{\text{Equity}}{\text{Current liabilities}}$$

The choice of ratios necessarily varies with the type of capital under analysis, e.g. working capital, capital employed, liquid capital.

Capital/assets ratio: An important measurement of banking companies' capital adequacy in respect of their loan books (assets).

Capital employed: The permanent capital used to run a business. The computation is:

Shareholders' funds
+
Long-term liabilities
+
Deferred taxation

Thus, capital employed may be a figure greater than net assets or 'balance-sheet totals'.

Cashflow basis interest cover: This measurement shows how far cash inflow can decline before current interest payments cannot be met. The computation is:

$$\frac{\text{Gross (or net) cashflow}}{\text{Interest payable}}$$

CD:
Current debt: Priority current liability items in urgency of settlement terms if not in legal terms. Generally composed of:

Overdraft
+
Current portions of loans
+
Leasing obligations and HP commitments
+
Current taxation due, e.g. corporation tax
+
Current portions of debenture interest
+
Current VAT liability and other collector taxes
+
Any documentary payments due, e.g. bills of exchange
+
Other taxation due/arrears, e.g. PAYE, NIC

Credit given: (Debt-turn) This computation indicates the approximate days' credit a company allows its customers:

$$\frac{\text{Trade debtors}}{\text{Sales}} \times 365$$

Credit taken: (Trade creditors' turnover) This computation shows the approximate days' credit allowed a company by its trade creditors:

$$\frac{\text{Trade creditors}}{\text{Direct costs of sales}} \times 365$$

Cumulative profitability ratio: There are many. A simple indicator showing the build-up of reserves is:

$$\frac{\text{Tangible net worth}}{\text{Total liabilities}}$$

Current ratio: An approximation of historical liquidity and solvency of trading position as at latest accounting date:

$$\frac{\text{Current assets}}{\text{Current liabilities}}$$

Debt ratio: A gearing indicator showing the relationship between borrowed capital and total capital used to run the operation:

$$\frac{\text{Loan capital}}{\text{Capital employed}}$$

Dividend cover: This ratio indicates the maximum amount of dividend plus tax credit a company can pay out of profits on a per share basis:

$$\frac{\text{Earnings per share}}{\text{Net dividend per share}}$$

Fixed assets turnover: A ratio showing how efficiently a company's investment in buildings, land and equipment are being used:

$$\frac{\text{Sales}}{\text{Net fixed assets}}$$

Forecast debt cover: This model shows on both historical and forecast bases the degree to which major surplus capital can decline before a company will be unable to meet its obligations including a proposed credit exposure. The computation is:

$$\Delta = 0.20 \left(\sum \mu X_{1-4} \right) + (Y)$$

Where: μ = harmonic mean and
$X_1 = >$ Gross cashflow-current debt/exposure
$X_2 = >$ Averaged free capital/exposure
$X_3 = >$ Normalized working capital/exposure
$X_4 = >$ Tangible net worth/total liabilities + exposure
$Y = >$ Pre-tax profit/capital employed

Harmonic mean: The harmonic mean of a set of numbers is the reciprocal of the arithmetic mean of their reciprocals, thus, letting μ stand for the harmonic mean and x and y as the numbers:

$$\mu = \frac{2xy}{x+y}$$

The computation throws a lower number than $\bar{x}$, the arithmetic mean.

Historic interest cover: This ratio shows the extent to which profit can decline before a company is unable to meet current interest charges from current profit:

$$\frac{\text{Profit before interest and taxation}}{\text{Interest}}$$

Liquid ratio: (Also quick and acid-test ratio) This measurement indicates the proportion of quickly realisable assets to total current obligations. The computation is:

$$\frac{\text{Current assets} - \text{stock}}{\text{Current liabilities}}$$

Monetary lag: The difference expressed in cashflow terms or in days between a company's cash collection period and its approximate payment turnover of trade creditors:

Debt-turn
Less
Trade creditors' turnover

NAV: (Net asset value) This quantity indicates the book value of assets per ordinary share:

$$\frac{\text{Ordinary shareholders' funds}}{\text{Ordinary shares issued}}$$

Normalized current debt: In accounting statements where no breakdown of current liabilities is given, current debt can be 'normalized' by taking an experienced-justified percentage of current liabilities to represent priority creditors. Fifteen per cent to 25 per cent tend to be the numbers used in the absence of other information.

Net cashflow: Gross cashflow less dividends.

Net current assets: (Working capital) Indicating surplus capital for the everyday requirements of a company. The computation is:

Current assets
Less
Current liabilities

And normalized working capital: Current assets
Less x% of stock and/or other slow-moving items
Less
Current liabilities

Net gearing: A solvency as well as gearing ratio. In terms of solvency, the ratio indicates a company's ability to meet total commitments from surplus funds. An example of a net gearing ratio is:

$$\frac{\text{Net current borrowings}}{\text{Surplus}}$$

Another is:
$$\frac{\text{Net borrowings}}{\text{Surplus}}$$

Prime ratio: This ratio indicates the return on capital used to run the company and is the chief indicator of profitability showing whether outputs are commensurate with resources invested. The computation is:

$$\frac{\text{Profit before taxation} + \text{interest}}{\text{Capital employed}}$$

Priority debt-service ability ratio: Indicating a company's ability to service current debt obligations from cash inflows. The computation is:

$$\frac{\text{Gross cashflow}}{\text{Current debt}}$$

Profit margin: This measurement shows the relationship between a company's sales and the cost of those sales with the margin expressed as a percentage:

$$\frac{\text{Profit before taxation} + \text{interest}}{\text{Turnover}}$$

Replacement value ratio (Fixed assets value ratio): Indicates the useful life of plant, machinery and tools as a percentage of original value:

$$\frac{\text{Net fixed assets}}{\text{Net f/assets book value}}$$

Sigma: (or Σ) standing for the sum of a group of numbers.

Smoothing divergences: Reduction of the divergence factor between two trend figures by computation of arithmetic or harmonic means.

Total liabilities: The sum of current, long-term, quantified contingent liabilities, and capital contracts entered into.

Tangible net worth: The computation is:

                                          Total assets
                                          Less
                                          Intangible assets
                                          Less
                                          Total liabilities

Trade creditors' turnover: (cf. credit taken)

Working capital: (cf. net current assets)

Working capital cover: This indicates the margin of liquid cover for a specific credit exposure. The computation is:

$$\frac{\text{Working capital}}{\text{Credit exposure}}$$

Working capital turnover: This ratio shows the utilisation of liquid surplus capital in generating sales. The computation is:

$$\frac{\text{Sales}}{\text{Working capital}}$$

Working worth: Coleshaw's measurement of surplus funds for credit purposes. The formula is:

$$\frac{\text{Current assets}}{\text{Current liabilities}}$$
$$+$$
$$\frac{\text{Quick assets}}{\text{Current liabilities}}$$
Less
$$\frac{\text{Current liabilities}}{\text{Equity}}$$

$$+\frac{\text{Total liabilities}}{\text{Equity}}$$

Or more clearly expressed: $(CA/CL + QA/CL) - (CL/E + TL/E)$

APPENDIX II

Glossary of reporting, analytical and accounting terms and references

Acceptances: When a bill of exchange has been drawn by the creditor, it must be accepted by the debtor. The bill is called an acceptance. For a fee, an acceptance house (normally a bank) will add its own acceptance to a bill making it more negotiable. Acceptance credits are a normal method of payment in international trade.

Accruals: Net profit is held to be the difference between revenue and expenses rather than the difference between cash receipts and expenditures. This is the accrual concept in accounting. Therefore, expenses in a period are not necessarily (or normally) the total of actual payments made. Accounting is based on the accrual concept, whereas credit analysis seeks, wherever possible, to convert accrual accounting figures into cashflow figures by constructing hybrid ratios, by normalizing quantities, and by restatement of accounting numbers.

Acid-test: Estimation of liquidity. Also called quick or liquid ratio. See table of computation (Appendix 1).

ACT: Advance corporation tax: Essentially the basic rate of income tax that would be payable on dividends were they grossed-up at the basic rate. ACT ranks as a current liability.

Added value: The difference between money generated by sales and money permitted to leave the company in terms of costs, or the difference between inflow and outflow.

Advances: In the UK, normally loans and overdrafts to supply industry and commerce with circulating capital as opposed to fixed capital.

Affiliated companies: A company associated with another, normally as a subsidiary (qv).

Aged debtor analysis: The segmentation of a company's trade debtors into groups by periods of credit taken. Ageing is normally done in days, e.g. 30, 60, or 90 days. This type of analysis indicates the efficiency of internal credit control and cash inflow management.

APAT: Attributable profit after taxation.

Associated or associate companies: Two or more companies with interlocking directorates enabling the companies to pursue a common policy. Such associations are alternatives to complete amalgamations or the setting-up of a holding company.

Bank information memoranda: Documents giving accounting figures, corporate data, forecasts and economic information as well as structural details of particular credits for the particular borrowers to whom the aforementioned data applies. The purpose of these memoranda is to provide participants in a credit with a reliable and wide collection of data on which to make their own credit decisions.

Bank of England risk categories for off-balance-sheet exposures: The Bank defines the comparative credit risks inherent in these financing instruments as:

    Full, medium, and low risk

GLOSSARY

Where these risk categories are intended to form points of reference against which capital requirements will come to be imposed on off-balance-sheet business.

Bonus: Financing instrument in the capital markets: 'Borrower's option for notes and underwritten standby'.

Breakdowns: Itemizations of accounting quantities, e.g. stock breakdowns into raw materials, WIP, and finished goods.

Breakeven: The point at which sales and cost of sales are equal.

CA: Current assets.

Capital market/s: In contrast to the money market which is the market for extremely short-term funds, the capital market is the market for medium-term and long-term corporate funding. This traditional view, however, is altering with a generally greater demand for liquid funds and the development of securitized debt.

Capitalized research and development (R&D): A company's research and development costs given a capital value as an asset in the balance sheet. For the computation of tangible net worth, capitalized costs of this type are netted-out as fictitious or intangible assets.

CCA: Current cost accounts/accounting—Accounts adjusted for inflation showing replacement values for quantities. This convention is currently falling into disuse as it has proved costly, unsatisfactory, and complicated for companies and the Inland Revenue to implement. (SSAP 16 refers).

CD: Currend debt (qv Appendix I).

CD: Certificate of deposit, ranking as a current asset.

CGT: Capital gains tax.

CL: Current liabilities.

CMO: Collateralized mortgage obligation, a form of asset-backed, highly tradeable security in the capital markets.

Collector taxes: VAT, PAYE and National Insurance Contributions for which companies are responsible for collecting and remitting.

Comfort margin: Difference between a monetary inflow, e.g. Gross cashflow, and an exposure or a set of exposures, e.g. a potential credit or total sum of liabilities.

Commercial paper: A note (debt) issuance programme by a company in which typically two or three dealers place the paper with investors.

Compensatory ratios: Ratios throwing outsized figures effectively cancelling out other outsized quantities to preserve overall and lower common-size. What the two ratios are measuring will be essential to the formula or model in which the ratios form part, but without compensating effects, these isolated measurements would grossly distort the model's findings.

Contingent liabilities: Liabilities that may or may not crystallize forming part of the notes to the accounts.

Days sales outstanding (DSO): The averaged or approximate amount of time in days of uncollected receivables (trade debtors' accounts) (cf. debt-turn, Appendix I).

Debenture: A company's written acknowledgement of debt normally given under seal and generally containing provisions as to payment of interest and repayment of principal. Debentures are normally long-term credit instruments and are frequently secured on some or all of companies' assets (fixed and floating charges).

Debenture cover: Measurements of a company's financial capacity to meet its debenture commitments.

Debenture formulas: Specifications laid down by banks as to acceptable financial and operational performance for the servicing of debentures.

Debenture statistics: Periodic financial data remitted to debenture-holders from borrowers. Debenture statistics constitute a potentially valuable and regular source of information for banks and other lenders.

Debt mix: The analysis of the constituent obligations in debt totals, e.g. current debt, current liabilities, or total borrowings.

Debt priority: The order in timing terms in which obligations are normally settled.

Delta: (Δ) Forecast debt cover (qv. Appendix I).

Denominator: The divisor in a fraction.

Depreciation: The amount by which the utility of a fixed asset has diminished.

Direct expenses/costs of sales: Expenses which can be directly attributable to the cost of producing particular goods or services as opposed to overhead expenses (establishment costs).

Domino effect: The failure of one company bringing about a chain reaction of failures in other companies.

DTI: Department of Trade and Industry.

e: Credit exposure.

ECGD: Export Credit Guarantee Department.

EEC: European Economic Community (Common Market).

Equity: Shareholders' funds composed of profit and loss account, reserves, and called-up (paid-up) share capital.

Eurocommercial paper: A non-underwritten or uncommitted note issuance programme where typically two or three dealers place the borrower's debt securities (paper).

Ex-ante (predictive): Truly predictive from historical or past data.

Expense creditors: Unpaid overheads.

Expert system: Computer program operable by non-experts to provide access to specialized, detailed, and holistic expert knowledge.

ED 29: Exposure draft 29; Accounting for leases and hire purchase contracts: published in 1981 as forerunner of SSAP 21, to prevent hidden gearing by capitalization of financial leases.

Extrapolation: Estimation of a value of a function or quantity beyond the known values by extension of a curve. Certain trend forecasting is thus based on extrapolation (cf. forecast debt cover/delta, Appendix I).

FDIC: Federal Deposit Insurance Corporation (US); Central banking deposit underwriting agency.

Finance/financial leases: Leases where both risks and rewards of ownership are substantially transferred to the lessee. Other types of leases are classified as operating leases.

Financial model: Extended formulas for use in forecasting, problem-solving, classification, and sensitivity analysis, etc.

Financial ratios: Ratios concerned with corporate gearing and liquidity.

Fixed and floating charges: In a fixed charge, the property to serve as security is specified in the loan/debenture agreement; With floating charges, the loan is secured on assets generally rather than on a particular item. The lender has priority of repayment from the fund of assets that exist, e.g. in the event of a receiving order against the company.

Funds flow (statement): (US) Statement of source and application of funds—the bridging statement in accounts between profit and loss account and balance sheet.

Gross cashflow: The sum of profit after taxation, depreciation, and increase/decrease in deferred taxation—a measure of operational inflow.

Gearing: External financial resources of a company in relation to internal financial resources, or commonly, loan capital, bank and other borrowings as a percentage of capital employed (Appendix I). Gearing is known as 'leverage' in the US.

Gross gearing: Total borrowings divided by surplus funds.

Gross profit: The excess of the realized proceeds of sales over their cost, before taking into account expenses incurred in selling, distributing, and administering the business.

Groups of companies/groups: In effect, a single business entity jointly controlled, normally consisting of one holding company and a number of subsidiary companies, sub-subsidiaries or associated companies.

Guarantee: An agreement to be answerable for debt, default, or miscarriage of another. This differs from an indemnity, which is a contract whereby one party agrees to suffer the loss of the other, e.g. credit insurance. Here, the indemnifier takes a primary liability. Under a guarantee, the guarantor assumes a secondary liability; and he must have no interest in the contract between debtor and creditor. A contract of guarantee must be accompanied by a memorandum in writing.

GUN: (Capital markets); acronym for grantor underwritten note: A floating rate note facility, akin to a Euronote facility, whereby a group of banks (grantors) commit to purchase any notes put back to them by investors on any floating rate note interest rate fixing date. But notes are then auctioned out to the market between the grantors.

Hard copy accounts: Company accounting statements printed-out from micro-film records provided by Companies' Registry (Companies' House); or printed/typed accounting statements.

Harmonic mean: The mean relating to numbers whose reciprocals form an arithmetic progression. In this text, harmonic mean is symbolized by μ (Mu)$_1$ and is used as an averaging and forecasting device yielding lower figures than $\bar{x}$ (X-bar), the arithmetic mean.

Harmonic ratios: Ratios whose component parts are composed of harmonically averaged numbers. Forecasting ratios, e.g. forecast debt cover model (cf. Appendix I).

Historical data: Past fact/supposition—audited and other. Historical accounting data is informed by the historical cost convention whereby assets are maintained at their original cost in the books and accounts of companies and where depreciation is charged accordingly.

Holistic: Adjective based on 'holism' which holds that the sum is greater than the sum of its parts. In this text, holistic interpretation of data, accounting and other, understands not only the philosophical meaning above, but also the treatment (interpretive) of data singly (in units), severally (in pairs or combinations of units), and simultaneously (all units taken at once). In this text, the adjectives holistic and synoptic are interchangeable.

HP: Hire purchase, e.g. an agreement (contract) in which the hirer agrees to hire goods from their owner in return for which a deposit is normally paid, and a series of periodic payments follow until the hire period terminates at which time, title (ownership) to the goods passes to the hirer. Title does not pass, therefore, until all payments have been made, including the nominal sum frequently payable as part of the final payment instalment.

Hybrid ratios: Ratios constructed for particular or special measuring purposes, e.g. Gross cash flow/current debt (measuring priority debt-service ability from operational inflows), as opposed to 'standard' financial/operational ratios, e.g. current assets/current liabilities (measuring solvency and liquidity).

Indenture review: A statement of the safety/comfort margins on ratio-based covenants interim loans, and any perceptions that may affect the decision to grant or to extend credit.

The indenture review forms part (Annexe or Appendix) to some bank credit analyses and loan agreements.

Indicated profit/(loss): Periodically estimated results obtained from debenture statistics (qv).

Initial and holdout samples: Accepted statistical testing formats used to minimise error, bias, and distortion of findings, and as a corroborative aid.

Input: Data entered in financial models, spreadsheets, and computer programs.

Insolvency: The inability to meet financial obligations as those obligations fall due.

Intangible assets: Incorrectly, 'fictitious assets'; Accounting term for invisible or impalpable assets which have value to a business and possibly, may have a sale value, e.g. goodwill, patents, trade-marks, technical know-how. Strictly, fictitious assets are assets appearing on a balance sheet, not because they have any particular value, but because double-entry bookkeeping demands that they should, e.g. a debit balance on a profit and loss account, or assets of no realizable value, e.g. formation expenses.

Intermediaries: persons or companies acting as agents or mediators between parties. Financial intermediaries are thus brokers, bankers of various kinds, and arrangers of deals between companies.

Inventories/inventory: (US) Stock.

Letter of comfort: Written intentions from parent companies to the effect that they will not ignore the debts of subsidiaries. Comfort letters are not the same as guarantees—which are legal instruments. Letters of comfort are increasingly used in international business between companies and banks/major suppliers. The most usual reason for accepting a letter of comfort is that competition among lenders/major suppliers has enabled buyers to use their financial muscle to avoid issuing a guarantee. Letters of comfort can be 'weak' or 'strong', depending upon phrasing, explicitness, and position of signatories.

Leverage: cf. Gearing.

Loan draw-downs: To request, take, and receive money forming part of a total loan facility at *ad hoc* or at specified intervals.

Loan workouts: The extension of credit and/or systematic collection of money on a troubled or non-performing loan account.

Long-term debt: Borrowings repayable after one year.

Marketable securities: Quoted corporate or government debt securities (stock, bonds, shares) for which a ready market for sale exists. Marketable securities rank as highly liquid current assets.

Matrix: In general, an environment in which something takes its origin and form. In mathematics, a rectangular array of elements set out in rows and columns used to facilitate the solving of problems. In credit analysis, probability and matrices can be used for forecasting purposes, e.g. the transformation of coordinate numbers. The spreadsheet is, in effect, a matrix from which synoptic scores take their origin and form.

MDA: Multiple discriminant analysis; a statistical-based analytical routine first used by Altman and developed by Taffler and others for corporate failure forecasting. MDA selects the amalgam of indicators that best discriminates between x and y conditions (say, solvent and insolvent companies), and provides a linear formula made up of the most discriminating component parts, e.g. ratios. The individual ratio weights are determined by MDA and the sum of the components or ratios provides a holistic 'score' which must then be viewed against a statistically computed array of other companies' scores to give significance to the score obtained.

Medium-term capital: Funds raised for a stated and limited period and not normally repayable at call. The period is generally less than five years. Funds raised for longer periods are long-term capital.

Mega-models: Holistic and comprehensive financially-orientated models driven by expert systems for forecasting and problem-solving purposes. Such models aim to treat disparate data, e.g. accounting information, as well as assessments of management capability, by means of various quantifying (scoring) procedures, and produce detailed (particular) as well as generalized (holistic and other) answers.

Merge and purge: The alignment, matching and elimination of items from two or more lists or sets with the purpose of providing a list or set of items in which no duplication occurs. Merge and purge operations are generally carried out on computer using lists on magnetic tape.

Minorities/minority interests/shareholders: Persons or entities holding shares in a company which is itself a subsidiary, though not themselves the holding company or its nominees.

Modified accounts: The bane of credit analysis. Small firms are granted reporting exemptions of certain key accounting figures by Schedule 8 of the Companies Act, 1985. The result is a gross and uninformative abbreviation of the full accounts which the same firms have to prepare in order to produce modified versions for lodgement at Companies House. The DTI has recently proposed further modifications and, in some instances, the scrapping of small companies' audit requirements.

MOF: Capital markets instrument; multi-option facility which is broader in scope than the underwritten Euronote facility (NIF) in that the banks' medium-term commitment is to backstop, not only the issuance of Euronotes, but a wide range of other short-term instruments, e.g. bankers' acceptances and short-term advances in various currencies.

Multiple: A form of ratio expression. When a ratio is expressed as a multiple, two or more numbers are involved, e.g. 2.123. Ratios are expressed either as multiples or as percentages.

Multiple sector models: Synoptic financial models driven by a variety of statistical and mathematical procedures that solve problems, highlight key flows, and/or forecast outcomes for companies trading in varying commercial/industrial sectors. Bathory's Model is an example of a multiple sector insolvency forecasting device.

Multivariate: Multivariate analysis employs a range of indicators, normally ratios, to drive formulas or financial models. Univariate analysis, on the other hand, examines one indicator, e.g. a ratio.

Net working assets: (NWA); A net current item introduced to credit analysis by Hale as a supposed substitute for working capital. NWA are held to be those items moving with the level of sales—in particular, accounts receivable and payable as well as stock (including WIP). NWA do not include short-term debt nor cash. The object of this measurement is to determine cash or lack of it from the processes of buying, manufacturing, selling, and collection.

Net worth: An accounting term for the sum of share capital and reserves or the difference between total assets and outside liabilities. The term is not considered satisfactorily informative in serious credit analysis, which prefers assessments of various 'worths', e.g. current worth, net assets, tangible net worth. Net worth is often mistaken for net assets and for capital employed.

Netting-out/off: In credit analysis, netting-out signifies the deduction of quantities that distort the significance of larger quantities, e.g. VAT should be netted-out of turnover if a significant idea of sales is to be gained. This example, of course, reflects accepted accounting practice in the posting of turnover in the profit and loss account. Netting-out, however, is not always the same as normalizing. The obtaining of 'net positions' is a basic principle in analysis.

NIF: Capital markets instrument; note issuance facility—a general description for all underwritten Euronote facilities.

Normalising: A process in credit analysis similar to netting-out. In normalizing, non-truly representative items are deducted from other items to leave a significant quantity. For instance, if the analyst wishes to gain an idea of a company's true working capital position, he might, given sufficient justification, deduct certain classes of slow-moving stock along with other current asset items from the total of current assets, before deducting current liabilities. In that case, normalized working capital would be a lower figure than net current assets (working capital).

NTA: Net tangible assets.

Numerator: The dividend of a fraction as opposed to the divisor (denominator).

Numerical scoring: Evaluative systems developed by Myers and Forgy and others for financial problem-based solutions, e.g. loan cover, and forecasting, e.g. solvency. Numerical scoring techniques can apply to non-numerical or unquantified data where assessments are made and numbers (scores) are assigned to the different classes of data on the basis of the assessments.

Obligations: Debts.

Off-balance-sheet business: Essentially business with an underwriting of risk element where some or all of the liabilities attached to the business are not recorded on the face of the balance sheet. An attraction of this type of business for banks is that additional capital has not always been required by the regulators to maintain statutory capital/assets ratios. Examples of such business are: NIFs and currency or interest rate swaps.

Operating leases: cf. Financial leases.

Operating/operational ratios: cf. Financial ratios.

Parent companies: An operating company having control over a number of others known as subsidiaries. By the Companies Act, 1948, a company is a subsidiary if that other company is a member of it and controls the composition of its board of directors; if that other company (parent) holds more than 50 per cent (in nominal value) of its share capital; or if it is a subsidiary of any company which is, in turn, a subsidiary of the first company. The parent company is often known as the holding company.

Pareto principle: Basically that 80 per cent of the value of receivables is concentrated in 20 per cent of accounts receivable (i.e. key customer accounts or trade debtors).

Pari passu: Latin for 'with equal rank, speed or progress'. For example, all shares of one class in a company rank *pari passu* as to receipt of dividends and return of capital.

PAYE tax: Pay As You Earn tax is the system whereby tax is deducted from salaries or wages by the employer before payment. State pension or National Insurance contributions (now called Social Security) are deducted with PAYE tax.

PBIT: Profit before interest and taxation.

PER: Price earnings ratio; The measure of a company's market rating or share price divided by earnings per share.

Per aval: In forfaiting, an aval is an irrevocable and unconditional guarantee to pay on the due date. The aval is written directly onto each bill of exchange or promissory note with the words 'per aval' and the signature of the avalizing party.

PLC: Public limited company.

Post-balance-sheet activity: An event the financial implications of which may be related and/or material to the financial condition of the company but which implications have not been included in the accounting statements as the event in question took place after accounting date.

Preferential debts: When a company is wound up, debts must be paid in a certain order. Secured creditors are paid first and unsecured creditors, second. While in general all unsecured creditors rank equally, certain debts must be given preference. By December 1986, preferential debts will in the UK be limited to employees' wages, holiday pay, and 'collector taxes' (namely, VAT for six months prior to winding-up; and PAYE/NIC deductions for twelve months prior). The Insolvency Act, 1985 abolishes the right of preference for rates and assessed taxes.

PRT: Petroleum revenue tax.

PTP: Pre-tax profit; correctly, profit before taxation.

Quick assets: Assets quickly realizable in cash, e.g. quoted shares.

Quick ratio: Also, acid-test ratio; a liquidity indicator (cf Appendix I).

Quoted investments: Securities quoted (listed) on stock exchanges. Quotation implies marketability.

R&D: Research and development (costs or expenditure); can be capitalized as an intangible asset.

Ratio: The relationship between two quantities.

RD: Risk description (grouping).

Receivables: Properly, accounts receivable or debtors (normally understood as trade debtors).

Recourse/non-recourse: The right to demand payment from the drawer or endorser of a bill of exchange or other negotiable instruments when the acceptor fails to pay. Non-recourse signifies a qualified endorsement on such negotiable instruments whereby the endorser protects himself from liability to subsequent holders.

REITS: US; real estate investment trusts.

Restatement of accounting numbers: A principle of credit analysis in which both the format and the figures of accounting statements can be altered, with sufficient justification, to provide more indicative answers to specific questions.

Retentions: Profits and other amounts retained within a company; a measure of permanent capital, i.e. called-up capital and reserves; and an indicator of capital adequacy.

Revocable commitment: An obligation which can be recalled or cancelled at any time without notice.

Rights issue: Invitation to existing shareholders to acquire additional shares in a company. The 'right' could be one new share for each two previously held. The rights issue is a means of raising capital.

Ripple effect: In credit analysis, the alteration of one accounting number entailing alterations in various other accounting numbers. The ripple effect powers sensitivity analysis.

ROCE: Return on capital employed; a measure of profitability (cf. prime ratio, Appendix I).

ROI: Return on investment; a measurement of yield.

Rollover relief: A company's election to have the gain arising on the disposal of an asset deducted from the cost of a new asset in lieu of paying tax on the gain.

RPI: Retail price index.

RUF: Capital market instrument; revolving underwriting facility. This is classically a medium-term commitment by a group of underwriting banks to purchase one, three, or six-month Euronotes at a fixed margin pegged to LIBOR (London interbank offered rate) should a sole-placing agent (typically, a bank) fail to sell the notes to investors at, or under, that margin. RUFs have subsequently been extended to tender panel placement facilities as well as sole-placing, though the tender panel facilities have proved cumbersome and costly in many cases.

Safety margin: The difference between debt and cover (realizable assets) for that debt. Also called comfort margin.

Sale and leaseback: The sale and reacquisition of an asset on a leasing arrangement in order to free capital to increase liquidity. Corporate headquarters typically are sold and leased back during troubled periods to restore levels of liquidity for the ordinary conduct of business.

Seasonality: Variation in trading levels and results according to seasons or times of the year. Certain trades are highly seasonal, e.g. toy manufacturers.

Securities: A misused term applied to corporate debt instruments, e.g. shares or debentures. Various species of corporate debt may or may not be 'secured' or backed with assets as a safeguard.

Securitization: The backing of corporate debt instruments with assets for the purpose of making the debt more tradeable.

Sensitivity analysis: The assessment of how alterations (generally, small) in key figures, e.g. price, may affect other key figures, e.g. profit before taxation.

Seven lending canons: A major bank provides the acronym 'CAMPARI' for character, ability, margin, purpose, amount, repayment, and insurance. The canons appear comprehensively refreshing.

Shareholders' funds: Equity; or the sum of paid-up capital, profit and loss account, and reserves.

Short-term facilities: Funds raised or available to cover temporary fluctuations, e.g. bank overdrafts.

SNIF: Capital market instrument; short-term note issuance facility. The SNIF is structurally the same as the RUF save as a means of distinguishing tender panel placement from sole-placing facilities.

Sovereign credits: Loans to sovereign states/governments.

Statistical deviation: Strictly, the difference between an observed value in a series of such values and their arithmetic mean. Forecast debt cover as calculated in this text will fall within n-points of deviance from actual results—single, several, and simultaneous.

Stock-turn/turnover: Approximate number (in days) it takes a company to shift (sell) total inventory (cf. Appendix I).

Subrogation: To put one person or entity in place of another in respect of a right or claim.

Sustainable funds flow: An inflation-adjusted funds flow measurement composed of profit before taxation and depreciation less taxation less capital maintenance requirements (Historical cost depreciation less additional CCA depreciation less cost of sales adjustment less monetary working capital adjustment).

Swaps: The exchange of one borrower's debt for another's. Swaps can be linked to interest rates and or currencies (circus swaps). At present, swaps are off-balance sheet business in respect of the liabilities attaching to them.

Synoptic: Single, several, and simultaneous interpretation of accounting and other data by a financial model or formula.

TA: Total assets.

Timing differences: Ref: Deferred tax; Timing differences arise where a company may be liable to pay the full rate of tax at some time but not in the year reported upon.

TL: Total liabilities.

TNW: Tangible net worth.

Trade creditor financing: An internal financing 'technique' whereby funds are kept (and/or interest can be maximized) by withholding payment from trade creditors beyond agreed credit terms.

Trading balance: In credit analysis, the relationship between trade debtors and trade creditors; or more generally, the relationship between current assets and current liabilities.

Transaction analysis: The delineation of separate transactions to determine the effect on cash. Hale advocates transaction analysis as a means for converting accrual accounting information into cashflow information.

Turnover: Sales net of VAT and other sales-based taxes, e.g. Excise duty.

Ultimate companies: A parent company may be controlled by an ultimate company.

VAT: Value added tax.

Verbatim: Word for word.

Warranties: A statement of fact in a contract, either express or implied. If it is unfulfilled the injured party cannot repudiate the contract but may be able to claim damages. A 'condition' is fundamental to a contract; a warranty is not.

WIP: Work-in-progress (normally posted under stock).

Y: The synoptic score given by Bathory's Model.

Z-Score: Zeta-Scoring and derivative forms of holistic insolvency forecasting techniques developed by Altman, Taffler and others. From Zeta analysis—based on MDA (qv).

INDEX

Ability to repay, 319
Accelerated capital allowances, 178
Accounting turnover, 28
Acid test ratio, 13, 36, 38–9, 45, 51–4, 90, 142, 352, 363
Acquisitions, 28
Added value effects on profits and cash-flows, 156–60
Added value modelling and forecasting, 160–2
Advance corporation tax (ACT), 176, 180, 305
Aged debtor analysis, 47
Ageing:
  of creditors, 313–14
  of debtors, 312–13
Amos Hinton & Sons PLC, 44
Amount of Advance, 320
Annual profitability, 58
Anticipatory Credit Policy, 262
Arbuthnot Factors Limited, 272–80
Arithmetic mean, 121, 359
Asset turnover, 32, 359
Attributable profit/loss after tax (APAT), 328
Audited accounts, 6, 24, 34, 75, 76, 77
Averaged capital cover, 61, 62, 65, 359
Averaged ratios, 359
Averaged views, 59

Bad debts, 295–6
Balance sheet analysis spreadsheet, 14, 324
Balance sheets, 29, 30, 31, 34, 43, 45, 51, 67, 77, 85, 89, 164, 170
  extrapolation of, 169
Bank account, 309
Bank analysts, 220
Bank analytical and forecasting routines, 319–43
  ability to repay, 319
  amount of advance, 320
  character assessment, 319
  margin, 319–20
  overall 'feel' for the operation, 323
  purpose of advance, 320
  repayment proposals, 320
  security requirement, 320
Bank computerized spreadsheet analysis, 339
Bank credit, applicants for, 24
Band credit facilities, 23–5
Bank data collection, 299
Bank of England, 192, 194, 196, 197, 215, 216, 218, 294, 297
Bank finance director, 295
Bank information memoranda, 207–12
Bank for International Settlements, 194, 196
Bank manual analytical spreadsheet, 323–38
Bank monitoring spreadsheets, 301–8
Bank references, 115, 205–6
Bank sector analysts, 293–4
Banker's ratio, 42, 360
Banking, off-balance-sheet, 191–5
Banking Supervision White Paper, 297
Banks, financial control, 44
Base index, 360
Bathory's Model, 59, 109–10, 114, 117–33, 168, 360
Bomin North Sea Limited 190
Borrowers and borrowing, 23–4, 32
Business expansion, 271

Capital adequacy, 58, 59, 81–2, 84, 89, 90
Capital adequacy ratio, 360
Capital allowances, 174–6
Capital assets ratio, 360
Capital employed, 43, 88, 360
  computation of, 29–31
Capital Gains Tax (CGT), 305
Capital reduction devices, 33
Cash acceleration, 33, 34
Cash inflow-outflow, 59
Cash injection effects on liquidity, 163–70

379

Cashflow, 28–9, 36, 38
Cashflow basis interest cover, 361
Cashflow contribution to deferred taxation, 182
Cashflow measurement, 57
Cashflow projections, 152–6
Cashflow resumés, 152–6
Catastrophe Policy, 262
Character assessment, 319
Collection periods, 34
Comfort margin, 58, 91
Commitments, 194
Common sense, 5, 6
Companies Act, 76, 156, 323
Companies' House data, 202–3
Companies' Registry, 222, 299
Company progress criteria, 81
Computational routines, 4
Computer programs, 4, 355
Confidential information, 204
Contingent liabilities, 188–91, 194
Cork Report, 119
Cost of sales, 16–18, 36–8
Cost sensitivity statement, 158–9
Credit analysis, 155, 201, 202, 293–318
    analytical assumptions, 4
    and current informational climate, 75–8
    as function of commercial credit management, 345–6
    basic assumptions, 4
    chief functions of, 5
    definition, 3
    dependence on good accounting, 353–4
    importance of dimensionality in, 351–3
    ingredients of ideal analysis, 348
    mirror the real world, 5
    need for full disclosure, 354–5
    'perfect', 344–56
    purpose of, 4
    questions answerable by, 22
    summary of assumptions, 21–2
    traditional, 26
    ultimate criterion, 5
    violation of common sense, 5
Credit analysis spreadsheet, 15
Credit assessment indicators, 288–9
Credit Committee, 280
Credit control, 35, 36
Credit decision, 285
Credit forms, 21–2

Credit given, 361
Credit insurance, 260–81, 285, 320
Credit management, 202
Credit Management Questionnaire, 263, 267
Credit opinions, 257–8
Credit paradox, 22–3
Credit rating system, 268–70
    general standing, 268
    history, 268–9
    liquidity, 269
    payment record, 269–70
Credit reporting companies, 222
Credit reports, purpose of, 219
Credit risk underwriting, information gathering for, 263–8
Credit risks, 193
    in currency and interest rate swaps, 216–17, 219
    in revolving underwriting facilities, 219
Credit sanction criteria, 298–9
Credit taken, 361
Credit Violation Report, 287
Creditor-turnover, 36, 38–9
Creditors, 311
    ageing of, 313–14
Creditors/sales ratio, 36
Creditworthiness, 23
Cumulative profitability, 58
Cumulative profitability ratio, 361
Currency rate swaps, 215–16
Currency swaps:
    credit risk in, 216
    exposure size in, 217–18
    frailties in exposure evaluations, 218–19
Current assets, 45, 51, 89, 328
    composition of, 46–8
Current cost accounts (CCA), 328–30
Current debt, 82–3, 361
Current liabilities, 45, 51, 64, 89, 90, 328
    composition of, 48–9
    imminence of, 49
Current ratio, 36, 38–9, 45–6, 50, 142, 352, 361
Current trading losses, 178–9

Data analysis, 270–80
Data assessment, 282–9
Data collection, 270–80, 282–9, 4–5, 219–21
    banks', 299

facilities and sources, 354
  requirements, 348–50
Data correlation, 202
Data interpretation, 202, 219–21
Data presentation, 10–21
Data simplification, 7–8
Data sources, 201–59, 354–5
  numerical, 3
Database reporting companies, 202–3
Debenture formula, 300–1, 304
Debenture statistics, 301–8
  and bank action, 317
  interpretation of, 306–8
  profitability assessment, 315–16
Debentures, as data sources, 300
Debt capacity, 91
Debt/capital employed ratio, 43
Debt-cover, computation, 117–32
Debt/equity ratio, 43, 45
Debt mix, 82–4, 91
Debt priority schedule, 49, 350
Debt ratio, 42–6, 362
Debt-service ability, 59, 61, 119, 120, 196
Debt swaps, 193
Debt-turn (debtors' turnover), 34–9, 361
Debtors, 308
  ageing of, 312–13
  financing, 33
Debtors' turnover (debt-turn), 34–9, 361
Debtors/sales ratio, 34
Decimal places, 13, 18
Decision-making, 5, 24
Deferred payment applications, forms of, 3
Deferred taxation, 43, 171–82
  accounting background, 171–2
  accounting periods on or after 1 April 1985, 176–7
  analytical treatment of accounts, 180–2
  cashflow contribution to, 182
  computation of, 172–3
    deferral method, 173
    liability method, 173, 176
  permanent differences, 171–2, 177
  provision for, 172
  related to losses, 178
  reversals of timing differences, 174
  timing differences, 172, 173, 175
  underlying principle, 171
Deloitte Haskins & Sells, 155
Department of Trade and Industry, 76–8

Depreciation, 16, 28, 86–8, 174–6, 354
Disclosures, 354–5
Dispassionate judgements, 6–7
Distortion, 121–2
Dividend cover, 362
Dun & Bradstreet, 204, 223–8, 230, 231–8, 263, 268, 283, 287
Dun's Financial Profiles (DFPs), 225

ECGD, 301
Economic background information, 205
EEC Fourth Directive, 157, 188
Emotive attributes, 7
Enquiry Listing sheet, 283, 285, 289
Expert systems, 346–8, 355
  characteristics suitable for, 347–8
  potentials of, 347
  principal strength of, 347
  role of, 347
  software, 348
Export Credit Policies, 262
Extel Statistical Services, 207

Factoring, 33, 34, 270–80, 301
FDIC, 196–7
Federal Reserve Board, 196
Finance leases, 184–5
  disclosures by lessees, 185, 186
Financial Accounting Standards, 188
Financial control, 44
Financial indicators, 19
Financial institution credit facilities, 23–5
Financial intelligence, 204
Financial intermediaries, 207
Financial models, 6, 8, 12, 20, 203, 351
Financial statements, accounting periods on or after 1 April 1985, 176–7
Fixed assets, 328
  investment levels in, 343
  revaluations, 179
Fixed assets turnover, 362
Fixed assets value ratio, 364
Ford Motor Company, 188
Forecast debt cover, 362
Forecasting, 4, 5, 202
  added value, 160–2
Forecasting programmes, 339
Forecasts, 152
Foreign exchange risks, 192

Foreign exchange transactions, 194
Forfaiting, 34
　of capital equipment/goods, 33
Free capital for day-to-day use, 59
Funds flow statements, 343
Future foreseeable capital needs, 7

Gearing, 7, 42–4, 353
Gearing ratio, 42, 352
Gross cash flow, 16, 19, 92, 181
Guarantees, 194

Hadson Petroleum International PLC, 190
Harmonic mean, 121, 122, 362
Harmonic ratio, 124
Hire purchase agreements, 309
Hire purchase commitments, 34, 306
Hire purchase debt, 303, 304, 312, 314
Historic interest cover, 362
Holistic analysis, 355
Human judgement, 4, 6

ICC Information Group Ltd, 205
Indenture review, 351
Indicators:
　operational, 39–41
　performance, 73–4
　profitability, 27
Industrial Performance Analysis, 205
Information augmentation, 203–7
Information availability, 207
Information companies' reports, 207
Information control, 286–7
Information gathering for credit risk underwriting, 263–8
Information sources, 75–6
Information updating, 203–7, 286–7
Insolvency, 35
　forecasting model, 105–37
　prediction, 105
　prediction model, 20
Insolvency Act (1985), 304
Institute of Credit Management, 24
Intelligent recommendations, 9–10
Interest cover ratio, 44–5
Interest rate risks, 192
Interest rate swaps, 215–16
　credit risk in, 216
　exposure size in, 217–18
　frailties in exposure evaluations, 218–19

Interest rate transactions, 194
Internal audit committees, 295
International Swap Dealers Association, 215
Investment levels in fixed assets, 343
Invoice discounting, 270, 301

Leases:
　analytical treatment of, 187–8
　see also Finance leases; Operating leases
Leasing agreements, 309
Leasing commitments, 183–4
Leasing of assets, 33–4
Legal commitments, 351
Lending applications, 293–318
Lending controls, 294–5
Lending criteria, 298
Leverage effect, 43
Liquid ratio, 363
Liquidity, 81, 82, 84, 89, 90, 101, 352, 353
　assessment, 328
　cash injection effects on, 163–70
　computations, 13
　evaluation, 269
　indicators, 33, 38
　injection, 271–2
　levels, 36
　maximization, 33
　measurement, 46, 52, 58, 87
　ratios, 42
　surplus/deficit, 314–15
Lloyds Bank, 220
Lloyds Bank International Economic Unit, 205
Loan maturity, 297
Loan portfolios, 293–318
London and Northern Group PLC, 189

Management control, 44, 297–8
Management information, 24, 115–16
Manufacturing companies, 41, 87
Margin, 319–20
Market information, 205
Market/position risk, 193
Mega-models, 221–2, 355
Merge and purge, 286–7
Model score, 18
Monetary lag, 363
Monsanto PLC, 17, 37, 64, 66–71, 127–30, 133–5, 150, 158–60, 189, 39

Multiple discriminant analysis (MDA), 105–8

National Insurance Contributions, 304
Net asset value (NAV), 363
Net assets, 29–31, 50, 83, 89
Net cash flow, 62–4, 363
Net current assets, 5, 62, 63, 363
Net current assets before inputting, 8–9
Net gearing, 363
Net profit, 50, 89, 90
Net totals generated from operations, 62–5
Net working assets, 138–42
Net worth, 83–4, 84
Non-specific or combined operations, 41–2, 87
Normalized current debt (NCD), 57, 363
Normalized gross cashflow (NGCF), 57
Normalized liquidity ratio, 52–3
Normalized working capital, 62–4, 90
Notes on the financial statements, 69–71
Numerical data sources, 3

OECD, 195
Off-balance-sheet banking business, 191–5
Off-balance-sheet commitments, 195–7
Off-balance-sheet exposures, 183–97
Operating leases, 185–6
Operational/control risks, 193
Outturns, 50–1
Overdraft borrowing, 328

Palmer Holdings International, 222
Pareto analysis, 202
PAYE, 304, 310–11
Performance indicators, 4, 89
Permanent differences. *See* Deferred taxation
Petroleum revenue tax (PRT), 171
Phillips Petroleum Products, 284, 308
Practical recommendations, 9–10
Preferential creditors, 304
Prime ratio, 27, 29, 352, 353, 364
Principal Accounts Datum Policy, 261
Priority debt-service ability, 58, 92
Priority debt-service ratio, 364
Private companies, 44, 75, 76
    reporting requirements for, 76
Profit and loss account, 17, 18, 28, 36–7, 66, 81, 156–8, 163, 175, 280, 354

Profit before interest and tax (PBIT), 328, 329
Profit before taxation (PBT), 328–9
Profit interpretations, 162–3
Profit margin, 27–8, 364
Profitability, 27–9, 32, 35, 81, 84, 89, 353
    assessment from debenture statistics, 315
    effects of growth of turnover on, 343
Profitability indicators, 27
Profitability measures, 89
Proprietorship ratio, 31, 42
Public companies, 44, 75
Purpose of advance, 320

Qui Credit Assessment Ltd, 222, 223–8, 230, 236–8

Rates, 311
Ratio-based models, 58, 61–72, 75–101
    as means of augmenting scanty information, 78–80
    linear form of, 84
    purpose and use of, 84
Ratios, 15, 18, 55–74, 138
    building, 57
    classical, 45
    composite, 58–73
    denominator, 57–8
    examination of, 26–54
    financial, 26, 42–8, 56
    hybrid, 56–7, 84
    key analytical criteria, 55
    numerator, 57
    operational, 26, 27, 31, 56
    selection of model, 89–94
    standard, 56
    trend in respect of, 73–4
    weighted, 60–1, 63
    see also under specific ratios
Recommendations, analytical, 9–10
Registry of Companies, 222, 299
Rejections, 285
Repayment proposals, 320
Replacement value ratio, 364
Retailing companies, 41, 87
Return on capital employed (ROCE), 7, 27, 29–39
Revolving underwriting facilities (RUF), 212–15, 219
    credit risk in, 212–15

Rights Issue, 166, 168–70
Ripple effect, 158
    forecasting, 119
Risk, 22–3
    quantified, 79
Risk classification:
    criteria, 321
    key questions in, 322
    modifiers, 321
Risk concentration within industries, 297
Risk description grouping, 84, 92–4
Risk description model, 79–80, 88, 92
    analysis of holdout sample, 98
    analysis of initial sample, 97
    averages of initial and holdout samples, 99–100
    statistical array, 96
    testing programme, 95
    underlying assumptions of, 80–1
Rollover relief, 179–80

Safety margin, 91
Sales:
    definition, 27
    working capital ratio, 40
Scrimgeour Vickers & Co, 293, 322
Seasonal effects, 308
Seasoned judgement, 6
Security requirements, 288, 320
Service companies, 41
Settlement time, 38
Short-term surplus funding, 138–70
Sigma, 364
Simplification, 7–8
Sinclair Research, 77
Small firms, 75
    accounting requirements, 78
    defining, 77
    reporting requirements, 76–7
Smaller accounts review, 287–8
Smaller Business Policy, 262
Smaller Exporters' Policy, 262
Smoothing divergences, 364
Social Security Contributions, 304
Solvency, 352
    measurement, 46
    models, 13
Source and application of funds, 165–7
Special Underwriting Unit, 262–3
Specific Account Policy, 261

Spreadsheets, 10–21, 72–3, 79
    balance sheet analysis, 324
    bank computerized analysis, 339
    bank manual analysis, 323–8
    building, 84–9
    credit analysis, 15
    credit analysts' most important tool, 18
    development of, 75
    essential questions of, 18
    model format, 81
    purpose of, 10–11
    purpose-built, 20
    raison d'être of, 21
    specimen layout, 13
    synthesis and antithesis in, 19
Stand-by financings, 33
Statement of source and application of funds, 68
Statement of Standard Accounting Practice 11 (SSAP 11), 173
Statement of Standard Accounting Practice 15 (SSAP 15), 171, 173, 178–80
Statement of Standard Accounting Practice 18 (SSAP 18), 188, 190
Statement of Standard Accounting Practice 21 (SSAP 21), 183–7, 328
Stock, 40–1, 87–8, 101, 303, 308–9, 316, 354
Stock index related transactions, 194
Stock treatment in normalized ratios and other quantities, 41–54
Summary of Standard Accounting Practice, accounting periods on or after 1 April, 176–7
Suspense accounts, 286
Synoptic analysis, 351–3, 355
Synoptic models, 203
Synoptic views, 58

Takeovers, 28
Tangible net worth (TNW), 83, 112–13, 364
Tax allowances, 172
Timing differences (See Deferred taxation)
Total liabilities, 364
Trade and Commercial Credit Corporation Limited, 204, 222, 239–59, 259
Trade credit facilities, 23–5
Trade creditors, 36, 38, 45, 46, 206, 311
Trade creditors' turnover, 17–18, 361, 364
Trade debtors, 34, 36, 45–7, 301
Trade Indemnity PLC, 205, 261–70

Trade references, 205
Trading balance, 40
Trading patterns, 49–51
Trading profit, 32
    definition, 27
Training techniques, 295–6
Transaction analysis, 140
Trend computations, 121
Turner & Newall, 190
Turnover and working capital relationship, 343
Turnover growth, 339

Unallocated cash review, 285–6
United Kingdom Mining Licences, 190
United Kingdom Production Licences, 190
United Kingdom Staple Removing Co. Ltd, 222

Value added tax (VAT), 155, 171, 303, 304, 310

Weightings, 60–1, 63
What if? type models, 59
Whole Turnover Policy, 261, 264, 266
Work-in-progress (WIP), 38, 303, 308–9, 316
Working capital, 5, 87, 363, 364
    and turnover relationship, 343
    cover, 365
    turnover, 39–40, 365
Working capital/sales ratio, 40
Working worth, 142–52, 365

Z-Score model, 55, 59, 105–7
Zeta Analysis, 105, 106